Popular prakashan

ENCYCLOPAEDIA
OF
INDIAN MEDICINE

लोकाः समस्ताः
सुखिनो भवन्तु ॥

SRI DHANVANTARI

DHANVANTARI

ENCYCLOPAEDIA OF INDIAN MEDICINE

VOLUME FOUR

Materia Medica - Herbal Drugs

Editor

Dr. S. R. SUDARSHAN

Popular Prakashan

On behalf of

Dr. V. PARAMESHVARA CHARITABLE TRUST, Bangalore

ENCYCLOPAEDIA
OF
INDIAN MEDICINE PROJECT

VOLUME FOUR

Sponsored by
Dr. V. P. Parameshvara Charitable Trust
Bangalore

Chairman
Dr. V. Parameshvara
M.B.B.S.,F.R.C.P. (London), F.A.C.C.,F.C.C.P.,F.I.C.A.,
F.I.S.E.,F.A.I.I.D.,M.S.A.,F.I.A.M.S.,F.I.C.N.

Editor
Dr. S. R. Sudarshan

First published 2005

ISBN : 81-7154-861-X

(3602)

Printed in India by:
Tarun Enterprises
20, Jaina Building,
Roshan Ara Road,
Delhi - 110 007

Published by RAMDAS BHATKAL for
Popular Prakashan Pvt. Ltd.
35-C Pandit Madan Mohan Malaviya Marg,
Tardeo, Mumbai-400 034

PREFACE

Indian religions are well known in the world. The philosophical systems that emerged on the Indian soil have also engaged the attention of scholars all over the world. India's achievements in the field of science and technology have also been recognised. However, the fact that India developed a system of medicine, thousands of years ago, has not received wide coverage in the world. And that the system thus developed is still prevalent among the masses of India is likewise not generally known, even to historians of medicine.

There are manifold reasons for this general ignorance of Indian medicine among historians of medicine, medical practitioners outside the country and intelligentsia interested in the problems of health and disease. One is absence of authoritative and well documented publications in English by Indians, dealing with this branch of medicine. The European indologists who have taken an interest in Indian medicine and have written on the subject do not seem to carry much credibility, because they are alien to the traditional details which are indispensable to the understanding of the spirit, outlook and value of Indian medicine. The literature available on this topic written in the traditional style of Indian languages have proved to be enigmatic to the modern reader. A great need is, therefore, felt for an authentic publication which communicates to the modern mind the traditional wisdom of India concerning medical practice.

The *Encyclopaedia of Indian Medicine* has been planned in six volumes to fulfill this need. The first three volumes have come out already (1985 and 1987), and the next three volumes are now being released. The first volume provided the historical perspective as well as an acquaintance with the classical medical literature in India. The second volume dealt with the basic ideas in Ayurvedic theory and practice. The third volume gave detailed account of clinical examination and diagnostic methods in Ayurveda. These volumes were prepared by Vidyalankara, Sastra-chudamani, Vachaspati Prof. S.K.Ramachandra Rao who hails from a family of traditional physicians and has been conversant with Ayurvedic texts from his boyhood. He was the president of the Ayurvedic Academy, Bangalore. He has also been a scientist, having headed the Department of Clinical Psychology in the National Institute of Mental Health and Neurosciences, where he was instrumental in opening a department in Ayurveda. He was also a visiting Professor at the

Centre for Theoretical Studies, Indian Institute of Science, and is a Senior Fellow of National Institute of Advanced Studies, Bangalore.

The three subsequent volumes which are now seeing the light of day were prepared by his son, Dr. S.R.Sudarshan, who is an alumnus of the Goverment College of Indian Medicine, Bangalore, and who has been a successful and popular Ayurvedic physician and consultant in Bangalore. He has also been an author of several volumes dealing with Ayurvedic theory and practice. The three volumes that have been included in the *Encyclopaedia of Indian Medicine* pertain to the Materia Medica of herbal and mineral drugs used in Ayurveda, and to the diseases and the therapeutic practices in Ayurveda.

It is hoped that the comprehensive and factual knowledge of Ayurveda, enshrined in these volumes of *Encyclopaedia of Indian Medicine*, will now be available to the world for the more efficient health-care programmes that are afoot. We are grateful to Prof. S.K.Ramachandra Rao and to Dr. S.R.Sudarshan for having spared their time and energy to complete the volumes we undertook. We also acknowledge the help of Messers Popular Prakashan, Mumbai in bringing out these volumes. We regret that due to several factors beyond our control the publication of the three later volumes which were ready for publication more than fifteen years ago was delayed beyond our expectation.

Bangalore

Dr. V.Parameshvara
Chairman
Dr. V. Parameshvara Charitable Trust,
Bangalore.

INTRODUCTION

The first three volumes of the *Encyclopaedia of Indian Medicine* edited by Prof. S. K. Ramachandra Rao and published in 1985 deal with the historical perspective, the basic concepts, and clinical examination and diagnostic methods respectively.

Of the subsequent volumes, the fourth one deals with the herbal drugs that have been described in the texts of Ayurveda. The information regarding the rasa, guna, virya, vipaka and the medicinal action has been taken from various nighantus and the samhitas; however the main text that has been referred to is the *Saligrama-nighantu*. All the herbs have been given the botanical names excepting those plants that have not been accurately identified, such as meda, mahameda and other plants that form the ashta-varga. I have tried to adopt a clinical approach by giving the therapeutic applications of numerous herbs that have been gleaned from the ancient classical texts like *Charaka-samhita* and *Susruta-samhita*.

The names of diseases have been given in English so as to make it more accessible, but they are only approximate. Thus dyspnoea and asthma are used as synonyms for the disease svasa while toxicosis refers to visha and drugs useful in toxicosis are those which are vishahara or vishaghna.

The fifth volume consists of the description and analysis of the metallic and mineral drugs that are used in Ayurveda, as well as an account of the animal products that have been mentioned in the Ayurvedic texts. The sixth volume contains a detailed account of the aetiology, pathogenesis, prodromal symptoms, symptomatalogy and treatment of all diseases that find a mention in the texts.

I am grateful to Dr. V. Parameshvara for having sponsored this work. I thank Mr. Prasad for the neat line drawings of the plants.

Dr. S. R. Sudarshan

CONTENTS

ABBREVIATIONS & MAJOR REFERENCES

AHṛ Ashṭanga-hṛdaya (Vagbhata, ed.A.M.Kunte, NS, Bombay, 1891).

AMD Āyurveda-rnahodadhi- an- napana-vidhi (Sushena, ed. S. Venkatasubrahmanya Sastri).

AP Āyurveda-prakaśa (ed. with comm. by Gulraj Sharma Miśra, C, Varanasi, 1962).

ARH Āyurveda-rasāyana (Hemadri on AHṛ).

AS Ashṭanga-samgraha (Vagbhaṭa, ed. Atrideva Gupta, NS, Bombay, 1951, with Hindi translation).

ASK Āyurvedīya-śabda-kosha (Veṇimādhav-śastri Joshī, Nārayaṇaharī Joshī, Bombay, 1968, in 2 volumes).

ASS Ānandaśrama Sanskrit Series, Puṇe.

BP Bhāva-prakaśa (Bhāvamiśra).

BPN Bhāva-prakaśa-nighaṇṭu.

BR Bhaishjya-ratnavali (ed. Govindadasa, Calcutta, 1893).

C Chowkhambha Series, Varanasi.

Chkp. Chakrapaṇi-datta (comm. on CS).

CS Charaka-samhita (ed. Yadavji Trikumji Acharya, NS, Bombay, 1941).

CSS Chikitsa-sāra-samgraha (Vanga sena, Calcutta, 1884).

CSSS Charaka-samhita: a scientific synopsis (P.Ray, et.al.. Indian National Science Academy, New Delhi, 1965, 1980).

DN Dhanvantari-nighantu (ASS, Pune, 1927, includes RN).

HHC History of Hindu Chemistry (P.C.Ray, Calcutta, 1902 and 1925, in 2 volumes).

HS Hārīta-samhita (Calcutta, 1887).

IMM Indian Materia Medica (N.M. Nadkarni, Popular Prakashan, Mumbai, revised and enlarged, 1976, in 2 volumes).

KS Kaśyapa-samhita (ed. Hemraj Sharma, C, Varanasi, 1953).

MI Minerals of India (D.N. Wadia, National Book Trust, India, Reprint Edition, 1988).

MMH Materia Medica of the Hindus (U.C.Dutta, Calcutta, 1922).

MPN Madana-pala-nighaṇṭu (Madana-pala).

NiS Nibandha-samgraha (Dalhana, on SS, NS, Bombay, 1915).

NS Nirṇaya-sāgar-press, Bombay RJN Rasa-jala-nidhi (Bhudev Mookerjee, Calcutta, 1926).

RN Rāja-nighantu (Abhidhāna chintāmani, ASS, Pune).

RRS Rasa-ratna-samucchaya (ed. Dattātreya Ananta Kulkarni, New Delhi, 1982, Vol.I, Dharmānanda Sharma, Motilal Banarsidass, 1958).

RSS Rasendra-sara-samgraha (ed. Naren-dranath Mitra, Motilal Banarsidass, 1976).

RT Rasa-tarangini

SaS Sārngadhara-samhita (ed. Paraśurama-sāstrī, NS, Bombay, 1931).

SdS Siva-dasa-sena

SN Śāligrama-nighantu (Lālā Śāligram, Varanasi, 1891).

SS Suśruta-samhita (ed. Yadavji Trikumjee Acharya, C, 1960).

SSS Suśruta-samhita : a scientific synopsis (P.Ray, et. al., Indian National Science Academy, New Delhi, 1980).

VSS Vaidyaka-śabda sindhu (Umesh Chandra Gupta, Calcutta, 1894).

YR Yoga-ratnākara (ASS, Pune, 1889; Mysore, 1899 in Kannada ch., with Kannada and Telugu Translations).

ENCYCLOPAEDIA OF INDIAN MEDICINE

Materia Medica – Herbal Drugs

A

Āḍhakī

Synonyms: Tuvarī, Tulyā, Karavīrā-bijā, Vṛtta bījah, Pīta-pushpah, Sūpyahah, Śāna-pushpikā.

Hin.	- Arahar, Tor
Kan.	- Togari
Ben. & Punj.	- Arhar
Mal.	- Tuvari
Bo.	- Tuver
Tam.	- Adagi, Tuvarai, Iyavai
Tel.	- Kandulu, Āḍhaki
Eng.	- Pigeon pea., Red gram

Botanical Name: Cajanas cajan (linn) Millsp.(Syn.C indicus Spreng; Cystisus Cajan Linn; C:Peudocajan Jaiq)

Natural Order: Leguminosae

Habitat: Cultivated through out India as a pulse crop.

Varieties: DN mentions three varieties, viz. white, red and black.

Medicinal Action:

Rasa : Astringent and sweet
Guṇa : Light and dry
Vīrya : Cold
Vipāka : Pungent

It alleviates kapha and pitta, improves complexion, slightly aggravates vāta, is constipative, appetizing and is useful in diseases of medas and vitiated blood.

Therapeutic Hints:

1. When taken with ghee, it alleviates all three doshas.
2. The pods used internally, either alone or in prescription, are useful in obesity, poisoning, rheumatism, etc. (CS, sūtra, 21, 26).

Ādityabhaktā

Synonyms: Varadā, Arkabhaktā, Suvarchalā, Sūryalatā, Arka-kāntā, Maṇḍūka-parṇī, Sura-sambhavā, Sourih, Arka-hitā, Ravīshṭa, Maṇḍūkī, Satyanāmnī.

Varieties: There is a bigger variety-Bṛhat-suvarchalā;

Medicinal Action:

Rasa : Bitter, astringent pungent and sweet.
Bitter, astringent and pungent (the leaves, and bṛhat - suvarchalā)
Guṇa : Heavy and dry
Light and dry (the leaves, and bṛhat-suvarchalā)
Vīrya : Cold
Hot (the leaves and bṛhat- survarchā)

It alleviates vāta and kapha, aggravates pitta, is a laxative, diuretic and is useful in skin diseases with itching, blotches on the skin, ulcers, fever with chill, urinary diseases, worms, constipation, ear-ache and grahas.

The leaves alleviate kapha and vāta, are laxative, beneficial to the voice, appetizing, bestow longevity and are used in fever, asthma, cough, skin diseases, pustular eruptions, urinary diseases, anorexia, dysmenorrhoea, urinary calculi, dysuria, anaemia, abdominal tumours and diseases of impure blood.

The Bṛhat-suvarchalā alleviates kapha and pitta, is a laxative and its actions and uses are similar to the leaves of the smaller variety.

Therapeutic Hints: The roots are used (along with other drugs) externally in grey hairs and headaches (CS chikitsā, 26, 268).

Agaruh

Synonyms: Lohah, Kṛmijah, Kṛmijagdhah, Anāryaka, Vishva-dhūpakam,Gandha-dhūmajam; Sudhūmyah.

Hin. - Agar
Mal. - Akil
Kan. - Agaru, Agilu-gandha
Arab. - Kalambak, Ud-el- ju
Eng . - Aloe-wood tree, Eagle-wood tree

Botanical Name: Aquilaria agallocha Roxb.

Natural Order: Thymelaeaceae

Habitat: E. Himalayas, Bhutan, parts of Bengal and particularly in Assam on the hill forests of Khasia, Garo, Naga, Cachar and Sylhet.

Description: This is a large evergreen tree with alternate, silky-glossy, linear lanceolate or oblong, usually glabrous leaves with a 2 mm long petiole. The flowers are small and greenish, having slender pedicels and forming umbels. The fruit is a compressed, hairy, tawny capsule with ovoid seeds.

Varieties: According to R N there are four varieties of Agaru, viz. Krshṇāgaru, Kāshṭāgaru, Dāhāgaru and Māngalyāgaru.

Parts Used: Stem, heart-wood and oil.

Medicinal Action:

Rasa : Pungent and bitter
Guṇa : Light, dry and tīkshṇa (sharp)
Vīrya : Hot
Vipāka : Pungent

It alleviates vāta and kapha, aggravates pitta, is beneficial to the skin, purifies septic wounds, and is useful in skin diseases, asthma, vomiting, catarrh and diseases of the eyes, ear and mouth.

Therapeutic Hints:

1. The powdered wood is used either alone or with other drugs, either externally or internally in fever, poisoning, skin diseases and rheumatism (CS, sūtra, 3, 28).
2. When applied externally, it is extremely useful in relieving cold and catarrh (CS, sūtra, 25, 40).

References: CS, chikitsā, 3, 267-269; sūtra, 5, 18; 45, 123.

Agastī

Synonyms: Agastyah, Śeeghrapushpah, Muni-pushpah, Muni-drumah, Vraṇārī, Deergha-phala, Vakra-pushpah, Surapriyah, Madhu-śigrū, Bakah.

Hin. - Basna; Agasta
Vernacular. - Agathiya (Ḍalhaṇa)
Ben. - Bak
Mal. - Agatti
Tel. - Avisecheṭṭu, Avisi
Kan. - Agase-mara; Chogachi
Mah - Hadga

Botanical Name: Sesbania grandiflora (Linn.) Pers. (Syn. Agati grandiflora Desv; Aeschynomene grandiflora Roxb; Coronilla grandiflora willd.)

Natural Order: Leguminosae

Habitat: Plains of Western Peninsula.

Description: This is a small, soft-wooded delicate tree reaching upto18 ft. high with a straight trunk. The young bark is smooth and light brown.The leaves are large and pinnate, while the flowers are either red or white.

Varieties: There are four varieties based on the colour of the flowers.They are: white, yellow, blue and red.

Medicinal Action:

Rasa : Sweet, bitter
Guṇa : Light and dry
Vīrya : Cold
Vipāka : Sweet

It alleviates all the doshas, increases intelligence and memory, is appetizing, a laxative and is useful in fatigue, pain, cough, intermittent fever, discolouration of skin, thirst, skin diseases, odema, catarrh, asthma, and diseases of the female sexual organs.

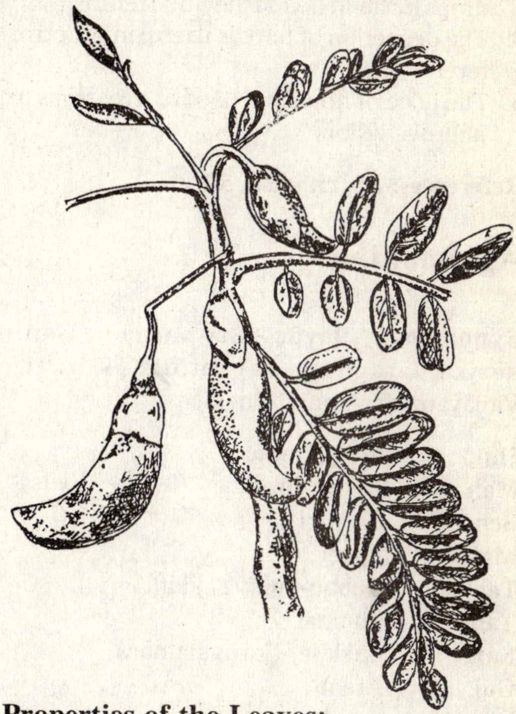

Properties of the Leaves:

Rasa : Pungent, bitter and sweet
Guṇa : Heavy
Vīrya : Hot

It alleviates pitta and kapha, is subtle, viśada, and is useful in diseases of impure blood, toxicosis, itching and worms.

Properties of Flowers:

Rasa : Bitter
Vīrya : Cold
Vipāka : Pungent

It alleviates all three doshas, is auspicious and is useful in cough, catarrh, night-blindness and emaciation.

Therapeutic Hints:

1. It is useful in night-blindness (SS, sūtra, 46, 282).

2. It relieves a certain variety of intermittent fever (AS, sūtra, 12, 89).
3. The juice of flowers and leaves is used as drops nasla in headache and rhinitis.
4. The decoction of bark is useful in eruptive fevers.
5. The juice of flowers is used as eye drops to īmprove vision.

References: AS, chikitsā, 50

Agnimanthā

Synonyms: Jayā, Śrī-parṇā, Gaṇikārikā, Vātaghnī, Jayanthih, Tarkāri, Vaijayantikā, Araṇī, Nādeyī.

Hin.	-	Arṇi, Agethu
Mah.	-	Takli, Airaṇ
Ben.	-	Gaṇiari
Mal.	-	Appel
Tel.	-	Gabbu-nelli; Takkali
Tam.	-	Munnai
Kan.	-	Takkile, Naruvalamara
Guj.	-	Araṇī
Vernacular.	-	Āgatha, Anga-śūra
Agni	-	vadhu (Ḍalhaṇa)

Botanical Name: Premna integrifolia Linn

Natural Order: Verbenaceae

Habitat: Near the sea from Mumbai to Malacca, Ceylon, Sri-Lanka and the Andamans.

Description: This is a large shrub or small tree reaching upto 9 metres high with yellowish bark. The young parts are glabrous or slightly pubescent; the trunk and large branches sometimes spinous. The leaves are entire or upper parts dentate, opposite, glabrous, broadly elliptic and very shortly acuminate. The flowers are small, greenish yellow with a disagreeable odour. The fruit is pearshaped and the endocarp ridged, bony and four seeded. The seeds are oblong.

Varieties: There are two varieties, the bigger one being Agnimantha and a smaller one called Tarkārī.

Ahiphenah

The inspissated juice of Papaver somniferum Linn.

Synonyms: Opium: Āphukah, Aphenakah, Poppy pods, Khasa-tilah, Sūkshma-bījah, Śubhra-pusphah, Latat-phalah, Tila-bhedah, Sūkshma-taṇḍulah.

Hin.	-	Postu (Poppy pods), Afyūm (Opium)
Ben.	-	Afīm (Opium)
Tam.	-	Gasagasā (Poppy pods) Abīni (Opium)
Tel.	-	Gasagasālu (Poppy pods) Abhini (Opium)
Kan.	-	Gasagase (Poppy pods), Afīmu (Opium)
Mal.	-	Kaśa-kaśa (Poppy pods), Kaśa-kaśa Karappu (Opium).

Natural Order: Papaveraceae

Habitat: Cultivated in U.P., districts of

Jullundur and Hoshiarpur in E. Punjab and various regions of Rajasthan and Madhya Bharat. Widely cultivated as ornamental plant in gardens.

Description: This is an annual herb with an erect, round, green, smooth stem, from 2 to 4 feet high. The leaves are large, oblong and green with toothed, wavy margin; the teeth sometimes are tipped with a rigid hair. The flowers are large, the calyx smooth, and the fruit a large smooth and globose capsule. The unripe capsule is marked in three or four places with longitudinal incisions from which the juice is obtained.

Varieties: There are four varieties-

a) Jāraṇa (with white flowers, digests food)
b) Māraṇa (with black flowers, causes death)
c) Dhāraṇa (with yellow flowers)
d) Sāraṇa (with flowers of variegated colours; is purgative)

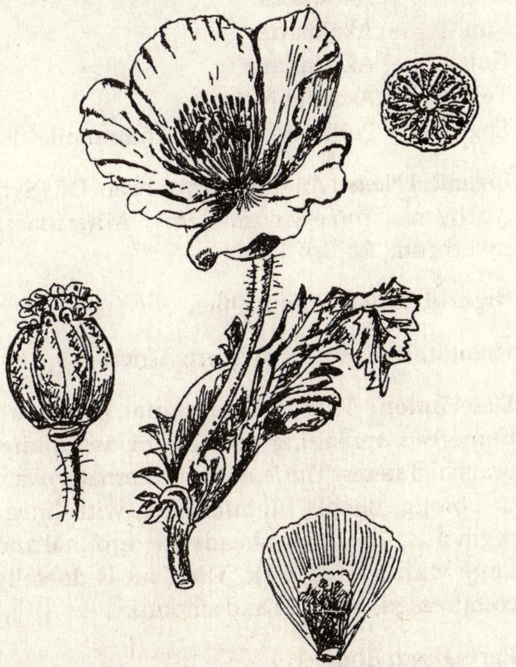

Parts Used: Khasa-tila (seeds within poppy pod); valkala (outer layer of poppy pod); ahiphena, aphūka (inspissated juice).

Medicinal Action:

Rasa : Bitter (ahiphena); bitter, astringent (valkala)

Guṇa : Heavy (khasa-tila); dry, light (ahiphena and valkala)

Vīrya : Cold (valkala); hot (ahiphena)

Vipāka : Sweet (khasa-tila), pungent (ahiphena)

The poppy seeds alleviate vāyu, aggravate kapha, increase strength and are an aphrodisiac.

The outer layer of poppy pods alleviates kapha, aggravates vāta, is constipative, dries up the dhātus, is narcotic, causes talkativeness, is an appetiser, and causes impotence.

The inspissated juice alleviates kapha, aggravates vāta and pitta, is subtle, constipative and exceedingly analgesic.

Therapeutic Hints:

1. Opium is purified if subjected to bhāvanā with ginger-juice for twenty- one times (RJN, Vol.III, p.349).
2. The poison of opium is destroyed if saindhava, pippalī and kernel of Madana fruit are made into a paste and drunk with hot water (ibid, p.352).

Ajamodah

Synonyms: Atyugragandhah, Modā,Hastimayūrakah, Kharāhvāh, Kāravī, Vallī, Vastimodah, Markaṭī, Dīpyakah, Gandha-dala, Hastikāravī,Gandha-patrikā, Māyurī, Modaḍhyah, Vahni-dīpikah, Bṛhma-kośī, Phala-mukhyā.

Hin. - Ajmod
Mar. - Ajamoda
Kan. - Ajmoda
Tel. - Vāmam
Ben. - Rāndhunī
Eng. - Indian celery

Botanical Name: Carum roxburghianum, Benth & Hook.f (Syn. Trachyspermum roxburghianum (DC.) Sprague; Apium graveolens Linn)

Natural Order: Umbelliferae

Habitat: Cultivated in many gardens.

Description: An annual, about 3 ft. high with a fusiform root. The upper segments of lower leaves are rather broad, while those of the upper are narrowly linear - lanceolate The fruit is hispid.

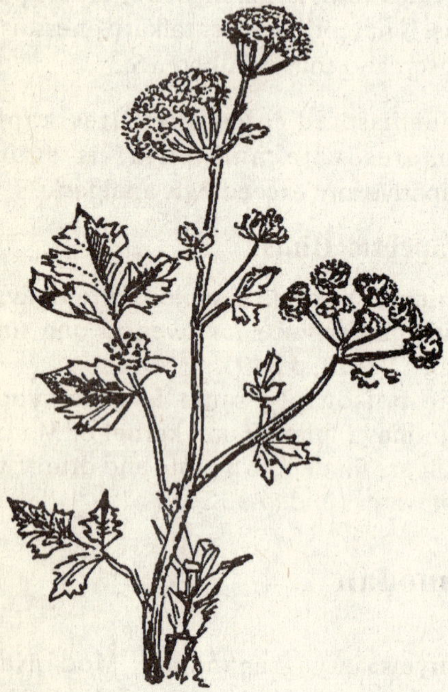

Parts Used: Seeds

Medicinal Action:

Rasa : Bitter and pungent
Guṇa : Light, dry and tīkshṇa
Vīrya : Hot
Vipāka : Pungent

It alleviates kapha and vāta, aggravates pitta, is appetising, constipative, an aphrodisiac and a heart-tonic and is useful in eye-diseases, worms, vomiting, hiccough, obesity, colic, distension of abdomen, anorexia, dysuria and pain.

Therapeutic Hints:

1. The powdered seeds are used, with other drugs, in urinary disorders, indigestion, jaundice, tumours, dysentery, etc. (CS, sūtra, 23, 20).
2. The roots are diuretic and tonic, and are useful in anasarca.
3. It should not be used by pregnant women.

References: CS, sūtra, 4, 9; 38, 22; AS, sūtra, 16, 40; AHṛ, sūtra, 15, 33).

Ākāra-Karabhah

Synonyms: Ākarakarā, Ākallakah

Hin. - Akarakara
Ben. - Akor-kora
Kan. - Ākalakare
Guj. - Akallakara
Tel. - Akarakaramu
Eng. - Pellitory, Spanish chamomile

Botanical Name: Anacyclus pyrethrum DC (Syn. Anthemis pyrethrum Linn; Matricaria pyrethrum, Baill.)

Natural Order: Compositae.

Habitat: Indigenous to North Africa.

Description: This is a perennial herb with numerous spreading prostate or ascending, branched stems. The leaves are alternate, ovate or oblong, deeply bipinnatisect, with linear segments. The flower heads are terminal and large with a wide disk. The fruit is dorsally compressed, obovoid and smooth.

Parts Used: Root

Medicinal Action:

Rasa : Pungent

Vīrya : Hot
Vipāka : Pungent

It alleviates vāta, increases strength and is useful in catarrh and oedema

Ākāśā - vallī

Synonyms: Kha-vallī, Dusparśā, Vyoma-vallikā, Amara-vallarī,

Hin. - Amarveli
Tel. - Antara-tāmara
Mah. - Ākāśbel
Kan. - Beḷu, Ākaśa-valli
Tam. - Kottan, Nandii

Botanical Names: Cassytha filiformis, Linn or Cuscuta reflexa Roxb (Convolvulaceae.)

Natural Order: (Convolvulaceae)

Habitat: A parasitic leafless twiner met with through out the greater part of India, especially near the west.

Description: A wiry, leafless parasite, sending numerous sucking roots by which it adheres to the host. The stem is 0.25 c.m. in diameter and is dark green. The flowers are small, sessile in spikes. The fruit is a globose, smooth, white drupe, enclosed in a fleshy perianth-tube. The plant flowers from September-April.

Medicinal Action:

Rasa : Pungent, sweet, bitter and astringent
Guṇa : Slimy

It alleviates pitta and kapha, increases the digestive fire, strength and semen, is a heart tonic, constipative and rejuvenative and is useful in diseases of the eye.

Akshoṭah

Synonyms: Akshodakah, Vṛnta-phalah, Kandarālah, Pṛthak-chadah, Rekhā-phalah, Parvatīyah, Phala-snehah, Guḍāśayah, Karparālah, Svādu-majjah. Pīluh.

Hin. - Akhrot
Tel. - Ākharotu
Ben. - Ākharot
Eng. - Walnut tree

Botonical Name: Juglans regia Linn (Juglandaceae)

Habitat: J. regia is found in the temperate Himalayas at 3,000 - 10,000 ft, Khasia Hills and Baluchisthan.

Description: A large, deciduous monoecious tree with grey, longitudinally fissured bark and tomentose shoots. The leaves are alternately imparipinnate with sub-sessile elliptic to oblong-lanceolate, usually entire leaflets. The flowers are small and yellowish green. The fruit is an indehiscent, ellipsoid-globose, green drupe with a leathery endocarp.

Medicinal Action:

Rasa : Sweet, slightly sour.
Guṇa : Unctous and heavy
Vīrya : Hot
Vipāka : Sweet

It alleviates vāta, aggravates kapha, increases strength and corpulence, is an aphrodisiac, constipative and appetising and is used in heart disease, diseases of impure blood, emaciation, haemoptysis and tuberculosis.

References: CS, sūtra, 27, 157; SS, sūtra, 46, 187; NIS on ibid.

Alābū

Synonyms: Tumbī, Lābukā, Piṇḍaphalā, Mahāphalā.

Hin. - Loukā, Khaddu, Tombī
Ben. - Lāu
Mah. - Dudhyā Bhopāḷ
Kan. - Kahi sorĕ
Tam. - Śurai, Kūḍembil
Tel. - Alābuvu, Surakāya, Ānapakāyi
Mal. - Kaippachuram
Eng. - White pumpkin, bitter bottle gourd

Botanical Name: Lagenaria vulgaris Ser. (Syn L. siceraria Standl; Cucurbita lagenaria. Willd.)

Natural Order: Cucurbitaceae

Varieties: There are two varieties, one bearing elongated fruits and the other roundish fruits.

Medicinal Action:

Rasa : Sweet
Guṇa : Heavy and unctous (the fruits) unctous (the stalks)
Vīrya : Cold

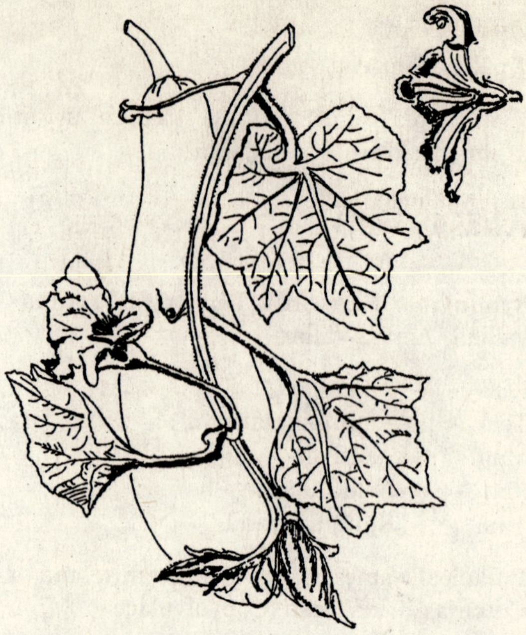

The fruit alleviates kapha and pitta, aggravates vāta, is a heart tonic, an aphrodisiac, appetizen, nutritive, strength giving and provides nourishment to the foetus if eaten by pregnant women.

The stalks alleviate kapha and pitta, aggravate vāta and are purgative.

References: CS, sūtra, 27, 112; SS, sūtra, 18, 16; 46, 2, 15.

Ālukah

Synonyms: Elavāluka

Hin. - Āluk
Kan. - Geṇasu;
Eng. - Yam

Botanical Name: Dioscorea

Natural Order: Dioscoreaceae

Habitat: Cultivated throūghout India.

Varieties:

1. Kāshṭāluka (which is hard; Hin. - Kaṭhālū)
2. Śankhālu (which is whitish in colour)
3. Hastyālu (which is long and thick)
4. Raktālu (which is reddish)
5. Piṇḍālu (which is roundish)
6. Madvālu (which is heavy, Hin-Dīrga-suthanī)

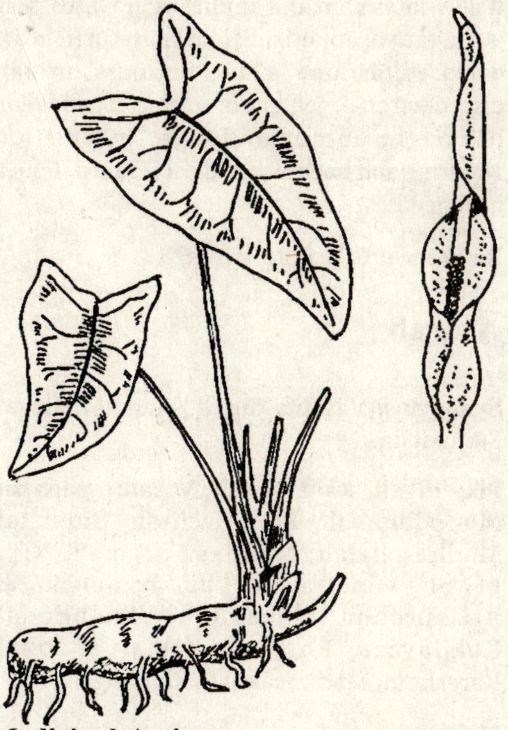

Medicinal Action:

Rasa : Sweet

Guṇa : Heavy and dry

Vīrya : Cold

It alleviates vāta and kapha, increases strength, is an aphrodisiac, increases lactation, is a laxative and diuretic, hard to digest and is used in haemoptysis. It is the most injurious to health among all tubers and is contraindicated in abdominal tumours.

References: CS, sūtra, 25, 39; SS, sūtra, 46, 298-299; uttara, 42, 75-76.

Āmalakah

Synonyms: Vayasthā, Dhātrīphalah, Amṛtaphalah, Śrīphalah, Śivah, Vṛshyā, Dhātrikā, Vṛttaphalah.

Hin. - Amla, Amlika

Ben.&Mah. - Āvaḷā

Tel. - Usiri-kāyi

Kan. - Nelli

Eng. - Emblic myrobalan

Botanical Name: Phyllantus emblica Linn; (syn. Emblica officinalis Gaertn.)

Natural Order: Euphorbiaceae

Habitat: Common in the mixed deciduous forests of India, ascending to 4,500 ft.

Description: A very handsome, medium sized deciduous tree with smooth grey bark and mottled stem. Leaves are pinnately compound with delicate small leaflets. Flowers are small, greenish in colour. The flowering time is from March to May. The fruits are round, green, becoming light yellow when mature. The fruiting season is from November to January.

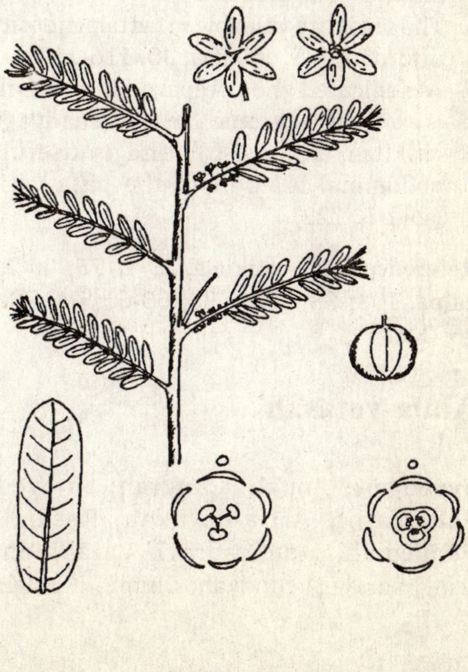

Parts Used: Root, leaves, fruit and seeds.

Medicinal Action:

Rasa : Sour, sweet, astringent, pungent and bitter
Guṇa : Light and dry
Vīrya : Cold
Vipāka : Sweet

It alleviates all the doshas, confers longevity and strength, promotes growth of hair, is appetising and an aphrodisiac and is useful in fever, constipation, urinary disorders (including diabetes), oedema, burning sensation, vomiting, excessive thirst, tuberculosis, haemoptysis, fatigue, eye-diseases and distension of abdomen.

Therapeutic Hints:

1. It is the best among rejuvenative drugs (CS, sūtra, 25, 40).
2. It is useful in relieving cough and skin diseases (CS, sūtra, 4, 11-13, 16).
3. It is best among the sour fruits (SS, sūtra, 46, 334)
4. Unripe fruits are used as collyrium in certain diseases (AS, uttara, 37).
5. The seeds are valuable in certain menstrual disorders (CS, chikitsā, 30, 116-117).
6. A medicated ghee prepared from āmalaki is excellent as a tonic and rejuvenative (CS, chikitsā, 1, 2, 4-6), and is useful in abdominal tumours of the pitta variety (ibid, 5, 122).

References: CS, chikitsā, 1, 1, 75; 1, 2, 7; kalpa, 108; SS, sūtra, 38, 60-61; 44, 70-71, 46, 206.

Amla-vetasah

Synonyms: Amlah, Chukrah, Śatavedhī, Sahasra-jit, Amla-nāyakah, Rasāmlah, Phalāmlah, Māmsa-drāvī, Varābhidhah, Śaṅkhadrāvī, Vedhakah, Bhīmā, Bhedanah, Raktasārah, Gulma-ketū, Vārāngī, Mahākshārah, Svara-bhedakah.

Medicinal Action:

Rasa : Exceedingly sour, astringent
Guṇa : Light, dry and tīkshṇa (sharp)
Vīrya : Hot

It alleviates vāta and kapha, aggravates pitta, is a laxative, appetizing and is useful in heart-diseases, asthma, colic, tumours, urinary disorders, enlargement of spleen, constipation, hiccough, anorexia, cough, indigestion, vomiting and haemorrhoids. It is said to liquefy iron needles.

Reference: CS, sūtra, 27, 152.

Āmrah

Synonyms: Vasanta-dūtah, Manmathālayah, Sumadanā.

Pika-rāgah, Kāma-śarah, Vasanta-pādapah, Madodbhavah, Para-pushṭah, Suphalah, Madhu-phalah, Mādhava-drumah, Nṛpa-priyah, Vanotsavah, Chūtah, Sahakārah, Atisourabha, Mākandah, Pika-bhudah, Kokilāvāsā, Rasālah, Kāma-vallabhah, Kāreshṭah, Madirāsakhah, Kāmāngah

Hin. - Āmb
Tel. - Māviḍi
Mal. - Mānga
Tam. - Māmaram
Kan. - Māvina mara
Eng. - Mango tree

Botanical Name: Mangifera indica - Linn (Syn. M. domestica Gaertn)

Natural Order: Anacardiaceae

Habitat: Found all over India

Description: A large, evergreen tree with rough, dark-grey bark. The leaves are lanceolate, purple-red or yellow green when young, dark green when mature and leathery. The flowers are bisexual or polygamous. The fruit is a one-seeded drupe. The tree flowers from January-March; fruits are borne in April-June.

Varieties: There are five varieties

1. Sādhāraṇāmra,
2. Kośāmra,
3. Rājāmra,
4. Mahā-rājāmra,
5. Rasālāmra

Parts Used: Bark, leaves, flowers, fruits and seed pods

Medicinal Action:

Rasa : Unripe fruit - astringent, sour and pungent
Ripe fruit - sweet
Seed - astringent, sweet and slightly sour
Bark and root - astringent

Guṇa : Unripe fruit - dry
Ripe fruit - unctous and heavy

Vīrya : Unripe fruit - excessively hot
Ripe fruit - cold

Unripe fruit aggravates all the doshas, is constipative, increases the digestive fire, and is useful in diseases of the throat. If eaten in excess, it causes loss of appetite, intermittent fever, eye-diseases, diseases of impure blood and a kind of ascites. It can however be eaten without any injurious effect, if milk or Sauvarchala salt or Jīraka is taken as anupāna.

The ripe fruit alleviates vāta, does not aggravate pitta, is appetizing, an aphrodisiac, constipative, promotes strength and complexion and is useful in urinary disorders, diseases of impure blood and ulcers.

If the fruit ripens on the tree itself, it is heavy, alleviates vāta and aggravates pitta. If it is ripened artificially it alleviates pitta.

If ripe fruit is eaten by sucking, it is appetising, strength-giving, light, cold, easily-digested, a laxative and alleviator of vāta and pitta.

The juice of the ripe fruit is a laxative, unctous, a digestive and increases strength and complexion.

The seed is useful in vomiting, diarrhoea and heart burn.

The bark and root are constipative and alleviate kapha and pitta.

Therapeutic Hints:

1. The flowers are used as collyrium in eye-diseases (SS, uttara, 17, 8-10).
2. The tender leaves relieve vomiting (CS, sūtra, 4, 14).
3. The stone is used as a constipative (CS, sūtra, 4, 15).
4. The fruits are used in polyuria (CS, sūtra, 4, 15).

5. It is useful in bleeding from internal organs (SS, uttara, 45, 23)

References: AS, sūtra, 7, 188-190).

Amlikā

Synonyms: Chukrikā. Chinchā, Tiṇṭidī, Śuktī, Chaṇḍikā, Dantaśatah, Ābdikā, Yamadūtikā, Gurupatrā, Suchukrikā, Panktipatrā, Bhuktā, Atyāmlā.

Hin.	-	Ambli, omli
Tel.	-	Chinta-cheṭṭu
Tam.	-	Puliya-maram
Mal.	-	Āmlam, chincha
Kan.	-	Huṇise-huḷi mara
Eng.	-	Tamarind tree

Botanical Name: Tamarindus indica Linn. (Syn. T. occidentalis Gaert; T. officinalis Hook.)

Natural Order: Leguminosae

Habitat: Cultivated throughout India.

Description: A large ever green tree with a grey, longitudinally fissured bark. The leaflets are in 10-15 pairs, oblong and sessile. The flowers are yellow, with pink streaks, in lax racemes. The fruit is a pod filled with acrid pulp, with brown seeds. The tree flowers in April-May; fruits are seen in February-March.

Parts Used: Fruits, seeds, leaves and flowers.

Medicinal Action:

Rasa : Unripe fruit - exceedingly sour.
Ripe fruit-sweet and sour
Flowers - astringent, sweet and sour

Guṇa : Unripe fruit - heavy
Ripe fruit - light and dry
Dried fruit - light
Flowers - light and viśada

Vīrya : Hot

The unripe fruit alleviates vāta and aggravates pitta, kapha and blood. The ripe fruit alleviates kapha and vāta, is appetizing and a laxative, diuretic and is useful in gṛhaṇi (sprue syndrome) and constipation. The dried fruit is a cardiac tonic and is useful in fatigue, giddiness, excessive thirst and worms.

The leaves are useful in oedema and diseases caused by impure blood.

The flowers are appetizers, alleviate kapha and vāta, increase the digestive fire and are useful in urinary disorders.

The ashes of the dried bark are used in colic and dyspepsia.

Preparations: Amlikā-pānam.

Therapeutic Hint: It is appetizing, a digestive and is used in diarrhoea, dysentery, etc. (CS, sūtra, 27, 121, 252).

References: CS, sūtra, 27, 121; vimāna, 8, 140; AHṛ, sūtra, 10, 25.

Āmrātakah

Synonyms: Āmra-taṭah, Tanu-kshīrī, Kapi-priyah, Pītanakhah, Kapichūtah, Pallīshah, Dru-phalah, Varsha-pākī, Markaṭāmrah, Amla-vāṭakah, Kapītanah, Rasāḍyah.

Hin. - Ambāḍa
Tel. - Aḍavi-māmiḍi, ambāṭapukāyā
Mal. - Ambālam
Kan. - Amaṭe mara
Tam - Kāṭṭuma
Eng. - Hog-plum tree
Vernaculae. - Āmrāṭakam (Ḍalhaṇa)

Botanical Name: Spondias mangifera Willd (Syn. S. Pinnata Kurtz; S. amara Lam; Evia amara Comm; mangifera pinnata Koen.

Natural Order: Anacardiaceae

Habitat: Sub-Himalayan tract and outer valleys upto 3,000 ft. Andamans and W. Peninsula.

Description: A medium-size tree with a handsome foliage. The fruits are oval shaped, of the size of a small hen's egg; the seed in the centre is enclosed by highly acid fibrous pulp which has the flavour of the mango.

Medicinal Action:

Rasa : Unripe fruit - astringent and sour
Ripe fruit - astringent, sweet and sour
Guṇa : Heavy; unctous (ripe fruit only)
Vīrya : Unripe fruit - hot
Ripe fruit - cold
Vipāka : Ripe fruit - sweet

Unripe fruit alleviates vāta, aggravates pitta, kapha and blood, is a laxative and appetizing, and is useful in diseases of the throat, rheumatism and dyspepsia.

The ripe fruit alleviates vāta and pitta, is constipative, strength-giving, refrigerant and an aphrodisiac, promotes the growth of dhātus, and is useful in traumatic ailments, burning sensation, emaciation and diseases of the blood.

The leaves are constipative and appetizing.

Therapeutic Hints:

1. It is one of the drugs which is a heart-tonics (CS, sūtra, 4, 10).
2. It is strength-giving, refreshing, and a tonic; it is hard to digest (SS, sūtra, 46, 155).
3. The stone of the fruit is used an a astringent (CS, sūtra, 4, 15-31).
4. It is especially useful in chronic diarrhoea (SS, uttara, 40, 70).

Note: The fruits resemble those of Āmra, NIS on SS, sūtra, 46,139.

Anannāsah

Synonyms: Pārvatī, koutukah

Hin. - Anānas
Tam. - Parangitālay
Eng. - Pine - apple

Botanical Name: Anannasa sativa Linn (Syn. Ananas comosus Merr.)

Natural Order: Bromeliaceae

Habitat: Cultivated in Assam, Bengal and along the W. Coast. Indigenous to Brazil.

Description: A perennial plant, 1 1/2 - 5 ft. high, with a very short stem hidden over by a rosette of long, narrow, stiff, fibrous leaves, usually spined. The fruit is borne on a stalk, which is an extension of the main stem, in the centre of the plant.

Medicinal Action:

Rasa : Ripe fruit - sweet.
Guṇa : Unripe fruit - heavy

The unripe fruit aggravates kapha and pitta, is appetizing, a heart tonic and is useful in fatigue, lethargy and anorexia.

The ripe fruit alleviates pitta and is useful in diseases of 'Rasa' dhatu and complaints brought on by hot weather.

Aākolah

Synonyms: Aṅkoṭah, Anguli-patrah, Dṛdha-mūlakah, Dīrgha-kīlah, Peeta-sārah, Bhū-sitā, Virechī, Nikochakah, Gupta-snehah, Śubhra-pushah, Tāmra-phalah, Kanṭakī, Vanavāsī, Gūḍhapatrah, Lamba-karṇah, Vishaghnah, Nedisṭhah, Rāmaṭhah.

Hin. - Ankol, Dhera
Mal. - Ankolam
Kan. - Ankole-mara
Eng. - Sage-leaved Alangium, Alangy.
Vernacular - Ankolla (Ḍalhaṇa)

Botanical Name: Alangium decapetalum Linn (Syn. A. lamarchii Thwaites; A. salviifolium (Linn. f.) Wang.)

Natural Order: Alangiaceae

Habitat: Throughout the drier parts of India, grows vigorously in the forests of S. India.

Description: This is a very variable, small and deciduous tree with spinescent branchlets. The bark is grey, smooth, orange-yellow when young, and fibrous. The leaves are alternate, simple, oblong-lanceolate, variable, entire and membranous, with prominent veins. The flowers are fragrant and white, in axillary fasicles. The fruit is a purplish-red globose berry, with one seed.

Parts Used: Root bark and seeds.

Medicinal Action:

Rasa : Pungent and astringent. sweet (fruit and seeds)
Guṇa : Unctous, sharp and light
Unctous and heavy (fruit and seeds)

Vīrya : Hot
Cold (fruit and seeds)
Vipāka : Sweet (fruit and seeds)

It alleviates vāta and kapha, is emetic and purgative, acts as antidote to the poisonous bites of dogs, mice etc, and is useful in worms, heart diseases, affections of the throat, colic, dyspepsia, oedema, diarrhoea, diseases of impure blood, rheumatic pains, herpes, and diseases caused by unseen agents (Graha).

The fruit alleviates all three doshas, is a laxative and strength-giving and is useful in emaciation, diseases of impure blood and burning sensations.

The seeds alleviate vāta and pitta, aggravate kapha, promote strength, are an aphrodisiac and a laxative, and are useful in emaciation, herpes, diseases of impure blood, toxicosis and burning sensations.

Therapeutic Hints:

1. The flowers antidote poison (SS, kalpa, 1, 72).
2. The fruits aggravate kapha and are hard to digest (CS, sūtra, 27, 159).
3. The roots are useful in poisoning caused by rat bites (AS, uttara, 46).

References: CS, chikitsā, 23, 244; NIS on SS, sūtra, 37, 12; kalpa, 1, 72; 7, 34; AHṛ, sūtra, 6, 120

Apāmārgah

Synonyms: Śikharī, Kiṇihā, Śekharikā, Pratyakpusphī, Mayūrakah, Kharamanjarī, Adhah-śalyā, Markaṭī, Vaśīrā, Kaṇṭhī, Durabigrahā, Kubjah.

Hin. - Latjīra
Tam. - Thirukaḍalāḍi
Tel. - Uttareṇe
Kan. - Uttaraṇe - giḍa
Mal. - Kaḍalāḍi
Mah. - Āghāḍa
Eng. - Prickly chaff flower
Vernacular - Andhaḍaka (Ḍalhaṇa)

Botanical Name: Achyranthes aspera Linn.

Natural Order: Amaranthaceae

Habitat: Throughout India upto 3,000 ft, Baluchistan.

Description: This is an erect shrub which grows to about a metre in height. The branches are many and have nodes. The leaves are simple, opposite and leathery. The flowers are small and pink. The fruit is oblong, containing brown seeds. The flowers are seen in the cold season.

Varieties: There are three varieties - white, red and black.

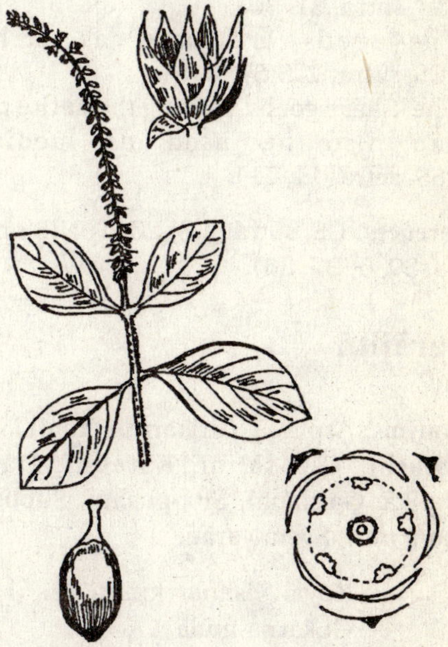

Parts Used: Root, leaves, seeds and ash of the whole plant.

Medicinal Action:

Rasa : Bitter and pungent
Guṇa : Dry and tīkshṇa (active)
Vīrya : Hot
Cold (Red variety)

It alleviatives kapha and vāta, is a laxative and emetic and is useful in diseases of impure blood, in haemorrhages, worms, haemorrhoids, itching, vomiting, obesity and heart disease. It is also used as errhine.

The leaves are used in haemoptysis and haemorrhages. The white variety is useful in ascites, haemorrhoids, bleeding, pain, obesity, skin-diseases, dyspepsia and swelling of glands. It promotes good complexion.

The red variety is emetic, and is useful in ulcers, toxicosis. skin diseases with severe itching and pain.

Therapeutic Hints:

1. The roots promote healing of ulcers (SS, sūtra, 37, 30).
2. The seeds are used as errhine (CS, sūtra, 2, 3-5).
3. The kshāra got by burning the entire plant can also be used as medicine (SS, sūtra, 11, 11).

References: CS, sūtra, 2,3; 20, 1; NIS on SS, sūtra, 39, 6; 37, 30).

Aparājitā

Synonyms: Āsphoṭā, Girikarṇī, Bhūmi-lagnā, Gavākshī, Giri-śālini, Kaṭabhī, Dadhi-pushpikā, Gardabhī, Sita-pushpī, Supushpī, Visha-hantrī, Śveta-varāṭī.

Hin.	-	Koyal, vishṇu - krānti
Mah.	-	Gokarṇa-mūlā
Kan.	-	Śankhu
Tam.	-	Kākkaṇam, kari-channi
Tel.	-	Dantina; gaṇṭina
Mal.	-	Āral

Botanical Name: Clitoria ternatea Linn (Syn. C. spectabilis Salis; Lathyrus spectabilis Forsk; Tenatea vulgaris H. B.)

Natural Order: Leguminosae

Habitat: A common garden plant.

Description: A very pretty climber or twining shrub with slender branches. Leaves are pinnately compound with either five or seven oval, parrot green leaflets. Flowers are solitary, short stalked with a beautiful bright blue or white colour, and with a characteristic shape. Fruit is a legume, 4-5 inches long, each legume containing 5-6 seeds. Seeds are oblong, about 6 mm long.

Varieties: Blue and white

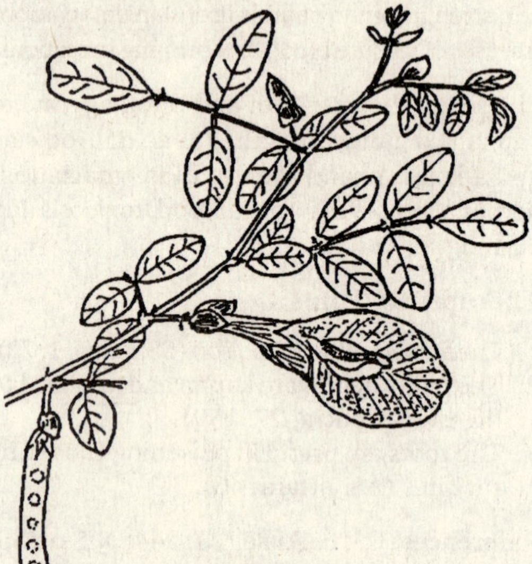

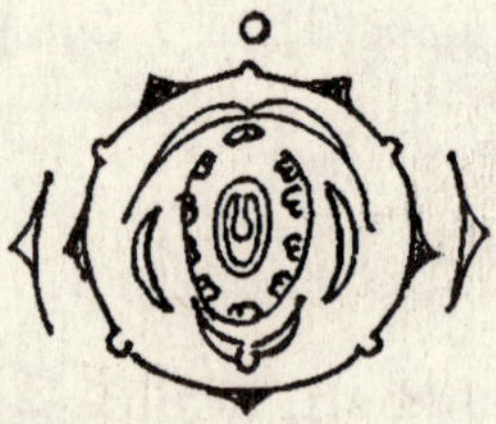

Medicinal Action:

Rasa : Bitter and pungent

Vīrya : Cold

It alleviates all the doshas, promotes intelligence and eye-sight, is beneficial to the throat, and is useful in cough, oedema, toxicosis, diarrhoea and diseases caused by unseen agent (grahas).

Āragvadhah

Synonyms: Rāja-vṛkshah, Sampākah, Kṛtamālakah, Vyādhi-ghātah, Karṇi-kārah, Pragrahah, Chaturāngulah, Ārogya-śimbī, Dīrgha-phalah, Rechanah, Hema-pushpah, Jvarāntakah, Svarṇa-pushpah, Kushtha-sūdanah

Hin.	- Amalatās
Kan.	- Kakke-mara
Mal.	- Konne
Mah.	- Bāhavā
Tam.	- Konrai
Tel.	- Relacheṭṭu tree
Eng.	- Pudding Pipe or Indian Laburnum

Botanical Name: Cassia fistula Linn, (Syn. C. rhomifolia Roxb)

Natural Order: Leguminosae

Habitat: Throughout India.

Description: A moderate or medium sized tree growing to about eight metres high, with a straight trunk and spreading branches. The younger branches are smooth and greenish in colour while the older ones are rough and dark brown. Leaves are pinnately compound and alternate, with three to eight pairs of opposite leaflets. Flowers are yellowish and fragrant, fruit is pendulous, cylindrical with many seeds imbedded in a soft pulp. The pulp is viscid with a sweet mucilaginous taste.

Parts Used: The fruit pulp, leaves, flowers and root-bark.

Medicinal Action:

Rasa	: Sweet and bitter
	Leaves - bitter
	Flowers - astringent
Guṇa	: Heavy and unctous
Vīrya	: Cold
Vipāka	: Sweet

It alleviates all three doshas, is a mild purgative suitable for all persons, and is useful in skin diseases, itching, fever, heart disease, gout, urinary disorders, colic and dysuria. The leaves alleviate kapha and are useful in diseases of medas.

The flowers aggravate vāta and are constipative.

The fruit-pulp alleviates vāta and pitta.

Therapeutic Hints:

1. It is one of the drugs used to treat skin diseases (CS, sūtra, 4, 11, 13).
2. The fruits are used for laxative purposes (ibid, 2, 10).
3. The decoction is used to clean wounds and abscesses (SS, chikitsā, 16, 24); while the root is used externally in skin diseases (ibid, 20, 50).

4. A medicated ghee prepared from this and certain other drugs is used to treat abdominal tumours caused by vitiated kapha (SS, uttara, 42, 37).

References: CS, kalpa, 8, 4-5; SS, sūtra, 38, 6-7; AHṛ. sūtra, 15, 18.

Arimedah

Synonyms: Viṭ-khadirah, Irimedah, Godhā-skandha, Ahi-mārah, Pūtimedah.

Hin. - Gandh-babul
Mah. - Śeṇyā-khair
Tam. - Pikkaruvel
Kan. - Kiri-jāli, Saṇṇa-jāli
Tel. - Kastūri-tumma.
Mal. - Pauvelam, Kari-velu
Eng. - Fragrant acacia; White babool tree
Vernacular - Arimanja (Ḍalhaṇa)

Botanical Name: Acacia farnesiana Willd; (Syn. Mimosa farnesiana Linn)

Natural Order: Leguminosae

Habitat: Throughout India

Description: This is a large thorny spreading bush or small tree bearing fragrant yellow flowers. The flowers are globular, and are seen in the cold season. The gum is met with in spheroidal tears or in stalactiform masses, of a pale-yellow or dark-reddish brown colour. It partly dissolves in water forming a gelatinous mucilage.

Medicinal Action:

Rasa : Astringent and bitter;
Sweet (the exudation)
Vīrya : Hot

It alleviates kapha, is auspicious and is used in oedema, diarrhoea, cough, herpes and skin diseases, diseases of impure blood, diseases of mouth and teeth, worms, toxicosis and ulcers.

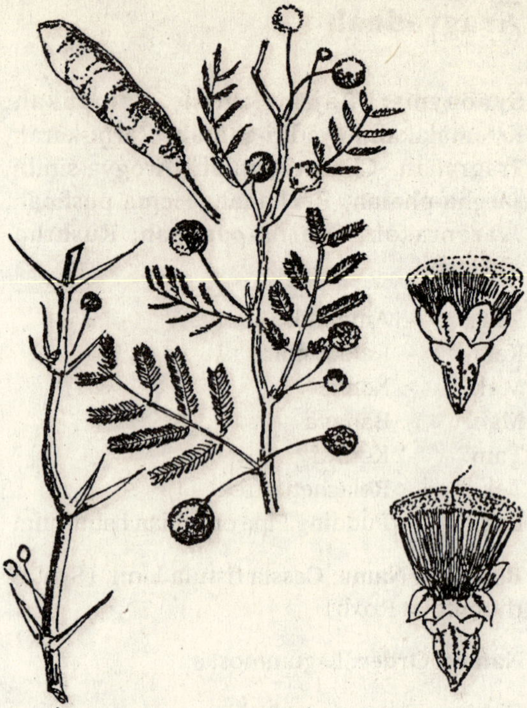

The milky exudation promotes strength and nutrition.

References: CS, sūtra, 4, 17, 18; SS, sūtra, 14, 36; Kalpa, 6,3

Arishṭakah

Synonyms: Māngalyah, Kṛshṇa-varṇah, Artha-sādhanah, Rakta bījah, Pīta-phenah, Phenilah, Garbha-pātaghnah, Gucchaphalah, Soma-valkalah, Kṛshṇa-vartula-phalah.

Hin. - Rīṭha
Tel. - Kunkuḍu, Phenilam
Mal. - Chavakāyi maram
Kan. - Araḍāla, Anṭa-vāla
Eng. - Soapnut tree
Tam. - Pūvandi
Vernacular - Arīṭhā (Ḍalhaṇa)

Botanical Name: Sapindus trifoliatus Linn (Syn. S. emarginatus Vahl.)

Natural Order: Sapindaceae

Habitat: South and West India, around the villages, cultivated in Bengal.

Medicinal Action:

Rasa : Pungent
Guṇa : Light, dry, active and emaciating
Vīrya : Hot
Vipāka : Pungent

It alleviates kapha and vāta, is abortifacient and is useful in grahas, burning pains, colic, threatened abortion, skin diseases and head aches.

The fruit is used in persons with worms and urinary disorders.

Note: Ḍalhaṇa describes the plant as having black rounded fruits (NIS on SS, śārīra,4,2,)

References: SS, uttara, 31,7; AS, uttara, 44.

Arjakah

Synonyms: Kuṭherakah, Kshudra-tulasī, Ugragandhā, Vaṭapatrah, Sūkshmapatrah, Madhu-manjarikah

Medicinal Action:

Rasa : Bitter and pungent
Guṇa : Light, dry and sharp
Vīrya : Hot
Vipāka : Pungent

It aggravates pitta, alleviates kapha, purifies the blood, increases salivation, is beneficial to eye-sight, and is useful in fever, skin diseases, vomiting, toxicosis, worms, pruritus, dysuria and swellings.

The root is used in menstrual disorders. The paste of the seeds is used externally. The stem and leaves aggravate pitta, are a heart tonic and appetizing.

Therapeutic Hints:

1. The leaves are used with other drugs to treat cough, dyspnoea and pain in the sides (CS, chikitsā, 11, 85).
2. The roots are used in menstrual disorders (AS, uttara,39).
3. A paste of the seeds is applied externally in kikkisa (stretch marks, as in pregnancy), (AS, śārīra, 36).
4. The plant is a heart tonic and refreshing (CS, sūtra, 27, 170).

References: (CS, sūtra, 14,, 32; SS, sūtra, 46, 235; NIS on SS, sūtra, 38, 18; AS, śārīra, 3).

Arjunah

Synonyms: Phālguṇah, Pārthah, Chitra-yodhih, Dhananjayah, Vairāntakah, Kirīṭī, Nadī-sarjah, Pāṇḍavah, Vīra-taruh, Kakubhah, Śambarah,

Indra-drumah, Karṇārī, Savya-sāchī, Dhavaḷah, Vīra-vṛkshah.

Hin. - Koh
Tam. - Marudayi
Tel. - Maddi-cheṭṭu
Kan. - Biḷi-mattiya mara
Mal. - Veḷu-marutu
Mah. - Sāra-ḍhol
Eng. - Arjuna tree

Botanical Name: Terminalia arjuna Bedd.

Natural Order: Combretacea

Habitat: Throughout the greater part of India.

Parts Used: Bark, leaves and heart-wood.

Description: A large evergreen tree growing upto 60ft. in height with a smooth grey bark. Internally the bark is reddish in colour. Leaves are short petioled, oblong and slightly serrated. Flowers appear in clusters, small and yellowish or red in colour. Fruit is about 1/2 inch in length, tan-coloured when dry. The flowering period is usually from March to June. The bark in quills is soft brown, scabrous and corky, easily seperable from the wood, breaking with a short fracture.

Medicinal Action:

Rasa : Astringent and sweet
Guṇa : Dry
Vīrya : Cold (hot according to a few texts)

It alleviates kapha and pitta, aggravates vāta, purifies the blood, promotes complexion and strength, is haemostatic, purifies wounds, and is useful in fractures of bones, toxicosis, traumatic affections, heart diseases, urinary disorders, disorders of medas, fatigue, excessive thirst, pain, anaemia, asthma and tuberculosis.

Therapeutic Hints:

1. It is used for external application in skin diseases (CS, sūtra, 3, 5).
2. It is one of the drugs used to relieve urticaria (udarda) (CS, sūtra, 4, 17).
3. It is used to treat heart-disease caused by vitiated kapha (CS, chikitsā, 26, 98).
4. A cold infusion of arjuna given internally is very useful in bleeding from internal organs (SS, uttara, 45, 23).
5. The flowers are used as collyrium in eye-diseases (SS, uttara, 12, 11).
6. It is used as fumigation in poisoning by organic and inorganic poisons (AS, sūtra, 81).

References: CS, sūtra, 4, 17; SS, sūtra, 38, 8, nidāna, 10, 12; AHṛ, sūtra, 15, 41.

Arkah

Synonyms: Kshīra-dalah, Tūla-phalah, Pratāpah, Kshīra-kāṇḍakah, Vikshīrah, Bhāskarah, Śuka-phalah, Sadāsumah, Vivasvān, Ahar-maṇī, Kshīra-parṇī, Vikartanah, Bhānuh, Mandārah, Divākarah, Śeeta-pushpakah, Suryāhvah, Āsphoṭakah.

Hin. - Madār, Āk
Tam. - Erukkai
Mal. - Errikai
Kan. - Ekka
Tel. - Jilleḍu
Eng. - Gigantic Swallow Wort; Madar

Botanical Name: Calotropis gigantea Br; (Syn. Asclepias gigantea Willd.)

Natural Order: Asclepiadaceae

Habitat: Common throughout India.

Description: A large, much-branched milky shrub, 3-6 ft. high and covered all over with soft, cottony hairs. Stem is erect, stout and round. Leaves are simple, opposite, sub-sessile with narrow base. Flowers are white or purplish with long pedicels. Fruits are large and fleshy with numerous flat seeds which have tufts of long. silky white hairs at the narrow ends.

Varieties: Most texts speak of two varieties - i.e. Arka and Alarka or red and white variety. A few texts speak of a variety, called Rājārka also.

Parts Used: Root-bark, whole plant.

Rasa : Pungent and bitter.
Pungent, sweet and bitter (the flowers)
Bitter and saline (the milky exutation)
Guṇa : Heavy
Vīrya : Hot

Both the varieties alleviate vāta and kapha, are appetizing and slightly purgative and are useful in haemorrhoids, oedema, ulcers, itching, skin diseases, worms, splenomegaly, toxicosis, tumours, ascites and affections of liver.

The flowers alleviate kapha and are used in toxicosis, skin diseases, worms, bleeding from various organs, tumours and oedema. The flowers of the white variety are an aphrodisiac, appetizing and useful in cough, asthma, haemorrhoids, anorexia, and salivation.

The milky exudation is a purgative and is used in skin diseases, tumours and ascites.

The root-bark is emetic, diaphoretic and useful in asthma and chancres and ulcers on the genital organs.

Therapeutic Hints:

1. The root of the white variety is used as errhine in headaches (SS, sūtra, 39, 6).
2. It is used, with ghee to purify (cleanse) ulcers and wounds (SS, sūtra, 37, 16).
3. Its tender leaves, root and bark relieve skin diseases (CS, chikitsā, 7, 112).
4. The bark is especially useful in wounds and ulcers infested with maggots (AHr, sūtra 29, 76).
5. The leaves are used to antidote poisons and cure worms (AS, sūtra, 8).
6. The milky exudation is used externally in skin diseases (CS, sūtra, 3, 12), and in bites of animals to remove the poison (SS, kalpa, 7, 51).
7. It is used in cases of snake bites to protect the heart (SS, kalpa, 5, 17).

Ārukam

Synonyms: Vīra-senam, Vīram, Vīrānakam.

Hin. - Aru, Ādu
Eng. - Peach tree

Botanical Name: Prunus persica Stokes (Syn. Amygdalus persica Linn; Persica vulgaris Nutt.)

Natural Order: Rosaceae

Habitat: Cultivated in the Himalayas, Kunawar upto 10,000 ft. Nilgiris at 6,000 ft., in the plains of N. India, Manipur and Baluchistan.

Description: A tree with elliptical leaves, about 4 inches long and 1½ inches broad, tapering to a sharp point above, with a short sharp point aboutabove, with a short leaf-stalk about ½ inch long; the margins are minutely serrate, with pale green under surface.

Varieties: There are four varieties.

Medicinal Action:

Rasa : Sweet (when ripe)
Astringent and sour (when unripe)

Guṇa : Heavy

Vīrya : Cold (not very hot according to Charaka)

It alleviates kapha and vāta, is constipative, a tonic and a digestive, cleanses the mouth and is useful in urinary disorders, haemorrhoids, tumours and diseases of impure blood.

When ripe, it aggravates kapha and pitta, is easily digested, appetizing and promotes the growth of all the dhatus.

Note: The ripe fruits are sweet, refreshing, nourishing and easy to digest (CS, sūtra, 27, 132).

References: SS, sūtra, 22, 8; NIS on ibid.

Asanah

Synonyms: Bījakah, Pīta-sārah, Pīta-sālakah, Bandhūka-pushpah, Priyakah, Mahā-sarjah, Paramāyudhah, Beeja-vṛkshah, Nīlakah.

Hin. - Āsan, Vijay-sār
Mal. - Mardu, Kari-mardu
Tam. - Kari-Mardu
Kan. - Baṇapu, Kari-matti, Hebhuluve
Ben. - Pīyā-sāb
Tel. - Naḷḷa-maddi

Botanical Name: Terminalia tomentosa Bedd (Syn. T. alata Roth; Pentaptera tomentosa Roxb)

Natural Order: Combretaceae

Habitat: Common throughout India.

Description: A large tree with the young parts covered with long, soft, hairs. The bark is rough, greyish-black with deep vertical fissures and transverse cracks. The leaves are alternate, leathery, elliptic-oblong, with many parallel nerves. The fruit is glabrous and large. The flowers appear in May.

Medicinal Action:

Rasa : Bitter and pungent

Vīrya : Hot

Vipāka : Sweet (of flowers)

It alleviates vāta and kapha, is beneficial to skin and hair, is a laxative, rejuvenative and is useful in pain, diseases of throat, skin-diseases, urticaria, herpes, leucoderma, urinary disorders, worms and bleeding from various organs.

The flowers aggravate vāta and are digestive.

Therapeutic Hints:

1. It is one of the drugs useful in urticaria (udarda).
2. The twigs are used for brushing the teeth (CS, sūtra, 5, 73).
3. It is useful in urinary disorders (including

diabetes) (CS, chikitsā, 11, 10).

4. It is found mostly in the eastern regions of India (NIS on SS, sūtra, 38, 8-9).
5. An arishṭa (alcoholic drink) prepared from this and certain other drugs is useful in anaemia, jaundice, urinary disorders, heart-diseases, cough, dyspnoea and intermittent fever (AS, chikitsā, 18).

References: NIS on SS, chikitsā, 9, 30; 25, 32; AS, chikitsā, 18).

Aśokah

Synonyms: Subhagah, Śoka-nāśah, Smarādhivāsah, Naṭah, Vichitrah, Karṇa-pūrakah, Kankelī, Hema-pushpah, Piṇḍa-pushpah, Vīta-śokah, Anganā-priyah, Madhu-pushpah, Rakta-pallavah, Rogi-taruh, Tāmra pallavah, Gandha-pushpah.

Hin.	- Aśok
Tam.	- Asogam
Tel.	- Aśoka
Kan.	- Kenkali mara.

Botanical Name: Saraca indica Linn (Syn. S. arborescens; Burm; Jonesia asoca Roxb; J. pinnata Willd.)

Natural Order: Leguminosae

Habitat: Central and E. Himalayas, E. Bengal and Western Peninsula.

Parts Used: Bark, flowers and seeds.

Description: A very handsome, small evergreen and erect tree with many branches spreading in all directions. The crown is dense and shapely, while the bark is smooth and brownish in colour. Young leaves are clustered together and drooping. The stems and branches bear the flowers which are slightly scented, changing in colour from yellowish orange to orange-scarlet. The bark internally is fibrous and of a pale reddish colour. Taste, astringent.

Medicinal Action:

Rasa	: Bitter, astringent and sweet
Vīrya	: Cold

It alleviates pitta, promotes complexion, is a heart tonic, constipative, hastens healing of fractured bones, and is useful in glandular enlargements, hamorrhoids, worms, toxicosis, tuberculosis, burning pains, fatigue, tumours, ascites, abdominal pain, flatulence, ulcers and menstrual disorders.

The bark is specific in menorrhagia and metrorrhagia.

Therapeutic Hints:

1. The seeds are valuable in cough (KS, chikitsā).
2. It is useful as a pain-reliever (CS, sūtra, 4, 18).
3. The flowers are used as collyrium in eye-diseases (SS, uttara, 17, 8).

References: NIS on SS, sūtra, 38, 14; 6, 27-29.

Asthi-saṁhārah

Synonyms: Vajra-vallī, Kuliśā, Śilārakah, Granthi-mān, Amarah, Asthi-śṛṇkhalā.

Hin.	-	Hadjosa
Ben.	-	Hād-bhang
Mah.	-	Kanḍu-vela
Kan.	-	Mangara-vaḷḷi
Tel.	-	Nalleru
Tam.	-	Arugani, Piranḍai
Mal.	-	Chanamparanḍa

Botanical Name: Vitis quadrangularis Wall (Syn. Cissus edulis Balz; C. quadrangularis Linn.)

Natural Order: Vitaceae

Habitat: The hotter parts of India.

Description: This is a climbing shrub with branched, leaf-opposed branches. The stems are fleshy, four-angled and constricted at the nodes. The old parts are leafless. The leaves are broadly ovate serrate and cordate at base. The flowers are red, in umbellate cymes. The fruit is a berry, red when ripe.

Medicinal Action:

Rasa : Sweet
Guṇa : Light and dry
Vīrya : Hot
Vipāka : Sour

It alleviates vāta and kapha, aggravates pitta, is a laxative, digestive, an aphrodisiac, promotes strength and complexion and is useful in fractures, dislocations of bones, haemorrhoids and eye diseases.

The plant with a four-angled stem is useful in flatulence, cataract, gout, epilepsy and diseases of vāta.

The plant with a three-angled stem aggravates vāta and is useful in haemorrhoids.

Therapeutic Hints: The fresh juice is given internally with milk in fractures of bones.

Aśvagandha

Synonyms: Vāji-gandhā, Kaṭukah, Aśvāvarohakah, Varāha-karṇī, Balyā, Turagī, Vāji-karī, Hayā, Balajā, Pushṭidā, Palāśa-parṇī, Vātaghnī, Kāma-rūpiṇī, Gandha-patrī, Kushṭa-gandhinī.

Hin.	-	Asgand
Tam.	-	Amukkira
Tel.	-	Penneru-gaḍḍa
Kan.	-	Hire-maḍḍina-giḍa, Angāra-geḍḍe
Eng.	-	Winter cherry

Botanical Name: Withania somnifera Dunal (Syn. Physalis flexuosa Linn; P. somnifera Wees; P. tomentosa Thunb.)

Natural Order: Solanaceae

Habitat: The drier parts of India.

Parts Used: Root, leaves and seeds.

Description: A small, erect, greyish, much branched under-shrub, growing to about 2 ft. high. The branches are soft and downy, while the leaves are simple, alternate and short petioled, with an entire margin. The small and axillary flowers are greenish or yellow in colour. The red fruit is round and smooth, containing very minute seeds, which are yellowish grey.

Medicinal Action:

Rasa : Pungent, bitter and astringent
Guṇa : Light
Vīrya : Hot

It alleviates vāta and kapha, promotes

nutrition, strength and complexion, is an aphrodisiac, bestows longevity and is useful in oedema, leucoderma, tuberculosis, cough, ulcers, toxicosis, worms, asthma, traumatic diseases and diseases of old age.

The leaves when externally applied as plaster are useful in tumours and glandular enlargements.

Therapeutic Hints:

1. It is strength-giving and promotes corpulency (CS, sūtra, 4, 9, 10).
2. The root can be used as an emetic (SS, sūtra, 39, 3).
3. It is one of the ingredients in a varti (plug) used to promote healing of wounds and ulcers (CS, sūtra, 37, 23).
4. It is used externally in pruritus, etc. (CS, sūtra, 6, 8).
5. The kshāra (alkali) of aśvagandhā is used in dyspnoea along with honey and ghee (CS, chikitsā, 17, 170).
6. An oil prepared from this drug is externally applied in diseases of the ear lobes (SS, chikitsā, 25, 26).
7. It is used as an ointment in swelling engendered by vitiated kapha (SS, sūtra, 37, 6).

References: CS, sūtra, 4, 10; SS, sūtra, 46, 433.

Aśva-karṇā

Synonyms: Jaraṇa-drumah, Sasya-samvaraṇah, Dhanyah, Dīrgha-parṇah, Kuśika-taruh, Kouśikah, Tārkshya-prasavah.

Tam. - Eṇṇei maram
Kan. - Eṇṇeya mara
Mal. - Varunga
Ben. - Teli-garjun
Eng. - Common gurjun tree or Wood oil tree
Vernacular - Gandha - munda (Ḍalhana)

Botanical Name: Dipterocarpus turbinatus Roxb (Syn. D. haevis Buch.)

Natural Order: Dipterocarpaceae

Habitat: Assam and Andamans.

Description: A lofty evergreen tree, reaching about 36.6. metres in height, clothed with tawny stellate pubescence. The bark is smooth and pale. The leaves are ovate and petiolate. The flowers are in axillary racemes, white, fragrant, 3.2 cm across. The fruit is globose, brown, 1.7 cm in diameter, enclosed in calyx-tube. The tree flowers in December-January; fruits are borne in April-May.

Medicinal Action:

Rasa : Pungent and bitter
Guṇa : Unctous

It is useful in putrid discharges, ulcers, fever, skin eruptions and headache.

Note: This is a tree resembling Aśvattha, found in eastesn regions (NIS on SS, sūtra, 11, 12.

Atasī

Synonyms: Picchilā, Devī, Mada-gandhah, madotkaṭah, Umā, Kshumā, Haimavatī, Su-nīlā, Nīla-pushpikā, Chaṇakā, Pārvatī, Tailottamā.

Hin. - Tisi
Vernacular - Alasi (Ḍalhaṇa)
Tel. - Atasī
Tam. - Aḷi-virai
Mah. - Aḷaśī
Mal. - Chirachaṇam vakku
Eng. - Common flax, linseed.
Ben. - Masinā - tisi

Botanical Name: Linum usitatissimum Linn.

Natural Order: Linaceae

Habitat: Cultivated throughout India upto 6,000 ft.

Medicinal Action:

Rasa : Sweet and bitter
Guṇa : Heavy and unctous
Vīrya : Hot
Vipāka : Pungent

It alleviates vāta, aggravates pitta, is constipative, promotes strength, decreases vision, causes sterility and is useful in ulcers, skin diseases, oedema and rheumatic pains.

The leaves alleviate kapha and vāta and are used in cough and dyspnoea.

Therapeutic Hints:

1. It is used as a poultice (upanāha) (CS, sūtra, 14, 36).
2. When applied externally, it relieves pain (CS, chikitsā, 29, 140).
3. It promotes suppuration in boils and abscesses (SS, sūtra, 37, 9).
4. The oil is beneficial as an article of diet in urinary disorders (including diabetes) (SS, chikitsā, 11, 6).

References: CS, sūtra, 3, 18; 13, 10; SS, sūtra, 45, 115; 46, 49.

Ativishā

Synonyms: Kāśmīrā, Vishā, Prativisha, Aruṇā, Ghuṇa-vallabhā, Śrngi, Mahoushadhah, Śveta-kanda, Visha-rūpa, Vīra, Amṛtah, Śveta-vacha, Śukla-kanda, Bhangura, Śiśu-bhaishajah, Śokhāpaha, Atisāraghni.

Hin. - Atees
Ben. - Ataicha
Tel. - Ativasa
Eng. - Indian aconite

Botanical Name: Aconitum heterophyllum Wall.

Natural Order: Ranunculaceae

Habitat: Common in the subalpine and alpine zones of the Himalayas, from the Indus to Kumaon, from 6,000 to 15,000 ft.

Description: The plant which is one to three feet high has erect branches, and oval, heart shaped, serrated leaves about two to three inches long. The blue flowers are small in size and the fruits are rounded with many seeds. The tubers are white internally, break with a resinous tracture and are very bitter. They do not cause tingling or numbness of the tongue.

Varieties: There are three varieties; white, black and brown.

Medicinal Action:

Rasa : Pungent and bitter
Guṇa : Emaciating
Vīrya : Hot

It alleviates all the doshas, is constipative, appetizing, and digestive, and is used in diarrhoea, cough, vomiting, oedema, fever, liver diseases, toxicosis, excessive thirst, haemorrhoids, catarrh, fever and worms. It is exceedingly useful in diseases of children.

Preparation: According to some texts, the root is to be boiled in a decoction of cowdung and later dried in the sun, before being used as medicine

Note: It is digestive, appetizing and alleviates all the doshas (CS, sūtra, 25, 40).

Reference: AHṛ, sūtra, 15, 35.

Ātma-gupta

Synonyms: Kapi-kacchuh, Kapi-priya, Śuka-piṇḍi, Kaṇḍūra, Śuka-simbika, Adhyaṇda, Pravrshāyini, Ṛshya-prokta, Markaṭi, Sadyah-śotha, Gātra-bhanga, Kacchu-mati, Ajāhvā, Vyāghra, Durabhi-priya, Kapi-roma-phala, Dusparśa, Romālu, Vṛshya.

Hin. - Kawanch
Ben. - Alkusa
Tam. - Punaikkali
Tel. - Pilli-aḍugu, Pedda-dūla-goṇḍa
Kan. - Nasagunni, Turachi
Mal. - Nayi-kuraṇa
Mah. - Kuhiti
Eng. - Cowhage, Cowitch

Botanical Name: Mucuna pruriens Bak (Syn. M. prurita Hook.)

Natural Order: Legumīnosae

Habitat: Distributed all over India.

Parts Used: Seeds, root and legumes.

Description: This is an annual twining herb. The leaves are pinnately three-foliate and stipellate, with ovate or rhomboid, membranous, leaflets which are almost glabrous above and silky pubescent beneath. The flowers are purplish, in racemes. The fruit is a turgid, longitudinally ribbed pod which is covered with dense, pale-brown, irritating scales. Flowers appear in February or March.

Medicinal Action:

Rasa : Sweet and bitter
Guṇa : Heavy
Vīrya : Cold

It alleviates all the doshas, promotes strength and growth, is an aphrodisiac and is useful in sterility, skin diseases, urticaria, disorders of impure blood, ulcers, menstrual disorders and emaciation (tuberculosis).

The seeds alleviate vāta and are a powerfully aphrodisiac. The fruits are also an aphrodisiac.

Note: The fruits have properties similar to those of Māsha (blackgram) (CS, sūtra, 27, 34; SS, sūtra, 46, 36).

References: CS, sūtra, 18, 4; SS, uttara, 52, 41.

B

Babbūlah

Synonyms: Mālāphalah, Yugma-kanṭah, Dṛdhāruhah, Ābhā, Kanṭaki, Sūkshma-patrah, Pīta-pushpah, Barbūrah, Kinkirātah, Yugalākshah, Tīkshṇa-kanṭakah, Pankti-bījah, Kaphāntakah, Dṛdha-bījah, Svarṇa-pushpah.

Hin.	- Bābul
Mal.	- Karuvelam
Tam.	- Karuvel
Kan.	- Kari-jāli, Gobbalimara
Tel.	- Nalla tumma
Eng.	- Indian gum arabic tree

Botanical Name: Acacia arabica Willd (Syn. Mimosa arabica Lam.)

Natural Order: Leguminoceae

Habitat: Naturalised in all parts of India; indigenous to Sind and the Deccan.

Parts Used: Bark, fruits, leaves and gum.

Description: A small or medium sized evergreen and thorny tree, about 25-30 ft. high. Leaves are pinnately compound, each leaf having 10-20 small, delicate leaflets. The flower heads are yellow. The fruit is a legume, with 8-12 seeds within. The flowering time is in August and September.

Medicinal Action:

Rasa : Astringent and bitter (the bark)
Astringent and sweet (the fruit)

	Pungent (the leaves)
Guṇa	: Unctous (the bark)
	Dry, heavy and viśada (the fruit)
Vīrya	: Cold (the gum, and fruit)
	Hot (the bark and leaves)

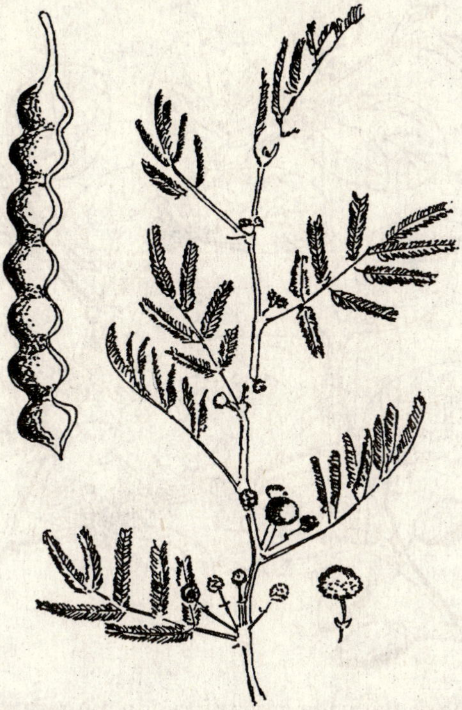

It alleviates kapha and pitta, is constipative and is useful in diarrhoea, haemorrhoids, skin diseases, toxicosis, worms, urinary diseases and burning sensation.

The leaves alleviate kapha and vāta, are constipative, stimutate the appetite, cause sterility and are useful in cough and haemorrhoids.

The fruit alleviates pitta and kapha, is constipative and emaciating.

The gum alleviates vāta and pitta, is constipative, styptic, promotes union of fractured bones and is used in diarrhoea, bleeding from various organs, urinary disorders, and bleeding from the vagina.

References: (AS, sūtra, 3, 20).

Bādāmah

Synonyms: Vātādah, Vātavairah, Netropamaphalah, Suphalah.

Hin. : Bādām

Botanical Name: Amygdalus communis Linn; (Syn. Prunus amygdalus Batsch)

Natural Order: Rosaceae

Habitat: Cultivated in the cooler parts of Punjab and Kashmir.

Description: This is a small tree with a pale purplish-brown, slightly wrinkled bark. The leaves are broadly or narrowly lanceolate, sharply serrate, acute, thin, stalked and bright-green. The flowers are nearly sessile, solitary or few, pale-pink in colour. The fruit is an irregularly ovoid drupe about 1 and 1/2 inches long. The seed is solitary, somewhat compressed, pointed at top and blunt at lower end, about 1 inch long.

Parts Used: Fruit and oil

Medicinal Action:

Rasa	: Sweet, sour and astringent
Guṇa	: Unctous and heavy (the fruit)
	Unctous and light (the oil)
Vīrya	: Hot (the fruit), cold (the oil)

The unripe fruit aggravates kapha and pitta and is a laxative.

The ripe fruit alleviates vāta and pitta, aggravates kapha, is an aphrodisiac and strength-giving.

The dried fruit alleviates vāta and pitta, aggravates kapha, promotes strength and nutrition and is an aphrodisiac.

The oil alleviates vāta and pitta, is a laxative

and an aphrodisiac, is useful in diseases of the head and burning sensation, and causes urinary disorders.

Badaram

Synonyms: Kolam, Karkanḍhū, Souviram, Phenilam, Picchila, Bālesṭham, Phala-saiśirah, Vṛtta-phalah, Ghoṇta, Guḍa-phalah, Dṛḍha-bīja, Kaṇṭaki, Vakra-kaṇṭaka, Surasa, Svādu-phalah, Ubhaya-kaṇṭakah.

Hin. - Ber
Ben. - Kul
Tam. - Hundai, Kullari
Tel. - Regu-cheṭṭu
Mah. - Bor
Kan. - Bogari, Elachi
Mal. - Ilanta, Kolam
Eng. - Jujube or Bhere fruit tree

Botanical Name: Zizyphus jujuba Lam (Syn. Z. mauritiana Wall; Z. sororia Schult; Rhamnus jujuba Linn)

Habitat: Indigenous and naturalized throughout India, and in the outer Himalayas upto 4,500 ft.

Description: This deciduous tree which grows upto 12 metres high has serrate, ovate to oblong oval or nearly lanceolate leaves, usually with two spines. The fruit which is a drupe is oblong to ovoid or sub-globose, 3 cms or less in length.

Varieties: There are three varieties of fruits : 1) a big variety called Souvīra, 2) a smaller variety called Kola and 3) a still smaller variety called Karkanḍhū

Parts Used: Fruits, bark and tender leaves

Medicinal Action:

Rasa : Sweet (souvīra and karkanḍhū)
Sour, sweet, astringent and bitter (karkanḍhū)

Guṇa : Heavy (all varieties), unctous (the ripe fruits)
Light (the dried and preserved fruits)

Vīrya : Cold (souvīra),
Hot (kola)

The souvira alleviates pitta, is a purgative, an aphrodisiac and nutritive and is useful in burning sensation, diseases of impure blood, tuberculosis and excessive thirst.

The kola alleviates vāta, aggravates kapha and pitta, is a laxative, stimulates the appetite and causes a burning sensation.

Karkanḍhū alleviates vāta and pitta.

The unripe fruits of all the three varieties aggravate kapha and pitta, while the ripe ones alleviate vāta and pitta and are laxatives. The dried fruits alleviate kapha and vāta, are laxative a and are used in thirst, fatigue and diseases of impure blood.

The leaves are used as a paste in fever and

burning sensation. The bark is useful in vesicles and other skin eruptions.

The seeds are useful in eye-diseases.

Therapeutic Hints:

1. It is used to relieve urticaria, fatigue and as a heart-tonic (CS, sūtra, 4, 10, 16, 17).
2. It is said to relieve hiccups (AS, sūtra, 15, 30) and vomiting (AS, sūtra, 15, 28).
3. The seeds relieve hiccups (CS, sūtra, 4, 14).
4. A soup prepared from badara relieves colic caused by vāta (SS, uttara, 42, 98).

References: CS, sūtra, 4, 13; 27, 132, 141; Kalpa, 1,8, 26; SS, sūtra, 38, 48; 39, 7,; 46, 139, 206; chikitsā, 17, 34; AS, sūtra, 9, 9; AHṛ, Sūtra, 6, 121.

Bākuchi

Synonyms: Somarājī, Avalgujā, Krimighnī, Sitāvarī, Krishṇa-phalā, Kushṭa-nāśinī, Somavallī, Kushṭa-hantrī, Kāmbhojī, Pūtigandhā, Kāntidā, Suparṇikā, Pūti-phalā, Vejānī, Asita-tvachā, Chandra-lekhā.

Hin.	- Babchi
Mah.	- Bāvachī
Ben.	- Latā-kasturi, Hākuch
Tel.	- Bhāvanchi, Kāla-ginjalu
Tam.	- Karpo-karishi, Bhoji-vidulu
Kan.	- Bāvanchi-bīja

Botanical Name: Psoralea corylifolia Linn.

Natural Order: Leguminosae

Habitat: Throughout India

Description: Śoḍhala Nighaṇṭu describes this plant as having darkish flowers, concealed fruits and four odourous blackish seeds.

This is an erect, sparsely hairy herb, about 1 metre high. The leaves are alternate, simple, broadly elliptic, obtuse, toothed, gland-dotted and sparsely hairy with persistent, lanceolate stipulates. The flowers are bluish purple or white, in condensed racemes. The fruit is an oblong or ovoid, black, closely pitted pod with a solitary small seed.

Varieties: A plant called Śvitrārī is another variety.

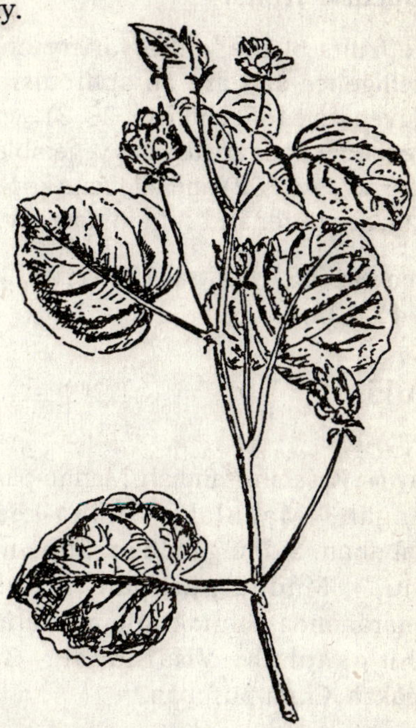

Parts Used: Seeds and oil of seeds.

Medicinal Action:

Rasa	: Sweet and bitter (the plant)
	Pungent and bitter (the fruit)
Guṇa	: Light and dry (the plant)
Vīrya	: Cold (the plant)
	Hot (the fruit)
Vipāka	: Pungent (The plant)

The plant alleviates kapha and pitta, promotes longevity, is a laxative and is useful in bleeding from internal organs, fever and ulcers.

The fruit alleviates kapha and vāta, aggravates pitta, is beneficial to the skin and hairs and is used in persons suffering from worms, skin diseases, toxicosis, dyspnoea, cough, oedema and anaemia.

The Śvitrāri variety alleviates all the three doshas, and is useful in rheumatism and skin diseases.

Therapeutic Hints:

1. The fruits of the white variety enhance intelligence and are an aphrodisiac and rejuvenative (SS, chikitsā, 28, 3).
2. The tender pods are used as vegetables (CS, sutra, 27, 96, 102) and alleviate kapha and pitta, are bitter and cold in potency.

References: (CS, chikitsā, 19, 32; 25, 15; SS, sūtra, 46, 235).

Bakulā

Synonyms: Keśarah, Kaṇṭhah, Madhu-panjarah, Tailāngah, Makulah, Simha-keśarah, Varalabdhah, Sīdhu-gandhah, Stree-mukha-madhu, Madhu-pushpah, Surabhi, Bhramarānanda, Sthirakusumah, Sārādikah, Sindhu-gandhah, Viśāradhah, Gūḍha-pushpakah, Chira-pushpah.

Hin.	- Mulari, Bakul
Tam.	- Magiḷa-maram
Tel.	- Pogaḍa
Kan.	- Renje, Pagaḍe-mara
Mal.	- Makura, Elani
Eng.	- Bakula tree

Botanical Name: Mimusops elengi Linn.

Natural Order: Sapotaceae

Habitat: Western Peninsula and the Andamans.

Description: A large, evergreen tree with dark grey, scaly, rough, deeply furrowed bark. The leaves are simple, entire, shortly-acuminate elliptic-oblong, glabrous, small in dry and large in damp localities. The flowers are white and fragrant, in fascicles. The fruit is a yellow, ovoid berry. The tree flowers in March-April. The bark is internally reddish-brown, brittle and breaks transversly. It has a rather disagreeable smell.

Medicinal Action:

Rasa	: Sweet and astringent (all parts)
Guna	: Unctous (flowers and fruits)
	Heavy (all parts)
	Dry and viśada (the fruits)
Vīrya	: Cold (all parts)
Vipāka	: Pungent

It alleviates kapha and pitta, is beneficial to the heart and is used in toxicosis, leucoderma, worms and diseases of teeth.

The flowers are fragrant and full of nectar, alleviate kapha and pitta, are appetite stimulants and constipative and are useful in diseases of impure blood.

The fruits alleviate kapha and pitta, aggravate vāta, are constipative, emaciating, bestow firmness of the teeth and cause flatulence.

The seeds are useful in headache and diseases of like teeth.

References: (SS, sūtra, 6, 27; AS, sūtra, 7, 182; 12, 86).

Balā

There are four varieties of Balā, viz.

I. Balā

Synonyms: Vāṭya-pushpah, Samāmśa, Vilala, Samanga, Odani, Bhadra, Balaḍhya, Śīta-pāki, Vāṭika, Khara-yashṭika, Vātaghni, Kanakah, Rakta-taṇḍulah, Phaṇi-jihvikah.

Hin.	- Khirayṭi
Mah.	- Laghu-chikaṇā
Ben.	- Beḍele
Tel.	- Muttuva-pulagamu
Kan.	- Visha-kaḍḍi, Kallangaḍale Chiṭṭāmuṭṭi-giḍa
Tam.	- Vattatiruppi
Mal.	- Malatāni, Chiru-paruva

Botanical Name: Sida cordifolia Linn.

Natural Order: Malvaceae

Habitat: Throughout the hotter parts of India.

Medicinal Action:

Rasa	: Sweet and bitter Sweet and astringent (the fruit)
Guṇa	: Unctous and heavy
Vīrya	: Cold
Vipāka	: Sweet

It alleviates vāta and pitta, is constipative, appetizing, and an aphrodisiac, promotes strength and nutrition and is useful in diarrhoea caused by pitta.

The fruit alleviates kapha and pitta, aggravates vāta, is constipative, emaciating and causes flatulence.

The root-bark is given with sugar and milk in polyuria (25, 40;).

Therapeutic Hints:

1. It is strengh-giving and constipative (CS, sūtra, 4, 10, 25, 40).
2. The plant is useful in diarrhoea (AS, sūtra, 7, 148).

II. Atibalā

Synonyms: Balika, Balya, Vikankata, Vāṭya-pushpika, Ghaṇṭa, Śīta, Śīta-pushpa, Bhūri-balā, Vṛshya-gandhika.

Hin.	- Kanghi
Mah.	- Kānsuli
Tam.	- Paṇiyāratuth
Tel.	- Tutturubeṇḍa, Nūgudeṇḍa
Kan.	- Kisangi, Hettuti
Mal.	- Kālūram, Veḷḷūram
Ben.	- Potari
Eng.	- Country Mallow

Botanical Name: Abutilon indicum G. Don (Syn. Sida indica Linn.)

Natural Order: Malvaceae

Habitat: Throughout the hotter parts of India.

Description: The plant grows upto 3ft high and has simple, alternately arranged and petiolate leaves, 1-2 inches long. The leaves have a whitish-green colour. The flowers are solitary and yellow in colour, with a slender pedical. The fruit is round with minutely furrowed, glabrous seeds.

Medicinal Action:

Rasa	: Bitter, pungent and sour
Vīrya	: Cold

It alleviates all the doshas, and is useful in fevers, toxicosis, urinary disorders, worms, burning sensation, vomiting and diseases characterised by exudation.

III. Mahābalā

Synonyms: Karambharā, Keśaruhā, Mṛgādani, Varsha-pushpā, Pīta-pushpā, Sahadevī, Jyesṭa-balā, Keśa-vardhanī, Prasādanī, Deva-bala, Sāriṇī, Gandha-vallarī, Mṛga-rasā, Mahāgandhā.

Hin.	-	Sahadeyi
Ben.	-	Beḍela
Mah.	-	Bhāurdi
Tel.	-	Muttavupulaga, Gūbataḍa
Kan.	-	Beṇṇe-garuḍa-giḍa
Mal.	-	Vaṭṭūram

Botanical Name: Sida rhombifolia Linn (Syn. S. rhomboidea Roxb.)

Natural Order: Malvaceae

Habitat: Throughout India.

Description: A shrubby weed with woody branches. The leaves are tapering or wedge-shaped at the base, broadened at top, with the upper part toothed, and the lower surface silvery with fine hairs. The stipule is longer than the petiole. The flowers are yellow and appear from October to December.

Medicinal Action:

Rasa : Sweet
Guṇa : Cold

It alleviates all the three doshas, is an aphrodisiac and is nutritive, promotes strength and is used in dysuria, flatulence, fever, heart-diseases, burning pains, haemorrhoids, oedema, intermittent fevers, and urinary disorders.

IV. Nāgabalā

Synonyms: Gāngeruki, Jhashā, Kharagandhini, Bhandroudani, Chatuhpalā, Mahāpatrā, Mahāphalā, Mahāśakhā, Anisṭah, Vishvadevā.

Varieties: There is a bigger variety called Bṛhan-nāgabalā.

Medicinal Action:

Rasa : Astringent and sweet (the fruit)
Sweet, sour, pungent and astringent (the root)
Guṇa : Heavy (the root)
Heavy and dry (the fruit)
Vīrya : Hot (the root)
Cold (the fruit)

It alleviates kapha and vāta, and is useful in ulcers, dysuria, diseases of traumatic origin, and skin diseases with itching.

The fruit aggravates vāta, is emaciating and constipative and causes flatulence.

The bigger variety alleviates all three doshas and is used in fevers with burning pains.

Bandhūkah

Synonyms: Bandhujīvah, Osṭhapushpah, Arka-vallabhah, Madhyandinah, Raktapushpah, Rāja-pushpah.

Hin. - Dupahariya, Gejuliya
Mah. - Dupāri
Tel. - Mankena-cheṭṭu
Ben. - Bāndhuli
Kan. - Kempu - gulābi
Tam. - Ucchitilakam
Vernacular. - Bādulī, Marunīyā (Ḍalhaṇa)

Botanical Name: Pentapetes phoenicea Linn.

Natural Order: Sterculiaceae

Habitat: Indigenous to NW India, Bengal, Gujarat. Planted in many places.

Varieties: There are four varieties based on the colour of the flowers.- white, dark, yellow and red.

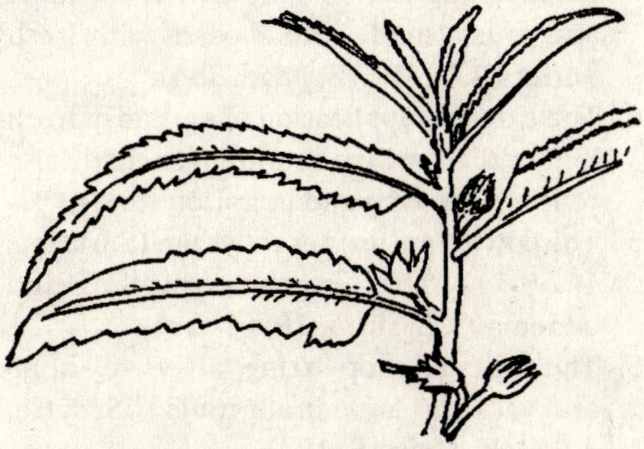

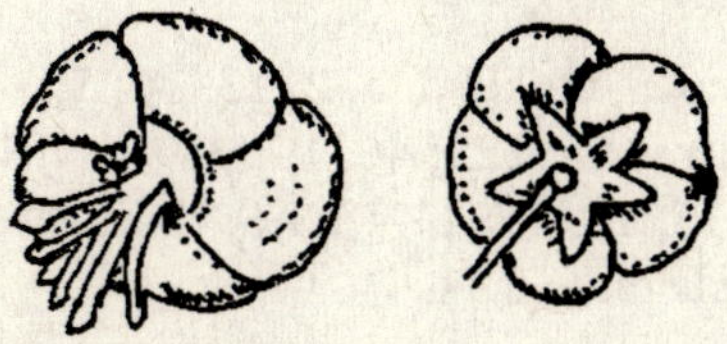

Parts Used: Flowers.

Medicinal Action:

Guṇa : Heavy
Vīrya : Hot

It aggravates kapha, is auspicious, constipative and is beneficial in fever.

Therapeutic Hints: The flowers aggravate kapha and are constipative (AS, sūtra, 12,90). The flowers are used as collyrium in certain eye-diseases (SS, kalpa, 1, 72).

Bhallātakah

Synonyms: Arushkarah, Śothahṛt, Vahnih, Vīra-taruh, Vraṇakṛt, Bhūta-nāshanah, Agni-mukhī, Anthah-satvā, Arśohitā, Nirdahanah, Tapanah, Krimighnah, Śyla bījah, Vātarī, Sphota-bījakah, Pṛthak-bījah, Dhanur-vṛkshah, Bījapādapah, Mahā-tīkshṇah, Sneha-bījah, Rakta-harah.

Hin. - Bhilāvā
Ben. - Bhelā
Mah. - Bibavā
Tel. - Jīḍi-cheṭṭu
Tam. - Śengotai-maram
Kan. - Gerkāyi, Kera-mara
Mal. - Cherumaram
Eng. - Marking-nut tree

Botanical Name: Semecarpus Anacardium Linn (Syn. Anacardium officinarum Gaertn.)

Natural Order: Anacardiaceae

Habitat: Throughout most parts of India.

Description: This is a deciduous tree with soft and hairy leaves and inflorescence. The bark is dark-brown and rough, exfoliating in very irregular patches. The leaves are alternate, coriaceous, exstipulate, oblong-obovate and rounded at the tip, with a thick petiole. The flowers are greenish-yellow, in panicles. The fruit is a purplish-black drupe with the pericarp rich in corrosive juice. The oil can be obtained by boiling the whole nut without depriving it of its pericarp.

Parts Used: Fruits, stalk and oil.

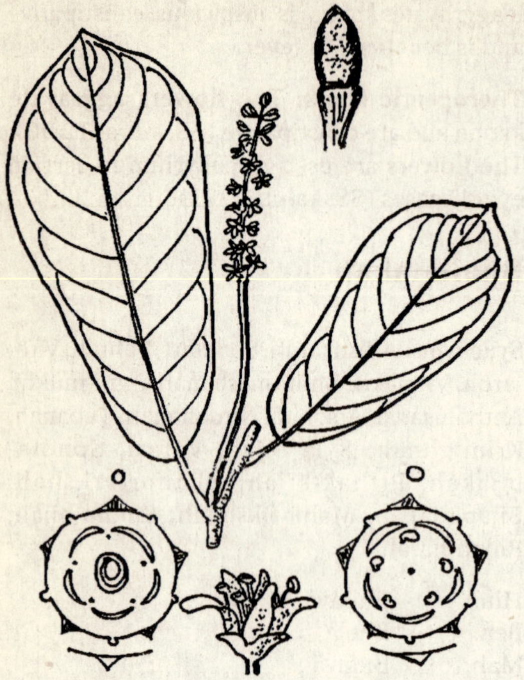

Medicinal Action:

Rasa : Pungent, bitter and astringent. Astringent and sweet (the fruit, stalk and oil)

Anurasa : Bitter (the oil)

Guṇa : Light, unctous and sharp

Vīrya : Hot

Vipāka : Sweet (the fruit)

It alleviates kapha and vāta, and is useful in persons suffering from worms, haemorrhoids, urinary disorders, constipation, sprue, tumours, fever, leucoderma and dyspepsia.

The ripe fruits alleviate kapha and vāta, are an aphrodisiac and constipative, strengthen the teeth, are digestive, appetizing, promote intelligence and are used in haemorrhoids, asthma, constipation, abdominal colic, ascites, flatulence, worms, ulcers, skin diseases, sprue, abdominal tumours, oedema and fever.

The fruit pulp alleviates vāta and pitta, promotes strength and complexion, is an aphrodisiac, is refreshing and is useful in burning pains, oedema, and anorexia.

The oil from the fruits is emetic, purgative, alleviates vāta and kapha, and is used in skin diseases, obesity, urinary disorders and worms.

The stalk aggravates vāta, alleviates pitta, is appetizing and beneficial to the hair (SS, sūtra, 46, 190).

Purification: The ripe fruits are collected and thrown into a trough of water. Only the fruits which sink to the bottom are collected and rubbed with pieces of brick. They can then be used for medicinal purposes.

Therapeutic Hints:

1. It is an aphrodisiac. (AS, uttara,49).
2. It is used in fever and constipation (SS, sūtra, 46, 196).
3. The toxic effect can be relieved by the external application of devadāru, sarshapa and musta made into a paste with fresh butter (RJN, Vol.III, page. 354).
4. The external application of a paste of fresh butter, tila, cow's milk and sugar candy also relieves swelling and irritation (ibid).
5. The flowers are used as collyrium (SS, kalpa, 1, 69-71). They engender swelling and oedema (CS, sūtra, 18,4).
6. The fruits are appetizing, alleviate kapha and vāta and are a brain-tonic (CS, sūtra, 4,9; AHṛ, sūtra, 6, 134).

References: CS, chikitsā, 1, 2, 13, 16; 5, 143-146; SS, sūtra, 45, 122; 46, 190, 196; NIS on chikitsā, 6 17, 18; 17, 41-42; AS, chikitsā, 19, 108; AHṛ, sūtra, 6, 134.

Bhaṅgā

Synonyms: Vijayā, Śakrāsanā, Jayā, Matkuṇārī, Vīra-patrā, Chapalā, Ajayā,

Ānandā, Harshiṇī, Mohinī, Bhrungī, Dhūrta-vadhū, Mātulānī, Neelī, Manoharā, Unmattinī, Yoginī, Kāmagnī, Tandrāruchi-vardhanī, Māyā.

Hin.	- Gānjā
Tam.	- Pañgi
Tel.	- Ganjāyi
Mal.	- Kanchāvu
Kan.	- Bhañgi
Eng.	- Hemp., Indian Hemp

Botanical Name: Cannabis sativa Linn.

Natural Order: Urticaceae

Habitat: More or less throughout India.

Description: This is a tall, erect, annual herb. The leaves are alternate or the lower ones opposite, serrate and palmate-nerved. Flowers are small, axillary, dioecious with the male ones occuring as short pendulous panicles and female ones crowded under leafy bracts. Achene is compressed with flattened seeds.

Medicinal Action :

Rasa	: Bitter
Guṇa	: Light, active and vikāsi
Vīrya	: Hot

It alleviates kapha and vāta, aggravates pitta, is appetizing, digestive and constipative, promotes longevity, strength and speech, stimulates the sexual urge, is an abortifacient, a sedative and is useful in skin diseases and convulsions.

Therapeutic Hints:

1. It is purified if it is fried with ghee after being boiled with milk (RJN, VOl.III, page, 350).
2. Troubles due to Bhañgā poison are remedied by partaking of a paste of śuṇṭhī mixed with curd prepared from cow's milk (ibid, page. 354).

Bhārngī

Synonyms: Brāhmaṇī, Padmā, Bhṛngajā, Angāra-vallarī, Mukha-dhoutā, Dūrvā, Brāhmaṇa-yashṭikā, Gardabha-śākā, Phanjikā, Barbarah, Bāleya-śākā, Vardhakah, Śāka-valeyah, Vāntārih, Vātārih, Kāsajit, Bhramareshṭah, Bhṛugu-bhavā, Khara-śākhā, Bhārgavī.

Hin.	- Bhārangi
Ben.	- Vāmun-hāṭī
Mal.	- Cheru-tekku
Tam.	- Thiru-tekku
Kan.	- Ganṭu-bhārangi

Botanical Name: Clerodendron serratum Spreng; (Syn. Volkameria serrata, Linn.)

Natural Order: Verbenaceae

Habitat: More or less throughout India.

Description: This is a shrub about 2 metres high, scarcely woody and not branched much. Stems are bluntly quadrangular and the young parts are usually glabrous. The leaves which are opposite are oblong or elliptic, acute, coarsely serrate and glabrous with an acute base. The flowers are numerous and showy, in pubescent cymes, pale blue in colour. The fruit which is a black drupe is succulent. The flowering period is from May to August. The root is light colored, often contorted, about an inch in thickness. The root bark is thin, faintly bitter; no peculiar odour.

Varieties: There are two varieties, one with white flowers and the other with blue ones.

Parts Used: Root and leaves.

Medicinal Action:

Rasa	: Pungent, bitter and astringent
Guṇa	: Dry and light
Vīrya	: Hot

It alleviates kapha and vāta, is constipative, appetizing, digestive and is useful in cough, asthma, abdominal tumours,diseases of impure blood, oedema, catarrh, fevers, hiccoughs, gout, tuberculosis and chancre.

The leaves alleviate all the doshas, and are used in fever, burning sensation and hiccoughs.

Therapeutic Hints:

1. It is used to correct unhealthy milk in lactating mothers (SS, chikitsā, 17, 44).
2. It is one of the drugs used in a prescription to cure epilepsy (SS, uttara, 61, 38).
3. The alkali (Kshāra) of the plant is used in cough of the kapha or vāta variety (AS, chikitsā, 4).

Bhavyam

Synonyms: Bhavam, Bhavishyam, Bhāvanam, Vakra-śodhanam, Picchila-bījam, Loma-phalam, Āvikā, Samputāngam, Kusumodaram.

Hin. - Chālta
Ben. - Chālta
Tam. - Uvā
Mah. - Karambaḷ
Eng. - Indian dillenia
Tel. - Uvva-kāyā

Botanical Name: Dillenia indica Linn

Natural Order: Dilleniaceae

Habitat: Evergreen forests of the Sub-Himālayan tract, from Kumaon and Garhwal eastwards to Assam and Bengal, and southwards to Central and South India.

Description: This is a large, evergreen tree with a red, smooth, moderately thick bark which peels off in small flakes. The leaves are large, upto 30 cms long, serrate, with prominent parallel nerves. The flowers are large, upto 15 cms across, solitary and white. The fruit big and fleshy.

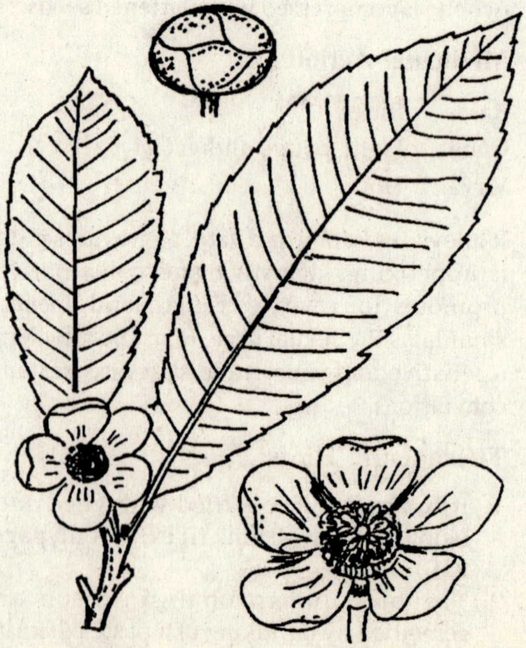

Parts Used: The fruit

Medicinal Action:

Rasa : Pungent, sour and astringent (the unripe fruit)
Sweet, sour and astringent (the ripe fruit)

Guṇa : Heavy

Vīrya : Hot (the unripe fruit)
Cold (the ripe fruit)

The unripe fruit alleviates kapha and vāta, is a heart-tonic and cleanses the mouth.

The ripe fruit aggravates kapha and pitta, is appetizing and constipative, cleanses the mouth, and is used in dysuria, fatigue, colic and toxicosis.

Note: It is constipative (CS, sūtra, 27, 131).

References: NIS on SS, sūtra, 46, 139; AS, chikitsā, 9).

Bheṇḍā

Synonyms: Bheṇḍātikā, Kshetra-sambhavah, Chatushpadah, Suśākah, Picchilah, Karaparṇaphalah, Chatush-puṇḍrah, Amalapatrah, Vṛtta-bījah.

Hin.	- Bhiṇḍī
Mah.	- Bheṇḍe, Rān-bheṇḍe
Kan.	- Bheṇḍe kāyi
Mal.	- Veṇḍa
Tel.	- Beṇḍ-kāya
Eng.	- Edible hibiscus, Esculent okra

Botanical Name: Abelmoschus esculenthus Moench (Syn. Hibiscus longifolius, Roxb; Hibiscus esculenthus Linn.)

Natural Order: Malvaceae

Habitat: Cultivated throughout India.

Description: This is a large herb cultivated as a garden crop for its fruits. The plant grows to about 3 to 8 feet high, with big, yellowish flowers, and palmately compound leaves. The fruit is a capsule 12-25 cms long, elongated and slightly angular with glabrous seeds.

Medicinal Action:

Rasa : Sour

Guṇa : Heavy and unctous

Vīrya : Hot

It alleviates vāta, aggravates kapha, is an aphrodisiac, strength-giving and appetizing. It is contra-indicated as an article of diet in cough, loss of appetite and catarrh.

Bhṛngāhvā

Synonyms: Bhramara - cchallī, Bhṛngamūlikah

Gin.	- Bhaulan
Mah.	- Bhramarasāli, Bhorsal
Tel.	- Dudippa
Tam.	- Vellai-kadambu

Botanical Name: Hymenodictylon excelsum Wall.

Natural Order: Rubiaceae

Habitat: Base of the Himalayas and Western Peninsula.

Description: A large decidous tree with thick branches and a greyish-brown, soft corky bark which is furrowed on old trees and smooth on branches. The leaves are broadly ovate, yellowish-green, petioled, with white veins. The flowers are pale-green. The fruit is a pendulous capsule with broadly winged seeds. The tree flowers in June-July; fruits are borne in March-April.

Medicinal Action:

Rasa : Bitter and pungent
Vīrya : Hot

It alleviates all three doshas, is appetizing and relieves sore-throat.

Bhṛngarājah

Synonyms: Mārkavā, Keśa-ranjanah, Pitr-priyā, Ranjakah, Keśyah, Kuntala-vardhanah, Kesa-rājah, Pankajātah.

The Yellow Variety: Svarṇa-bhṛngārah, Harivāsah, Devapriyah, Vandanīyah, Pāvanah.

The Blue Variety: Mahānīlah, Sunīlakah, Śyāmalah

Hin - Bhāngarā
Ben. - Bhamirāj
Kan. - Garuga
Tam. - Karisalānkaṇṇi
Mah. - Mākā
Tel. - Gunṭa-kalagara
Mal. - Kaiyanta-kara
Eng. - Trailing eclipta

Botanical Name: Eclipta alba Hassk; (Syn. E. erecta Linn; E. prostrata Roxb; E. adpressa Moech)

Natural Order: Compositae

Habitat: In most places throughout India

Description: This is a small, erect or prostrate, many branched, annual herb growing upto 2 ft. in height. The stems and leaves are covered with appressed hairs. The leaves are simple, dark green, opposite, sessile and ablong-lanceolate with a sub-acute or acute tip. The flowers are white, small, axillary or terminal.

Varieties: There are two varieties

1. ith yellow flowers
2. With blue flowers.

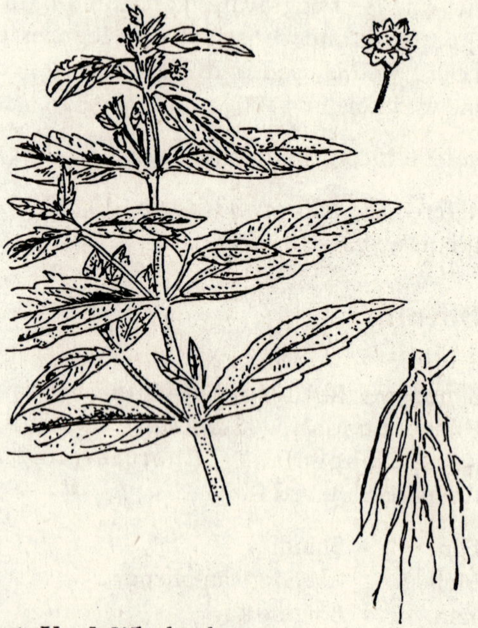

Parts Used: Whole plant

Medicinal Action:

Rasa : Pungent and bitter
Guṇa : Dry and sharp
Vīrya : Hot

It alleviates kapha and vāta, causes rejuvenation, promotes intelligence, is beneficial to the skin, hair and teeth, and is useful in fevers, diseases of the skin, eyes and head, cough, asthma, worms, anaemia, heart-disease, hernia, indigestion, toxicosis, baldness and greying of hair.

Therapeutic Hints: The oil prepared from this plant is useful in cough and dyspnoea, when given internally (SS, uttara, 51, 30).

References: CS, vimāna, 7, 21; SS, chikitsā, 7, 24; kalpa, 8, 56).

Bhūmyāmalakī

Synonyms: Tāmalakī, Śivā, Tālī, Kshetrāmalī, Jhārikā, Bahupushpī, Adhyaṇḍah, Ajaṭā, Sūkshma-phalā, Vitunnakah, Aphalā, Mālā, Dhṛḍapādi, Vituntikah, Bhū-dhātrī, Vṛshyā, Vishaghnī, Bahupatrikā, Ahimapadā, Vīrā, Vishva-parṇī, Bhū-parvā, Dalasparśinī, Choraṭā.

Hin.	- Bhui-āmlā
Tam.	- Kīḷa-nelli
Tel.	- Nela-usirike
Mal.	- Kiḷa-nelli
Kan.	- Kiru-nelli, Nela-nelli

Botanical Name: Phyllanthus niruri Linn (Syn. Nymphanthus niruri Lour; Urinaria erecta Medic.)

Natural Order: Euphorbiaceae

Habitat: Throughout the hotter parts of India.

Description: The plant is a glabrous, annual herb, 1-2 ft. high. Branchlets are slender and spreading. They look very much like compound leaves. Leaves are simple, alternate and oblong. Flowers are small, axillary, yellowish in colour, and hanging below the branchlets. The fruit is a capsule, depressed and smooth.

Parts Used: The whole plant

Medicinal Action:

Rasa	: Astringent, sour and sweet
Guṇa	: Light
Vīrya	: Cold

It alleviates kapha and pitta, aggravates vāta, promotes conception, is appetizing and useful in urinary disorders like dysuria and retention, cough, asthma, skin diseases, diseases of impure blood, anaemia, tuberculosis, traumatic affections, thirst, hiccoughs, burning pains and toxicosis.

The seeds are beneficial in menstrual disorders.

Therapeutic Hints:

1. It is valuable in cough and dyspnoea (CS, sūtra, 4).
2. It is one of the ingredients of a medicated ghee useful in chronic fevers, tuberculosis, cough, head-ache, pain in the sides, and malignant jaundice (CS, chikitsā, 3, 219-220; SS, uttara, 39, 219).

Bhūnimbā

Synonyms: Chirāyatā, Chira-tiktā, Kirātah, Rāma-senakah, Anārya-tiktah, Tiktah, Kāṇḍa-tiktah.

Hin. - Chirāyata
Ben. - Chirata
Tam. - Chirāyatu
Tel. - Nela-vemu
Kan. - Nela bevu
Mal. - Kiriyāttu
Mah. - Kirayita
Eng. - Gentian, Chiretta

Botanical Name: Swertia chirata Ham; (Syn. Gentiana chirayata Roxb; G. chirata Wall; Agathotes chirata D. Don.)

Natural Order: Gentianaceae

Habitat: Native of temperate Himālayas, 4,000 - 10,000 ft. from Kashmir to Bhutan and Khasia Hills, 4,000-5,000 ft.

Description: An annual or perennial herb with robust stems. The root is woody and knotty īrregularly, giving off several small rootlets. Leaves are opposite, broadly lanceolate and acute. Flowers occur in terminal corymbs, and are greenish-yellow coloured, with a tinge of purple. Fruit is a capsule with many minute compressed seeds.

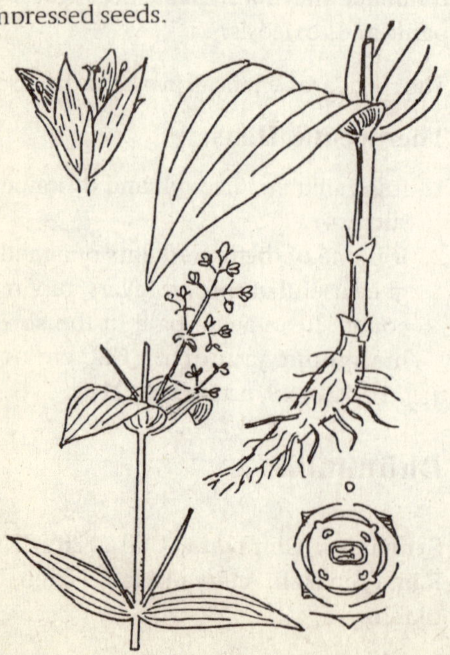

Varieties: There is another variety called Naipāla which has the synonyms : Jvarāntakah, Tṛṇa-nimbah, Nāḍī-tiktā, Nidrārī and Sannipātakah.

Parts Used: The whole plant. The root is medicinally more active.

Medicinal Action:

Rasa : Bitter
Guṇa : Light and dry
Vīrya : Cold
Slightly hot (the Naipāla nimba)

It alleviates kapha and pitta, aggravtes vāta, is a laxative, purifies the milk in lactating women, heals wounds and is used in fevers, thirst, skin diseases, itching, oedema, worms, burning pains, colic, urinary disorders, ulcers, asthma, cough, vaginal bleeding and haemorrhoids.

The Naipāla variety alleviates kapha and pitta, is yogavāhī, and analgesic, causes insomnia and is used in fever and diseases of impure blood.

Bhūrjapatrah

Synonyms: Bhūrjah, Charmī, Bahu-valkalah, Chada-patrah, Valka-drumah, Chitra-tvak, Bindu-patrah, Rakshā-patrah, Bhūtaghnah, Mṛdu-patrah, Mṛdu-charmī, Śailendrasthah, Śibī, Sthiracchadah, Dala-nirmokah, Patra-pushpakah, Bahupaṭah, Bahu-tvak.

Hin. - Bhoj-patra
Eng. - Bhojapatra tree

Botanical Name: Betula bhojpatra Wall (Syn. B. utilis D. Don.)

Natural Order: Betulaceae

Habitat: Temperate Himālayas from Kashmir, 7,000-12,000 ft. to Sikkim, 9,000-14,000 ft and Bhūtan.

Medicinal Action:

Rasa : Astringent and pungent
Vīrya : Hot

It alleviates all three doshas, promotes strength, is auspicious and is useful in mental diseases, ear-ache, bleeding from internal organs, diseases of impure blood and medas, and toxicosis.

References: (CS, śārīra, 8, 38; chikitsā, 26, 227)

Bhūstṛṇaṃ

Synonyms: Guhya-bījah, Bhū-tīkah, Sugandham, Gomayapriyam, Chattrā, Māla-tṛṇam.

Medicinal Action:

Rasa : Pungent and bitter
Guṇa : Light, sharp and dry
Vīrya : Hot

It aggravates pitta, is appetizing and digestive, cleanses the mouth, increases the amount of faeces, causes burning sensation and sterillity, vitiates the blood and is harmful to the eyes.

References: CS, sūtra, 27, 172; vimāna, 7, 17; NIS on SS, sūtra, 38, 18-19, 46, 235)

Bījapūrah

Synonyms: Mātulungah, Rūchakah, Phala-pūrakah, Amla-keśarah, Pūrṇa-bījah, Sukeśarah, Bīja-phalakah, Jantughnah, Dantura-cchadah.

Hin. - Bijoura
Ben. - Tāvā-levu
Mah. - Mahā ḷung
Kan. - Mādaḷa
Tel. - Mādīphalamu
Mal. - Madulungam
Eng. - Citron, Adam's apple tree

Botanical Name: Citrus medica Linn

Natural Order: Rutaceae

Habitat: Cultivated in many parts of India.

Description: This is a small tree armed with strong, axillary spines. The leaves are alternate, one foliate with a winged petiole; the leaflets are elliptic or ovate-lanceolate, usually serrate, coriaceous, glabrous and gland dotted. The flowers are bisexual, white and fragrant, solitary or in axillary cymes. The fruit is an avoid, oblong or globose berry. The flowering season is in April or May.

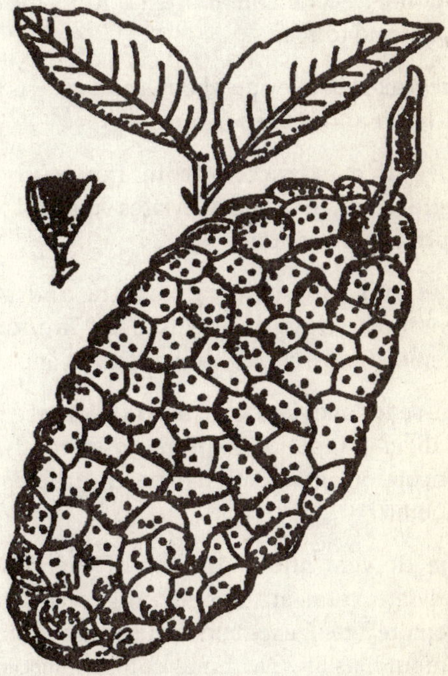

Medicinal Action:

Rasa : Sour and pungent (the unripe fruit)
Sour and sweet (the ripe fruit)
Bitter (the seeds and skin)
Sweet (the pulp and juice extracted from the skin)
Guṇa : Light (the fruit and flower)
Heavy (the seeds)

Unctous and heavy (the pulp and skin)

Vīrya : Hot (the fruit, skin and seed)
Cold (the pulp, flowers and juice extracted from skin).

Vipāka : Sweet (the pulp)

The unripe fruit aggravates all the three doshas and engenders impurity of blood.

The ripe fruit alleviates kapha and vāta, promotes nutrition, complexion and strength, is a cardiac-tonic and is used in indigestion, constipation, asthma, cough, oedema, abdominal colic and anorexia. It purifies the throat and tongue.

The fruit-skin alleviates kapha and vāta, is hard to digest and is used in worms.

The juice extracted from the fruit-skin aggravates kapha and alleviates vāta and pitta. It promotes nutrition.

The fruit pulp alleviates pitta and vāta, promotes strength and is used in worms, haemorrhoids, cholera, constipation and colic.

The seeds alleviate the three doshas, are hard to digest, appetizing, promote strength and conception and are used in haemorrhoids and oedema.

The flowers and filaments of the flowers alleviate vāta, are appetizing, constipative, promote intelligence and are used in abdominal tumours, ascites, asthma, cough, hiccoughs, alcoholism, constipation, bleeding from internal organs, haemorrhoids and tuberculosis (CS, sūtra, 27, 154; SS, sūtra, 46, 149-151, 334).

Note: It relieves vomiting (CS, sūtra, 4, 14) and when applied externally is useful in swellings of Vāta type. (SS, sūtra, 37, 3).

References: (CS, sūtra, 46, 149-152, 344, 433; AS, chikitsā, 5, 38; CS, sūtra, 27, 154).

Bilvah

Synonyms: Mahā-kapitthah, Śrī-phalah, Go-harītakī, Pūti-vātah, Māngalyah, Mālūrah, Tri-śikhā, Śāndilyah, Śulushah, Kapītanah, Mahā-phalah, Hṛdya-gandhah, Śalyah, Śalātuh, Karkaṭah, Śūlapatrah, Śiveshṭah, Patra-śresṭah, Tri-patrah, Gandha-patrah, Lakshmī phalah, Durāruhah, Tri-śākhapatrah, Sudā-phalah, Sunītikah, Sameera-sārah, Adharāruhah, Kaṇṭakāḍhyah, Sitānanah, Nīla-mallikah, Pīta-phalah, Soma-harītakī.

Hin. - Bel
Kan. - Bela-patre
Tel. - Śrī-phalamu, Māreḍu
Tam. - Vilvam
Mal. - Kūvalam
Eng. - Bengal quince

Botanical Name: Aegle marmelos Corr; (Syn. Crataeva marmelos Linn; Feronia pellucida Roth.)

Natural Order: Rutaceae

Habitat: All over India.

Description: This is a glabrous, spiny, deciduous tree with the spines being sharp, straight and axillary; the bark grey and corky. The leaves are alternate, three foliate with a resinous odour. The leaflets are 2.5 to 5 cms long, usually ovate-lanceolate, acuminate and gland dotted. The flowers are greenish-white and fragrant, occuring in short lateral panicles. The fruit is a woody berry with many seeds embedded in orange coloured aromatic pulp.

Parts Used: Root, bark, leaves, fruits and oil.

Medicinal Action:

Rasa : Sweet, astringent, bitter and pungent

Guṇa : Heavy and dry
Light (the root)

Unctous and heavy (the unripe fruit)

Vīrya : Hot

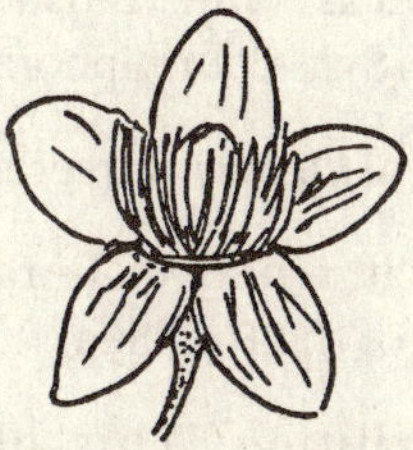

The root alleviates all the doshas, especially vāta, and is used in vomiting, colic and dysuria.

The unripe and young fruits alleviate kapha and vāta, are constipative, appetizing and digestive, used in abdominal colic, sprue and diarrhoea.

The ripe fruit aggravates vāta and pitta, alleviates kapha, is hard to digest, constipative and causes indigestion.

The leaves alleviate vāta and pitta, alleviates kapha, is hard to digest, constipative and causes indigestion.

The flowers are useful in diarrhoea, thirst and vomiting. The flower buds alleviate kapha and vāta, are constipative and relieve colic.

The oil extracted from the pulp alleviates vāta.

Therapeutic Hints:

1. The young fruits of Bilva are to be preferred to ripe ones, as they are medicinally more active (CS, sūtra, 27, 138).
2. It is useful in haemorrhoids and swellings (CS, sūtra, 4, 11-16).
3. It is valuable in diarrhoea of pitta and kapha types (CS, sūtra, 2, 20).
4. Its twigs are not to be used for brushing the teeth (AS, sūtra, 3, 20).
5. The flowers are used as collyrium for eye diseases (SS, uttara, 12, 11).
6. The kshāra of the fruit is useful in ascites (CS, chikitsā, 13, 170).

References: CS, sūtra, 5, 64; 25, 40; 27, 107, 138; kalpa, 12, 92; siddhi, 3, 70; 7, 53; SS, sūtra, 38, 46; 46, 174, 254; NIS on chikitsā, 5, 7; chikitsā, 8, 13; 37, 46; uttara, 40, 44; AHṛ, sūtra, 6, 167; AS, uttara, 47).

Bimbī

Synonyms: Tuṇḍikerī, Rakta-phalah, Tumbī, Oshṭopamaphalah, Pīluparṇī.

Hin. - Kandūri
Ben. - Tālākuchā
Tan. - Kovai, Vimbam
Tel. - Doṇḍatīga
Mah. - Toṇḍalī
Kan. - Toṇḍe
Mal. - Kova
Eng. - Kunch tree
Vernacular - Tiṇḍurika (Ḍalhaṇa)

Botanical Name: Cephalandra indica Schrader; (Syn. Coccinia indica W & A; Momordica monadelpha Roxb; Bryonia grandis Linn.)

Natural Order: Cucurbitaceae

Habitat: Throughout India

Description: A prostrate or climbing, branched herb with a thick taproot. Branches are glabrous, grooved with simple tendrils. Leaves are alternate, simple, ex-stipulate, broadly ovate, cordate at the base with five lobes. Flowers are solitary, axillary and white in colour. Fruit is an oblong, ovoid berry, bright scarlet when ripe.

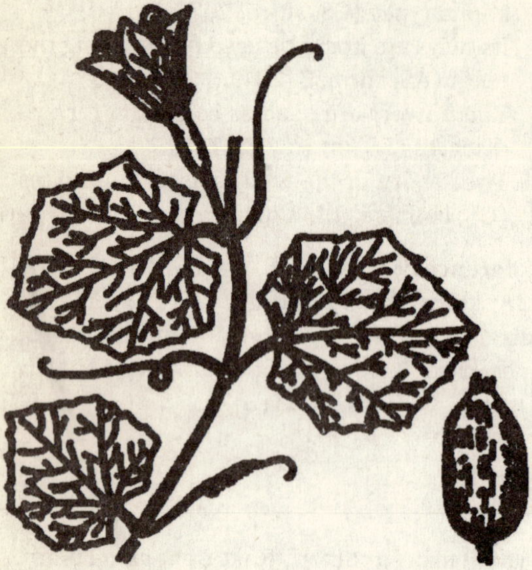

Parts Used: Fruit

Medicinal Action:

Rasa : Sweet

Guṇa : Heavy

Vīrya : Cold

It alleviates kapha and pitta, is constipating, appetizing, emaciating, a lactagogue and is used in vomiting, ulcers, nausea, skin diseases, diseases of impure blood, oedema, anaemia, fever, asthma, cough and bleeding from internal organs. It causes flatulence (SS, sūtra, 46, 164).

Note:

1. The fruits are of two kinds, bitter and sweet. The sweet variety is used for culinary purposes (CS, sūtra, 27, 142).
2. The root is emetic and is used as errhine (CS, sūtra, 1, 78).

References: SS, sūtra, 46, 164, 176; AS, sūtra, 7).

Bolam

Synonyms: Gandha-rasam, Piṇḍam, Nirloham, Bārbaram, Sugandham, Nālakam, Pouram, Sitā, Raktāpaha, Muṇḍam, Surasam, Piṇḍakam, Visham, Sourabham, Mahāgandham, Viśvam, Vraṇārihī, Prāṇa, Gopakam, Gosaśaśa, Gāndhāra, Maśi-vardhanam.

Hin. - Hirā-bol
Ben. - Hira-bol
Mah. - Boḷ
Eng. - Myrrha

Botanical Name: Balsamodendron myrrha T. Ness; (Syn. Commiphora myrrha (Nees.) Engl.)

Natural Order: Burseraceae

Habitat: A native of Arabia and of the African coast of the Red Sea.

Description: This plant has a shrubby arborescent stem, spiny branches, a very pale gray bark and yellowish-white wood. The leaves are compound with obovate leaflets.

Parts Used: Gum-resin.

Medicinal Action:

Rasa : Pungent, bitter and astringent

Vīrya : Hot

It alleviates the three doshas, especially kapha and pitta, is digestive, appetizing, fragrant, a brain tonic, and a uterine stimulant. It purifies the blood and is useful in skin diseases, excessive uterine bleeding, epilepsy, urinary diseases, dysmenorrhoea, fever, perspiration and bleeding from the anus. It causes impotence.

Brahmadaṇḍī

Synonyms: Aja-daṇḍī, Kaṇṭapatraphalā

Medicinal Action:

Rasa : Pungent and bitter
Vīrya : Hot

It alleviates kapha and vāta and is useful in oedema and swellings.

Brāhmī

Synonyms: Vayasthā, Matsyākshī, Surasā, Somavallarī, Sarasvatī, Soumyā, Suraśreshṭā, Suvarcchalā, Kapotavegā, Vai-dhātrī, Divya tejah, Mahoushadhih, Svāyambhuvī, Maṇḍūkī, Medhyā, Bhāratī.

Hin. - Brāhmī, Charelī
Ben. - Brāhmī, Thālkuni
Tel. - Maṇḍūka-brāhmi-cheṭṭu
Tam. - Vallārai
Mal. - Muttaḷ
Kan. - Ondelaga, Ili-kivi-baḷḷi
Eng. - Indian pennywort

Note: The properties of Brahmī are supposed to be identical with those of Maṇḍūka-parṇī (Botanical name : Hydrocotyle asiatica Linn; = Centella asiatica (Linn) Urban; Eng. - Indian Penny wort; Natural order : Umbelliferae).

Botanical Name: Herpestis monniera (Linn) H.B. & K (Syn. Gratiola monniera Linn; Bacopa monnieri (Linn) Pennell; Monniera cuneifolia Michx.)

Natural Order: Scrophulariacae

Habitat: Throughout India in wet, damp and marshy areas.

Description:

1. Hydrocotyle asiatica Linn. (Syn. Centella asiatica Urban).

A slender, prostrate or creeping perennial herb growing upto 3 or 6 inches long, with a fairly long, slightly tuberous root. Leaves are simple with an elongated petiole, each leaf being 3-6 inches in length. The petiole is channelled, and the leaves are parrot green in colour. Flowers are sessile and small. It is in flower nearly all throughout the year.

2. Herpestis monniera Linn

A somewhat succulent, glabrous, prostrate annual herb with many branches which are opposite, round and smooth. Each branch has nodes from which arise leaves which are simple, almost sessile and opposite. Flowers are solitary, alternate, pedicelled and small, with blue or blush-white colour. Fruit is a capsule containing many minute seeds.

Medicinal Action:

Rasa : Astringent, bitter and sweet
Guṇa : Slimy
Vīrya : Cold

It alleviates the three doshas, especially kapha, is appetizing, a laxative, brain-tonic, heart tonic, causes rejuvenation, is beneficial to the throat and voice, and is useful in skin diseases with itching, anaemia, urinary disorders, cough, oedema, fever, enlargement of spleen, gout, anorexia, asthma, toxicosis, tuberculosis, insanity, fistulous ulcers, and diseases of impure blood (SS, chikitsā, 7, 24; uttara, 62, 30).

Therapeutic Hints:

1. It is useful in sterility (CS, sūtra, 4, 18).
2. The juice of the plant is useful in the mental disorder called atattvābhinivesha (hysteria?) (CS, chikitsā, 10, 62).
3. When used as an ingredient in medicated ghee, it is useful in skin diseases (AS, chikitsā, 21).

References: SS, chikitsā, 7, 24; 28, 5, 6; uttara, 62, 30).

Bṛhatī

Synonyms: Mahatī, Simhī, Prasahā, Hingulī, Kulī, Ākrāntā, Kshudra-Vārtākī, Rakta-pākī, Latā, Rāshṭrikā, Sthūla-kaṇṭā, Kshudra-bhaṇṭā, Bhaṇḍākih, Bahupatrī, Kaṇṭatanuh, Kaṇṭāluh, Kaṭphalā, Parāvedih

Hin. - Bārhaṇṭa, Katāyi
Ben. - Vyākud
Tel. - Tella-mulaka
Tam. - Muḷḷichadi, Cheruchuṇṭa
Kan. - Hegguḷḷa, Kiri-guḷḷa
Mal. - Cheru-chuṇḍa
Mah. - Doraḷī
Eng. - Indian nightshade

Botanical Name: Solanum indicum Linn (Syn. S. canescens Blum; S. violaceum Jacq.)

Natural Order: Solanaceae

Habitat: Throughout tropical India.

Description: This is a much branched, prickly undershrub. The branches are star shaped and downy, armed with recurved prickles. The leaves are ovate, acute, sub-entire, or lobed, sparcely pricky and often unequal-sided. The flowers are blue, in racemes. The fruit is a globose berry, yellow when ripe and glabrous. Flowers appear in October.

Parts Used: Root and fruits.

Varieties: There are two other varieties -(1) A small variety (Kshavikā) and (2) A white variety (Śveta-bṛhatī).

Medicinal Action:

Rasa : Pungent and bitter
Guṇa : Light (the kshavikā and the fruits)
Vīrya : Hot

The root alleviates kapha and vāta, is a cardiactonic, constipative and digestive, and is useful in anorexia, indigestion, skin diseases with itching, fever, asthma, colic, cough, heart disease, vomiting, worms, and nausea.

The fruits alleviate vāta and kapha, and are used in worms, herpes, and skin diseases characterized by itching.

The kshavikā variety also alleviates vāta and kapha, and is used in dyspnoea, abdominal colic, fever, vomiting, heart diseases and indigestion.

The white variety also alleviates vāta and kapha, and is appetizing. It is used as collyrium (añjana) in cases of eye-diseases (SS, sūtra, 38, 31; AHṛ sūtra, 6, 76).

Therapeutic Hints:

1. It is useful in swellings, hiccoughs, body-pain and for improving the voice (CS, sūtra, 4, 17).
2. It is one of the ingredients of a medicated oil used to cleanse (and purify) ulcers and wounds (SS, sūtra, 37, 18).
3. The flowers are used as collyrium in eye-diseases (SS, uttara, 12, 11).
4. It is useful in preventing abortion (SS, śārīra, 10, 61).

References: SS, sūtra, 38, 31-32, 36; 46, 267; AHṛ, sūtra, 6, 76).

C

Cchatrakam

Synonyms: Samsvedajam, Bhumi-cchatram, Śilīndhrakam.

Hin. - Bhuī-cchatta, Cchatonā, Khumī
Ben. - Koḍak-cchātā
Mah. - Alambe
Guj. - Bilāḍīno-rom
Kan. - Nāyi-koḍe
Tel. - Tukka-goḍugu
Eng. - Mushroom

Botanical Name: Agaricus campestris Linn. (Syn. Psalliota campestris (L.) Fr.)

Natural Order: Agaricaceae.

Habitat: Common in many parts of India, chiefly in cattle-fields of central Punjab after the rains, barren desert tracts of central and southern Punjab and also Baluchistan.

Medicinal Action:

Rasa. - Sweet
Guṇa. - Heavy and slimy
Vīrya. - Cold

It aggravates kapha, and causes vomiting, purgation, fever and indigestion. However, mushrooms which are white in colour, and which are found growing on logs of wood, bamboo stems and cowdung are not excessively dangerous to health.

Note: All varieties of mushrooms other than the sarpa-cchatra are sweet, cold in potency, hard to digest, and aggravate catarrh. (CS, sūtra, 27.)

Cchikkanī

Synonyms: Kshavakṛt, Ghrāṇaduhkhadā, Ugrā, Kshavakah, Krūranāsā, Samvedana-paṭuh.

Hin. - Nāgcchikanī
Ben. - Hānchuṭī
Mah. - Nāgaśikaṇ

Botanical Name: Centipeda minima (Linn) A Br et Aschers. (Syn. C. orbicularis Lour.)

Natural Order: Compositae

Habitat: Throughout the plains of India in moist places.

Medicinal Action:

Rasa : Pungent and astringent
Guṇa : Light, dry and sharp
Vīrya : Hot

It alleviates kapha and vāta, aggravates pitta, purifies the blood, is appetizing, emetic, has a strong odour and is useful in worms, skin diseases, white patches on the skin, dyspnoea, cough and toxicosis.

Chakramardah

Synonyms: Prapunnāṭah, Dadrughnah, Meshalochanah, Padmātah, Eḍagachah, Chakrī, Tarkiṇah, Kharjūghnaha, Uraṇākshakah, Dṛḍha-bījah.

HIn. - Chaka-vad, Pavāḍ
Ben. - Chākundā
Mah. - Taṅkālā, Tākaḷā
Kan. - Tagache, Chagache-giḍa
Tel. - Tagirisa
Tam. - Tagarai

Botanical Name: Cassia tora Linṇ. (Syn. C. foetida Salisb; Senna tora, Roxb, C. gallinaria Collad.)

Natural Order: Leguminosae

Habitat: Throughout India.

Description: This is an undershrub, which is an annual. It is erect and sparcely branched. Leaves are alternate, pinnate, about 8 cms long with entire, rounded leaflets. The leaves when full grown are mucilaginous with a nauseous taste. Flowers are fairly large, yellowish in colour and almost sessile. Fruit is a long, narrow, nearly cylindrical pod, containing about twenty seeds.

Parts Used: Root, fruits, seeds, leaves and stalks.

Medicinal Action:

Rasa : Sweet, pungent and bitter
Sour (the leaves and stalks)
Guṇa : Light and dry
Vīrya : Cold (the root)
Hot (the leaves, stalks and fruits)

It alleviates all the three doshas, is a heart-tonic, constipative, decreases urination, and is used in urinary disorders, dyspnoea, cough, skin diseases, scabies, worms, headache, ulcers, diseases of medas, fever and anorexia.

The fruits and seeds alleviate kapha and vāta, are constipative, and are useful in skin diseases with itching, scabies, abdominal tumours, cough, asthma, worms, oedema, gout and toxicosis.

The leaves and stalks alleviate kapha and vāta, aggravate pitta, and are beneficial in skin diseases with itching, scabies, psoriasis, cough and dyspnoea.

Champakah

Synonyms: Sukumārah, Surabhih, Śītalah, Chāmpeyah, Hemapushpah, Kānchanah, Shadpadātithih, Kusumādirāṭ, Puṇyagandhah, Atigandhakah.

Hin. - Champak
Tam. - Champakam
Kan. - Sampige
Tel. - Sampenga

Botanical Name: Michelia champaca Linn; (Syn. M. suaveolens Pers; M. Rheedi Wight.)

National Order: Magnoliaceae

Habitat: Throughout India

Description: A large tree with green bark, olive-brown heart wood, and distinct annual rings. The leaves are ovate-ianceolate, acuminate, shining and petiolate. The flowers are yellow and sweet-scented. The fruit is an aggregate of follicles, with oval, brown seeds. The tree flowers in May; fruits are borne in November-December.

Varieties: There are five varieties - (1) Śveta, (2) Nāga, (3) Sultāna, (4) Nīla and (5) Bhūmi.

Parts Used: Bark, flowers.

Medicinal Action:

Rasa : Pungent, bitter, astringent and sweet
Astringent (the flowers)
Vīrya : Cold
Vipāka : Sweet (the flowers)

It alleviates kapha and vāta, is an aphrodisiac and cardiac tonic and is useful in worms, dysuria, bleeding from internal organs, burning sensation, skin diseases with itching, ulcers and toxicosis.

The flowers alleviate Kapha and Pitta, purify the blood and are used in bleeding from internal organs, dysuria, skin diseases and toxicosis.

Therapeutic Hints: It is valuable in bleeding from internal organs (SS, sūtra, 46, 288).

Chaṇakah

Synonyms: Hari-manthah, Vāji-manthah, Jīvanah, Sugandhah, Kṛshṇa-chanchukah, Bāla-bhojyah, Vāji-bhakshyah, Sakala-priyah.

Hin. - Chane, Chanā
Ben. - Cholar-gācch
Kan. - Kaḍale
Tel. - Senagalu
Mah. - Harbhare
Tam. - Kaḍalai
Eng. - Bengal gram

Botanical Name: Cicer arietinum Linn.

Natural Order: Leguminosae

Habitat: Largely cultivated in most parts of India.

Description: This is an erect or spreading, much-branched, hairy, annual herb, one to two feet high, with pinnately compound leaves and small, oval leaflets. The pods are oblong with one or two rounded seeds with pointed anterior ends and smooth or wrinkled coats. The seeds are brown, yellow or white in colour.

Varieties: There is another variety called Kṛshṇa Chaṇaka (Black Chaṇaka).

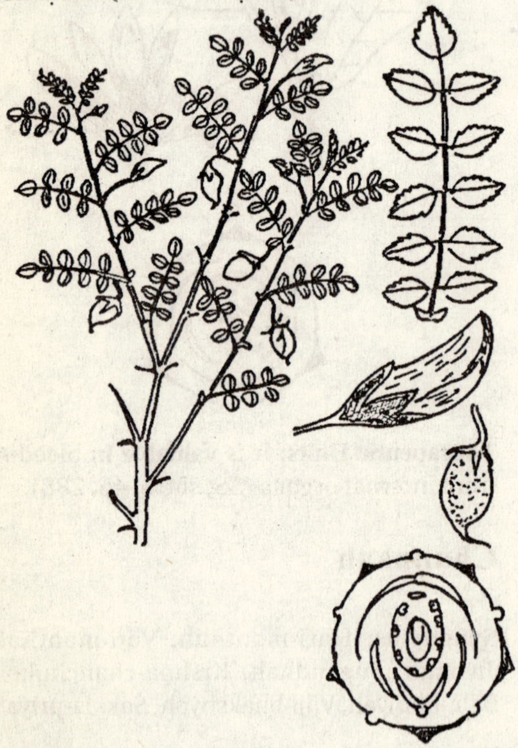

Medicinal Action:

Rasa : Astringent and sweet
Astringent and slightly sour (the leaves)
Sweet (the black variety)

Guṇa : Light and dry
Excessively dry (that which is fried when dry)

Vīrya : Cold

The peas alleviate kapha and pitta, aggravate vāta, are constipative, appetizing, strength-giving, promote complexion and are useful in skin diseases, urinary disorders, diseases of impure blood and fever. They however cause impotence and flatulence.

The peas which are fried when wet are strength giving, appetizing and an aphrodisiac. They increase the amount of blood, but cause aches and pains.

The peas which are fried when dry aggravate vāta and cause skin diseases.

The peas which are steam-cooked alleviate kapha and pitta.

The raw, uncooked peas alleviate kapha and pitta, aggravate vāta, are constipative, nutritive and appetizing. They cause impotence. They are useful in thirst, burning sensation, urinary calculi and tuberculosis.

The soup of the gram alleviates vāta, aggravates kapha and are useful in bleeding from internal organs.

The peas are soaked in water, and the water is later allowed to ferment. This water is nutritive and useful in bleeding from internal organs.

The plant slightly aggravates vāta, is constipative, appetizing, nutritive and hard to digest. It is used in swelling of the gums.

The black variety alleviates pitta, is strength giving, a tonic and is useful in dyspnoea, cough and diarrhoea.

Reference: CS, sūtra, 27, 28.

Chanchū

Synonyms: Vijalā, Chira-patrikā, Kalabhī, Bhīru-patrikah, Suśākah, Kshetra-sambhavah, Dīrgha-patrī, Chinchā.

Hin. - Chanchu, Chevunā
Ben. - Chechako, Titapat
Mah. - Thor-chanchū

Botanical Name: Corchorus acutangulus Lam; (Syn. Corchorus aestuans Linn.)

Natural Order: Tiliaceae

Habitat: Throughout the hotter parts of India.

Description: A branching undershrub or annual with ovate, acute, serrate, almost glabrous leaves. The flowers are small, yellow in leaf opposed cymes. The fruit is a six-angled capsule with a three branched beak. The tree flowers after the rains.

Varieties:

I Mahā-chanchuh

Synonyms: Vishārī, Bṛhat-chanchū, Dīrgha-patrī, Divya-gandhā.

II Kshudra-chanchuh

Synonyms: Śunaka-chanchukā, Tvaksārā, Bhedanī, Kaṭukā, Kaṭu-patrikā.

Parts Used: The leaves, stem and seeds.

Medicinal Action:

Rasa : Astringent and pungent (Mahā-chanchuh)
Astringent, pungent and sweet (Kshudra-chanchuh)
Pungent (the seeds)
Guṇa : Sharp
Vīrya : Hot

Both varieties are beneficial in ascites, abdominal tumours, constipation, sprue and haemorrhoids.

Mahā-chanchuh is constipative, bestows longevity, and is useful in abdominal colic and toxicosis.

Kshudra-chanchuh is appetizing.

The seeds of both varieties are used in abdominal tumours, colic, ascites, discolouration of skin, pruritus. and toxicosis.

Chandanam

Synonyms: Śrī-khaṇḍam, Chandra-kānthah, Go-śīrsham, Bhogi-vallabham, Bhadra-sāram, Malayajam, Gandha-sārah, Bhadra-śrīh, Śveta-chandanam, Tila-parṇakam, Mangalyam, Gandha-rājam, Sarpāvāsam, Śītalam.

Hin. - Chandan, Śvet-chandan
Kan. - Śrī-gandha
Eng. - Sandal-wood tree

Botanical Name: Santalum album Linn. (syn. S. myrtifolium Roxb)

Natural Order: Santalaceae

Habitat: Western Peninsula. Cultivated elsewhere.

Description: This is a small evergreen tree with slender drooping branches. The sap wood is white and odourless, the heartwood yellowish-brown and strongly-scented. The leaves are glabrous, opposite, elliptic-lancealate, entire with an acute base, and petiolate. The flowers are brownish-purple, hermaphrodite, inodorous, occuring as paniculate cymes. The fruit which is a sub globose drupe is purple-black with a hard endocarp.

Varieties: There are several classifications of Chandana:

I. Into two kinds: (a) Beṭṭa Chandana, (b) Sukvaḍi Chandana.
II. Into seven kinds: (a) Śrī-khaṇḍa, (b) Śavara-chandana, (c) Pīta Chandana, (d) Pataṅga, (e) Rakta chandana, (f) Barbara and (g) Hari-chandana.

Rakta Chandanam

Synonyms: Tāmra-sāram, Rakta-sāram, Ku-chandanam, Tāmrābham, Kshudra-chandanam, Hari-chandanam, Arka-chandanam.

Hin.	- Lāl-chandan
Kan.	- Rakta-chandana
Tam.	- Śen-chandana
Eng.	- Red Sandal wood

Botanical Name: Pterocarpus santalinus Linn. f.

Natural Order: Leguminosae

Habitat: Deccan, in the hills of Cuddapah, S. Kurnool, N. Arcot and Chinglepet, upto 1,500 ft.

Characteristics: The Chandana which is superior is said to be bitter to taste, yellow when rubbed, red internally, white externally, full of knots and lumps and hollow within.

All the varieties of Chandana have similar properties.

Medicinal Action:

Rasa	: Bitter, astringent and slightly pungent
Guṇa	: Light and dry
Vīrya	: Cold

It alleviates kapha and pitta, is a heart-tonic, promotes complexion, is refreshing and an aphrodisiac, and is useful in fevers, vomiting, thirst, burning, diseases of impure blood, syncope, dysuria, cough, worms, vertigo, fatigue, tuberculosis, diseases of gums and teeth and toxicosis.

Pīta Chandana (Yellow Sandal) is especially useful in scabies, eczema and skin diseases characterised by itching.

Rakta Chandana alleviates all the doshas, is strength giving, beneficial to the eyes and useful in ulcers, skin diseases and bleeding from internal organs.

Therapeutic Hints:

1. It relieves pruritus (CS, sūtra, 4, 11), body pain (ibid, 4, 17), bleeding from rectum (CS, chikitsā, 19, 86), and enhances complexion (CS, sūtra, 4, 10).
2. It is used as collyrium (SS, uttara, 17, 27) and in a few urinary disorders (SS, chikitsā, 11, 9).
3. It is also useful in menstrual troubles (AS, śārīra, 1, 38).

References: CS, sūtra, 5, 21; 25, 40; chikitsā, 3, 258; SS, uttara, 10, 10; 12, 13, 14).

Chandra-śūrah

Synonyms: Chandrikā, Charma-hantrī, Paśu-mehana-kārikā, Nandinī, Kāravī, Bhadrā, Vāsu-pushpā, Suvāsarā, Rakta-rājī, Siddha-prayojanā, Dara-kṛshṇah, Ahālimam

Hin.	- Hālo hālim
Mah.	- Āhā ḷīm
Ben.	- Halim
Tam.	- Aliverai
Eng.	- Common Cress

Botanical Name: Lepidium sativum Linn.

Natural Order: Cruciferae

Habitat: Cultivated throughout India.

Description: This is an annual glabrous herb. The leaves arising from the underground portion of the stem are divided pinnately, while those arising from the stem above the ground are sessile, deeply lobed or lanceolate. The flowers are small and white, in long racemes. The fruit is a pod, winged at the margins, with two seeds.

Medicinal Action:

Rasa : Bitter
Vīrya : Hot

It alleviates vāta and kapha, promotes strength and nutrition, is an aphrodisiac, lactogenic and is used in rheumatism, gout, diarrhoea, abdominal tumours, diseases of impure blood, skin diseases, eye diseases and bruises.

Chāngerī

Synonyms: Amlikā, Chukrā, Cchatrāmlikā, Chatuh-cchadā, Amla-loṇikā

Hin. - Khaṭṭi-tipatti
Ben. - Amrūl
Mah. - Ambutī
Tam. - Puḷiyārai
Tel. - Pulichinta, Puḷi. - Chanchali
Kan. - Puḷḷam-purachi
Eng. - Yellow Wood Sorrel
Vernacular. - Amla - chāngerī, (Ḍalhaṇa)

Botanical Name: Oxalis corniculata Linn (Syn. O. pusilla Salisb.)

Natural Order: Geraniaceae

Habitat: Throughout the warmer parts of India.

Description: It is a small herb with the stem loosely covered with soft hairs. Leaves are palmately trifoliate with a long, slender hairy petioles. Flowers are yellow in colour, with a long peduncle. Seeds are numerous, broadly ovate, brownish-black with transverse striations.

Parts Used: Plant

Medicinal Action:

Rasa : Sour and slightly astringent
Vīrya : Hot

It alleviates vāta and kapha, is constipative, appetizing and digestive, useful in sprue, haemorrhoids and diarrhoea (CS, sūtra,27, 93).

Therapeutic Hints:

1. It is useful in sprue and haemorrhoids, of the vāta and kapha types (SS, sūtra, 46, 273; CS, sūtra, 2, 19).
2. A medicated ghee prepared from Chāngerī is useful in rectal prolapse (CS, chikitsā, 19, 42-43).
3. A gruel prepared from the stem and leaves is useful in alleviating Vāta (KS, khila, 4, 53).

References: CS, sūtra, 2, 19; 27, 93; SS, sūtra, 46, 273.

Chavikā

Synonyms: Chavyam, Chavaṇam, Ucchishṭam, Kola-vallikā, Kaṭu-pākini, Gandha-nākulī, Kṛkarah.

Hin. - Chavya
Ben. - Chayi gāch
Mah. - Chāvaḷ
Tel. - Chavyam

Botanical Name: Piper chaba Hunter.

Natural Order: Piperaceae

Habitat: Cultivated in various parts of India.

Parts Used: Root and flowers. The fruits are called Gaja-pippali.

Medicinal Action:

Rasa : Pungent
Guṇa : Light
Vīrya : Hot

It alleviates kapha and vāta, is appetizing, useful in worms, cough, asthma, abdominal colic, haemorrhoids and fever.

The flowers are used in cough, tuberculosis, dyspnoea and toxicosis.

Therapeutic Hints: It is appetizing, useful in anorexia, haemorrhoids and abdominal colic (CS sūtra, 4, 9, 11-17).

References: (NIS on SS, sūtra, 38, 22-23).

Chichiṇḍah

Synonyms:

Hin. - Chachinga
Tam. - Puḍal
Tel. - Poṭla
Mal. - Paṭolam
Kan. - Paḍavala
Eng. - Snake gourd

Botanical Name: Trichosanthus anguina Linn.

Natural Order: Cucurbitaceae

Habitat: Extensively cultivated throughout the hotter parts of India.

Medicinal Action: It alleviates vāta and pitta, is appetizing, strength giving and extremely beneficial in tuberculosis.

Chīnakah

Synonyms: Kāka-kanguh, Su-ślakshnah, Kangu-bhedah.

Hin.	- Chīna, Chinnā
Ben.	- Chine
Tam.	- Pani Varagu
Mah.	- Varo, Vari-vav
Kan.	- Baragu
Tel.	- Varigalu
Eng.	- Common Millet, Hog Millet

Botanical Name: Panicum miliaceum Linn.

Natural Order: Gramineae

Habitat: Throughout the hotter parts of India.

Description: This is an erect annual, from 30 to 100 cm. high with shallow roots. The panicles are slender, upto 45 cm. long, either open or compact. The spikelets are rather large, glabrous and green or brownish-green in colour. The kernel or grain is white and broadly ovate, the ripe grain shedding easily.

Medicinal Action: Its action and properties are similar to those of Kanguh.

Chirapoṭa

Synonyms: Dīrghapatrā, Kuntalī, Tiktakā, Parpoṭī Raktahantrī, Jvarakāriṇī.

Medicinal Action:

Guṇa : Dry
Vīrya : Cold

The ripe fruits aggravate kapha and pitta, are purgative, and beneficial in dyspnoea and cough and cause fever.

Chirbhaṭam

Synonyms: Gorakshakarkaṭī, Dhenudugdham, Chitraphalā, Suchitrā, Pāṇḍuphalā, Pathyā, Rochanaphalā.

Hin.	- Phūṭ
Mah.	- Chibhaḍe, Phūṭ

Botanical Name: Cucumis momordica Roxb.

Natural Order: Cucurbitaceae.

Habitat: Cultivated in many parts of India.

Description: A variety with short, smooth, oval or cylindrical fruits, about 1-2 ft. long, which resemble the cucumber, and are dark green when immature, lemon-yellow when ripe.

Medicinal Action:

Rasa : Bitter and slightly sour (the unripe fruits)
Sweet (the ripe fruits)
Guṇa : Heavy and dry
Vīrya : Cold (the unripe fruit)
Hot (the ripe fruit)

The unripe fruits alleviate pitta and kapha, aggravate vāta and are constipative.

The ripe fruits aggravate pitta.

The flowers alleviate vāta and pitta and aggravate kapha.

Therapeutic Hints: It is useful when taken along with unctous substances in dysentery (CS, chikitsā, 19, 32).

References: CS, sūtra, 27, 112; AS, sūtra, 7, 135; nidāna, 1, 15; AHṛ. sūtra, 6, 87).

Chitrakah

Synonyms: Analah, Pāṭhī, Vyālah, Ūshaṇah, Śārdūlah, Jyotishkah

Hin.	- Chitā
Tam.	- Chittiramūlam, Koḍiveli
Kan.	- Kempu-chitramūlamu, Chitramūlamu
Kan.	- Kempu-chitramūla, Biḷī-chitramūla
Mal.	- Chekki koṭuveri, Tumpa koṭuveli
Eng.	- Rose-coloured lead wort, Ceylon lead wort

Botanical Name: Plumbago rosea Linn (Syn. Indica Linn;)

Natural Order: Plumbaginaceae

Habitat: Found all over India.

Description: This shrub grows to about 2 metres high. The leaves are alternate, simple, crowded on short branches, ovate and lanceolate, acute, obtuse, narrow at base, dark green above and paler below. The flowers are glandular and whitish in terminal racemes. The fruit is an oblong capsule. The fresh root exudes a yellow juice. The dried root is in pieces from 2 to 4 inches long, cylindrical and as thick as the little finger, odour acrid and disagreeable.

Varieties: There are two views regarding the varieties -According to one authority there are two varieties - (1) Śveta and (2) Rakta. According to another, there are three varieties- (1) Pīta, (2) Śveta and (3) Kṛshṇa.

The Rakta variety is said to be superior.

Medicinal Action:

Rasa : Bitter and Pungent
Guṇa : Light, Dry and Sharp
Vīrya : Hot
Vipāka : Pungent

It alleviates all the three doshas, especially kapha and vāta, is appetizing, constipative, a carminative and tonic, and is useful in sprue, skin diseases with itching, oedema, haemorrhoids, worms, dyspepsia, ascites, enlargement of liver and emaciation.

The black variety is useful in curing grey hair.

Therapeutic Hints:

1. The root is used in some kinds of urinary disorders (SS, chikitsā, 11,9).
2. It is purgative (SS, sūtra, 39, 40) and hastens suppuration of abscesses (SS, sūtra, 37, 10).
3. It alleviates kapha (CS, sūtra, 27, 106), is appetizing, emaciating, purgative, pain-relieving, and useful in anorexia and haemorrhoids (CS, sūtra, 4, 9-17).
4. A medicated ghee prepared from its root is valuable in swellings (CS, chikitsā, 12, 58), and ascites (ibid, 13, 116).

References: CS, sūtra, 2, 18; SS, sūtra, 11, 11).

Chopchīnī

Synonyms: Dvīpāntara vachā

Hin. - Chobchini
Eng. - China

Botanical Name: Smilax china Linn

Natural Order: Liliaceae

Habitat: A native of Japan and China.

Description: This is a large perennial climber with a large, short, nodular, subterranean rhizome. The stems are numerous, semi-woody, erect at the base and prickly. Leaves when fully grown are very large, alternate, stalked and nearly evergreen.

Medicinal Action:

Rasa : Pungent and astringent
Sweet (the leaves)
Vīrya : Hot

It alleviates vāta, is appetizing, a laxative, diuretic, tonic, an aphrodisiac, nutritive and strength giving, promotes conception, purifies the blood and is used in syphilis, rheumatism, pain in the limbs, skin diseases, tuberculosis, constipation, abdominal colic, distension of abdomen, epilepsy, insanity, ulcers and chancres, paralysis, glandular enlargements, impotence, eye-diseases, parkinsonism and spondylitis.

Diet : While taking chopchīnī, the patient must avoid alcoholic drinks, oil, leafy vegetables and food which is sour, saltish, bitter or acidic.

D

Dāḍimah

Synonyms: Kuṭṭimah, Phalashāḍavah, Karakah, Rakta-bījah, Suphalah, Danta-bījakah, Madhu-bījah, Kucha-phalah, Rochanah, Śuka-vallabhah, Maṇi-bījah, Valka-phalah, Vṛtta-phalah, Nīla-patrah.

Hin.	- Anār
Tam.	- Tuchagam
Kan.	- Dāḷimbe
Mal.	- Uruyāmpaḷam
Tel.	- Dāḍimamu, Dānimma
Eng.	- Pomegranate tree

Botanical Name: Punica granatum Linn,

Natural Order: Lythraceae (Punicaceae)

Habitat: Cultivated in many parts of India.

Description: This is a deciduous shrub with spinescent branches. The bark is grey and thin, peeling off in small flakes. The leaves are opposite, extipulate, simple and in clusters. The flowers are bisexual and regular, with five to seven petals. The fruit is a berry with many angular seeds which have an edible aril. The plant flowers in April-May.

Varieties: There are three varieties based on the taste of the fruit: (1) Sweet, (2) slightly sour and (3) sour.

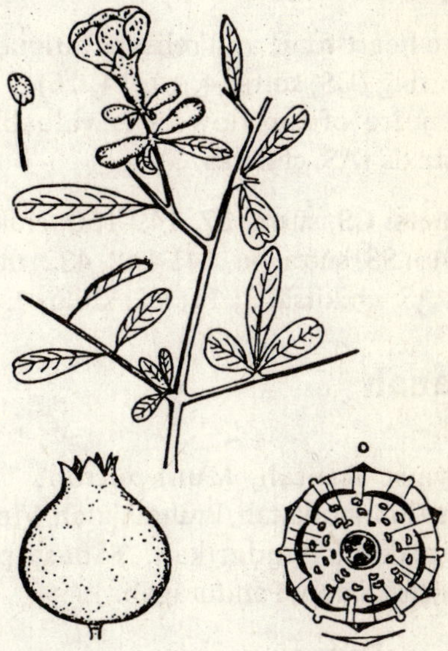

Parts Used: Fruit, flowers, bark, rind.

Medicinal Action:

Rasa	: Sweet, slightly sour
Anu-rasa	: Astringent
Guṇa	: Light and unctous
Vīrya	: Cold

The sweet variety alleviates all the three doshas, is nutritive, strength-giving, refrigerant, an aphrodisiac, constipative, promotes intelligence and is used in thirst, burning, fever, diseases of the throat, heart and mouth, syncope, diseases of impure blood, vertigo, vomiting, anorexia, dyspepsia, fatigue, cough and debility.

The slightly sour variety slightly aggravates pitta, and is appetizing.

The sour variety alleviates kapha and vāta and aggravates pitta.

The flowers are useful in epistaxis. The fruit-rind and the bark are constipative and are used in worms, dysentery and bleeding from the rectum.

Therapeutic Hints:

1. It is a heart-tonic and relieves fatigue and vomiting (CS, sūtra, 4, 10, 14, 16)
2. The juīce of the flowers is valuable in epistaxis (AS, chikitsā, 3)

References: CS, sūtra, 27, 149-150; chikitsā, 16, 44-46; SS, sūtra, 46, 141-142, 432; uttara, 12, 42; AS, chikitsā, 3; 11; KS, khila, 4, 36).

Damanah

Synonyms: Dantah, Muni-putrah, Tapo-dhanah, Gandhotkaṭah, Brahmajaṭah, Vinītah, Kulapatrakah, Puṇḍarīkah, Tāpasa-patrī, Pushpa-chāmarah, Pāṇḍurāgah.

Guj.	-	Damaro
Hin.	-	Devana, Dounā
Punj.	-	Dona
Mah.	-	Davana
Ben.	-	Donā

Botanical Name: Artemisia vulgaris Linn

Natural Order: Compositae

Habitat: The mountain district of India, ascending upto 5,000 — 12,000 ft. in the Western Himalayas and upto 5,000 — 8,000 ft in Sikkim and Khasia, Mount Abu in Rajasthan and Western Ghats from Konkan southwards to Sri Lanka.

Description: A perennial, aromatic shrub with a creeping root. The stem is angular, about 1 m. in height and furrowed longitudinally. The leaves are dark green above, alternate, pinnatisect, with five to seven lobes, erect, deeply incised, silvery white and hairy beneath.

Varieties: There are two other varieties, viz. (1)Vanya-damana and (2)Agni-damana.

Medicinal Action:

Rasa	: Bitter, astringent and pungent Pungent (Agni-damana)
Guṇa	: Dry (Agni-damana)
Vīrya	: Cold Hot (Agni-damana)

It alleviates all the three doshas, is an aphrodisiac, a cardiac tonic and aromatic, and is used in blisters, sprue, skin diseases with oozing and itching, and toxicosis.

The vanya-damana retards ejaculation, is strength-giving and is useful in indigestion.

The Agni-damana alleviates vāta and kapha, is appetizing, a cardiac tonic and is used in abdominal tumours and enlargement of the spleen.

Daṇḍotpalā

Synonyms: Sahadevā, Vishamajvara-nāśinī

Ben.	- Daṇḍakalas
Kan.	- Karīhiṇḍi, Sahadevi
Tam.	- Naichiṭṭe
Mal.	- Pirinā, Pūvankuruntala
Eng.	- Ash coloured fleabane
Tel.	- Sahadevi

Botanical Name: Vernonia cinerea Less

Natural Order: Compositae

Habitat: Throughout India, ascending to 8,000 ft in the Himalayas, Khasia and Peninsular Hills.

Description: An erect annual growing to 2-3 ft. in height with the stem stiff, striate and slightly pubescent. The leaves are alternate, upper leaves smaller, shape varying from elliptic to lanceolate, obtuse or acute, and irregularly toothed. The flowers are pinkish white. The fruit is an achene, oblong, not ribbed, narrowing towards the base, with white hairs.

Varieties: There are three varieties : (1) Yellow variety called Govandinī, Devasahā, (2) Red variety called Viśvadevā and (3) White variety called Devikā.

Medicinal Action: It is appetizing and beneficial in cough, dyspnoea and tuberculosis.

Dantī

There are two varieties of Danti viz. (1) Kshudra-dantī (the small variety) and (2) Bṛhat-dantī (the larger variety).

Synonyms of Kshudra-danti: Udumbara-parṇī, Pratyak-parṇī, Śvetaghaṇṭā, Nikumbhī, Nihśalyā, Nishkumbhā, Śīghrā, Nāgasphoṭā, Upachitrā, Rūkshā, Rechanī, Anukūlā, Rakta-dantī, Vishalyā, Madhu-pushpā, Eraṇḍa-phalā, Eraṇḍapatrikā, Ākhukarṇī.

Hin.	- Danti,
Ben.	- Danti-ghācch
Mah.	- Laghu-danti
Eng.	- Wild Croton

Synonyms of Bṛhat-danti: Guccha-phalā, Dugdha-garbhā, Virechanī, Vishabhadrā, Bhadra-dantī, Jyotishka.

Hin.	- Mugalāyi
Mah.	- Thor-danti

Botanical Name: Baliospermum axillare blume (Syn. B. montanum Muell-arg; Croton polyandrus Roxb.)

Natural Order: Euphorbiaceae

Habitat: Outer ranges of the Himālayas from Kashmir to Bhutan upto 3,000 ft; Assam, Khasia Hills, N. and E. Bengal, Bihar, from central and western India to Travancore.

Description: This is a leafy, stout undershrub with herbaceous branches from the root and is usually glabrous. The leaves are alternate, toothed, the upper ones small and lanceolate while the lower ones are large and broad. The flowers occur as racemes. The fruit, a capsule is abovoid, usually hairy with ellipsoid, smooth and mottled seeds.

Medicinal Action:

Rasa	: Pungent Sweet (the fruit and seeds of Kshudra-danti) Bitter, pungent and astringent (the oil)
Guṇa	: Dry and sharp, vikāsī and āśukāri Heavy and unctous (the seeds)
Vīrya	: Hot Cold (the fruit of Kshudra-dantī)
Vipāka	: Pungent Sweet (the fruits and seeds of Kshudra-dantī)

It is appetising, cleanses the body, alleviates kapha and vāta and relieves ascites, haemorrhoids, ulcers, calculi, āma, colic and skin diseases.

References: CS, sūtra, 2, 9; chikitsā, 16, 51; SS, sūtra, 45, 124; AS, chikitsā, 16).

Darbhā

Synonyms: Kuśah, Barhih, Sūchyagrah, Yagnya-bhūshanah.

There is another variety called Dīrgha-patrā and Kshura-patrā.

Hin. - Kuśā, Dābh
Ben. - Kuśa
Mah. - Thor-darbha
Mal. - Āṭṭu-darbha
Kan. - Kuśa-darbha, Darbhe-hullu
Eng. - Large variety of sacrificial grass

Botanical Name: Eragrostis cynosuroides Beauw (Syn. Poa cynosuroides Linn; Desmostachya bipinnata Stapf.)

Natural Order: Graminae

Habitat: Throughout India in hot and dry places.

Description: The leaves are long, broad and rough. (NIS on SS, sūtra, 37, 75).

Varieties: There are two varieties, the small and the bigger. The bigger variety is called Sita-darbha or Dīrgha-patra and is supposed to be medicinally superior.

Medicinal Action:

Rasa : Sweet and astringent
Guṇa : Unctous
Vīrya : Cold

It alleviates all the three doshas, is appetizing, purifies the blood and semen, and is used in dysuria, habitual abortion, urinary calculi, thirst, renal colic, menorrhagia, bleeding from internal organs, fatigue, sterility, dyspnoea, jaundice, vomiting, syncope and herpes.

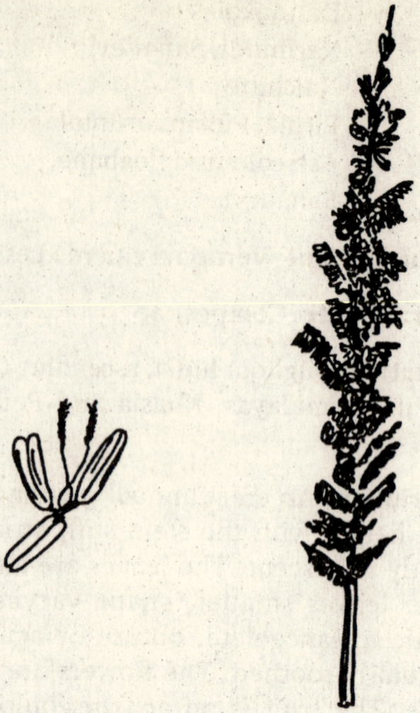

The root is used especially in cough, jaundice and dyspnoea.

Therapeutic Hint: It increases breast-milk in lactating mothers (CS, sūtra, 4, 12; SS, sūtra, 38, 75-76).

References: AS, chikitsā, 8; AHṛ, sūtra, 6, 171; 15, 21).

Dāru-haridrā

Synonyms: Dārvī, Dvitīyābhā, Kapītakam, Pachampachā, Parjanyā, Kāshṭā, Marmarī, Pītikā, Pīta-dāru, Sthira-rāgā, Kāminī, Kaṭankaṭerī, Dāru-niśā, Kāmavatī, Dāru-pītā, Pīta-tvak, Kāshṭa-rajanī, Haimavatī.

Hin. - Daru-haldī
Mah. - Dāru-haḍd
Tel. - Mānu-pasupu
Tam. - Mara-manjalu
Mal. - Mara mannal
Kan. - Doḍḍa maradarishaṇa
Eng. - Tree turmeric, Indian barberry

Botanical Name: Coscinium fenestratum Colebrooke; or Menispermum fenestratum Gaert of Menispermaceae is used in S. India. Berberis aristata DC of Berberidaceae is used in N. India.

Natural Order: Menispermaceae or Berberidaceae

Habitat:

Description:

C. fenestratum: This is a climbing shrub with branches that are yellow-tomentose when young. The lamina is coriaceous, shining and smooth above, minutely tomentose beneath, broadly cordate and sinuate. The inflorescence is supra-axillary, finely tomentose, with yellow petals. The fruit is a subreniform-globose slightly tomentose drupe.

B. aristata: This erect, spinescent and glabrous shrub has a light brown, corky soft bark. The leaves are simple, fascicled in the axils of spines, obovate or lanceolate. The flowers are yellow, in panicles or racemes. The fruits are spindle shaped, red shining berries with few seeds. The plant flowers in March-April.

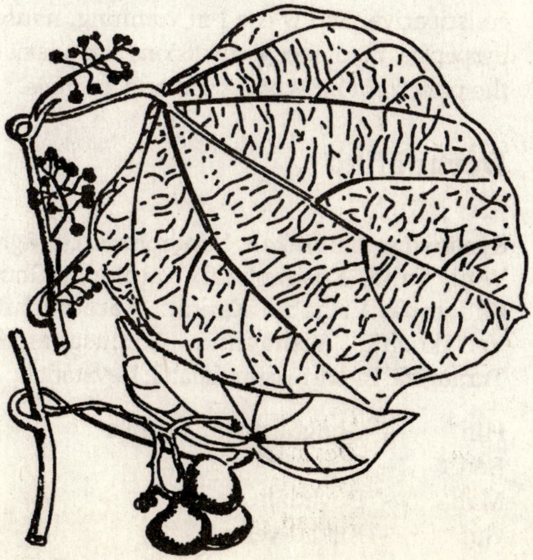

Medicinal Action:

Rasa : Bitter and pungent
Vīrya : Hot
Guṇa : Light and dry

It alleviates kapha and pitta and is useful in oedema, toxicosis, ulcers, urinary diseases, skin diseases with itching, herpes and diseases of ears, eyes and mouth. Most of its properties are similar to those of Haridrā.

Therapeutic Hints:

1. It is emaciating, and relieves pruritus and haemorrhoids (CS, sūtra, 4, 9-11).
2. The bark is very useful in diarrhoea (CS, chikitsā, 19, 80).
3. A medicated ghee prepared from dāru-haridrā is useful in certain skin diseases (CS, chikitsā, 7, 135).
4. Its extract is used as an errhine (CS, sūtra, 2, 5).

Preparations: Rasāñjana :

Synonyms: Rasa-garbham, Tārkshyajah, Bālabhaishajyam

Hin. - Rasot
Ben. - Rasavat

Method of Preparation: A decoction of the bark is boiled with an equal quantity of milk until a semi-solid mass remains. This mass is called rasāñjana.

Purification: The rasanjāña is dissolved in boiling water, strained through a cloth and dried by exposing it to the sun.

Medicinal Action:

Rasa : Bitter and pungent
Guṇa : Sharp
Vīrya : Hot

Rasāñjana is a tonic, an aphrodisiac, beneficial to the eyes, and is useful in diseases of the eyes, ears and mouth, vomiting, bleeding from internal organs, ulcers, hiccough, toxicosis, haemorrhoids and asthma.

Note: It is used as errhine in headache (CS, sūtra, 2, 5).

Dāru-sitā (See also Tamāla-patra)

Synonyms: Tvacham, Bhṛngam, Varaṅgam, Rāmeshṭam, Uṭkaṭam, Mukhaśodhanam, Vanyam, Surasam, Rāma-vallabham, Cholam, Guḍa-tvacham, Chocham, Surabhi-valkalam, Hṛdya-tvak, Saimhalam, Vijjulam, Tanu-tvak.

Hin. - Dālchini
Tel. - Dālchini
Tam. - Karrushā
Kan. - Dālchini
Mal. - Karuva

Botanical Name: Cinnamomum zeylanicum Blume (Syn. Laurus cassia Burm; Laurus cinnamomum Roxb; Laurus nitida Wall.)

Natural Order: Lauraceae

Habitat: Found in most parts of India.

Description: An evergreen tree, with all parts glabrous. Leaves are oblong-lanceolate to lanceolate and caudate-acuminate with the petiole being about 10 cms long. Flowers are small, occurring as slightly silky, cymose panicles. Fruit is a drupe, the size of a pea, and glabrous.

Parts Used: Bark, leaves (see Tamāla-patra), oil from bark.

Medicinal Action:

Rasa : Sweet, bitter and pungent.
Guṇa : Dry and light.
Vīrya : Hot (cold according to some texts)

It alleviates vāta, is aromatic, nutritive, diuretic, an aphrodisiac, promotes complexion, and is useful in dryness of the mucous membranes, thirst, cough, catarrh, worms, indigestion, anorexia, hiccough, diseases of heart, bladder and throat, and toxicosis.

The oil alleviates vāta, is emmanagogue, constipative, and is used in vomiting, nausea, dyspepsia, flatulence, convulsions and alleviates the pain from bites of insects and animals.

Devadālikā

Synonyms: Jīmūtakah, Kaṇṭaphalā, Garāgarī, Veṇī, Sahā, Koshaphalā, Kaṭphalā, Ghorā, Kadambā, Vishadā, Karkaṭī, Sāramūshikā, Vṛttakoshā, Vishaghnī, Lomaśapatrikā, Turangikā, Tarkārī, Āśhuvishahā, Devatāḍah.

Hin. - Ghagharbala, Saniiya
Ben. - Devātāḍā
Mah. - Devadāli
Guj. - Kukaḍ-velya

Tel. - Devatala, Ḍāvara-ḍangi
Kan. - Devaḍangarī
Eng. - Bristly Luffa

Botanical Name: Luffa echinata Roxb.

Natural Order: Cucurbitaceae

Habitat: Cultivated throughout the greater part of India.

Description:

Varieties: There are three varieties, viz. (1) white variety, (2) red variety and (3) yellow variety.

Medicinal Action:

Rasa : Bitter and pungent
Bitter (the fruit)
Guṇa : Sharp
Vīrya : Hot

It alleviates kapha, is an emetic and is useful in anaemia, haemorrhoids, asthma, cough, jaundice, rat poison, indigestion, oedema, fever, anorexia, hiccoughs, worms, diseases of traumatic origin and toxicosis.

The fruit alleviates kapha and vāta, is laxative and is used in abdominal tumours, worms, colic, jaundice and haemorrhoids.

Deva-dāru

Synonyms: Dru-kilimam, Bhadra-dāru, Surāhvayam, Pīta-dāru, Devakāshṭhah, Pittadru, Bhadravat, Masta-dāru, Amara-daru, Snigdha-dāru, Bhūta-hārī, Indra-dāru, Sneha-viddham, Sukāshṭakam.

Hin. - Devdār

Botanical Name: Cedrus deodara (Roxb) Loud; (Syn. Cedrus libani Barrel; Pinus deodara Roxb.)

Natural Order: Pinaceae

Habitat: North-Western Himālayas from Kashmir to Garhwal, at 4,000-10,000 ft.

Description: A large evergreen tree with dark, almost black, rough bark. Shoots are long with solitary needles. Leaves are long, needlelike and short-pointed. Flowers are usually monoecious. Seeds are long, pale brown, wing longer than the seed.

Varieties: (1) Snigdha-dāru and (2) Kāshṭa-dāru.

Parts Used: Heart - wood and oil.

Medicinal Action:

Rasa : Bitter
Bitter, pungent and astringent (the oil)
Guṇa : Unctous and light
Dry (Kāshṭha-dāru)
Vīrya : Hot
Vipāka : Pungent

It alleviates kapha and vāta, purifies breastmilk, and is used in constipation, flatulence, oedema, indigestion, lassitude, hiccoughs, fever, urinary diseases, catarrh, cough, itching and diseases of impure blood.

The Kāshṭha-dāru, when applied externally removes moles and other discolourations of the skin.

Note: It is an aromatic tree (CS, sūtra, 3, 25).

Therapeutic Hints:

1. It is used to fumigate ulcers and wounds (SS, Sūtra, 37, 21).
2. The oil is bitter, astringent, pungent, cleanses wounds and ulcers, alleviates kapha and vāta, and is useful in worms and skin diseases (SS, sūtra, 45, 123).

Dhām-1rgavah (See also Kośātakī)

Synonyms: Pīta-ghoshā, Mahā-kośātakī, Hasti-ghoshah, Mahā-phalā, Ghoshakah, Hastiparṇah, Sapītakā, Bṛhat-kośātakī, Grāma-kośatakī.

Hin. - Nenua, Ghiatarui
Mah. - Ghosāḷi
Ben. - Hasti-ghoshā, Dhunnul
Mal. - Tureippirku
Tam. - Pichukku
Eng. - Sponge gourd

Botanical Name: Luffa aegyptica Mill-ex Hook f. (Syn. Luffa cylindrica (Linn.) M. roem)

Natural Order: Cucurbitaceae

Habitat: Cultivated throughout the greater part of India.

Medicinal Action:

Rasa : Sweet
Guṇa : Unctous

It alleviates vāta and pitta, is a laxative, an aphrodisiac, purifies the blood and is used in flatulence, abdominal tumours, ascites, cases of toxicosis, worms, wounds and diseases of the throat.

Therapeutic Hints: The fruit is an emetic (CS, vimāna, 8, 135).

References: CS, kalpa, 4; Chkp on CS, kalpa, 4, 3; SS, sūtra, 43, 8; uttara, 47, 37; AHr, kalpa, 1, 35).

Dhanvanah

Synonyms: Picchilatvak, Dhanur-vṛkshah, Mahābalah, Rakta-kusumah, Svāduphalah, Badarīsadṛśapatrah.

Hin. - Dhāmin
Mah. - Dhāmin, Dhāmaṇ
Ben. - Dhāmanā
Tam. - Unu, Thadasal
Mal. - Chadachi
Tel. - Taḍa-cheṭṭu
Kan. - Taḍasalu, Buttele, Kaṭankuṭlc-haṇṇu

Botanical Name: Grewia tiliaefolia Vahl.

Natural Order: Tiliaceae

Habitat: Sub-Himalayan region from the Jumna to Nepal upto 4,000 ft., M.P., all districts of T.N., Bihar, and Orissa.

Description: A medium sized tree with a tough, blackish-brown bark. The leaves are broadly ovate to oblique-ovate, serrate, three-nerved at the base and petiolate. The flowers are yellow, with thin, linear or lanceolate petals. The fruit is a two-lobed drupe. The tree flowers in February-April; fruits are borne in May-June.

Medicinal Action:

Rasa : Sweet and astringent (the fruit)
Pungent, astringent and sweet.
Guṇa : Light and dry
Cold (the fruit)
Vīrya : Slightly hot.

It alleviates kapha and vāta, purifies the blood, is constipative, nutritive, promotes healing of wounds, is strength giving and is useful in diseases of the throat, catarrh, burning pains and tuberculosis.

The fruits alleviate kapha and vāta and are employed in preparing āsavas.

Therapeutic Hints: The gum (or ghee medicated with the fruits) is used in extracting a dead foetus from the womb (SS, chikitsā, 15, 9).

References: CS, sūtra, 25, 49; NIS on SS, chikitsā 15, 9; AS, sūtra, 14, 2; śārīra, 4, 38).

Dhānyakam

Synonyms: Dhanyākam, Dhanikam, Dhanyam, Chavalikā, Kustumbarī, Cchātrā, Tumburu, Vitunnakam, Śāka-yogyah, Kunaṭī, Dhanā,

Hṛdya-gandhā, Sugandhih, Sūkshma-patrah, Janapriyah.

Hin. - Dhaniya
Ben. - Dhane
Tam. - Kottumalli
Kan. - Kottambari giḍa
Tel. - Kotimiri, Dhaniyālu
Mal. - Kottampālari
Eng. - Coriander

Botanical Name: Coriandrum sativum Linn.

Natural Order: Umbelliferae

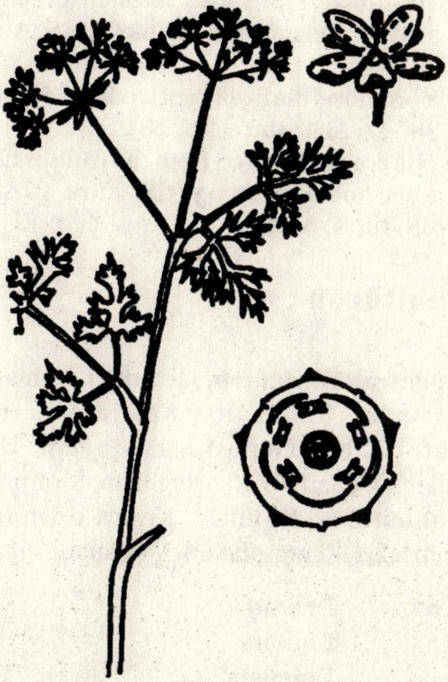

Medicinal Action:

Rasa : Sweet and astringent (when fresh) Sweet, astringent and slightly pungent (when dry)
Guṇa : Light and unctous
Vīrya : Cold
Vipāka : Sweet

The fresh plant alleviates pitta, is aromatic and a heart tonic and is useful in thirst, burning pains, vomiting, dyspnoea, cough, emaciation and worms (CS, sūtra, 27, 173).

The dried plant alleviates all the three doshas, is a diuretic, appetizing, constipative, digestive and is useful in catarrh, fever with chill, cough, thirst, vomiting and anorexia and when taken continuously suppresses the sexual urge (AS, sūtra, 16; CS, sūtra, 27, 307).

Therapeutic Hints:

1. It is useful in cold and catarrh (CS, sūtra, 4, 17), and in relieving thirst (CS, sūtra, 4, 14).
2. It is used externally to relieve pruritus (CS, sūtra, 3, 8).
3. The water in which the fruits are steeped for some time is useful in alleviating thirst. (CS, chikitsā, 22, 61).

References: CS, sūtra, 3, 8; 27, 173, 307; AS, sūtra, 16; 12).

Dhātakī

Synonyms: Tāmra-pushpī, Dhātrī, Dhātu-pushpikā, Vahni-pushpī, Agni-jvālā, Subhikshā, Dāhanī, Pārvatī, Bāhu-pushpikā, Kumudā, Sīdhu-pushpī, Kunjarā, Madya-vāsinī, Guccha-pushpī, Lodhra-pushpiṇī, Madya-pushpā.

Hin. - Dhay
Ben. - Dhai
Mah. - Dhāyaṭī
Tel. - Āre-puvvu

Botanical Name: Woodfordia floribunda Salisb (Syn. W. fruticosa Kurtz)

Natural Order: Lythraceae

Habitat: Throughout India and Baluchisthan.

Description: This is a large, deciduous, ornamental shrub, more or less downy, with a fluted stem. The bark is very thin and grey, peeling off in thin scales. The leaves are opposite, sometimes in whorls of three, sessile from a broad base, simple, lanceolate, with the underside white with black dots. The flowers are bright, brick-red and numerous covered with calices. The fruit is a capsule.

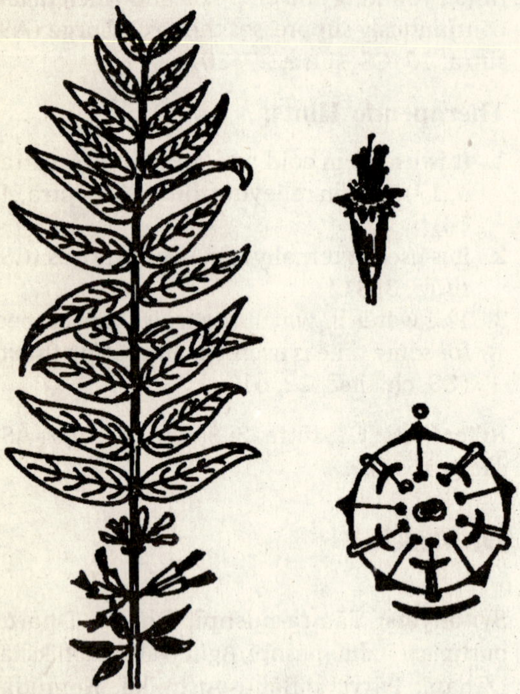

Parts Used: Root and flowers.

Medicinal Action:

Rasa : Pungent, bitter and astringent sweet (the flowers)

Guṇa : Light
Dry (the flowers)

Vīrya : Cold

It alleviates pitta, is constipative, promotes conception, causes intoxication, and is useful in thirst, toxicosis, diarrhoea, bleeding from internal organs, worms, herpes, dysentery, ulcers, diseases of impure blood and wounds. It turns high coloured urine colourless. The flowers are used in bleeding from internal organs, diarrhoea and toxicosis.

Therapeutic Hints:

1. It is valuable in promoting the union of fractured bones and lacerated wounds (CS, sūtra, 4, 9; AS, sūtra, 15, 10).
2. The flowers are used in relieving high-coloured urine (CS, sūtra, 4, 15); and as a constipative (CS, sūtra, 4, 15).
3. It is used externally in swellings caused by poisonous bites and stings (SS, kalpa, 1, 49).
4. The flowers are used as collyrium in some forms of conjunctivitis (SS, uttara, 12, 11-12).
5. The flowers are also used in preparing āsavas (fermented drinks) (CS, sūtra, 25, 49).
6. It promotes the healing of wounds (SS, sūtra, 38, 47; AHṛ, sūtra, 15, 38).
7. The āsava prepared from the fruits is heart-tonic and appetizing (CS, sūtra, 27, 188; AS, sūtra, 6, 121).

Dhattūrah

Synonyms: Dhustūrah, Madanah, Unmattah, Kitavah, Kanakah, Kalabhonmattah, Mātulakah, Kālapushpah, Khalah, Hara-vallabhah, Śaṭhah, Kharjūghnah, Śiva-priyah, Mahāmohī, Devikā, Khara-dūshaṇah, Dhūrtakṛt, Kaṇṭa-phalah, Mohanah.

Hin. - Dhatūra
Ben. - Dhuturā
Kan. - Ummatta
Tam. - Ummattai
Tel. - Ummatta-cheṭṭu
Mal. - Ummattam
Eng. - Thorn apple

Botanical Name: Datura fastuosa Linn (Datura stramonium Linn; Datura metel Linn; Datura alba Nees)

Habitat: Throughout India.

Natural Order: Solanaceae

Description: The plant is a foetid-smelling, robust herb, 1/2 - 2 feet high with forking, zigzag branches. Stem is rather round and softly hairy. Leaves are simple, alternate and petioled. Flowers are solitary, purplish in colour. Fruit is a sub-globose capsule on a stout stalk, covered all over with short spines. Seeds are many, compressed and yellowish - brown in colour.

Varieties: There are five varieties based on the colour (1) white, (2) blue, (3) black, (4) red and (5) yellow. The black variety is said to be superior.

Medicinal Action:

Rasa : Sweet, bitter, astringent and pungent.
Guṇa : Heavy
Vīrya : Hot

It alleviates kapha, aggravates vāta and pitta, is analgesic, poisonous, an intoxicant, appetizing, enhances complexion, and is useful in fever, skin diseases with itching, scabies, lice, worms, ulcers, jaundice, haemorrhoids, diseases of impure blood and fatigue. It is emetic and causes vertigo.

Therapeutic Hints:

1. The seeds are soaked in cow's urine for sixteen hours, and then are divested of their outer layers and cut into small pieces. They are thus purified (AP, 6, 114).
2. The toxic effects of impure seeds are tremors, salivation, intoxication, vomiting, loss of memory and vertigo. The person also sees everything as being yellow (AS, uttara, 40).

Antidotes:

1. Four palas of the juice of seeds of vṛntāka (brinjals) are to be taken (RJN, Vol. III, page 352).
2. Cows's milk if taken with sugar-candy also serves as an effective antidote (ibid).

Reference: AS, uttara, 40.

Dhavah

Synonyms: Pichācha-vṛkshah, Śakaṭah, Dhurandharah, Dhavalah, Madhura-tvak, Nandi-taruh, Gourī, Dṛdha-taruh, Śukla-vṛkshah, Indra-vṛkshah.

Hin. - Dhāvā
Ben. - Dhauyāgāch
Mal. - Marukinchiram
Mah. - Dhāvḍā
Tam. - Vellai-nāgai
Kan. - Sirivaru, Dinḍige

Botanical Name: Anogeissus latifolia Wall (Syn. Conocarpus latifolia Roxb)

Natural Order: Combretaceae

Habitat: Common in dry deciduous forests throughout India, except Assam. Found in the sub-Himalayan tract, Bihar, Madhya Pradesh and southwards to Sri Lanka.

Description: A large, deciduous tree with drooping branchlets and smooth, pale-brown bark mottled with white, and exfoliating in thin, rounded scales. The leaves are elliptic or sub-orbicular, obtuse, pubescent, copper-coloured when young, glabrous and dullgreen when mature. The flowers are greenish, sessile, in globose spikes or heads, in short, axillary racemes. The fruit is a compressed, nearly orbicular, narrowly two-winged drupe. The tree flowers in December-January and June-July.

Parts Used: Root and fruits.

Medicinal Action:

Rasa : Pungent and astringent
Sweet and astringent (the fruits)
Guṇa : Dry
Vīrya : Cold (the fruits)

It alleviates kapha and vāta, aggravates pitta, is appetizing and is useful in anaemia, urinary disorders and haemorrhoids.

The fruits alleviate kapha and pitta, aggravate vāta, and are constipative.

Therapeutic Hints:

1. It is used for external application in skin diseases (CS, sūtra, 3, 3).
2. It is useful in abdominal tumours, urinary calculi, and impotence (SS, sūtra, 38, 20-21; AS, sūtra, 16, 16; AHṛ, sūtra, 15, 32).
3. The bark is applied in upadamśa (chancre) SS, chikitsā, 19, 33). It also promotes healing of wounds (SS, sūtra, 37, 28).
References : CS, kalpa, 1, 8; SS, sūtra, 38, 8-9, 39, 28; NIS on chikitsā, 34, 17; AS, sūtra, 3, 20; AHṛ, sūtra, 15, 19.

Ḍiṇḍaśah

Synonyms: Roma-phalah, Muni-nirmitā

Hin. : Tiṇḍā

Botanical Name: Citrullus vulgaris var. fistulosus (Stocks) Duthie and Fuller.

Natural Order: Cucurbitaceae

Habitat: Cultivated largely in Uttar Pradash, Punjab and Bombay for its fruit which is used as a vegetable.

Medicinal Action:

Guṇa : Dry
Vīrya : Cold

It alleviates kapha and pitta, aggravates vāta, is appetizing, a laxative, diuretic and is beneficial in urinary calculi.

Drākshā

The three varieties of Drākshā are:

1. Kṛshṇa which has the synonyms : Chāruphalā, Svādvī, Madhurasā, Mṛdvīkā, Yakshmaghnī and Gostanī.

2. Kapila-drākshā which has the synonyms : Harita, Madhūlih, Madhu-vallī, Dīrgha-phalā, Amṛta-rasā, Pathikā, Gostanī, Mṛdvīkā, Hārahūrā, Mṛdvī, Kāśmīrī and Śata-vīryā.
3. Kākalī-drākshā which has the synonyms : Nirbījah, Laghu-drākshā, Jāmbukā, Suvṛttā and Ruchi-kāriṇī.

Hin. - Dākh, Angur
Tel. & Kan. - Drākshā
Mah. - Drakh

Botanical Name: Vitis vinifera Linn.

Natural Order: Vitaceae

Habitat: Cultivated in many parts of India.

Varieties: (1) Kṛshṇā (black grapes), (2) kākalī (seedless grapes) and (3) kapila

Medicinal Action:

Rasa : Sweet and slightly astringent (ripe grapes)
Sour (those grown on mountains)
Guṇa : Heavy and unctous (ripe grapes)
Viśada and heavy (unripe grapes)
Vīrya : Cold (ripe grapes)
Hot (unripe grapes)
Vipāka : Sweet (ripe grapes)

Ripe grapes alleviate vāta and pitta, aggravate kapha, are a laxative, diuretic, nutritive, an aphrodisiac, beneficial to the voice and eyes, appetizing and are useful in fever, thirst, gout, jaundice, dysuria, bleeding from internal organs, syncope, burning pains, emaciation, tuberculosis, alcoholism, diseases of traumatic origin, vomiting and dyspnoea.

Grapes grown on mountains aggravate kapha and pitta and cause diseases of impure blood.

Seedless grapes alleviate all three doshas, especially kapha and pitta, are an aphrodisiac, appetizing, a cardiac tonic, a laxative, and are useful in hoarseness, tuberculosis, fatigue, burning pains, syncope, cough, fever, diseases of impure blood, thirst, palpitation, diseases of traumatic origin and dyspnoea.

Unripe grapes aggravate pitta, cause diseases of impure blood and are inferior in medicinal qualities.

Raisins (dried grapes) are nutritive, strength-giving, analgesic and are useful in fatigue.

Therapeutic Hints: They have an affinity for the throat (CS, sūtra, 4, 10). They relieve cough, are laxative (CS, sūtra, 4, 10, 16; AS, sūtra, 15, 36, 14, & 4) and are useful in fevers (CS, sūtra, 4, 16) and fatigue (ibid)

References: SS, sūtra, 46, 334, 183-184, AHṛ, 6, 115-117).

Droṇa-pushpī

Synonyms: Kshava-patri, Droṇā, Phela-pushpī, Kumbha-yonih, Pālindī, Kurambikā, Chitra-patrikā, Cchatrāṇī, Dīrgha-patrā, Supushpā.

Hin. - Gūmā, Gomā
Mal. - Tumpa
Ben. - Ghalghase
Tam. - Tumbai
Kan. - Tumbe
Mah. - Kumbhā
Tel. - Enugatumbe, Tummi

Botanical Name: Leucas cephalotes Spreng (Syn. Leucas linifolia Spreng; Phlomis linifolia Roth)

Natural Order: Labiatae

Habitat: More or less found throughout India.

Description: The plant is a diffusely branched herbaceous annual growing to a height of 18 inches. The stem is square, and covered with coarse hairs. Leaves are simple, opposite and shortly stalked. The blade is linear lance-shaped. Flowers are white and sessile. Fruit consists of four brown and smooth nutlets.

Varieties: There is another variety called Mahā-droṇā, which has the synonyms of : Deva-pūrvakā, Kurambhā, Divya-pushpi and Devī-kāṇḍā.

Parts Used: Root and leaves.

Medicinal Action:

Rasa : Sweet, saltish and pungent
Pungent and bitter (Mahādroṇā)
Guṇa : Heavy, dry and active
Vīrya : Hot
Vipāka : Sweet

It alleviates kapha and vāta, aggravates pitta, is a purgative and is used in dyspepsia, jaundice, oedema, dyspnoea, worms, haemorrhoids, paralysis and intermittent fever.

The juice of the plant is used as collyrium in jaundice.

The leaves are purgative and used in fever, urinary disorders, oedema and jaundice.

The Mahā-droṇā variety alleviates kapha and vāta, bestows intelligence, is an analgesic and useful in indigestion.

Durālabhā

Synonyms: Dhanvayāsah, Dhanva-yavāsah, Durālambhā, Samudrāntā, Rodinī, Gāndhārī, Kacchurā, Anantā, Kashāyā, Durabhi-grahā, Dusparśā, Ātmamūlī, Padma-mukhī, Idamkāryā, Tāmrā-mūlī, Dhanvī, Prabodhinī, Sūkshma-dalā, Virūpā, Durlabhā, Dushpraharshā, Marujjanmā, Ushṭra-bhakshyā, Mṛdu-parṇā, Prāhlādinī, Ajā-bhakshyā, Phaṇihārī.

Hin. - Dhamāsā, Durālā
Mah. - Dhamāsā
Kan. - Dūlagoṇḍi, Turuche-baḷḷi, Valli-duruve
Mal. - Koṭlattūva, Choriyaṇam
Tel. - Dūlagoṇḍi, Dūla-koṇḍi
Tam. - Kāyanchori, Sendoṭṭi
Eng. - Nettle?

Botanical Name: Fagonia arabica Linn (Syn. F. cretica Linn.)

Natural Order: Zygophyllaceae

Habitat: Most parts of India.

Description: A small green, spiny under-shrub with woody, erect, more or less quadrangular branches and one to three foliate opposite leaves. Leaflets are entire, elliptic or linear, acute, petiolate with spiny stipules. Flowers are small, pink and solitary. Fruit is a globular capsule. Thorns are conical, longitudinally furrowed and a little below the apex, jointed and reddish in colour.

Varieties: There is another variety called Kshudra-durālabhā or small durālabhā.

Medicinal Action:

Rasa : Pungent, bitter, sweet, astringent and sour.

It alleviates all the three doshas, is an analgesic, and is useful in fever, abdominal tumours, toxicosis, urinary disorders, diarrhoea, diseases of impure blood, dyspnoea, herpes, skin diseases, intermittent fevers, thirst, vomiting, syncope and vertigo.

Therapeutic Hints:

1. A fermented drink prepared from this plant is used in sprue, anaemia, haemorrhoids, etc. (CS, chikitsā, 15, 152-155).
2. The plant is useful in haemorrhoids (CS, sūtra, 4, 11) and excessive thirst (CS, sūtra, 4, 14).

Dūrvā

There are three varieties:

1. Nīla-dūrvā (bluish in colour)

Synonyms: Śashpam, Śadvalam, Haritam, Śataparvā, Śīta-kumbhī, Śītalā, Vāminī, Śambhavī, Śyāmā, Dhūrtā, Amṛtā, Śata-granthī, Anuvallikā, Śivā, Mangalā, Jayā, Bhūta-hantrī, Śata-mūlā, Mahoushadhi. Gourī, Śāntā, Tikta-parvā, Kaccha-ruhā, Asitā-latā, Amarā.

2. Śveta-dūrvā (whitish in colour)

Synonyms: Gaṇḍālī, Śata-vīryā, Śakulakshakah, Golomī, Śata-parvā, Sitā-latā, Chaṇḍā, Bhadrā, Bhārgavī, Durmarā, Gourī, Vighneśāna-kāntā, Vidyā, Śveṭa-kāṇḍā, Prachaṇḍā, Sahasra, Kāṇḍā, Sura-vallabhā, Suparvā, Sitacchadā, Svacchā, Kacchānta-ruhā.

3. Gaṇḍa-dūrvā

Synonyms: Gaṇḍālī, Tīvrā, Matsyākshikā, Jalasthā, Granthiparṇī, Bahlī, Śakulādanī, Atitīvrā, Granthilā, Vāruṇī, Mati-netrā, Śyāma-granthī, Sūchipatrā, Śyāma-kāṇḍā, Kalāyā, Chitrā.

Hin. - Dūva
Ben. - Dūrvā
Mah. - Haraḷi
Tam. - Arugu, Muyarpul
Tel. - Garike
Mal. - Karuka pullu
Kan. - Garike, Ambaṭe-hullu
Eng. - Hariali or Doub Crass

Botanical Name: Cynodon dactylon Pers (Syn. C. linearis Willd; C. maritimus H. B. ; Dactylon officinale Vill ; Panicum dactylon Linn.)

Natural Order: Gramineae

Habitat: Throughout India, ascending to 8,000 ft. in the Himālayas.

Description: A very hardy, much branched, leafy grass with numerous stems below and above soil. The aerial branches are either ascending or prostrate and rooting at the nodes. The underground stems are hard, brittle and thick. Leaves are 1-2 inches or more long in two rows, narrow and pointed.

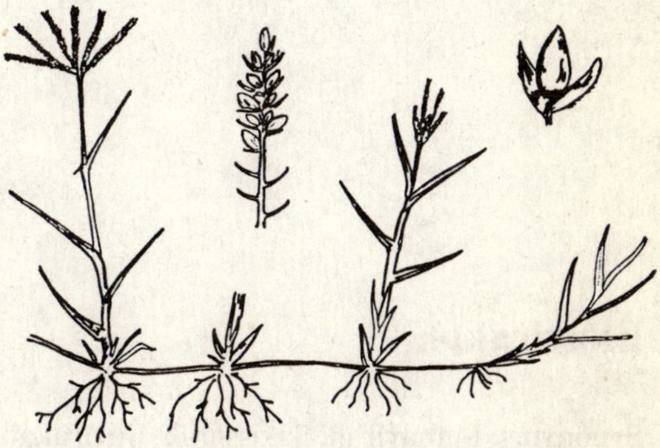

Medicinal Action:

Rasa : Sweet, bitter and astringent
Guṇa : Light (Gaṇḍa-dūrvā)
Vīrya : Cold
Vipāka : Pungent (Gaṇḍa-dūrvā)

All the varieties of Dūrvā have certain properties in common : They alleviate kapha and pitta, facilitate conception, beautify the complexion, are useful in anorexia, thirst, vomiting, vertigo, burning pains and fatigue.

Nīla-dūrvā is appetizing, an analgesic, purifies the blood and is useful in bleeding from internal organs, skin diseases with itching, diarrhoea, fever, vomiting, thirst, burning and herpes.

Śveta-dūrvā has the same action as Nīla-dūrvā. It is in addition beneficial in cough.

Gaṇḍa-dūrvā is constipative and beneficial in fever, vertigo, thirst, fatigue, diseases of impure blood and skin diseases with burning.

References: CS, sūtra, 3, 27.

E

Ekavirakah

Synonyms: Mahāvīrah, Sakṛtvīrah, Suvīrakah

Medicinal Action:

Rasa : Pungent and bitter
Vīrya : Hot

It alleviates vāta and is beneficial in rheumatism, sciatica, abdominal colic, back pain, paralysis and pricking pain.

Elā

Varieties: There are two varieties, viz. Sthūlailā (big variety) and Sukshmailā (small variety) (SS, sūtra, 38, 24)

Synonyms:

1. Sthūlā, Bahulā, Māleyā, Tāḍakīphalā, Bṛhadelā, Tripuṭā, Tridivodbhavā, Surabhi-tvak, Mahilā, Kumārikā, Pṛthvī, Goupṭā, Kāyasthā, Kāntā, Ghṛtāchī, Garbha-sambhavā, Indrāṇī, Aindrī, Divya-gandhā, Nishkuṭī, Charma-sambhavā, Bālā.
2. Sūkshmā, Vayasthā, Tīkshṇa-gandhā, Drāviḍih, Truṭih, Upakunchikā, Korinjī, Bhṛnga parṇikā, Tutthā, Tripuṭā, Cchardikā-ripuh, Tvachi-sugandhā, Chandrasambhavā, Kapota-varṇī, Divodbhavā, Chandra-bālā, Kunaṭī, Nishkuṭih, Gourangī, Gandha-phalikā, Śvetailā.

Hin. - Ilayachi
Mah. - Elā
Mal. - Elattari
Tam. - Elam, Chittelam
Kan. - Elakki-giḍa
Tel. - Elakkāyi
Eng. - Cardamom plant

Botanical Name: Elettaria cardamomum Maton. (Syn. Alpinia cardamomum Roxb; Zinziber ensal Gaert; Amomum cardamomum Linn; Amomum racemosum Lam; Amomum subulatum Roxb).

Natural Order: Zinziberaceae

Habitat: Cultivated in many parts of India.

Description: The plant has stems growing upto seven feet in height. The leaves are sub-sessile, broadly lanceolate or oblong-lanceolate and wide, about 30 to 60 cms long, and 5 to 7 cms broad. The flowers are in small panicles, small and violet coloured. The fruit is a sub-globose or oblong capsule about an inch long, with fine ribs, containing many small, dark seeds.

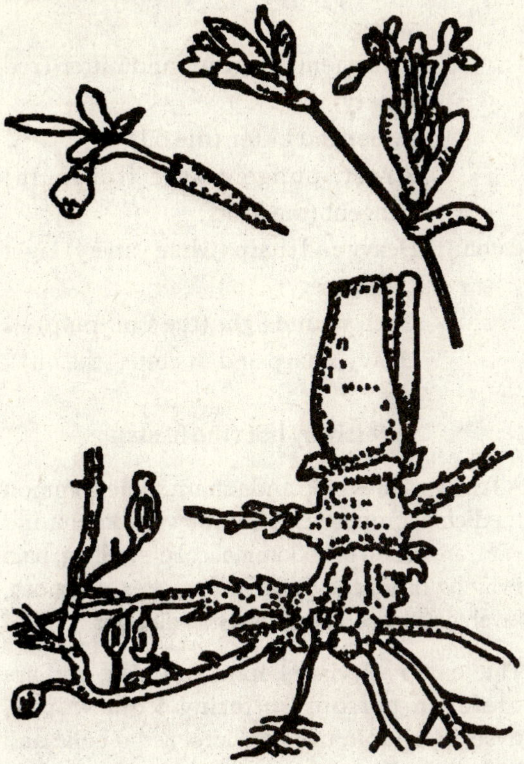

Medicinal Action:

Rasa : Pungent and bitter (Sūkshmailā)
Guṇa : Dry, light and active (Bṛhadelā)
Light and dry (Sūksmailā)
Vīrya : Hot (Bṛhadelā)
Cold (Sūkshmaila)
Vipāka : Pungent (Bṛhadelā)

Bṛhadelā alleviates kapha and pitta, is appetizing, aromatic, digestive, and is useful in bleeding from internal organs, vomiting, thirst, seminal calculus, diseases of impure blood, renal colic, diseases of mouth, headaches, cough, dyspnoea, constipation, colic and toxicosis.

Sūkshmailā alleviates kapha and vāta, aggravates pitta, is aromatic, abortifacient, and is useful in dyspnoea, cough, haemorrhoids, dysuria, diseases of mouth, tuberculosis, renal colic, sore throat, urinary calculi, ulcers, itching, breaking pain all over the body and toxicosis.

Therapeutic Hints:

1. The seeds are used as an emetic (CS, sūtra, 2, 7).
2. It is externally applied in headaches (CS, sūtra, 3, 24) and catarrh (ibid, 3, 28).
3. It relieves dyspnoea (CS, sūtra, 4, 16) body pain (CS, sūtra, 4, 17) and is used for smoking (CS, sūtra, 5, 21).
4. The smaller variety is used as an errhine (CS, sūtra, 2, 4).
5. It is externally applied with honey in sores or ulcers on the genitals (AS, uttara, 39).
6. The bigger variety antidotes poison (CS, sūtra, 4, 11).
7. The small variety is used externally in the disease anjana-nāmikā (SS, uttara, 14, 6).

Eliyakam

Synonyms: Kṛshṇa-bolam, Sāratodbhavah, Kumārī

Medicinal Action:

Rasa : Pungent
Vīrya : Cold

It alleviates kapha and vāta, is purgative and is beneficial in abdominal colic, flatulent distension of the abdomen, worms and abdominal tumours.

Eraṇḍah

Synonyms: Vyāghra-pucchah, Chitrakah, Triputī-phalah, Panchāngulah, Śūla-śatruh, Vātārih, Dīrgha dantakah, Gandharva-hastakah, Vardhamānah, Dīrgha-patrakah, Chitrabījah.

Hin. - Aṇḍa
Ben. - Bherāṇḍā
Tam. - Āmanakku
Tel. - Āmudāla-cheṭṭu
Mal. - Chiṭṭāmanakku
Kan. - Haraḷu, Auḍala-giḍa
Eng. - Castor-oil plant

Botanical Name: Ricinus communis Linn (Syn. R. vulgaris Mill)

Natural Order: Euphorbeaceae

Habitat: Cultivated throughout India.

Description: This is a tall, glabrous and glaucous annual, sometimes shrubby or tree-like. The leaves are alternate, broad and palmately-lobed, with seven or more lobes. Flowers are monoecious, rather large and in terminal racemes. The fruit is a prickly capsule with oblong seeds. The testa of the seeds is crustaceous, albumen fleshy and cotyledons broad and flat.

Varieties: There are three varieties : (1) Sthūla (big), (2) Rakta (red coloured) and (3) Śukla (white coloured).

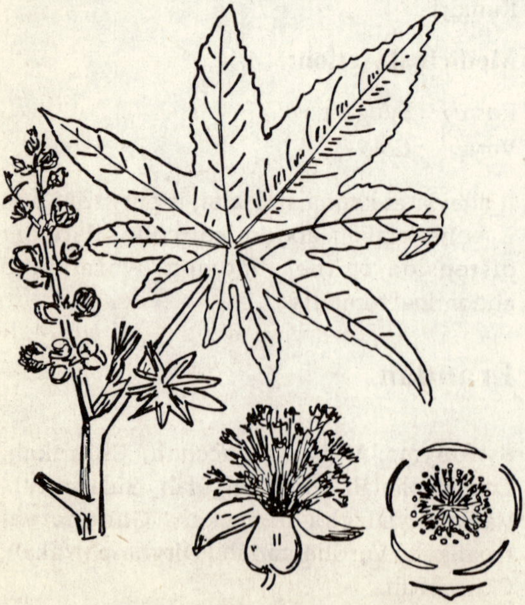

Medicinal Action:

Rasa : Sweet, bitter and pungent (white variety)
Astringent, pungent and bitter (red variety)
Sweet and bitter (the oil)
Sweet, pungent (the fruit-pulp)
Pungent (the fruits)

Guṇa : Heavy and sharp (white variety) Light (red variety)
Unctous and light (the fruit-pulp)
Heavy, sharp and unctous (the oil)

Vīrya : Hot
Excessively hot (the fruits)

All the varieties of Eraṇḍa share some common medicinal properties: They alleviate kapha and vāta, are useful in abdominal colic, swelling, pain in limbs, headache, renal colic, ascites, dyspnoea, fever, flatulence, cough and skin diseases.

The leaves alleviate kapha and vāta, and are useful in persons suffering from worms, dysuria, abdominal tumours, renal colic and hydrocele. They are contraindicated in bleeding from internal organs.

The fruits alleviate vāta, are appetizing, and are useful in abdominal tumours, colic, enlargement of liver and spleen, abdominal tumours and colic.

The fruit-pulp alleviates vāta and kapha, is a purgative and beneficial in ascites, haemorrhoids, enlargements of the spleen and liver, abdominal tumours and colic.

The roots alleviate vāta and kapha, are an aphrodisiac and analgesic.

The flowers alleviate vāta and kapha, are analgesic and used in haemorrhoids, growths in the rectum, abdominal tumours, flatulence and dysuria. They are contraindicated in bleeding from internal organs.

The white variety alleviates all three doshas, is a laxative and specially useful in constipation, hernia (inguinal?), abdominal tumours, enlargement of spleen, indigestion, urinary disorders, gout, diseases of Medas and prolapse.

The red variety alleviates vāta and kapha, and is particularly useful in worms, haemorrhoids, hernia, anaemia, diseases of impure blood, anorexia and vertigo.

The oil of any variety alleviates vāta and kapha, is a laxative, a cardiac tonic, an aphrodisiac, appetizing, analgesic, promotes intelligence, bestows longevity and is beneficial in persons suffering from worms, skin diseases, gout, heart diseases, abdominal tumours, indigestion, fever, hernia, ascites, intermittent fever, swellings, dysmenorrhoea and pains in the limbs.

Therapeutic Hints:

1. The root alleviates vāta and is an aphrodisiac (CS, sūtra, 25, 40), and relieves body pain (ibid, 4, 17).
2. The leaves are applied in ulcers of the vāta type (SS, chikitsā, 1, 112)
3. The seeds and pulp are used as purgative (ibid, sūtra, 39, 4).
4. The oil is an excellent purgative (CS, sūtra, 13, 12; SS, sūtra, 44, 75; 45, 114; 27, 289).
5. Regular use of castor oil is of use in hernia, abdominal tumours and wind colic (AS, sūtra, 13).
6. The kshara (ash) of the leaves relieves cough (CS, chikitsā, 18, 171).
7. Milk medicated with the tender leaves, root or bark is used as an eye wash in conjuctivitis (ophthalmia) of the vāta type (SS, uttara, 9, 11-12).

Ervārukah

Synonyms: Karkaṭī, Hasti-danta-phalā, Vyāla-patrā, Lomaśī, Bṛhat-phalā, Sthūlā, Toya-phalā, Cchardāpanikā, Pīnasā, Mutralā, Mūtra-phalā, Trapushā, Hasti-parṇī, Lomaśa-kāṇḍā, Bṛhat-kandā, Karkatākshah, Śāntanu, Grīshma-karkaṭī

Hin. - Kakaḍī
Ben. - Kākud
Mah. - Kānkadī
Tel. - Dosakāyā
Kan. - Soute-baḷḷi
Mal. - Veḷḷarikai
Eng. - Snake cucumber

Botanical Name: Cucumis utilissimus Roxb (Syn. C. melo var. utilissimus Duthie & Fuller.)

Natural Order: Cucurbitaceae

Habitat: Cultivated throughout India.

Varieties: There are two other varieties viz. (1) Araṇya-karkaṭī (those grown in forests) and (2) Tikta-karkaṭī (bitter variety).

Medicinal Action:

Rasa : Sweet and slightly bitter (when tender)
Bitter (Araṇya and Tikta-karkaṭī)
Pungent (the outer skin)

Guṇa : Light and dry (when tender)
Heavy (when ripe)

Vīrya : Cold (when tender)
Hot (ripe ones and Araṇya-karkaṭī)

Vipāka : Pungent (Tikta-karkaṭī and Araṇya-karkaṭī)

Tender cucumbers alleviate pitta, are appetizing, constipative, diuretic, purify the blood and are useful in vomiting, fatigue, fever, syncope, dysuria and bleeding from internal organs. When excessively used, they aggravate vāta.

Ripe cucumbers aggravate Pitta, are appetizing and are beneficial in fatigue and thirst.

The outer skin is appetizing, a digestive, constipative, and is beneficial in dysuria, urinary calculi, vomiting, burning pains and fatigue. If overused, they cause sterility.

Araṇya-karkaṭī alleviates kapha and pitta, is a laxative and is useful in fever, worms and pruritus.

Tikta-karkaṭī alleviates vāta, is emetic, diuretic and beneficial in dysuria, flatulence and Ashṭīlā.

Cucumbers grown in the rainy season and Śarad ṛutu are to be avoided as they are injurious to health.

Those grown in winter (Hemanta ṛtu) alleviate pitta, are appetizing and beneficial.

Therapeutic Hints: The seeds are given with a little rock-salt, (in water) in cases of retention of urine (SS, uttara, 55, 27) and dysuria (ibid, 58, 29).

References: SS, sūtra, 45, 120; 46, 219; CS, sūtra, 27, 110-111; SS, chikitsā, 31, 5).

G

Gaja-pippalý

Synonyms: Śreyasī, Ibha-kaṇā, Kapillikā, Vasirah, Gajāhvā, Ibhoshaṇā, Kunjara-pippalī, Chavyajā, Cchidra-vaidehī, Dīrgha-granthih, Gaja-kṛshṇā.

Hin. - Gaja-pīpal,
Ben. - Gaja-pipul
Kan. - Aḍake-bīlu-baḷḷi, Dodda - hippali
Mal. - Anaittippili,
Guj. - Mottopiper
Tel. - Aenuga-pippaḷḷu

Botanical Name: (According to some authorities, Gaja-pippalī is the name given to the fruits of Chavikā) Scindapsus officinalis Schott (Syn : Pothos officinalis Schott Melet)

Natural Order: Araceae

Habitat: Tropical Himālayas, from Sikkim eastwards, Bengal, Chittagong and the Andaman Islands.

Description: This is a large epiphytic climber, clinging to trees and rocks by adventitious aerial roots. Leaves are 15-25 cm. long, obliquely ovate-oblong, cuspidate and leathery. The spadix of bisexual, greenish-yellow flowers are enclosed in an oblong spathe, green without and yellow within. The fruit, cut into transverse pieces and dried, appears a greyish colour.

Part Used: Root and fruits

Medicinal Action:

Rasa : Pungent
Guṇa : Dry and sharp
Dry (the fruits)
Vīrya : Hot (the root)
Cold (the fruits)
Vipāka : Sweet (the fruits)

It alleviates kapha and vāta, is constipative, digestive, appetizing, a lactogogue, and is useful in diarrhoea, dyspnoea, worms and diseases of the throat. It is said to cause an increase in the size of breasts.

The fruits aggravate vāta, are constipative and hard to digest, and are beneficial in bleeding from internal organs.

Gambhārẏ

Synonyms: Kāśmarī, Sarvatobhadrā, Madhuparṇikā, Śrī-parṇī, Bhadra-parṇī, Gopabhadrikā, Bhadrā, Kumudā, Krishṉa-phalā, Katphalā, Kṛshṇa-vṛntikā, Hīra, Snigdha-parṇī, Kshīriṇī, Vidāriṇī, Aśvetā, Sthūla-tvachā, Madhumatī, Modinī, Sudṛḍhatvachā, Vātaḥā.

Hin. - Kumbher
Ben. - Gābhār
Guj. - Śavanya
Mah. - Śivaṇa-gambhāri
Tam. - Perungumil, Kāṭṭaṇam
Tel. - Gummuḍu-cheṭṭu
Mal. - Kumaḷu
Kan. - Kūli-mara, Śivanī-mara

Botanical Name: Gmelina arborea Roxb

Natural Order: Verbenaceae

Habitat: Throughout India

Description: A moderate sized unarmed deciduous tree reaching 18 metres high. Its bark is greyish-yellow and rather corky. The young parts are covered with fine, white hairs. The leaves are opposite, broadly ovate, acuminate and entire; the flowers, which usually appear in small cymes of about three, are brownish-yellow in colour. The fruit which is a succulent ovoid drupe is smooth and orange-yellow when ripe. The seeds are oblong in shape.

Parts Used: Root-bark, flowers, fruits, fruit-pulp and oil.

Medicinal Action:

Rasa : Astringent, bitter and sweet (the root and fruit-pulp
Bitter and sweet (the ripe fruits)
Astringent and sour (the unripe fruits)
Astringent, sweet and bitter (the flowers)
Astringent and sweet (the oil)
Guṇa : Heavy (the root)
Heavy and unctous (the fruits)
Vīrya : Hot (the root)
Cold (the fruits, flowers and fruit-pulp).
Vipāka : Sweet (the fruits and flowers)

The root-bark alleviates all three doshas, is

appetizing, digestive, a brain tonic, a laxative, and is beneficial in vertigo, emaciation, thirst, dyspepsia, abdominal colic, haemorrhoids, burning, fever, oedema, urinary disorders, worms, insanity and toxicosis.

The fruits alleviate vāta and pitta, are diuretic, nutritive, constipative, an aphrodisiac, bestow longevity, promote growth of hair and are useful in thirst, diseases of impure blood, tuberculosis, burning sensation, gout, diseases of traumatic origin and menorrhagia.

The fruit-pulp alleviates kapha and pitta, aggravates vāta, is an aphrodisiac, strength-giving, constipative and is used in menorrhagia.

The flowers aggravate vāta, alleviate pitta and are useful in burning pains, bleeding from internal organs and diseases of impure blood.

The oil extracted from the seeds alleviates kapha and pitta.

Therapeutic Hints:

1. The leaves are given internally in haemorrhages and septic wounds and ulcers (SS, chikitsā, 1, 113).
2. The fruits are a heart-tonic, beneficial to hair, a brain-tonic, rejuvenative and relieve constipation and haemorrhages (SS, sūtra, 46, 185).

References: SS, kalpa, 6, 18: sūtra, 46, 185; 38, 39; CS, sūtra, 4, 16).

Gaṇḍa-gātrā

Synonyms: Ātṛpyam, Sītāphalam, Vaidehi-vallabham, Kṛshṇa-bījam, Bahubījakah

Hin. - Sarīphā
Ben. - Ātā
Tam. - Āttamaram
Kan. - Sītāphala
Tel. - Sītāphalamu
Mal. - Ātta-chakka
Eng. - Custard Apple tree

Botanical Name: Annona squamosa Linn

Natural Order: Annonaceae

Habitat: Occurs wild and is also cultivated throughout India.

Description: A small, widely spread tree with oblong-elliptic, obtuse leaves; the flowers are solitary, leaf-opposed and yellowish-white.

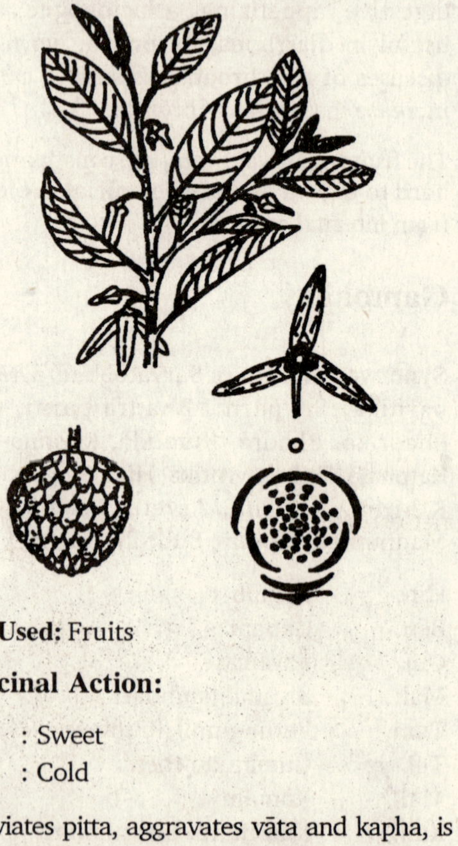

Parts Used: Fruits

Medicinal Action:

Rasa : Sweet
Vīrya : Cold

It alleviates pitta, aggravates vāta and kapha, is nourishing, strength-giving, aphrodisiac and cardiac tonic, and is useful in thirst, vomiting, nausea, burning and bleeding from internal organs.

Gandha-nākulī

Synonyms: Bhujangākshī, Sarpākshī, Nāga-sugandhā, Nakuleṣṭā, Surasā, Visha-nāśinī, Sarvagandhā, Rakta-patrikā, Iśvarī, Ahibhuk, Sarpādinī, Vyāla-gandhā, Vishamardanikā.

Hin.	- Nāyi
Ben.	- Nākuli
Tam.	- Chovannamil-pori
Mah.	- Mungas-vel
Tel.	- Pātāla-gandhi
Mal.	- Vaṇḍu-vāra
Kan.	- Sūtranābhi

Botanical Name: Rauwolfia serpentina Benth (Syn : Ophioxylon serpentinum Linn).

Natural Order: Apocynaceae

Habitat: Distributed in most parts of India.

Description: This is a herbaceous undershrub, about 60 cms. high. The leaves are in whorls of three, lanceolate or elliptic-lanceolate, acute or acuminate, thin, bright-green above, pale beneath and tapering to-wards the base. The flowers are pink or white in cymes. The fruit is a drupe, purplish-black when ripe. The flowers are seen in November or December.

Varieties: There is another variety called Nākulī.

Medicinal Action:

Rasa : Astringent, bitter and pungent
Vīrya : Hot

It alleviates all three doshas, and is said to be extremely useful in bites of poisonous insects and snakes. It is also beneficial in fever, worms and ulcers.

Gandha-palāśikā

Synonyms: Śaṭhī, Shaḍgranthā, Suvratā, Gandha-mūlikā, Gandārikā, Gandha-vadhū, Pṛthu-palāśikā, Gandha-mūlī, Palāśa-śaṭī, Gandha-śaṭī, Karchūrah, Jīmūta-mūlah, Kacchorā, Himajā, Amla-niśā, Samudrā.

Hin.	- Gandha-palāśī, Kapura-kacharī
Ben.	- Gandha-śaṭī
Mah.	- Kāpur-kācharī, Āve-halḍ

Botanical Name: Hedychium spicatum Ham. ex Smith

Natural Order: Zinziberaceae

Habitat: Subtropical Himalayas, Nepal and Kumaon, 5,000 -- 7,000 ft.

Description: This is a herb with perennial tuberous root stock. The leaves are oblong, lanceolate, or oblong, very variable, glabrous, reaching to 30 cms or more. The flowers are white, ascending and imbricate. The fruit is a globose, glabrous capsule.

Medicinal Action:

Rasa : Astringent, bitter and pungent
Guṇa : Light and sharp
Vīrya : Neither cold nor-hot

It alleviates kapha and vāta, slightly aggravates pitta, is constipative and beneficial if there is a bad taste in the mouth, oedema, cough, vomiting, ulcers, abdominal colic, hiccough, fever, abdominal tumours, diseases of impure blood and dyspnoea.

Gandha-tṛṇam (See also Bhūs tṛṇam)

Synonyms: Sugandha-bhū-tṛṇam, Rouhisham, Bhū-tṛṇam, Gomaya-priyam.

Medicinal Action:

Rasa : Sweet and slightly bitter
Guṇa : Unctous
Vīrya : Cold

It alleviates kapha and pitta, is aromatic, bestows longevity and is beneficial in vertigo and general debility.

Therapeutic Hints: It is pungent, hot, cleanses the mouth and causes impotence (CS, sūtra, 27, 172).

Garjaram

Synonyms: Gājaram, Gṛnjanam, Nāranga-varṇakam, Pītakam, Svādumūlam, Supītam, Pīta-mūlakam, Pinga-mūlam.

Hin. - Gājar
Bin. - Gājar
Kan. - Kempu-mūlangi,
Eng. - Carrot

Botanical Name: Daucus carota Linn. var sativa, DC.

Natural Order: Umbelliferae

Description: This is an annual or biennual herb with an erect, much branched stem, from one to four feet high, and a thick, fleshy tap-root. The leaves are pinnately compound, while the flowers are whitish or yellow, borne on branched umbels. The fruits are oblong, with bristly hairs along the ribs.

Habitat: Cultivated throughout India.

Medicinal Action:

Rasa : Sweet, bitter and slightly pungent
Guṇa : Light and sharp
Vīrya : Hot

It alleviates kapha and vāta, is appetizing, and constipative, and is beneficial in flatulence, distention of the abdomen, worms, abdominal colic, burning, thirst, bleeding from internal organs, haemorrhoids and sprue.

Gavedhukā

Synonyms: Gojihvā, Gundra-gutthā.

Hin. - Gar-heduā, Gurlu, Sankru
Ben. - Gurgur, Gargaredhān
Mah. - Ranmakkai
Tam. - Net pavalam
Tel. - Aḍavi-godhūmalu

Botanical Name: Coix lachryma-jobi Linn (Syn. Coix lachryma Linn)

Natural Order: Gramineae

Habitat: Throughout the hotter and damper parts of India upto 5,000 ft., wild or cultivated.

Description: This is a tall, erect, annual, monoecious grass, from 3 to 6 feet high with broad leaves and large, shining pear-shaped fruits which contain a whitish or light brownish grain resembling rice.

Medicinal Action:

Rasa : Pungent and sweet

It alleviates kapha and is emaciating.

Note: It is of two varieties, town-grown and forest-grown (CS, sūtra, 27, 17).

References: CS, sūtra, 2, 25; SS, sūtra, 46, 21; AS, uttara, 42.

Godhūmah

Synonyms: Bahu-dugdhah, Arūpah, Mleccha-bhojanah, Yavanah, Nistushah, Kshīrī, Rasālah, Sumanah

Hin. - Gehū
Ben. - Gam
Mah. - Gahū
Kan. - Godhi
Tel. - Godhūmalu
Tam. - Godhumai

Mal. - Kotampam
Eng. - Wheat

Botanical Name: Triticum vulgare Villars (Syn. Triticum aestivam Linn)

Natural Order: Gramineae

Habitat: Cultivated through-out the greater part of India.

Description: This is an annual grass, usually 60-150 cm in height with stems tufted, erect or semi-erect to prostrate and generally hollow with thin walls. Nodes are generally 5-7, wholly or partially covered by leaf sheaths. Leaves are long and narrow, with prominent parallel veins, glabrous or hairy on one or both surfaces. The inflorescence is a spike of spikelets with a tough rachis.

Varieties: There are three varieties, viz. (1) Mahā-Godhūma (2) Madhūli (which is slightly smaller) and (3) Dīrgha-godhūma (which is devoid of bristles)

Medicinal Action:

Rasa : Sweet and slightly astringent
Guṇa : Heavy and unctous
Vīrya : Cold

It alleviates all the doshas, especially vāta and pitta, is an aphrodisiac, strength-giving, nutritive, appetizing, and improves the complexion. It aids the healing of wounds and fractures and is beneficial in ulcers with burning pains.

Therapeutic Hints:

1. It is used externally in some diseases of the blood (CS, sūtra, 3, 23).
2. It is used as an aphrodisiac (AS, uttara, 25)
3. Although it improves eye-sight in its natural state, it destroys eye-sight when cooked with oil (AS, sūtra, 7).

References: CS, sūtra, 27, 21; chikitsā, 15, 226; SS, sūtra, 37, 11).

Gojihva

Synonyms: Dārvikā, Gobhī, Kurasā, Dārvi-patrikā, Kharapatrī, Adhomukhā, Adhah-pushpī, Vātonā.

Medicinal Action:

Rasa : Pungent, bitter, astringent and sweet.
Guṇa : Sharp and light
Vīrya : Cold
Vipāka : Sweet

It alleviates pitta and kapha, aggravates vāta, is constipative, a cardiac tonic, heals ulcers and wounds and is useful in skin diseases, fever, dysuria, urinary disorders such as polyuria, diseases of the teeth, diseases of impure blood, cough and anorexia.

Therapeutic Hint:

1. It is useful in destroying the poison in wounds inflicted by four-legged animals (CS, chikitsā, 23, 220).

References: CS, sūtra, 27, 97; 46, 264.

Gokshurah

Synonyms: Palankashā, Bhakshaṭah, Shaḍangah, Kaṇṭī, Kshurakah, Ikshu-gandhā, Śvadamshṭrā, Svādu-kaṇṭakā, Gokanṭakā, Sthala-śṛngāṭakah, Vana-śṛngāṭakah, Trikaṇṭah, Vyāladamsṭrakah

Hin. - Gokhrū, Choṭa-gokhru
Ben. - Gokhrī
Kan. - Neggilu-muḷḷu
Tam. - Nerungil, Acchuram
Tel. - Palleru
Mal. - Nerinil
Eng. - Small calotrops

Botanical Name: Tribulus terrestis Linn

Natural Order: Zygophyllaceae

Habitat: Throughout India.

Description: It is a procumbent, much branched, spreading herb with densely silky-hairy stems, 4 to 6 inches long. Leaves are opposite, compound, evenly pinnate and shortly petiolate. Flowers are axillary and yellow in colour. The fruit is a dry woody subglobose schizocarp breaking into 4-5 hard bits each containing 4-6 seeds and armed with spines on the back.

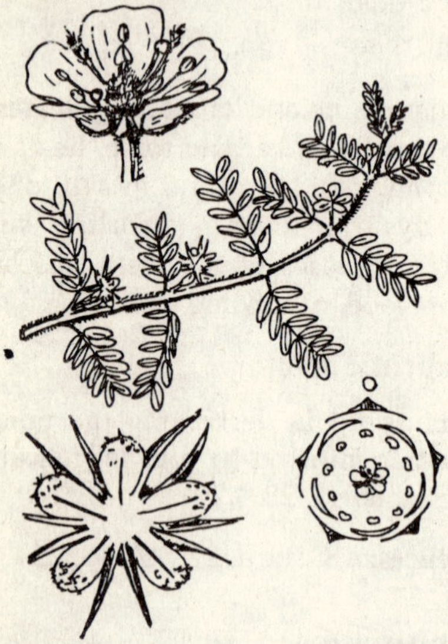

Varieties: There is a bigger variety, said to be medicinally superior.

Hin.	- Baḍa-gokhruū,
Tel.	- Eruga-palleru, Pedda-palleru
Tam.	- Āne-nerinjil
Mal.	- Kāka-mulla
Kan.	- Āne-neggilu

Botanical Name: Pedalium murex Linn

Natural Order: Pedaliaceaes.

Description: This is a diffuse, more or less succulent herb with rather foetid-smelling, slime-secreting glands. The leaves are ovate or ovate-oblong while the flowers are bright yellow, solitary and axillary. The fruit is spinous and bluntly four-angled with oblong, black seeds.

Parts Used: Whole plant, roots, fruits and seeds.

Medicinal Action:

Rasa : Sweet
Bitter (leaves and stem)
Vīrya : Cold
Vipāka : Sweet

It alleviates all three doshas, but particularly vāta, is appetizing, an aphrodisiac, nutritive, strength-giving, diuretic and analgesic, bestows longevity, and is beneficial in abdominal colic, heart disease, dysuria, urinary disorders, urinary calculi, burning sensation, cough, haemorrhoids, worms, skin diseases and dyspnoea.

The leaves and stems are an aphrodisiac and cleanse the channels of the body.

The seeds are beneficial in oedema, dysuria and urinary disorders.

Note: It is a diuretic and relieves dropsical swellings (CS, sūtra, 4, 15, 16; 25, 40).

References: CS, sūtra, 4, 13; 23, 12; chikitsā, 11, 44; SS,sūtra, 46, 433; chikitsā, 2, 48).

Goraṇī

Synonyms: Dṛḍhabījā, Niśāndhyaghnī, Bākuchī, Suśākā, Vakra-śimbī, Goraksha-phalinī

Hin.	- Gvārki-phalī
Mah.	- Bāvachyā
Kan.	- Gorī-kayī-ballī, Chavlī-kāyi
Tel.	- Gorchikuḍu,
Guj	- Guwar

Tam. - Kūṭavarai
Mal. - Pantalavara

Botanical Name: Cyamopsis tetragonoloba (Linn.) Taub (Syn. C. psoralioides DC.)

Natural Order: Leguminosae

Habitat: Cultivated in many parts of India.

Description: This is a robust, erect annual, from 3 to 10 feet high, bearing clusters of thick, flesh, pods, each containing 5 to 12 seeds.

Medicinal Action:

Rasa : Sweet
Guṇa : Heavy and dry

It alleviates pitta, aggravates kapha and vāta, is a laxative and appetizing.

The leaves alleviate pitta and are useful in night-blindness.

Guḍūchī

Synonyms: Amṛta-vallī, Madhuparṇī, Kuṇḍalī, Chakra-lakshaṇā, Soma-vallī, Viśalyā, Tantrī, Nirjarā, Vatsādanī, Amṛtā, Cchinna-ruhā, Jīvantikā, Vātaraktārī, Pamaroddhārā, Pittaghṇī, Varā, Jvarārī, Śyāmā, Sura-kṛtā, Rasāyanī, Cchinnodbhavā, Somalatikā, Vayasthā, Nāgakumārikā, Chandrahāsā, Dhīrā, Chakrāngī

Hin. - Giloy
Ben. - Gulanchā
Mah. - Gulaveḷi
Kan. - Amṛta-baḷḷī
Tam. - Amṛda-vallī
Tel. - Tippatīge
Mal. - Chiṭṭāmṛtam
Eng. - Heart-leaved Moonseed

Botanical Name: Tinospora cordifolia Miers (Syn. Cocculus cordifolius Dec; Menispermum cordifolium Willd; Cocculus verrucosus Wall)

Natural Order: Menispermaceae

Habitat: Distributed throughout India.

Description: This is a climbing succulent shrub, with a bark that is papery at first and later corky, and grey or creamy-white in colour.

The leaves are simple, roundish to ovate, deeply cordate, alternate and petiolate. The flowers are yellow, in slender racemes or panicles on old wood. The fruit is a red, sessile drupe. The flowering period is in November.

Varieties: There are 2 varieties viz. (1) Vallī-guḍūchī and (2) Kanda-guḍūchī.

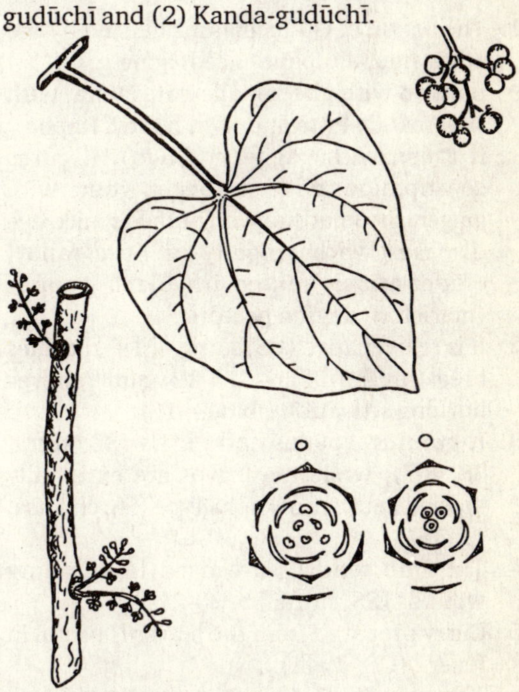

Parts Used: Stems, leaves and extract (satva).

Medicinial Action:

Rasa : Bitter and astringent
Guṇa : Light
Vīrya : Hot
Vipāka : Sweet

It alleviates all the three doshas, particularly vāta, is an aphrodisiac, strength-giving, a brain tonic, constipative, emaciating, appetizing, bestows longevity of life and purifies the blood. It is beneficial in fever, intermittent fever, worms, bleeding piles, skin diseases, thirst, anaemia, gout, rheumatism, vomiting, obesity, pruritus, herpes, burning, vertigo, jaundice, cough, dysuria, heart diseases and dyspnoea.

The leaves alleviate all the doshas and are useful in diseases of the eyes. Taken along with buttermilk, they are especially of use in jaundice.

Therapeutic Hints:

1. The action of Guḍūchī is influenced by the adjuvants (anupāna) used. For e.g.
   If taken with ghee, it alleviates Vāta, with sugarcandy Pitta and with honey, Kapha.
   If taken with gaggery (Guḍa), it cures constipation; with castor-oil, gout; with ginger, rheumatism; with buffalo's milk, eye diseases; with gingelly oil (tila taila), elephantiasis, and with black pepper (maricha), angina pectoris.
2. It is rejuvenative (CS, sūtra, 4, 18), purifies breast-milk (ibid, 4, 11-12) and relieves burning sensation (ibid, 4, 17).
3. It purifies wounds and ulcers (SS, sūtra, 38, 6-7); while the leaves are externally applied in ulcers of kapha type (SS, chikitsā, 1, 115).
4. The fine tendrils are used in stitching wounds (SS, sūtra, 25, 20-21).
5. Curry prepared from the leaves is useful in fever., (CD, 1, 41).
6. The powder taken with powdered black pepper and hot water is efficacious in chest pain (angina pectoris) (CSS, page 320).
7. Milk boiled with the expressed juice of guḍuchi is useful in vata-rakta (gout) (AHṛ, chikitsa, 22, 7).
8. The decoction of guḍuchi is taken with honey in bilious vomiting, (AHṛ, chikitsā, 6, 14).
9. The cold infusion of guḍuchi is to be taken every morning with honey, in jaundice, (AHṛ, 16, 43).

Guggulū

Synonyms: Kāla-niryāsah, Mahishākshah, Palankashah, Jaṭāyuh, Deva-dhūpah, Śivah, Purah, Kumbhī, Rakshohā, Durgah, Kouśikah, Niśāṭakah. Yātughnah, Marudeśyah, Yavanadvishṭah.

Botanical Name: Balsamodendron mukul Hook. (Syn. Commiphora mukul Engl)

Natural Order: Burseraceae

Habitat: Bellary, Mysore, Deccan, Khandesh, Kathiawar, Rajasthan Desert, Sind and Balushisthan.

Description: This is a small resinous thorny tree, about 6 ft. in height, with a greenish-yellow outer bark. The leaves are alternate, simple or three-foliate, exstipulate with a smooth margin. The flowers are small, reddish in colour, and solitary. The fruit is a drupe which is fleshy and roundish.

Varieties: There are five varieties -

1. Mahishākshah (which is blackish in colour) and

2. Mahā-nīlā (which is blue in colour), both of which are used mostly in diseases of elephants.
3. Kumudā (which is reddish in colour) and
4. Padmā (which shines like a ruby), both of which are used mostly in diseases of horses; and
5. Hiranyākshah (which is golden in colour) which is used in diseases of human beings.

Parts Used: Gum-resin, leaves and stems.

Medicinal Action:

Rasa	: Pungent, bitter, astringent and sweet (gum resin) Sweet (leaves and stems)
Guṇa	: Light, sharp and unctous (gum resin) Heavy and dry (leaves and stems)
Vīrya	: Hot (gum resin) Cold (leaves and stems)
Vipāka	: Pungent (gum resin)

The fresh gum resin alleviates kapha and vāta, aggravates pitta, is a laxative, appetizing, nutritive, an aphrodisiac, bestows long life, heals wounds, enhances the complexion, and strengthens the voice. It is beneficial in urinary calculi, skin diseases with exudation, syncope, oedema, herpes, diseases of impure blood, tumours, warts, ulcers, glandular swellings, pimples, dyspepsia, pruritus, worms, cough, ascites, haemorrhoids and ascites.

The old gum resin is emaciating.

The leaves and stems aggravate kapha and vāta, are a laxative and diuretic (SS, chikitsā, 5, 40-45, sūtra, 15, 32; AS, uttara, 49).

Purification: The gum resin should be powdered, boiled in milk and dried, before being used.

Test for Excellence: Pure gum resin burns in fire, melts when exposed to the sun and forms a milky emulsion with hot water. Fresh gum resin is aromatic and sticky, while old resin is dry and foul-odored.

Therapeutic Hints:

1. Patients using guggulū should avoid sour, and heavy foods, alcohol, suns rays, anger, coitus and over-exertion.
2. It hastens suppuration in boils and abscesses (CS, chikitsā, 25, 53).
3. It can also be purified by boiling it in a decoction of guḍūchī or milk or triphalā in a dolā yantra and later drying it in the sum (RJN, Vol. III, page. 359).

Toxic Effects: It causes vertigo, dryness of the mouth and throat, impotence, emaciation, urinary disorders (including diabetes), debility and dryness of skin (AS, uttara, 49).

Gundrah

Synonyms: Paṭerakah, Racchah, Śṛngaverābha-mūlakah, Pṛthulah, Nīrajah, Mṛdu-darbhah.

Hin.	- Gond-pater
Ben.	- Hogla
Mah.	- Pān-gavat
Kan.	- Jambu-hullu
Eng.	- Elephant Grass

Botanical Name: Typha elephantina Roxb (Syn. Typha angustura Bory & Chaub)

Natural Order: Typhaceae

Description: This is a tall, robust, marshy, perennial up to four metres high, with a creeping, branched rhizome. The leaves are semi-cylindrical, often longer than the flower-stalks and spongy. The spikes are cylindrical, bearing male and female flowers, sometimes on different plants.

Medicinal Action:

Rasa	: Astringent and sweet
Vīrya	: Cold

It alleviates pitta, purifies breast-milk and semen, is a diuretic and is useful in dysuria, bleeding from internal organs and sterility.

Gunjā

Synonyms: Chūdamaṇih, Raktikā, Kākajanghā, Śikhaṇḍini, Kṛshṇalā, Rākiṇī, Kakshā, Kanīchih, Kākaṇantikā, Śāngushṭhā, Kākatuṇḍikā, Soumyā, Aruṇā, Tāmrikā, Śītapākī, Ucchaṭā, Bhīla-bhūshaṇā, Vaktraśalyā, Vāyasādanī, Kāmbhojī, Angāra-vallarī.

Hin. - Ghughachī
Ben. - Kuch
Kan. - Gulaganji-baḷḷi
Tam. - Kunri, Guṇḍumaṇi
Tel. - Guriginja, Gulivinda
Mal. - Kunai.

Botanical Name: Abrus precatorius Linn (Syn. Abrus minor Desv)

Natural Order: Leguminosae

Habitat: Throughout the greater part of India.

Variety: There are two varieties, one with red seeds and the other with white seeds.

Description: This is a beautiful, perennial, wiry twiner with paripinnate leaves. There are 10 to 20 pairs of leaflets which are opposite and oblong. Flowers are white or pink, in racemes. The fruit is a pod, from 2 to 4 inches long with a sharp beak, and contains 3-5 seeds which are globose, bright scarlet with a black patch on hilum.

Parts Used: Root, seeds and leaves.

Medicinal Action:

Rasa : Bitter, astringent and sweet
Vīrya : Slightly hot

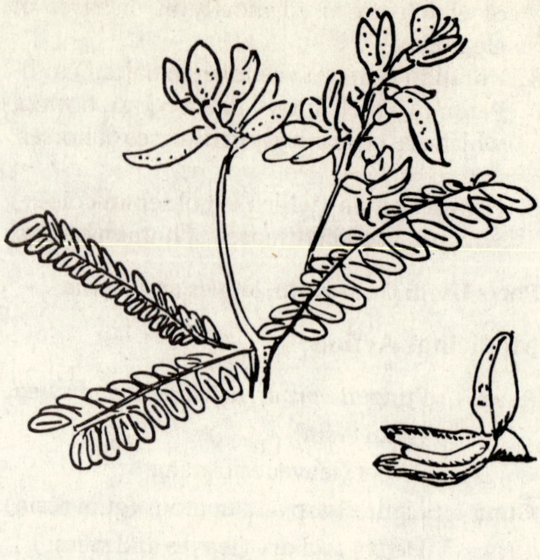

It alleviates kapha and pitta, promotes ejaculation, is strength giving, appetizing, is beneficial to the eye-sight, hair and skin, and is used in alopecia, pruritus, skin diseases, ulcers, worms, fever, headache, diseases of mouth, vertigo, thirst, dyspnoea and toxicosis.

The seeds are emetic and are useful in abdominal colic. The leaves are useful in toxicosis.

Therapeutic Hints:

1. It is useful in herpes of the kapha type (SS, chikitsā, 17, 15).
2. The root is an aphrodisiac (ibid, 26, 34).
3. The root is also poisonous (AS, uttara, 40).
4. It is purified by boiling it with kānjī in a dolā yantra for three hours (AP, 6, 112).

H

Hamsapādī

Synonyms: Godhāpadikā, Kīramātā, Tripādī, Madhusravā, Suvahā, Tridaḷā, Haimavatī, Chitrapadā, Raktapādī, Ghṛtamaṇḍalikā, Viśvagranthī, Vipadikā, Kīṭamārī, Karṇāṭī, Vikrāntā, Padāngī, Śītāngī, Sūtapādikā, Sanchāriṇī.

Hin. - Hamsapādī
Ben. - Goyale-latā
Guj. - Ins-rājā
Kan. - Chelakoṇḍi, Ānekivi, Navilina-bāla
Tam. - Mailikoṇḍe
Mah. - Lāl-Lājaḷu
Eng. - Walking Maidenhair Fern

Botanical Name: Adiantum phillipense Linn. (Syn. A. lunulatum Burm).

Natural Order: Polypodiaceae

Habitat: Throughout India in moist places.

Description: A graceful fern. The stipes are 6-15 cm long, tufted, wiry, glabrous, polished and dark chestnut-brown. The fronds are 15-30 cm long, simply pinnate, often elongated and rooting at the apex.

Medicinal Action:

Rasa : Pungent
Guṇa : Heavy
Vīrya : Cold

It purifies the blood, bestows longevity, and is used in ulcers, herpes, burning, diarrhoea, vertigo, epilepsy, skin diseases and toxicosis.

References: CS, sūtra, 4, 10; SS, sūtra, 38, 4)

Hapushā

Synonyms: Vapushā, Viśrā, Visra-gandha, Vigandhika (first variety).

Aśvattha-phalā, Matsya-gandhā, Plīha-hantrī, Vishaghnī, Dvānksha-nāśinī, Kaphaghnī, Aparājitā (second variety).

Hin. - Hauber, Abhal
Ben. - Havūshā
Mah. - Hosh, Śeraṇī
Kash. - Betar
Kumaon - Chichia
Eng. - Juniper

Botanical Name: Juniperus communis Linn

Natural Order: Cupressaceae

Habitat: Western Himalayas from Kumaon westwards, 12,500-- 14,000 ft.

Description: This is a dense, more or less procumbent shrub rarely ever attaining the height of a tree, with very close branches and reddish brown bark which peels of in papery shreds. The leaves are in whorls of three, linear, long, sharply pointed with the upper surface concave, bluish-white in colour. The flowers are usually dioecious and axillary, while the fruit is sub-globose, bluish-black when ripe.

Medicinal Action:

Rasa : Pungent, bitter and astringent
Guṇa : Heavy
Vīrya : Hot

It alleviates kapha and vāta, is appetizing and beneficial in sprue, abdominal colic, abdominal tumours, haemorrhoids, ascites, dyspepsia, worms, catarrh, constipation and menorrhagia.

The second variety is useful in toxicosis, dysuria and enlargement of spleen (SS, uttara, 52, 38).

Varieties: There are two varieties based on the fruits :

1. The fruits are fish shaped with an odour of raw meat.
2. The fruits are shaped like the fruit of the peepul tree, but with a fleshy odour.

Haridrā

Synonyms: Niśā, Pītā, Yuvatī, Hema-rāginī, Kānchanī, Kshaṇadā, Gourī, Mehaghnī, Varavarṇinī, Yāminī, Kshapā, Tamasinī, Gandhapalāśikā, Suvarṇa-varṇā, Mangala-pradā, Umā, Gharshaṇī, Vishagnī, Yoshitpriyā, Jvarāntikā, Śiphā, Kṛmighnī, Dīrgha-rāgā, Hṛd-vilāsinī.

Hin. - Haldi
Ben. - Halud
Tam. - Manjal, Kānchani
Tel. - Pasupu
Kan. - Ariśiṇa
Mal. - Mannal
Eng. - Long-rooted Turmeric

Botanical Name: Curcuma longa Linn (Syn. Amomum curcuma Murs).

Natural Order: Zinziberaceae

Habitat: Cultivated all over India.

Description: This is a tall herb with a large ovoid rootstock which has sessile, cylindrical, internally orange coloured tubers. The leaves are very large, in tufts upto 4 ft. long, including the petiole which is about as long as the blade, oblong-lanceolate, and tapering to the base. The flowers are in autumnal spikes, 4 to 6 inches long.

Varieties: There are four varieties (three according to SS, sūtra, 14, 35):

1. Haridrā (Curcuma longa Linn)
2. Karpūra-haridrā

Synonyms: Āmra-gandhā, Surabhi-dāru, Padma-patrā, Suranāyikā.

Hin. - Kapur-haldi
Ambīyā-haldi
Ben. - Āmādā
Mah. - Āvale-haḷad
Tel. - Māmiḍallam
Kan. - Karpūra-arisina
Tam. - Māngai-inji
Eng. - Mango ginger

Botanical Name: Curcuma amada Roxb

Descriptions: This herb has a large rootstock with thick, cylindric or ellipsoid, sessile tubers. The leaves are in tufts, long, petiolate, oblong, lanceolate, acute-or acuminate, narrowed to the base, glabrous and green on both sides. The flowers are white or very pale yellow.

3. Vana-haridrā

Synonyms: Araṇya-haridrā. Śolī, Vanārishṭā,

Hin. - Van-haldi,
Janglī-haldi
Ben. - Van-halud
Mah. - Rān-haḷad
Tam. - Kasturi-manjal
Tel. - Kasturi pasupu
Mal. - Kaṭṭu-mannal
Kan. - Kāḍarasina, Kastūri-ariśina
Eng. - Cochin turmeric,
Wild turmeric, Yellow Zedoar

Botanical Name: Curcuma aromatica Salisb

Description: The rhizome is very hard, oblong, rather ovate, 2 to 3 inches long, and 11/2 to 2 inches in diameter; the surface is wrinkled and hairy, marked with circular disks or rings. It exudes a fragrant odour.

4. Dāru-haridrā - See Dāru-haridrā.

Medicinal Action:

Rasa : Pungent and bitter (haridrā and vana-haridrā) bitter (karpūra-haridrā)
Guṇa : Dry (haridrā)
Light (karpūra-haridrā)
Vīrya : Hot (haridrā)
Cold (karpūra-haridrā)

Haridrā alleviates kapha and vāta, enhances the complexion and is beneficial in skin diseases, discolouration of the skin, urinary disorders such as polyuria, diseases of impure blood, swellings, anaemia, ulcers, pruritus, worms, catarrh, anorexia, glandular swelling, elephantiasis and toxicosis.

Karpūra-haridrā alleviates pitta, aggravates vāta, is appetizing and is useful in pruritus, ulcers, cough, fever, hiccoughs, contusions nd dyspnoea.

Vana-haridrā alleviates vāta, purifies the blood, is appetizing and is used in skn diseases.

Therapeutic Hints:

1. Haridrā antidotes poison and is useful in skin diseases (CS, sūtra, 4, 11).
2. The rhizome is useful in diseases of Vāta (SS, sūtra, 39, 7).
3. It is used for external application in pain in the sides (CS, sūtra, 3, 25).
4. It is especially useful in urinary disorders (including diabetes) (AS, sūtra, 13) and in pishṭha meh. (SS, chikitsā, 11, 9).
5. A combination of haridra and triphala is considered useful in anaemia (SS, uttara, 44, 17).

Haridrakah

Synonyms: Pītadāruh, Śrīmān, Gouradrumah, Kadambakah, Supushpah

Hin. - Ladivā, Haludavā
Ben. - Keli-kadam
Mah. - Haḷadiv
Tam. - Manja-kadambai
Tel. - Pasupu-kadamba
Mal. - Manja-kadamba

Botanical Name: Adina cordifolia (Roxb.) Benth & Hook, fo.

Natural Order: Rubiaceae

Habitat: Most parts of India.

Description: A large deciduous tree, upto 42 metres high and 5.2 metres girth with a buttressed stem and grey bark exfoliating in patches. The leaves are orbicular-cordate, shortly acuminate, glabrous above and pubescent below and petiolate. The flowers are yellow and downy. The fruit is a capsule with many oblong, minute, winged seeds. The tree flowers from May-August; fruits are borne in October-November. The tree is leafless in February-May.

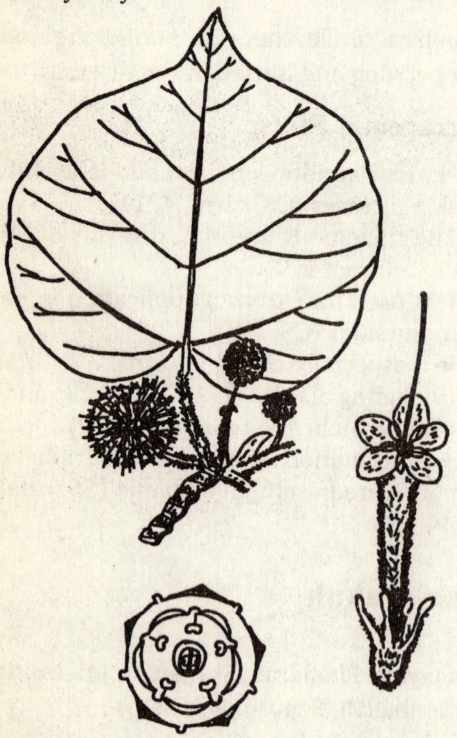

Medicinal Action:

Rasa : Astringent, pungent and bitter
Guṇa : Light
Vīrya : Hot
Vipāka : Pungent

It alleviates kapha, is strength-giving, enhances the complexion, facilitates healing of wounds, prevents suppuration and is used in skin diseases.

Harītakī

Synonyms: Abhayā, Pathyā, Pramathyā, Pūtanā, Amṛtā, Balyā, Jayā, Avyathā, Haimavatī, Vayasthā, Chetakī, Śivā, Sudhā, Prāṇadā, Nandinī, Rohiṇī, Vijayā, Śreyasī, Jīvapriyā, Jīvanikā, Bhishagvarā, Kāyasthā, Devī, Vahni-netra-mitā.

Hin.	-	Harar
Mah.	-	Hiraḍā
Tam.	-	Ankanam, Kaḍakay-maram
Mal.	-	Kaṭukkāmaram
Tel.	-	Karakkāya
Kan.	-	Aḷale-kāyi-mara
Eng.	-	Ink-nut tree, Chebulic myrobalan

Botanical Name: Terminalia chebula Retz (Syn. Terminalia reticulata Roth; Myrobalanus chebula Gaertn)

Natural Order: Combretaceae

Habitat: Abundant in N. India from Kangra and Kumaon to Bengal, and southwards to the Deccan table-lands at 1,000 — 3,000 ft; higher forests of the Bombay Ghats, Satpuras, Belgaum and Kanara.

Description: This is a medium-sized to large, deciduous tree with a short bole and round crown. The young parts are covered with rusty hairs. The bark is dark-brown with numerous, shallow, vertical cracks, exfoliating in woody scales. The leaves are sub-opposite, ovate-elliptic or oblong-ovate, acuminate, and glabrous when full grown. The flowers are sessile, dull white with an offensive smell.

Varieties: There are seven kinds of fruits : (1)

Abhayā, (2) Chetakī, (3) Pathyā, (4) Pūtana, (5) Harītakī, (6) Jayā and (7) Haimavatī.

Parts Used: The fruits and seeds.

Medicinal Action:

Rasa : Astringent, sour, sweet, bitter and pungent (the pulp is sweet, the fibres and stone sour, the skin pungent, stalk bitter and stone astringent)

Guṇa : Dry
Heavy (the seeds)

Vīrya : Hot

Vipāka : Sweet

It alleviates all the three doshas, is a laxative, nutritive, a brain tonic, appetizing, strength-giving, promotes vision and bestows longevity. It is beneficial in cough, urinary disorders, haemorrhoids, skin diseases, swellings, ascites, worms, anorexia, sprue, constipation, diarrhoea, intermittent fever, abdominal tumours, distention of abdomen, thirst, vomiting, hiccough, pruritus, heart diseases, jaundice, abdominal colic, dyspnoea, flatulence, enlargement of spleen and liver, calculi, dysuria, toxicosis, retention of urine, discolouration of skin, headaches, eye-diseases, hoarseness, chronic fevers, anaemia, tuberculosis, diseases of the ear, ulcers, and rheumatism (CS, chikitsā, 1, 25-30).

It is contraindicated in acute fever, dyspepsia, pregnant women, in very emaciated people and in cases of tetanus.

The seeds alleviate vāta and pitta and improve eyesight.

Adjuvants: Haritaki ensures longevity and health if taken as follows :

With salt in the rainy season, with sugarcandy in autumn, with ginger in the later part of winter, with pippalī in the earlier part of winter, with honey in spring and with jaggery in summer.

If taken with salt, it alleviates kapha, with sugarcandy pitta, with ghee vāta, and with jaggery all three doshas (BP, 6, 33).

Haritaki, if chewed is appetizing, if taken in paste form is a laxative, if steam-boiled is constipative and if fried alleviates all three doshas (BP, 6, 36).

Test of Excellence : That fruit which is fresh, smooth, dense, rounded, heavy and which sinks in water is of good quality.

Therapeutic Hints:

1. It ensures longevity (CS, sūtra, 4, 18) and is used in skin diseases (ibid, 4, 11), cough, hiccough and fever (ibid, 4, 16).
2. It is considered the best among the substances which are pathyā (CS, sūtra, 25, 40).
3. A linctus prepared from Harītakī and other drugs is useful in cough and dyspnoea (CS, chikitsā, 18, 163).

Hijjalah

Synonyms: Ijjalah, Nichulah, Ambujah, Jalajah, Nadī-kāntah, Raktah, Vidulah, Dīrgha-patrakah, Kārmukah.

Hin.	-	Samudraphal
Tam.	-	Radami
Kan.	-	Samudrakāyi, Kempu-kaṇagina, Gaṇigilatora
Tel.	-	Kanapu-cheṭṭu, Kaṇigi
Mah.	-	Mānkumba, Piwar

Botanical Name: Barringtonia acutangula Gaertn (Syn. Eugenia acutangula Linn)

Natural Order: Myrataceae

Habitat: Common in the Sub-himalayan tracts, Bihar, Orissa, Bengal, Assam, Madhya Pradesh and South India.

Description: This is a middle sized evergreen tree with a dark brown bark. The leaves are oblong-ovate and serrate. The flowers occur in racemes which are pendulous and red in colour. The fruit is a berry which is bluntly four angled. The tree flowers from January to March.

Parts Used: Root, leaves and fruits.

Medicinal Action:

Rasa : Pungent
Vīrya : Hot

It alleviates kapha and vāta, is auspicious, a purgative, emetic and used in vertigo, worms and toxicosis.

The leaf-juice is given with honey in diarrhoea.

The fruit-juice is used as collyrium in jaundice and eye diseases.

Note: The properties of Hijjala are greatly similar to those of Jala-vetasa.

Hilamochikā

Synonyms: Trivritparṇī, Vishagnī, Jala-brāhmī, Śankhadharā, Matsyākshī.

Hin.	-	Hurkuch, Harkuch
Ben.	-	Hinchā

Botanical Name: Enhydra fluctuans Lour (Syn. Hingtsha repens Roxb)

Natural Order: Compositae

Habitat: Bengal, Assam and Bihar.

Description: This is a prostate herb with sessile, opposite, linear-oblong leaves, from 1 to 3 inches long.

Parts Used: Whole plant.

Medicinal Action:

Rasa : Bitter

It alleviates kapha and pitta, is laxative and is beneficial in skin diseases and swellings.

Hinguh

Synonyms: Rāmaṭham, Bahlīkam, Jatukam,

Sahasravedhī, Jantughnam, Sūpāngam, Śūlahrt, Sūpa-dhūpanam, Ugragandham, Agūḍha-gandham.

Hin.	- Hing
Tam.	- Perungāyam
Mal.	- Perunkāyam
Tel.	- Rāmaṭhamu, Inguā
Kan.	- Ingina-giḍa
Eng.	- Asafoetida

Botanical Name: Ferula foetida Regal (Syn. Ferula narthex Boiss)

Natural Order: Umbelliferae

Habitat: Eastern Persia and Western Afghanisthan.

Description: This is a strong smelling plant growing to 6-8 ft. high with soft, serrated leaves. The flowers are small, yellow, the umbels arising from the sheath of the lower leaves.

Varieties: There are two varieties, black and white.

Parts Used: Gum-resin

Medicinal Action:

Rasa	: Pungent and bitter
Guṇa	: Light, unctous and sharp
Vīrya	: Hot
Vipāka	: Pungent

It alleviates kapha and vāta, aggravates pitta, is a cardiac tonic, appetizing, a digestive, a laxative, promotes vision and is beneficial in abdominal colic, worms, abdominal tumours, constipation, flatulence, distention of abdomen, dyspepsia, syncope, dyspnoea, heart-diseases, cough, ascities and dental caries.

Purification: Hingu is fried with ghee in an iron vessel till it becomes slightly reddish in colour.

Therapeutic Hints:

1. It relieves dyspnoea (CS, sūtra, 4, 16), is useful as an errhine (SS, sūtra, 39, 6), and in fainting spells (CS, sūtra, 4, 18).
2. It is very useful as a laxative, is appetizing, cchedana and alleviates Kapha and Vāta (CS, sūtra, 25, 40).

Hrīveram

Synonyms: Vālā, Bālakam, Vāridam, Kacham, Pingam, Kuntalam, Vārī, Udīchyam, Keśanāmakam.

Hin.	- Sugandha bālā
Tam.	- Perāmuṭṭe, Āvibattam
Tel.	- Nāga-muttuva-pulagamu
Mal.	- Kuruntotti
Kan.	- Balarakkasī, Balarākshasī-giḍa
Ben.	- Vālya
Mah.	- Vāḷā

Botanical Name: Pavonia odorata Willd (Syn. P.odoratus Roxb)

Natural Order: Malvaceae

Habitat: North-Western India, Bundelkhand, Sind, Baluchisthan, W. Rajputana, Bengal, Konkan, Deccan and Carnatic.

Description: A pubescent herb with leaves cordate-ovate, shallowly 3-5 lobed, dentate or the lower ones entire. The flowers are axillary, fragrant, and pink or white in colour. The root is 7 to 8 inches long, twisted, gives off numerous thin fibres, having a delicate musky odour.

Medicinal Action:

Rasa	: Sweet and bitter
Guṇa	: Light and dry
Vīrya	: Cold

It alleviates kapha and pitta, is appetizing, a digestive, and is beneficial in nausea, anorexia, herpes, heart-diseases, diarrhoea, vomiting, thirst, skin diseases, fever, ulcers, salivation, diseases of impure blood, bleeding from internal organs, burning, pruritus, leucodema, alcoholism, haemorrhoids, diarrhoea of children and dyspnoea.

Reference: CS, sūtra, 5, 21.

I

Ikshuh

Synonyms: Dīrgha-cchadah, Bhūrirasah, Guḍamūlah, Asipatrah, Madhu-tṛṇah.

Hin. - Gannā
Tam. - Karumbu, Uggira gandhi
Ben. - Āk
Tel. - Cheruku, Rasālamu
Mah. - Ūsa
Kan. - Kabbu,
Mal. - Karimbu
Eng. - Sugar-cane

Botanical Name: Saccharum officinarum Linn

Natural Order: Graminea

Habitat: Cultivated in most parts of India.

Description: This is a very large perennial herb with a thick, solid, jointed rhizome, giving off root-fibres above each joint. The stems are erect, numerous, and succulent within. The leaves are very large, numerous and close placed.

Varieties: There are a number of varieties, all of which however have similar medicinal properties.

Parts Used: Stems and roots.

Medicinal Action:

Rasa : Sweet and slightly astringent.
Sour (fermented juice)
Guṇa : Unctous and heavy
Vīrya : Cold
Hot (juice expressed by machine)
Vipāka : Sweet

It alleviates vāta and pitta, aggravates kapha, is strength giving, nutritive, aphrodisiac, diuretic, appetizing, and is beneficial in fatigue, bleeding from internal organs, diseases of impure blood, ulcers, oedema, emaciation, burning, suppression of urine, and dysuria.

The juice, when squeezed out by chewing alleviates vāta and pitta, aggravates kapha, is aphrodisiac, laxative, nutritive, diuretic, strength giving, promotes eyesight and is useful in tuberculosis, fatigue, bleeding from internal organs, etc.

The juice which is expressed by machines is mixed with the juice of the skin and nodes. It is therefore constipative and heat producing.

The fermented juice alleviates vāta, aggravates pitta and kapha and is diuretic.

The juice that is boiled alleviates kapha and vāta, slightly aggravates pitta and is useful in abdominal tumours and constipation.

Sugarcane alleviates pitta if taken before meals and aggravates vāta if taken after.

Products of Sugarcane (SS, sūtra, 45, 159):

1. Phāṇitah: The juice which is heated till it becomes slightly dense. This alleviates vāta and pitta, aggravates kapha, is heavy, nutritive, abhishyandī, diuretic and aphrodisiac.
2. Matsyandī: This is the juice further subjected to heat till it becomes semi-solid. This alleviates vāta and pitta, is sweet, light, strength-giving, laxative, nutritive and aphrodisiac
3. Guḍa (Jaggery): This alleviates vāta, slightly aggravates pitta, increases kapha, is heavy, unctous, aphrodisiac, diuretic, strength-giving and causes growth of worms. Guḍa which is old, alleviates vāta and pitta, is appetizing, heart tonic, sedative, light and is beneficial in fever, urinary disorders, pruritus and fatigue. It is prescribed as an article of diet in haemorrhoids, jaundice, tuberculosis, urinary disorders, polyuria, abdominal tumours, anaemia and in diseases of vāta and Pitta. Guḍa which is fresh aggravates kapha, is heavy, hot, unctous, laxative, appetizing, causes worms, dyspnoea and dyspepsia.

Therapeutic Hints:

1. Sugarcane is diuretic, relieves fatigue and is useful in impotence (CS, sūtra, 4, 12, 16; 25, 40).
2. The juice is excellent in anaemia (SS, uttara, 44, 18), in all forms of ascites (AS, chikitsā, 17) and in bleeding from external organs (haemorrhages) (CS, chikitsā, 4, 9; SS, sūtra, 46, 431).
3. CS also gives a recipe of sugarcane juice which is useful as an aphrodisiac (CS, sūtra, 27, 269).

References: SS, sūtra, 45, 148, 149, 155, 159.

Indra-vāruṇī

Synonyms: Viśālā, Goja-chirbhiṭā, Mṛgervārū, Kshudrasahā, Chitraphalā, Aindrī, Gavakshī, Bharā, Mṛgādanī, Aruṇā, Govādanī, Vishaghnī, Sūryā, Gaṇakarṇikā, Sukarṇikā, Tārakā, Vṛshabhākshī, Pīta-pushpā, Hemapushpā, Bālakapriyā, Raktervaruh, Vishalatā, Indra-vallarī.

Hin.	-	Indrāyan
Tam.	-	Pedikāri, Āttuttummaṭṭi
Tel.	-	Pāparabuḍamu, Ḳārkārukamu, Puccha - cheṭṭu
Kan.	-	Hāvumekke, Doḍḍa-hālmekke-baḷḷi, Kāḍu-kavaḍe
Mal.	-	Paikummṭi, Kāṭuveḷḷari
Eng.	-	Bitter apple, Colocynth

Botanical Name: Citrullus colocynthis Schrad (Syn. Cucumis colocynthis Linn)

Natural Order: Cucurbitaceae

Habitat: Occurs wild throughout most parts of India.

Description: A perennial, slight rough herb with rather long, angular and rough branches trailing on the ground. Tendrils are simple, leaves are deeply divided, lobed and very rough below. The middle lobe is the longest. Flowers are yellow, solitary and axillary. Fruit is a globose berry, blotched with green and white.

Varieties: There is a bigger variety called Mahā-indravāruṇī.

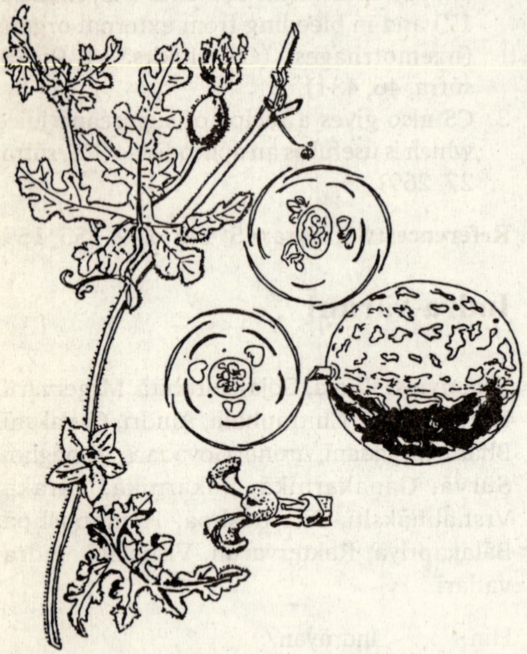

Parts Used: Fruits, root and oil from seeds.

Medicinal Action:

Rasa : Bitter and pungent
Guṇa : Light
Vīrya : Cold
Vipāka : Pungent

It alleviates kapha and pitta, is a purgative, diaphoretic, and is used in ascites, abdominal tumours, worms, skin diseases, fever, ulcers, cough, polyuria, tendency to abortion, jaundice, enlargement of spleen, prolonged pregnancy, enlargement of glands, constipation, anaemia, dyspnoea and toxicosis.

Mahā-indravāruṇī is beneficial in sore throat and elephantiasis.

The oil from the seeds is useful in blackening grey hair.

References: SS, chikitsā, 37, 34.

Ingudī

Synonyms: Angāra-vṛkshah, Tiktakah, Tāpasadrumah, Taila-phalah, Tīkshṇa-kaṇṭakah, Hingupatrah, Vishakaṇṭah, Kroshṭu-phalah, Anilāntakah, Supatrah, Śūlarih, Pūtigandhah.

Hin. - Hingoṭ
Ben. - Hingan
Mah. - Hinganbet
Tam. - Nanjuṇḍan
Tel. - Gāra
Mal. - Nanjuṇḍa
Kan. - Ingaḷa, Ingalīka-mara, Ingalukke

Botanical Name: Balanites roxburghii Planch (Syn. Ximenia aegyptiaca Roxb; Balanites aegyptiaca (Linn) Delile)

Natural Order: Simarubaceae

Habitat: Drier parts of India

Description: A small, thorny tree with an yellowish-grey bark. The leaves are alternate, two-foliate with ashy-green, entire leaflets. The flowers are small, greenish, fragrant, in axillary cymes. The fruit is a large, oily drupe, up to 5 cm long with five distinct grooves. The tree flowers in Ferbuary-March; fruits are borne in September-October.

Parts Used: Root-bark, fruits, flowers and oil of seeds.

Medicinal Action:

Rasa : Pungent and bitter
Sweet and bitter (flowers and oil)
Guṇa : Light
Unctous (flowers and oil)

Vīrya : Hot
Cold (oil)
Vipāka : Pungent

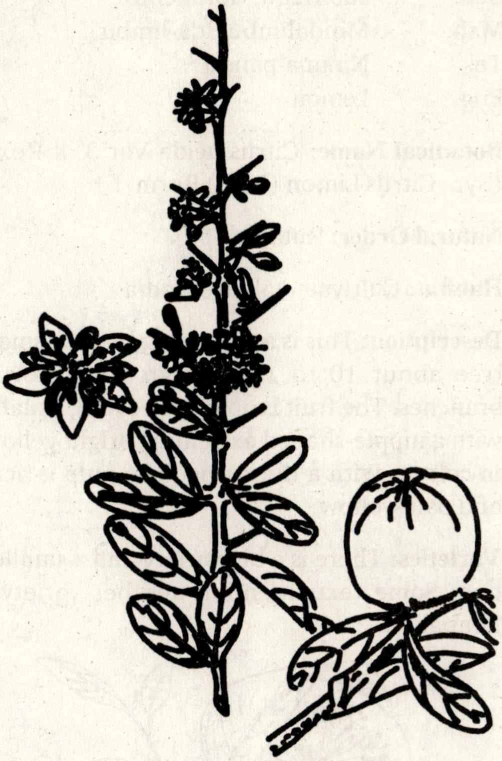

It alleviates kapha and vāta, bestows longevity, and is beneficial in worms, ulcers, skin diseases, leucoderma, abdominal colic, dyspepsia, knotty growths and toxicosis. The flowers alleviate kapha and vāta. The oil alleviates pitta, aggravates kapha, is strengthening, enchances complexion and promotes growth of hair.

Therapeutic Hints:

1. This bark is used as an errhine in headaches, etc. (SS, sūtra, 39, 6).

References: CS, sūtra, 27, 146, chikitsā, 1, 3, 15; SS, sūtra, 45, 115; chikitsā, 11, 6; 25, 22; uttara, 45, 26; 52, 22; AS, uttara, 35).

Īshad-golah

Synonyms: Snigdha-bījah, Aśvakarṇabījah, Slakshṇajīrah.

Hin. - Isphaghūl
Tam. - Ishappa^bolvirai
Mal. - Isabgol
Tel. - Isabagālaviṭṭulu
Kan. - Isabagolu

Botanical Name: Plantago ovate Forsk (Syn. Plantago ispaghul Roxb)

Natural Order: Plantaginaceae

Habitat: Punjab plains and low hills from the Sutlej westwards, Sind and Baluchistan.

Description: This is a stemless or nearly stemless softly hairy or wooly annual herb. Leaves are narrowly linear, finely acuminate, entire or distantly toothed and usually 3-nerved. Flowers are greenish, occurring in ovoid or cylindric spikes. Fruit which is a capsule is ellipsoid, membranous and glabrous; while the seeds are 3 mm long, boat-shaped, smooth and yellowish-brown.

Parts Used: Seeds

Medicinal Action:

Rasa : Sweet and astringent
Guṇa : Slimy
Vīrya : Cold

It slightly aggravates vāta, alleviates pitta and kapha, is aphrodisiac, constipative and is beneficial in bleeding from internal organs, dysentery and burning.

J

Jala-vetasah (see also Vetasah)

Synonyms: Vānīrah, Nikunchakah, Parivyādhah, Jalasambhavah, Nādeyah, Vyādhighātah, Śākhālū, Vṛttapushpah.

Hin.	- Jalabet
Ben.	- Jalavet
Mah,	- Thorvet, Vanjhā
Tel.	- Nīti-prabbali

Botanical Name: Salix tetrasperma Roxb

Natural Order: Salicaceae

Habitat: Throughout tropical and subtropical India.

Varieties: There is a bigger variety called Bṛhad-jalavetasah.

Medicinal Action:

Rasa	: Astringent and bitter
Guṇa	: Dry
Vīrya	: Cold

It alleviates kapha and pitta, aggravates vāta, is constipative, promotes healing of wounds, and is beneficial in bleeding from internal organs, ulcers and diseases of impure blood.

References: AS, uttara, 46.

Jambīrah

Synonyms: Danta-śaṭhah, Jambhah, Rochanakah, Mukha-śodhī, Jāḍyārī, Jantu-jit, Danta-harshaṇah.

Hin.	- Jambīrī-nimbu, Pahārī-nīmbu
Ben.	- Jabīrlebu, Gorānebu
Mah.	- Moiḍalīmbu, Iḍa-limbu
Tel	- Nimma-panḍu
Eng.	- Lemon

Botanical Name: Citrus acida Var 3 of Roxb (Syn. Citrus Limon (Linn) Burm. f.)

Natural Order: Rutaceae

Habitat: Cultivated all over India

Description: This is a straggling bush or small tree about 10 to 12 ft. high with thorny branches. The fruit is oblong or ovoid, usually with a nipple-shaped extremity, bright yellow in colour, with a thick rind. The pulp is acid and pale-yellow.

Varieties: There is a big variety and a smaller one. Some texts mention another variety - Limpākah.

Parts Used: Fruits and leaves.

Medicinal Action:

Rasa : Slightly sweet and very sour (unripe fruits of the small variety); sweet (ripe fruits)
Sweet and slightly sour (Limpāka)
Sour, astringent and bitter (fruits of the big variety)

Guṇa : Heavy
Sharp (the leaves)

Vīrya : Hot

It alleviates kapha and vāta, aggravates pitta, is aromatic, difficult to digest, strength-giving and appetizing, and is beneficial in constipation, abdominal colic, nausea, vomiting, cough, thirst, dyspepsia, bad taste in the mouth, chest pain, worms, rheumatic pains, dyspnoea and toxicosis.

When ripe, the fruits alleviate kapha and pitta, are sedative, nutritive, appetizing, strength-giving, refreshing, and purify the blood.

The fruits of the big variety alleviate kapha and pitta, are a laxative and digestive.

The leaves alleviate kapha and vāta, are appetizing, aromatic and cleanse the mouth.

The Limpāka fruits alleviate vāta and kapha, do not aggravate pitta in excess, are aromatic, a heart-tonic and are useful in vomiting.

References: SS, sūtra, 46, 162.

Jambū

Synonyms: Surabhipatra, Nīlaphalā, Śukrapriyā, Śyamalā, Mahāskandhā, Rājārhā, Rājaphalā, Megha-modinī.

Hin. - Jāmun
Ben. - Kālā Jām
Tam. - Nāval
Mal. - Kiḷakkan-neral
Tel. - Nereḍu
Kan. - Nīraḷe-mara
Eng. - Jambul, Black Plum

Botanical Name: Eugenia jambolana Lam (Syn. Syzygium jambolanum Dec : S. cumini (Linn.) Skeels) Calyptranthes jambolana Willd).

Natural Order: Myrtaceae

Habitat: Throughout India.

Description: It is a large evergreen tree with a dark stem and shining green foliage with a dense crown, and smooth greyish bark. Leaves are leathery and opposite, having a characteristic vein pattern with translucent dots visible against light. Flowers are dirty-white, fragrant and crowded in short racemes. Fruits are purplish-black, smooth and shining when young.

Varieties: There are three main varieties;

1. Rāja-jambū

Synonyms: Mahājambū, Svarṇamātā, Mahāphalā, Kokileshṭā, Mahā-nīlā, Bṛhat-phalā.

2. Kāka-jambū

Synonyms: Kāka-phalā, Nādeyī, Kāka-vallabhā, Bhṛgeshṭā, Kāka-nīlā, Dhvāṇksha-jambū, Ghana-priyā.

3. Bhūmi-jambū

Synonyms: Hrasva-phalā, Bhṛnga-vallabhā, Bhramareshṭā, Pika-bhakshā, Kāshṭha-jambu.

Parts Used: Fruits, seeds, bark and leaves.

Medicinal Action:

Rasa : Astringent (the bark)
Astringent, sweet and sour (fruits of Bhūmi-jambu).
Astringent and sweet (Rāja-jambu)
Astringent, sour and bitter (Kāka-jambu).
Sweet (the fruit pulp)

Guṇa : Dry (all parts)
Heavy (the fruits)

Vīrya : Cold
Hot (Rāja jambu)

Vipāka : Sweet

Jambu alleviates kapha and pitta, is constipative, appetizing and beneficial to the throat. It is useful in burning, worms, cough, tuberculosis, diarrhoea, diseases of impure blood, ulcers, and dyspnoea.

The tender leaves restore normal colour to faeces, decrease the amount of urine and cure vomiting.

Bhūmi-jambu (leaves and bark) is heart tonic, nutritive, and aphrodisiac. The tender leaves cause flatulence.

The fruits aggravate vāta, are emaciating, cause flatulence and sore throat.

Rāja-jambu is useful in fatigue and anorexia.

Kāka-jambu is nutritive, strength-giving and aphrodisiac.

The fruit-pulp is especially useful in diabetes.

Therapeutic Hints:

1. The leaves are used in the form of decoction in certain eye diseases (SS uttara, 19, 13).
2. The stone of the fruits is constipative (CS, sūtra, 2, 28) and is used for external application in diseases of the mouth (SS, kalpa, 1, 48-49).

Reference: CS, sūtra, 4, 14, 15; 27, 140; SS, uttara, 45, 23; AHṛ, sūtra, 6, 128).

Japā

Synonyms: Oṇḍra-pushpah, Rakta-pushpī, Arka-Priyā, Prātika, Hari-vallabhā.

Hin.	-	Jāsand, Oḍahul
Ben.	-	Jābā
Mah.	-	Jāsavand
Kan.	-	Dāsavāḷa
Tam.	-	Śembarattai
Tel.	-	Dāsana-cheṭṭu
Mal.	-	Champarutti
Kon.	-	Dasaṇe-phula
Eng.	-	Shoe flower, China Rose, Chinese Shoe Flower

Botanical Name: Hibiscus rosa-sinensis Linn.

Natural Order: Malvaceae

Habitat: Throughout India

Description: This is an evergreen, woody, glabrous, showy shrub, from 5 to 8 feet high, with bright green, ovate leaves, entire below and coarsely toothed above. The flowers are solitary, axillary, large and bell-shaped with pistil and stamens projecting from the centre. The fruit is a roundish capsule with many seeds.

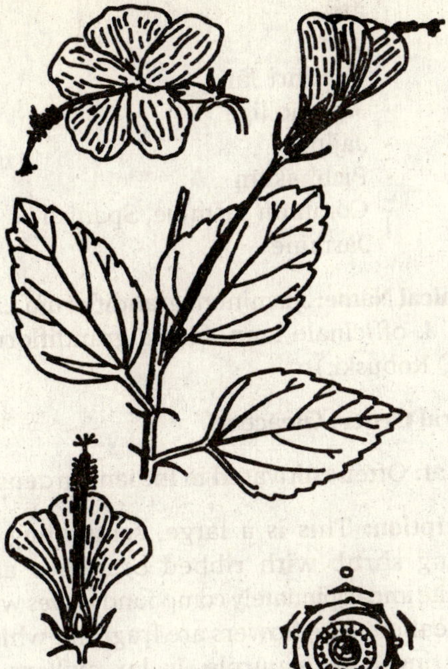

Medicinal Action:

Rasa : Sweet (pungent according to RN)
Bitter (the flowers)
Guṇa : Unctous and light
Vīrya : Cold (hot according to RN)

It is nutritive, nourishes the foetus if taken by pregnant women, is constipative, engenders worms, is emetic, and is beneficial in burning pains, urinary disorders, haemorrhoids, menstrual disorders and falling hair.

The flowers when fried with ghee and administered are said to ensure easy menstruation.

Jaṭāmāmsī

Synonyms: Jaṭā, Peshī, Lomaśā, Jaṭilā, Misih, Tapasvinī, Himsrā, Chakravartini, Vahninī, Kṛshṇa-jaṭā, Kirātinī, Bhūtajaṭā, Mālā, Kravyādī, Piśitā, Peśinī, Tāmasī, Amṛtajaṭā, Mṛgabhakshā.

Hin. - Bālchad
Tel. - Jaṭāmāmsi
Tam. - Namattam
Kan. - Jaṭāmāmsi, Sugandha-muste
Eng. - Indian Spikenard

Botanical Name: Nardostachys jatamanysi DC (Syn. Valeriana jatamansi Wall)

Natural Order: Valerianaceae

Habitat: Alpine Himālayas, 11,000--15,000 ft., extending eastwards from Kumaon to Sikkim, 17,000 ft. and Bhutan.

Description: This perennial plant has a stem from 4-24 inches high which lies partly underground and partly above. The root stock is woody, long and stout, clothed with fibres from the stalks of the dead leaves. The leaves are oblong, lanceolate and hairy. The flowers are pink and small, in clusters. The fruit is small, with white hairs pointing upwards.

Varieties: There are two other varieties:

1. Gandha-māmsī;

Synonyms: Laghu-māmsī, Keśī, Lomaśā, Piśāchī

2. Ākāśa-māmsī:

Synonyms: Nirālambā, Svasambhavā, Sūkshmapatrī, Gourī, Parvatavāsinī.

Parts Used: Root

Medicinal Action:

Rasa : Bitter, astringent, sweet and pungent. Bitter (Gandha-māmsī)

Guṇa : Unctous

Vīrya : Cold

It alleviates all the doshas, purifies the blood, enhances intelligence, restores consciousness, and promotes strength and lustre. It is beneficial in skin diseases, discolouration of skin, herpes, toxicosis and burning. It's paste applied externally brings down fever.

The Gandha-māmsī alleviates kapha and vāta, promotes growth of hair, enhances the complexion and is useful in fever, diseases of the throat, bleeding from internal organs and toxicosis.

The Ākāśa-māmsī is analgesic, enhances the complexion, repels insects and is of use in herpes, ulcers, oedema, abscesses, measles and other eruptive fevers.

Test for Excellence: The root which is fresh, unctous and reddish-brown in colour is to be used.

Jātī

Synonyms: Sumanā, Mālatī, Chetakī, Surapriyā, Sandhyā-pushpī, Sukumārī, Surabhi-gandhā, Manoharā, Rājaputrī, Manognyā, Tailamālinī, Janeshṭā, Hṛdya-gandhā, Priyamvadā, Vasantajā, Vārshikā, Prahasantī, Vāsantī.

Hin. - Jai
Ben. - Jātī
Mah. - Paṇḍhri Jāi
Kan. - Jāji mallige
Tel. - Jājipu
Mal. - Pichhakam
Eng. - Common Jasmine, Spanish Jasmine

Botanical Name: Jasminum grandiflorum Linn (Syn. J. officinale Linn. forma grandiflorum (Linn) Kobuski.)

Natural Order: Oleaceae

Habitat: Often cultivated in Indian gardens.

Description: This is a large, scrambling or twining shrub with ribbed branches and opposite imparipinnately compound leaves with 7-11 leaflets. The flowers are fragrant, white, often tinged with purple, in lax axillary or terminal cymes, longer than leaves.

Varieties: There is another variety called Svarṇa-jātī- with reddish flowers.

Parts Used: Leaves, flowers and flower-buds.

Medicinal Action:

Rasa : Astringent, pungent and bitter
Guṇa : Light
Vīrya : Hot (the leaves)
Cold (the flowers)

The leaves alleviate kapha and vāta, and are beneficial in ulcers in the mouth, toothache, headache, toxicosis, diseases of the eye, skin diseases, diseases of impure blood, ulcers and worms.

The flowers-buds are useful in ulcers, vesicles, boils, skin diseases and diseases of the eyes.

The flowers alleviate kapha and pitta and are aromatic.

Svarṇa-jātī is used in toothache, earache, excessive suppuration, and diseases of impure blood.

Therapeutic Hints:

1. Its tender leaves are used to cleanse ulcers in arbuda (AS, uttara, 35).
2. An oil medicated with this drug is used for massage in menstrual disorders caused by Vāta. A tampon saturated with this oil is also made use of (CS, chikitsā, 30, 59).
3. It is valuable in septic wounds and ulcers (SS, sūtra, 38, 64).
4. The flowers are used for culinary purposes (SS, sūtra, 46, 286; AS, sūtra, 87, 88).

Jātīphalah

Synonyms: Koshakah, Sumanah-phalah, Jātiśasyah, Mālatīphalah, Majjasārah, Śālūkah, Putah.

Hin. - Jāyphal
Tam. - Jādikāy
Tel. - Jāikāya
Kan. - Jājikāyi-mara
Mal. - Jādikai

Botanical Name: Myristica fragrans Houtl (Syn. Myristica moschata Thunb; Myristica aromatica Lam)

Natural Order: Myristicacea

Habitat: A native of E. Moluccas, cultivated in the Malay Peninsula and the Malay Islands. Grown in some parts of India.

Description: This is a lofty evergreen tree with slender branches. Leaves are alternate, entire, usually lanceolate, acuminate and pale yellow-brown in colour. Flowers are small, dioecious and bracteolate. Fruit is ovoid, subglobose and 3-8 to 5 cms long. Seeds are erect and enclosed in a membranous, often aromatic aril.

Parts Used: The seeds (Jātīphala); Mace (Jātīpatrī) - the layer covering the seeds; and Oil. Jātīpatrī is also called Jātīkoshā and Jātīphalatvak. Hin. - Jāvitrī, Ben. - Jaitrī, Mah. - Jaypatrī, Eng. - Mace.

Medicinal Action:

Rasa : Astringent, bitter and pungent (Jātīphala).

Pungent, bitter, and sweet (Jātīpatrī)
Guṇa : Sharp and light (Jātīphala)
Unctous and light (Jātīpatrī)
Vīrya : Hot

Jātīphala alleviates kapha and vāta, is an aphrodisiac, constipative, appetizing, digestive, analgesic, heart tonic and is beneficial in anorexia, bad taste in the mouth, foul smelling stools, blackish stools, worms, cough, vomiting, tuberculosis, catarrh, angina pectoris, thirst, abdominal colic, diseases of the throat, diarrhoea, polyuria, herpes and dyspnoea.

Jātīphala made into a paste and applied removes moles, freckles and cracking of the skin.

The oil is stimulant, appetizing, strength giving, and is of use in chronic diarrhoea, flatulence, convulsions, abdominal colic, rheumatism and gum boils.

Jātīpatrī alleviates kapha, antidotes poison, is appetizing, enhances the conplexion, is aromatic, cleanses the mouth and is useful in cough, vomiting, thirst, worms, drowsiness and dyspnoea.

Test: The fruit which is heavy, unctous and produces sound when shaken is to be used.

References: SS, sūtra, 46, 202-203.

Jayantī

Synonyms: Balāmoṭā, Sūkshma-mūlā, Vijayā, Haritā, Sūkshma-patrā, Vikrāntā, Aparājitā.

Hin. - Jait, Jayanti
Mah. - Śevārī
Tel. - Jalugu, Suriminta
Kan. - Kari-jīnāngi mari
Tam. - Karumśembai, Champai

Botanical Name: Sesbania sesban (Linn) Merr. (Syn. Sesbania aegyptiaca Poir; Aeschynomene sesban Roxb)

Natural Order: Leguminosae

Habitat: Plains from the Himalayas to Ceylon, ascending to 4,000 ft. in north-west.

Description: A soft wooded shrub with a brown bark. The leaves are pari-pinnate with 20-30 leaflets which are linear-oblong, pale-green and glabrous. The flowers are yellow or reddish-yellow, in racemes. The fruit is a twisted pod, 15-23 cms long, slightly constricted between seeds. The plant flowers in October-November.

Parts Used: Roots, leaves, flowers and seeds.

Varieties: There are two other varieties: Kṛshṇa (black) variety and Śveta (white) variety.

Medicinal Action:

Rasa : Bitter and pungent
Guṇa : Sweet (the leaves)
Vīrya : Hot cold (the leaves)

It alleviates vāta, and is useful in goitre, dysuria, diseases of the throat and diseases caused by unseen agents and toxicosis.

The leaves promote vision and are beneficial in cases of Gara-visha (slow poisoning).

The root of the white variety, if taken with milk is of value in leucoderma.

The Kṛshṇa variety bestows longevity.

Jayapālah

Synonyms: Sārakah, Tintiḍi-phalam, Dantī-bījam, Mala-drāvī, Rechakah, Nikumbhā.

Hin. - Jamālagoṭ
Ben. - Jaypāl
Mah. - Jepāḷ
Tam. - Nervāḷam

Mal. - Nīrvāḷam
Tel. - Nepāḷavema
Kan. - Jāpāḷa-giḍa
Eng. - Croton oil plant, Purging Croton

Botanical Name: Croton tiglium Linn (Syn. Croton Jamalgota Hamit)

Natural Order: Euphorbiaceae

Habitat: Naturalized and cultivated in Bengal, Assam and South India.

Description: This evergreen tree whose young shoots are covered with hairs has a smooth, ash-coloured bark. The leaves are oblong to ovate-lanceolate, petioled, alternate, toothed, acuminate, membranous and yellowish-green. The flowers are small, monoecious, both sexes in glabrous racemes. The fruit which is a capsule is oblong, almost glabrous with smooth seeds about 13 mm long.

Parts Used: Seeds and oil.

Medicinal Action:

Rasa : Pungent
Guṇa : Sharp, heavy and unctous
Vīrya : Hot

It alleviates kapha and vāta, is a purgative, appetizing and is used in worms.

The oil is a purgative and beneficial in fever, constipation, ascites, coma, headaches, paralysis, tetanus, insanity, rheumatism and cough. If rubbed on the chest, it relieves cough.

Purification: The seeds are divested of the outer layer and boiled in milk in a dolā yantra. Later, the embryo also is removed. Only then can it be used internally.

Note: The adverse effects caused by the use of unpurified seeds are antidoted by the internal use of a paste of Dhānyaka, sugar candy and curds. (RJN, Vol. III, page. 357).

Jhaṇḍuh

Synonyms: Sthūlapushpah

Hin. - Lāl-muragā, Makhmalī
Mah. - Jheṇḍū
Gu. - Mukhmal
Eng. - French Marigold

Botanical Name: Tagetes erecta Linn

Natural Order: Compositae

Habitat: Grown in gardens in India.

Medicinal Action:

Rasa : Astringent and pungent

It is auspicious and relieves fever.

Jhillah

Synonyms: Raktāpahah, Nīlah, Mṛdupatrakah.

Hin. - Jhil
Mah. - Murakuṭ

Botanical Name: Indigofera oblongifolia Forsk (Syn. I. pauciflora Del)

Natural Order: Leguminosae

Habitat: Throughout the plains of India and Baluchisthan.

Medicinal Action:

It is cooling, appetizing and is useful in gout.

Jhāvukā

Synonyms: Pichulah, Aphalah, Bahu-granthikah

Medicinal Action:

Rasa : Pungent and bitter

It is beneficial in dysuria.

Jhinjhiriṇṭikā

Synonyms: Jhinjhirīṭā, Kaṇṭaphalī, Pītapushpā, Vṛttā, Jinjhirā.

Hin. - Chikti
Ben. - Bunokra
Tam. - Puramutti
Tel. - Chirusitrika

Botanical Name: Triumfetta bartramia Linn (Syn. T. rhomboidea Jacq)

Natural Order: Tiliceae

Habitat: Throughout tropical and subtropical India.

Description: This is a herbaceous perennial, up to 1.5 metres high with ovate, rhomboid or cordate, leaves usually three-lobed and irregularly serrate. The flowers are yellow, in dense cymes, while the fruits are globose or ovoid, pea-shaped with smooth, hooked spines.

Medicinal Action:

Rasa : Pungent and astringent
Vīrya : Cold

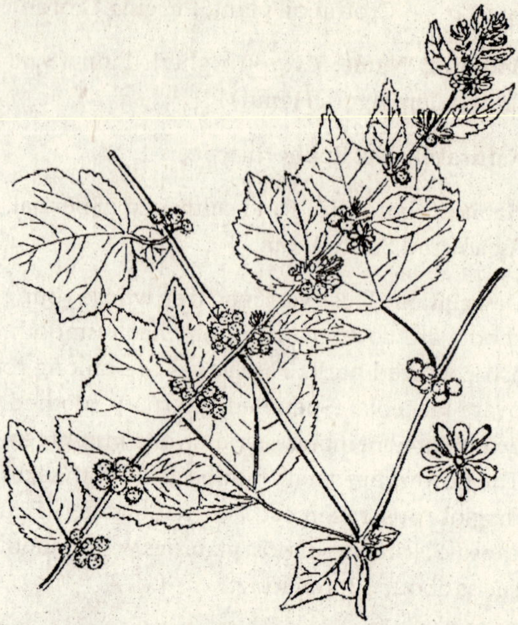

It is nutritive, strength-giving, an aphrodisiac, and is useful in diarrhoea and dysentery. It is said to increase the milk in buffaloes.

Jinginī

Synonyms: Su-niryāsā, Pramodinī, Guḍa-manjarī, Pārvateyā, Sunirghoshā, Madana-manjarī.

Hin. - Jinginī
Mah. - Moi, Mok
Tel. - Oḍḍimānu
Tam. - Odiyamaram
Kan. - Uḍi-mara, Sintimara
Mal. - Oti
Ben. - Jiol

Botanical Name: Odina woodier Roxb (Syb. Lannea grandis (Dennst.) Engl.)

Natural Order: Anacardiaceae

Habitat: Common in deciduous forests throughout India.

Description: It is a large, deciduous tree with stout branchlets and prominent leaf-scars. The bark is thick and grey, exfoliating in small, rounded flakes. The leaves are imparipinnate, crowed at tips of branchlets. The flowers are greenish-yellow and small, in racemes. The fruit is a red, avoid drupe. The tree sheds its leaves and flowers from January to April.

Medicinal Action:

Rasa : Sweet, pungent and astringent
Vīrya : Hot
Vipāka : Pungent

It alleviates kapha and vāta, is emmanogogue and is useful in ulcers, heart diseases, angina pectoris, diarrhoea and bad breath.

References: SS, sūtra, 38, 14; CS, chikitsā, 30, 83.

Jīrakam

Synonyms: Ajājī, Dīpyakah, Jaraṇā, Kaṇā, Māgadhah, Śveta-jīrakā.

Hin.	-	Jīrā
Ben.	-	Jīre, Sādā-jīre
Mal.	-	Jīrakam
Mah.	-	Pāḍhare-jīra
Tel.	-	Jīlakarra
Tam.	-	Chīrakam
Kan.	-	Jirige, Biḷiya-Jīrige
Eng.	-	Cumin seed

Botanical Name: Cuminum cyminum Linn

Natural Order: Umbelliferae

Habitat: Cultivated throughout India, except Bengal and Assam.

Description: This is a glabrous, annual herb, varying from 1 to 3-ft. in height, with the stem arising almost from the base. The lower leaves are slender, short petioled and feathery, while the upper ones have winged petioles. The flowers are small, in long stalked umbels.

Varieties: According to some authorities there are five kinds of Jīraka : (1) Śveta-jīraka, (2) Kṛshṇa-jīraka, (3) Sthūla-jīraka, (4) Sūkshma-jīraka and (5) Vana-jīraka.

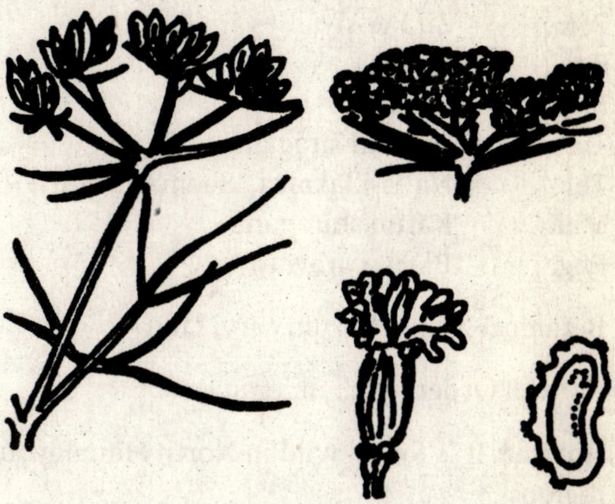

According to BP, there are three varieties (1) Śveta-jīraka, (2) Kṛshṇa-jīraka and (3) Sthūla-jīraka.

1. Śveta-jīrakah

Synonyms: Goura-jīrakah, Śuklājājī, Kaṇa-jirakah, Dīrghakah, Jīrakah.

Eng. - Cumin seeds.

Medicinal Action:

Rasa : Pungent, sweet and bitter
Guṇa : Light, dry and sharp
Vīrya : Slightly hot.
Vipāka : Pungent

It alleviates vāta and kapha, is anthelmintic, appetizing, digestive, constipative, aromatic, strength-giving, and purifies the uterus. It helps eyesight and is beneficial in vomiting, distension of abdomen, fever, anorexia, toxicosis, tuberculosis, diseases of impure blood, diarrhoea, colic, and abdominal tumours.

2. Kṛshṇa-jīrakah

Synonyms: Kṛshṇājājī, Jaraṇā, Sugandhā, Kālajīrakah, Varshā-kālī, Hṛdyā, Udgāra-śodhinī, Bhedinī, Nīla-kaṇā, Kaśmīra-jīrakah, Vānti-śodhinī.

Hin.	-	Kālā-jīrā, Syah-jīrā
Pers.	-	Zirake-siyah
Ben.	-	Kāl-jīra
Mah.	-	Śyājiro
Tam.	-	Shemai-śiragam
Tel.	-	Nalla-jilakarra, Seema-jilakara
Mal.	-	Karun shiragam
Eng.	-	Black caraway

Botanical Name: Carum carvi Linn

Natural Order: Umbelliferae

Habitat: It is found wild in North Himalayan regions.

Description: This is a perennial or biennial herb, from 1 to 3-ft. high, with thick tuberous roots and compound leaves with linear segments, The flowers are small and white, borne in dense umbels.

Medicinal Action:

Rasa : Pungent
Guṇa : Dry
Vīrya : Hot

It alleviates kapha, is aromatic, appetizing, promotes vision and is useful in sprue, fever, dyspepsia, oedema, headache and skin diseases.

3. Sthūla-jīrakah

Synonyms: Kalājājī, Pṛthivī, Pṛthukā, Kunjikā, Kāravī, Dīvyā, Manogynā, Jāriṇī, Sushavī, Taruṇī

Hin.	-	Kalaoji, Mangrelā
Ben.	-	Moṭākāle-jīre
Tel.	-	Nalla-jilakara
Mah.	-	Kalaonjī-jīra
Kan.	-	Kari-jīrige
Eng.	-	Small fennel, Black cumin, Nigella seed.

Botanical Name: Nigella sativa Linn

Natural Order: Ranunculaceae

Habitat: Punjab, Bihar and other parts of India, cultivated and an occasional weed of cultivation.

Description: This is a small herb with leaves 2-3 pinnatisec, cut into linear-lanceolate segments. The flowers are pale-blue, without an involucre, on solitary long peduncles. The seeds are trigonous, black, rugulose-tubular.

Medicinal Action:

Rasa : Bitter and pungent
Vīrya : Hot

It alleviates all the three doshas, is aphrodisiac, appetizing and uterine tonic. It is useful in dyspepsia, flatulence, abdominal tumours, worms and neuralgia.

4. Vana-jīrakah

Synonyms: Araṇya-jīrakah, Bṛhat-pālī, Kshudra-patrā, Kanā.

Hin.	-	Kālā-jīre
Ben.	-	Van-jīre, Som-rāj
Mah.	-	Kaḍū-jīre
Eng.	-	Purple fleabane

Botanical Name: Centratherum anthelminticum (Willd) Kuntze (Syn. Vernonia anthelmintica. Willd)

Natural Order: Compositae

Habitat: Throughout India upto 5,500 ft in the Himalayas and Khasia Hills.

Medicinal Action:

Rasa : Pungent and astringent

It alleviates kapha and vāta, is constipative and is used in ulcers.

Jīvakah

Synonyms: Kshvedah, Hrasvāngah, Dīrghāyuh, Śrngakah, Priyah, Śṛnga-kūrchah, Madhurakah, Chiranjīvakah, Prāṇadah, Bhṛngāhvah, Vṛddhidah, Baladah

Habitat: According to some texts, this plant is found in the Himalayas. According to some other texts, it is found in South India in marshy places (ānūpa-deśa).

Description: The plant is small, full of thorns and milky. The underground stem resembles that of Laśuna (garlic). The leaves are thin, sharp, and similar to those of Jīvantī. The plant resembles a brush in shape.

Medicinal Action:

Rasa : Sweet
Vīrya : Cold

It alleviates vāta and pitta, aggravates kapha, is aphrodisiac, nutritive, purifies the blood and is beneficial in tuberculosis, fever, bleeding from internal organs and burning pains.

Note: If Jīvakah is not to be found, Vidārī can be used in its place.

Reference: CS, sūtra, 4, 9, 13; 3, 22; SS, sūtra, 46, 274.

Jīvantī

Synonyms: Jīvadā, Sukhankarī, Raktāngī, Prāṇadā, Bhadrā, Mangalyā, Madhusravā, Payasvinī, Śāka-śreshthā, Yaśasyā, Kānjikā, Śaśa-śimbika.

Hin. - Jīvanti, Ḍoḍi
Ben. - Jibai
Kan. - Sihi-hāle, Oṇa-hāle
Tam. - Palakudai
Tel. - Palatīge

Botanical Name: Leptadenia reticulata W and A

Natural Order: Asclepiadaceae

Habitat: Punjab and Western Penisula.

Description: A climbing plant with a round, slightly hairy stem which contains pale-yellow, watery juice. The leaves are upto 2.5 to 3.5 inches, simple, opposite, ovate, acute and entire; the base is rounded or somewhat cordate. The flowers are many, greenish-yellow, in umbellate cymes which are usually solitary. The fruit is somewhat woody with flat, ovate-acute seeds with tufts of fine silky hairs at the tips.

Varieties:

There are four varieties:

1. Jīvantī
2. Bṛhat-jīvantī (Syn. Putra-bhadrā, Madhurā, Jīvapushpā)
3. Svarṇa-jīvanti (Syn. Svarṇa-latā, Hema-pūrṇā, Hema-vallī, Hema-kshīrī, Soumyā). Hin. - Sunaharī jīvantī, Kan. - Hoṇa-hāle.
4. Tikta-jīvantī (Bitter jīvantī)

Parts Used: Whole plant.

Medicinal Action:

Rasa : Sweet
Guṇa : Light and unctous
Heavy (the fruits)
Vīrya : Cold

It alleviates vāta and pitta, aggravates kapha, is aphrodisiac, nutritive, constipative, strength-giving, lactogogue, promotes vision, conception and voice, and purifies the blood. It is beneficial in bleeding from internal organs, tuberculosis, burning pains, fever, cough, thirst, diarrhoea, ulcers in the mouth, rheumatic pains, dyspnoea and toxicosis.

The fruits are very nutritive.

According to CS, Jīvantī is the best among all

the leafy vegetables (CS, sūtra, 25, 38; also AS, sūtra, 7, 138; SS, sūtra, 46, 252).

Therapeutic Hints:

1. It confers longevity, and is useful in dyspnoea (CS, sūtra, 4, 9, 13, 16, 18).
2. A medicated ghee prepared with this drug is useful in all forms of tuberculosis (CS, chikitsā, 8, 111-113).

References: SS, sūtra, 45, 120; chikitsā, 37, 23-26.

Jyotishmatī

Synonyms: Pūtilatā, Laganā, Sphuṭabandhanī, Pārāvatapadī, Piṇyā, Pīta-taila, Kanguṇī, Nishphalā, Ingudi, Svarṇalatā, Anala-prabhā, Dīptā, Medhyā, Matidā, Durharā, Kaṭabhī, Amṛtā, Triparṇī, Supingalā, Agni-bhāsā, Lavaṇoktā.

Hin.	-	Mālkānguni
Ben.	-	Latāphatkī
Kan.	-	Gangungebīja
Tel.	-	Bekkuḍu-toge
Eng.	-	Staff tree
Tam.	-	Vāludai

Botanical Name: Celastrus paniculatus Willd

Natural Order: Celastraceae

Habitat: Sub-himālayan tract from the Jhelum eastwords, upto 6,000 ft. throughout the hilly parts of Bombay, south of Gujarat, of Madhya Pradesh and Tamil Nadu.

Description: According to Śiva nighaṇṭu :

Pakva raktaphalā gucchā pītatailā cha vartulā I

Panktipatrā raktabījānupushpā vanajā smṛtā II

This is a large, climbing shrub with lenticellate branches, and an yellow, corky bark. The leaves are alternate, obovate, crenulate and petiolate. The flowers are greenish, in lax, terminal panicles. Fruit is a three-valved yellow capsule with three to six brown seeds. The flowering time is from March to July.

Varieties: There is a bigger variety called Mahā-jyotishmatī.

Medicinal Action:

Rasa	:	Bitter, astringent and slightly pungent
Guṇa	:	Dry, Unctous and sharp
Vīrya	:	Excessively hot

It alleviates kapha and vāta, is appetizing, brain-tonic, laxative, emetic, nutritive, aphrodisiac, enhances complexion and causes burning pains. It is beneficial in ulcers, anaemia, herpes, boils and colic.

The oil alleviates vāta, aggravates pitta, is brain tonic and is useful in ascites.

The leaves are useful in amenorrhoea.

Therapeutic Hints:

1. It is used as an errhine (CS, sūtra, 4, 13; SS, sūtra, 39, 6).
2. The milky exudation is purgative (AS, sūtra, 14).

K

Kadalī

Synonyms: Rambhā, Suphalam, Mochā, Rājeshṭā, Vāraṇa-vallabhā, Sukumārā, Charmaṇvatī, Amśumatphalā, Kāshṭhelā, Satṛtphalā, Guchha-phalā, Bālaka-priyā, Urustambhā, Bhānu-phalā, Vanalakshmī, Ambu-sārā, Dīrgha-patrā, Nih-sārā, Hasti-vishāṇī, Guchcha-dantikā.

Hin.	- Kelā
Ben.	- kalā
Mal.	- Vāla
Tam.	- Vāḷai
Kan.	- Bāḷe-giḍa
Tel.	- Araṭi-cheṭṭu, Kadalamu
Eng.	- Plantain or Banana Tree

Botanical Name: Musa paradisiaca Linn. var sapientum, Kuntze; (Syn. Musa sapientum Linn.)

Natural Order: Musaceae

Habitat: Cultivated all over India.

Habitat: There are many varieties which have similar properties.

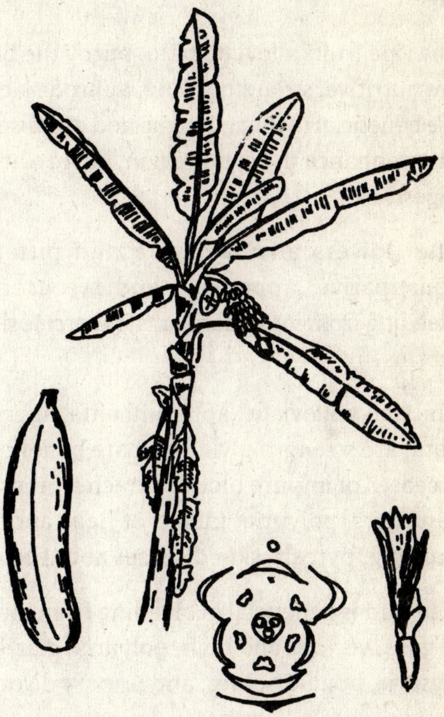

Parts Used: Fruits, flowers, stalk, sap of the stem.

Medicinal Action:

Rasa	: Sweet, astringent and sour (the tender fruits) Sweet and astringent (the ripe fruits) Sweet, astringent and Bitter (the flowers)
Guṇa	: Heavy and unctous (the fruits and flowers) Heavy and dry (the stalks)
Vīrya	: Cold (all parts)

The tender fruits alleviate pitta and are appetizing.

The slightly ripened fruits are constipative, and are useful in thirst, bleeding from internal organs, fever and dysentery. They cause indigestion.

The unripe fruits aggravate vāta and kapha, are constipative, strength-giving, and hard to digest.

The ripe fruits alleviate pitta, purify the blood, are nutritive, strength-giving, aphrodisiac, and are beneficial in thirst, fatigue and eye-diseases. They enhance the complexion, but are hard to digest.

The flowers alleviate vāta and pitta, are constipative, appetising and are useful in bleeding from internal organs, tuberculosis and worms.

The stalks alleviate kapha and pitta, aggravate vāta, are strength giving and are beneficial in diseases of impure blood, earache, menstrual disorders, polyuria, falling of hair, anorexia, burning, pyrosis, skin diseases and worms.

The sāra is beneficial in bleeding from internal organs, vesicles and boils, polyuria, diarrhoea, dysuria, bone-diseases, and urinary disorders.

The juice of the stem is constipative, and is useful in ear-ache, dysuria, diarrhoea, diseases of the bones, menstrual irregularities, tuberculosis, boils, burning pains, bleeding from internal organs and urinary disorders.

Therapeutic Hints:

1. The kshāra (ash) got by burning the plant is drunk with goat's milk in urinary calculi (SS, chikitsā, 7, 22). It is also applied externally in skin diseases (SS, chikitsā, 7, 89).
2. The leaves are used as bandage in haemorrhages (CS, chikitsā, 4, 107).
3. The fruits should not be taken regularly with milk or butter-milk (AS, sūtra, 9; AHṛ, sūtra, 7, 35).

References: AHṛ. sūtra, 15, 26; CS, kalpa, 1, 8; Cckp. on CS, chikitsā, 21 73.

Kadambah

Synonyms: Surabhih, Lalanā-priyah, Kādambaryah, Sindhupusphah, Madāḍhyah, Karṇapūrakah, Hari priyah.

Hin.	-	Kadamā
Ben.	-	Kadam-gācch, Keli-kadom
Tel.	-	Nīpamu, Prekhaṇamu
Tam.	-	Kadambam
Kan.	-	Kadava
Mal.	-	Kaṭambu
Eng.	-	Cadamba Tree

Botanical Name: Anthocephalus cadamba Mig (Syn. Anthocephalus indicus A. Rich; Nauclea cadamba Roxb)

Natural Order: Rubiacae

Habitat: Sub-Himalayan tract from Nepal eastwards to Burma, and in the south in N. Circars and W. Ghats.

Description: A large, deciduous, fast-growing tree with horizontal, spreading branches. The bark is grey, smooth in young trees, dark-grey in old trees with numerous vertical fissures, exfoliating in small rectangular places. The leaves are simple, entire, ovate, shining above, pubescent beneath, with prominent venation. The flowers are 1.5 cm long and yellow. flowers are 1.5 cm long and yellow. The tree flowers in May-July; The fruits are borne in August-September.

Varieties: There are three varieties

1. Dhārā-kadambah

Synonyms: Prāvṛshyah, Pulakī, Bhṛnga-vallabhah, Meghāgama-priyah, Nīpah and Kadambakah.

2. Dhūlī-kadambah

Synonyms: Kramuka-prasūnah, Rāja-kadambah, Parāga-pushpah, Bala-bhadrah, Vasanta-pushpah, Makaranda-vāsah, Bhṛnga-priyah and Reṇu-kadambah.

3. Bhūmi-kadambah

Synonyms: Bhūnimbah, Bhūmijah, Bhṛnga-vallabhah, Laghu-pushpah.

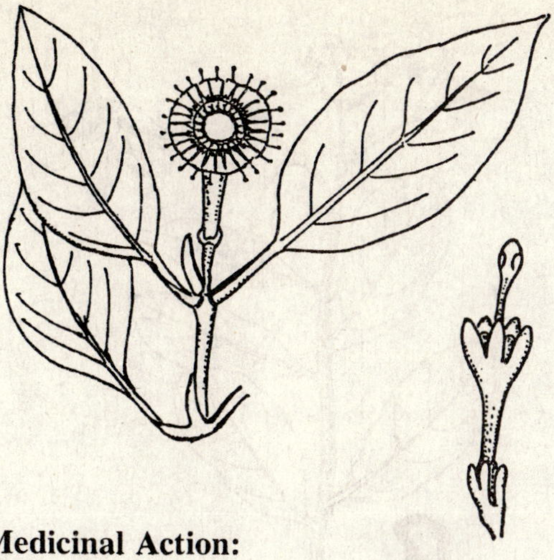

Medicinal Action:

Rasa : Bitter, astringent and pungent
Astringent (the tender sprouts)
Guṇa : Heavy and dry
Light (the tender sprouts)
Vīrya : Cold
Hot (the unripe fruits)

The three varieties of Kadamba share many common properties: They alleviate all the three doshas, are constipative, lactagogue, enhance the complexion, are aphrodisiac, increase spermatogenesis and are beneficial in menstrual disorders, dysuria, diseases of impure blood, ulcers, burning pains and toxicosis.

The tender sprouts are appetizing and are useful in anorexia, diarrhoea and bleeding from internal organs.

The ripe fruits alleviate all the three doshas.

Dhūli-kadamba is beneficial in oedema.

Bhūmi-kadamba is beneficial in worms and urinary disorders.

Note: The tree is said to flower in the rainy season (SS, sūtra, 6, 32; 38, 14).

Therapeutic Hints:

1. It is pain-relieving (CS, sūtra, 4, 18).
2. The exudation is useful in impotence (CS, sūtra, 4, 12).

References: SS, sūtra, 38, sūtra, 38; CS, sūtra, 27, 114).

Kaiḍaryah

Synonyms: Mahānimbah, Ramaṇah, Girinimbah, Mahārishṭah, Śukla-sārah, Cchardighnah, Priya-sālah, Varatiktah.

Hin. - Miṭhanīm
Ben. - Barsunga
Mah. - Kaḍhyānimb
Kan. - Karibevu
Tel. - Karivepāku
Mal. - Karivepu

Botanical Name: Murraya koenigii Spreng

Natural Order: Rutaceae

Habitat: Found in most parts of India.

Description: This deciduous shrub has a grey bark with shallow fissures. The leaves are pinnately compound and alternate; the leaflets being ovate or lanceolate and oblique at the base. The flowers are white, occuring in panicles. The berry is sub-globose and black when ripe. The plant flowers in March-April.

Medicinal Action:

Rasa : Pungent, bitter and astringent
Guṇa : Light
Vīrya : Cold

It purifies the blood, and is beneficial in fever, tuberculosis, skin diseases, vomiting, worms, burning pains, haemorrhoids, abdominal colic, swellings, pruritus and toxicosis

References: AS, uttara, 6.

Kājūtakah

Synonyms: Vṛttapatrah, Gucchapushpah, Pārvati, Snigdhapittaphalah, Pṛthakbījah, Arushkarah.

Hin. - Kāju
Mah. - Kājū
Tam. - Mundirika;
Tel. - Jīḍimāmiḍi,
Mal. - Kappamāvu,
Kon. - Kajju-ruku
Kan. - Geru, Turuke-geru mara.

Botanical Name: Anacardium occidentale Linn.

Natural Order: Anacardiaceae

Habitat: Distributed mostly in coastal distrct of India.

Description: This small, evergreen tree with a rough bark and simple, obovate, pale-green and leathery leaves has polygamous, yellowish flowers, in panicles. The fruit is a kidney-shaped nut; the hypocarp is pear-shaped, large, crimson and fleshy.

Medicinal Action:

Rasa : Astringent and sweet
Guṇa : Light
Vīrya : Hot

It alleviates kapha and vāta, is nutritive, and is beneficial in abdominal tumours, fever, ascites, worms, ulcers, wounds, dyspepsia, skin diseases, leucoderma, sprue, haemorrhoids and flatulence.

Kāka-janghā

Synonyms: Kākāngi, Kākānchī, Kākanāsikā, Kāka-kalā, Prachībalā, Dvānksha-janghā, Sulomaśā, Vāyasi, Pārāvatapadī, Dāsī, Nadī-kāntā, Surangi.

Medicinal Action:

Rasa : Bitter, pungent and astringent
Vīrya : Hot

It alleviates kapha. enhances the complexion, and is beneficial in bleeding from internal organs, toxicosis, deafness, ulcers, worms, dyspepsia, intermittent fever, pruritus and traumatic diseases.

If the root is placed under the head at night, it is said to produce sleep. If tied to the body, it cures certain type of intermittent fevers (Ekāhita-jvara).

Therapeutic Hint: Its ash (kshāra) is useful in elephantiasis (SS, chikitsā, 19, 63)

Kākamāchi

Synonyms: Dhvānksha-māchī, Vāyasī, Ghanāghanā, Kākā, Sarvatiktā, Bahu-phalā, Kaṭu-phala, Rasāyanī, Guccha-phalā, Svādu-pākā, Tiktakā, Jaghanaphalā, Kushṭhaghnī, Sundarī, Varā, Matsyākshī.

Hin.	- Makoy, Sabayyā
Ben.	- Madan, Guḍ - kāmāy
Kan.	- Gaṇikeya-giḍa
Mah.	- Laghu-kāvaḷe
Tel.	- Kānchi-punḍu
Tam.	- Mannātākāli-puttum
Eng.	- Black Night shade

Botanical Name: Solanum nigrum Linn

Natural Order: Solanceae

Habitat: Throughout India, upto 9,000 ft in the W. Himalayas

Decription: An erect herb with ovate, lanceolate, usually lobed leaves and clusters of small, round, black or red berries on lateral peduncies, Flowers are white.

Varieties: There are two varieties i.e. white and red. According to some texts, there are five other varieties (See Gunjā): (1) Kāka-janghā, (2) Kāka-nāsā, (3) Kākādanī, (4) Chūḍāmaṇih and (5) Śveta-kāmbhojī.

Parts Used: Mostly berries; all parts can be used. The plant is also used as a vegetable.

Medicinal Action:

Rasa	: Bitter and pungent
	Bitter, pungent, astringent and sweet (the white variety)
Guṇa	: Unctous and light
Vīrya	: Slightly hot
	Cold (the white variety)

It alleviates all the doshas, is appetizing, a laxative, heart-tonic, aphrodisiac, nutritive, bestows longevity and enhances vision and voice. It is beneficial in skin diseases, dyspnoea, pruritus, swellings, haemorrhoids, fever, urinary disorders, hiccough, vomiting, heart-diseases, abdominal colic, diseases of the ear, vomiting, cough, anorexia, worms, paralysis of lower limbs, premature greying of hair and alopecia.

The red variety is useful in anaemia also.

Therapeutic Hints:

1. The leaves are externally applied in skin diseases (CS, sūtra, 3, 17).
2. The leaves and stem are harmful if taken with jaggery (SS, sūtra, 20, 11).

Note: The fruits are considered to be very tasty (NIS on SS, sūtra, 38, 18).

Reference: CS, sūtra, 27, 89; SS, sūtra, 40, 5; 46, 266; AHṛ, sūtra, 6, 74.

Kāka-nāsā

Synonyms: Kākāngī, Kāka-tuṇḍa-phalā, Vāyasī, Dvānksha-nāsā, Surangī, Taskara-snāyuh, Dhvānksha-tuṇḍa phalā, Sunāsikā, Kāka-prāṇā, Kāka-śmaśrū, Śiro-balā, Dhvānksha vallī.

Medicinal Action:

Rasa : Astringent, bitter and pungent.
Vīrya : Hot
Vipāka : Pungent

It alleviates kapha, is an emetic, and is beneficial in skin diseases, leucoderma, haemorhoids and oedema.

Note: The fruits resembles a crow's beak in appearance (NIS on SS, chikitsā, 37, 20).

Kāka-tiṇḍukah

Synonyms: Jalajah, Dīrgha-patrakah, Kāka-sphūrjah, Kākendukah, Kapīluh, Kāka-pīlukah, Markaṭa-tindukah, Kāka-bījakah.

Hin. - Makar-teduā, Kāka-tendu,
Ben. - Mākrā-kendu, Mākdā-tendu,
Mah. - Kūkaṭe bhurṇī,

Botanical Name: Diospyros melanoxylon Roxb (Syn. Diospyros tomentosa Roxb).

Natural Order: Ebenaceae

Habitat: Deciduous forests of Madhya Pradesh, Nagpur, Bihar and W. Peninsula.

Medicinal Action:

Rasa : Bitter, astringent and sour
Sweet (ripe fruits)
Guṇa : Light
Heavy (the fruits)
Vīrya : Cold
Vipāka : Pungent

It alleviates kapha and pitta, aggravates vāta, purifies the blood and is constipative.

The ripe fruits slightly aggravate kapha and alleviate vāta and pitta.

(See Tiṇḍuka)

Kākodumbarikā

Synonyms: Phalgū, Rājiphalguh, Śivāṭikā, Phalguṇī, Phala-sambhārī, Malayūh, Chitrabheshajā, Kharapatrī, Udumbarī, Kaṭhinā, Kushṭhagnī, Ajākshī.

Hin. - Konea-dumbur, Kagsha
Mal. - Peragam
Ben. - Kāk-ḍuınur
Kan. - Kāḍ-atti
Tam. - Peyatti, chona-atti
Tel. - Brammadi

Botanical Name: Ficus hispida Linn, f.

Natural Order: Moraceae

Habitat: More or less throughout India.

Description: A small, weak tree with a tough grey, bark which peels off in irregular flakes. The leaves are opposite, rarely alternate, elliptic-ovate, oblong, obovate or obovate-oblong, acute, 3-5, ribbed, serrate or dentate and coriaceous. The fruits are borne all through the year, especially in January-February.

Medicinal Action:

Rasa : Pungent and sour
Astringent (the fruit-skin)
Guṇa : Heavy (the fruit-skin)
Vīrya : Cold

It alleviates kapha, is constipative and is useful in skin diseases, pruritus, ulcers, bleeding from internal organs, swellings and anaemia.

The bark relieves diarrhoea.

The fruit skin promotes lactation, protects the foetus and is beneficial in ulcers.

Therapeutic Hints: The leaves are used to cause bleeding, in diseases of the mouth (SS, chikitsā, 22, 19).

Kakoli

Synonyms: Śītapākī, Payasyā, Vāyasolikā, Kshīrī, Vīrā, Dhīrā, Vayasyā, Svādumāmsī, Dhamankshikā, Jīvantī, Madhura, Śukla-kshīrī.

The stem is similar to that of Śatāvarī and exudes a strong-smelling fluid. It is considered to be darker than Kshīra-kākolī.

Habitat: Kakoli is found in the same regions where Mahāmedā grows.

Varieties: There is another variety called Kshīra-Kākolī.

Synonyms: Vayasyā, Mahāvīrā, Payasvinī, Kshīra-śuklā, Ashṭamī, Kshīra-vishāṇikā, Jīvavallī, Kshīrā, Kshiravallī, Kshīra-madhurā, Dugdhāḍhyā.

Habitat: Kshīra-kākolī is to be found near the places where Kākolī is distributed.

Medicinal Action:

Rasa : Sweet and bitter
Guṇa : Unctous and heavy (Kākolī)
Unctous and light (Kshīra-kākolī)
Vīrya : Cold
Vipāka : Sweet

Both the plants alleviate vāta and pitta, aggravate kapha, bestow longevity, are aphrodisiacs and are useful in tuberculosis, bleeding from internal organs, burning pains, fever, diseases from impure blood and toxicosis.

Kshīra-kākolī has the additional action of promoting lactation.

Note: If Kākolī and Kshīra-kākolā can not be obtained, Aśvagandhā can be made use of in their place.

References: CS, sūtra 4,9,12,13,17.

Kalambī

Synonyms: Upodakī, Śataparvā, Picchila-chadā, Mohinī, Mada-śākah.

Hin. - Kalmī-śāk, Karenbu
Tel. - Toṭa-kūra
Ben. - Kalmī-śāk
Mah. - Nālīchī-bhājī
Tel. - Tome-vacchalicheṭṭu
Tam. - Sarkarei-valli, Vettai-keerai
Eng. - Swamp cabbage

Botanical Name: Ipomea reptans (Linn) Poir, (Syn. Ipomea aquatica, Forsk)

Natural Order: Convolvulaceae

Habitat: Throughout India, espeically in Maharashtra, Bihar, Orissa, Bengal, and S. India.

Description: This is an aquatic, trailing or floating, herbaceous perennial, sometimes annual, with a long, hollow stem, rooting at the nodes. The leaves are elliptic or ovate-oblong, cordate or hastate at the base. The flowers are infundibuliform, white or pale purple, solitary or in five-flowered cymes. Fruit is a capsule, ovoid and smooth.

Varieties: There are two other varieties :

1. kshudra-kalambī (the small variety of Kalambi) and
2. Vana-upodakah (the kalambī which grows in forests)

Medicinal Action:

Rasa : Sweet, pungent and astringent
Guṇa : Heavy
Vīrya : Hot

It aggravates kapha, promotes lactation, spermatogenesis and sleep.

Kalāyah

Synonyms: Muṇḍa-chaṇakah, Hareṇū, Reṇukah, Satīlakah, Tripuṭah, Ativartulah, Satīnakah.

Hin. - Maṭar, Kerāb
Ben. - Maṭhar
Mar. - Vāṭāṇ
Kan. - Baṭāṇi
Tel. - Guṇḍu-sanagalu
Eng. - Field Pea, Garden Pea

Botanical Name: Pisum sativum Linn

Natural Order: Leguminosae

Habitat: Cultivated generally.

Varieties: There are two varieties, tripuṭa and vartulah (SS, sūtra, 46, 30).

Description:

Medicinal Action:

Rasa : Astringent and sweet
Bitter (according to CS)
Guṇa : Dry
Vīrya : Cold
Vipāka : Sweet (pungent according to CS)

It aggravates vāta, alleviates kapha and pitta, purifies the blood, is strength-giving, nutritive, appetizing and relieves burning pains.

Therapatic Hints: It increases the formation of pus, and is not to be used in ulcers and abscesses (SS, sūtra, 19, 16).

References: CS, sūtra, 27, 97; 27, 29.

Kālingam

Synonyms: Kṛshṇa-bījam, Suvartalam, Kālindam, Madhuraphalam, Māmsaphalam, Chitraphalam, Śīrṇavṛntam, Bṛhatgolam, Rakta-bījam, Mūtralam.

Hin. - Tarbjūj, Sardā-tarbūj
Ben. - Tarmuj
Tam. - Kommaṭṭi, Vattākku
Mah. - Kaliṇgaḍ
Tel. - Darbūji
Kan. - Bachchangāyi
Mal. - Vattakka
Eng. - Water Melon

Botanical Name: Citrullus vulgaris Schrad (Syn. Cucumis citrullus Dec; Cucurbita citrullus Linn)

Natural Order: Cucurbitaceae

Habitat: Largely cultivated throughout India.

Description: This is a trailing or climbing hispid annual with alternate, ovate, three-lobed, cordate leaves and axillary, solitary flowers, yellow in colour. The fruit is globose, large and greenish, with small, numerous compressed seeds.

Parts Used: Fruits and leaves.

Medicinal Action:

Rasa : Sweet
Bitter (the leaves)
Guṇa : Heavy (the unripe fruits)
Light (the ripe fruits)

Vīrya : Cold (the unripe fruit)
Hot (the ripe fruit)

The unripe (tender) fruits aggravate kapha, alleviate pitta, are constipative, nutritive, anaphrodisiac and harmful to the vision.

The ripe fruits alleviate kapha and vāta, aggravate pitta, are acidic (kshāra), aphrodisiac, strength-giving, nutritive and useful in fatigue.

The fruit-pulp is appetizing, strength-giving and nutritive

The leaves are styptic and increase the quantity of blood.

Reference: AHṛ, sūtra, 6, 87.

Kamalam

Synonyms: Pankajam, Nalinam, Ambujam, Kuśeśayam, Rājīvam, Aravindam, Saroruham.

Hin. - Kamal
Ben. - Padma
Tam. - Tāmarai
Mal. - Aravindam
Kan. - Tāvare
Tel. - Tamara
Eng. - Sacred Lotus

Botanical Name: Nelumbo nucifera Gaertn (Syn. Nelumbium speciosum Willd; Nymphaea nelumbo Linn)

Natural Order: Nymphaeaceae

Habitat: Throughout the warmer parts of India.

Varieties: There are three varieties.

1. Puṇḍarīkam (White Lotus)

Synonyms: Śveta-kamalam, Mahāpadmam, Dṛśopamam, Hari-netram, Śāradam, Śambhu-vallabham, Śatapatram.

Hin. - Safed-kamal

2. Kokanadam (Red Lotus)

Synonyms: Rakta-kamalam, Ravi priyam, Saroruham, Nalinam, Pushkaram.

Hin. - Lāl-kamal

3. Nīlakamalam (Blue Lotus)

Synonyms: Mṛdūtpalam, Sougandhikam, Kuvalayam, Indra-vīram, Tāmarasam.

Parts Used: All parts. (The entire plant including the root, stems and flowers is called Padmini)

Medicinal Action:

Rasa : Sweet, bitter and astringent (Puṇḍarikam and the receptacle for the seed)
Sweet, bitter and pungent (Kokandam)
Sweet (Nīla-kamalam and leaf stalk)
Sweet, bitter, astringent and slightly saltish (Padmini)

Bitter and astringent (the tender leaves)
Astringent, sweet and pungent (the filaments round the base of the receptacle)
Sweet, astringent, bitter and pungent (the seeds)

Guṇa : Heavy and dry (the entire plant)
Light (the receptacle for the seed)

Vīrya : Cold (all parts)

Vipāka : Sweet (the leaf-stalk)

The entire plant (Padmini) alleviates kapha and pitta, aggravates vāta, purifies the blood, strengthens the breasts, is constipative, and beneficial in worms, tuberculosis, vomiting, vertigo, fever, oedema, dysuria and toxicosis.

The tender leaves are useful in burning pains, thirst, dysuria, haemorrhoids and bleeding from internal organs.

The receptacle for the seed alleviates kapha and pitta, purifies the blood and cleans the mouth.

The filaments alleviate all the doshas, purify the blood, are aphrodisiac, constipative, appetizing, enhance the complexion and are used in haemorrhoids, thirst, toxicosis, burning pains, oedema, fever, ulcers in the mouth and tuberculosis. They remove the tendency to repeated abortions.

The seeds alleviate kapha and pitta, are constipative, aphrodisiac, strength giving, appetizing, digestive, emaciating, facilitate conception, purify the blood and are used in vomiting, burning pains and bleeding from internal organs.

The leaf-stalk alleviates pitta, aggravates vāta and kapha, is constipative, hard to digest, aphrodisiac and purifies the blood. It improves lactation.

The honey from the flowers alleviates all the doshas, is very nutritive and removes all eye diseases.

The white lotus plant is especially useful in eye-diseases, oedema, ulcers, fever and blisters and boils.

The red lotus plant alleviates all the doshas, is nutritive, aphrodisiac and blood-purifier.

The blue lotus plant is aromatic, appetizing, beneficial to the hair, strength-giving and bestows longevity.

Kampillakah

Synonyms: Karkaśah, Rechanakah, Chandrah, Raktāngah, Rakta-chūrṇakah, Nadī-vāsah, Rakta-phalah, Bahu-pushpah, Bahu-phalah.

Hin. - Kabīlam, Kambīlā
Ben. - Kamalā
Mah. - Kapilā
Tam. - Kamala
Tel. - Kampillamu
Kan. - Kapileya-hiṭṭu
Eng. - Kamala dye tree

Botanical Name: Mallotus philippinensis Maell-Arg (Syn. Rottlera tinctoria Roxb)

Natural Order: Euphorbiaceae

Habitat: Throughout tropical India.

Description: This is a small, many-branched tree with the young leaves and flowers covered with soft tawny hairs. The leaves are alternate, ovate-lanceolate or ovate, acuminate, glabrous above and pubescent below and variable in size. Flowers are dioecious and small. The male ones are clustered in erect terminal spikes often longer than the leaves. The fruit is a capsule, covered with a bright red, powder consisting of small hairs and fine grains of a red resinous substances.

Parts Used: The red powder covering the capsules; the stems and leaves are also used.

Medicinal Action:

Rasa : Pungent
Bitter (the stem and leaves)
Guṇa : Light
Vīrya : Hot
Cold (the stem and leaves)

It alleviates kapha and pitta, purifies the blood, ia appetizing, purgative and is beneficial in toxicosis, ulcers, worms, cough, abdominal tumours, ascites, urinary disorders, flatulence, distention of the abdomen, oedema and urinary calculi.

The stem and leaves aggravate vāta, are constipative and appetizing.

Tests for Excellence: The powder is said to have the colour of powdered brick pieces.

Note:

1. It is considered to be purgative (CS, vimāna, 8, 136)
2. It is used as a dusting powder in pruritus, scabies, etc. (CS, sūtra, 3, 10).
3. It is useful in abdominal tumours (SS, sūtra, 38, 29).
4. The fruits are described as being covered with reddish powder (NIS on SS, chikitsā, 4, 27).

Kānchanārah

Synonyms: Rakta-pushpah, Kāntārah, Kanaka-prabhah, Suvarṇārah, Girijah, Karakah, Yugma-patrah, Mahā-pushpah, Gaṇḍārī, Śona-pushpakah, Chamarikah, Tāmra-pushpah, Champa-vidalah.

Hin. - Kachnār
Ben. - Kānchan
Kan. - Kempu-mandāra
Mah. - Koral
Tel. - Deva-kānchanamu
Tam. - Śemmandārai
Eng. - Purple Bauhinia

Botanical Name: Bauhinia variegata Linn

Natural Order: Leguminosae

Habitat: Sub-Himālayan tract from the Indus eastwards; also the dry forests of Eastern, Central and South India.

Description: It is a small tree with an openly branched irregular crown, and slightly rough, brownish bark. Leaves are split down the middle. The tree is bare in February when all the leaves fall. Flowers are large, white or pink in colour and orchid shaped. The fruit is a pod with ten to fifteen seeds.

Varieties: There are two other varieties:

1. Śveta-kānchanah (white flowered Bauhinia)

Synonyms: Kovidārah, Kuddālah, Kuṇḍalī,

Kulī, Āsphoṭah, Svalpakeśarah, Chamarī, Pākārī and Aśmantakah.

Hin. - Safed-kachnār
Kan. - Biḷe-mandāra
Tam. - Koppu-mandārai

2. Pīta-kānchanah (yellow flowered Bauhinia)

Parts Used: Bark and flowers. The leaves of Kovidāra are said to be the best among the leafy vegetables.

Medicinal Action: The three varieties have many properties in common.

Rasa : Astringent
Astringent and sweet (the flowers of Purple Bauhinia and all parts of the white variety)
Guṇa : Light and dry.
Vīrya : Cold
Vipāka : Sweet (the flowers)

They alleviate kapha and pitta, are constipative, appetizing and are beneficial in worms, skin diseases, prolapse of the rectum, ulcers and glandular enlargements.

The red variety is beneficial also in bleeding from internal organs. The flowers are useful in cough, diseases of impure blood, tuberculosis and menorrhagia.

The white variety is useful also in bleeding from internal organs, dyspnoea, cough, tuberculosis and menorrhagia. The flowers have similar properties.

The yellow variety alleviates kapha and vāta, heals wounds and is useful in dysuria.

Therapeutic Hints:

1. It is considered to be an emetic (CS, sūtra, 4, 13).
2. The flowers, leaves and stems are useful in bleeding from internal organs (SS, sūtra, 46, 281).
3. It is used to protect the heart in cases of snake-bites (CS, kalpa, 5, 17-18).

Kaṅguh

Synonyms: Priyanguh, Kangunī, Pīta-taṇḍulah, Asthi-sambhandhanah, Sukumārah.

Hin. - Kangunī
Ben. - Kāngunī
Mah. - Kāng
Kan. - Navaṇe-akki
Tel. - Korralu
Tam. - Tinai
Mal. - Tina
Eng. - Italian Millet

Botanical Name: Setaria italica Beauv. (Syn. Panicum italicum Linn; Panicum glomeratum Moench)

Natural Order: Graminae

Habitat: Cultivated throughout India and upto 6,000 ft. in the Himālayas.

Description: This is an erect, often robust, tufted annual grass with fasciculated and prominently jointed culms branching somewhat from the stem. The leaves are flat, linear or lanceolate, tapering to a point and glabrous. Panicles are erect or nodding, continuous and cylindrical or more or less lobed having 2-4 spikelets in each involucre.

Varieties: There are four varieties i.e. white, black, red and yellow. The yellow variety is considered superior.

Parts Used: Grains

Medicinal Action:

Rasa : Sweet and astringent
Guṇa : Heavy and dry
Vīrya : Cold

It alleviates kapha and pitta, aggravates vāta, is appetizing, nutritive and accelerates healing of fractured bones. It is beneficial in abortion and burning pains. It is considered a very useful drug in ailments of horses.

Therapeutic Hints:

1. It is beneficial as an article of diet for all living beings (SS, sūtra, 20, 5)
2. The powder is valuable as a healing agent (SS, sūtra, 37, 28).

References: SS, chikitsā, 31, 5; AHṛ. sūtra, 6, 11).

Kankolakam

Synonyms: Kolaka, Taila-sādhanam, Kṛta-phalam, Kaṭ-phalam, Dvīpa-sambhavam, Sugandhi-phalam, Sthūla-maricham, Kanda-phalam, Chūrṇam, Maricham.

Hin. - Śītal-chīnī, Kabāb-chīnī
Ben. - Kānkala
Mah. - Kankoḷ, Kāpur-chīnī
Kan. - Bāla meṇasu, Gandha-meṇasu
Tam. - Vila-metlāku
Tel. - Kabāk-chīnī
Eng. - Cubeb Pepper

Botanical Name: Piper cubeba Linn. f.

Natural Order: Piperaceae

Habitat: Cultivated to some extent in India.

Description: This is a perennial plant, with a climbing stem, round branches about half inch in breadth, ash-coloured and rooting at the joints. The leaves are from 4 to 6.5 inches long, ovate-oblong, acuminate and very smooth. The flowers are arranged in spikes at the end of the branches; the fruit is a berry.

Varieties: There is a bigger variety, viz. Bṛhat-kankolakam.

Medicinal Action:

Rasa : Pungent and bitter
Guṇa : Light and sharp
Vīrya : Hot

It alleviates kapha and vāta, is appetizing, digestive, aromatic, aphrodisiac, heart-tonic and is beneficial in anorexia, bad taste in the mouth, heart diseases, worms, blindness, thirst and dyspepsia.

References: SS, sūtra, 46, 485; CS, sūtra, 5, 77; AS, sūtra, 12, 84-85.

Kaṇṭakārī

Synonyms: Kulī, Kshudrā, Kāsaghnī, Spṛhī, Dhāvanikā, Vyāghrī, Du-sparśā, Dush-pradharshiṇī, Nidigdhikā, Prakodinī, Bhaṇṭākī, Simhī.

Hin. - Kaṭerī
Ben. - Kaṇṭakāri
Mah. - Ringṇi
Tam. - Kaṇḍan-kattari
Tel. - Vrākuḍu, Nela-mulaka
Mal. - Veḷḷottuvaḷutina
Kan. - Nela-guḷḷa

Botanical Name: Solanum xanthocarpum Schrad & Wendl

Natural Order: Solanaceae

Habitat: Throughout India.

Description: The plant is a very conspicuous herb with a very deepseated woody root. Branches are rather short, spreading and prostrate on the ground. The numerous long, yellow spines all over the plant make it very prominent. Leaves are simple and alternate, flowers rather showy, purplish-blue in colour and fruit is a globose berry.

Varieties: There is a white variety called Lakshmaṇā.

Parts Used: All parts, especially the root.

Medicinal Action:

Rasa	: Bitter and pungent
Guṇa	: Light and dry
Vīrya	: Hot
Vipāka	: Pungent (the fruits)

It alleviates kapha and vāta, is laxative, appetizing, digestive, analgesic and is beneficial in cough, fever, catarrh, heart diseases, rheumatic pains, dysuria, oedema, hiccough, dyspepsia, abdominal colic, worms, anorexia, diseases of the throat, urinary calculi and dyspnoea.

The fruits alleviate kapha and vāta, aggravate Pitta, are laxative, appetizing and are useful in pruritus, fever, dyspnoea, worms and urinary disorders.

The white variety (Lakshmaṇā) alleviates kapha and vāta, is appetizing, promotes vision and facilitates conception. It can be substituted for Kaṇṭakārī.

Therapeutic Hints:

1. It has an affinity for the throat, relieves hiccough, body pain, cough, cold and catarrhs, and swellings (CS, sūtra, 4, 10, 14, 16, 17).
2. It is considered as one of the best drugs for cough (AS, sūtra, 13, 2).
3. It is useful, with Tribulus terrestris (gokshūra) in dysuria (CS, sūtra, 2, 22).
4. It is especially useful in dysuria of the Vāta type (SS, uttara, 59, 17).
5. The fruits are used for culinary purposes (SS, sūtra, 46, 262).
6. A medicated ghee prepared from this drug is valuable in cough of the Kapha and Vāta type (CS, chikitsā, 18, 35, 125).
7. Milk (preferably that of a goat) which is medicated with the root is used as eye-wash in ophthalmia of the Vāta type (SS, uttara, 9, 11-12).

Kanthārī

Synonyms: Katharī, Durdharshā, Tīkshṇa-kaṇṭakā, Tīkshṇa-gandhā, Krūragandhā, Dushpraveshā.

Medicinal Action:

Rasa	: Pungent and bitter
Vīrya	: Hot

It alleviates kapha and vāta, purifies the blood, is appetizing and is useful in swellings, knotty tumours and affections of tendons and ligaments.

Kapitthah

Synonyms: Dadhitthah, Pushpa-phalah, Kapi-priyah, Danta-śāṭhah, Granthi-phalah, Grāhī, Kucha-phalah, Gandha-phalah, Kāṭhinya-phalah, Karabha-vallabhah, Mālūrah, Nīlamallikā, Chira-pākī, Karaṇḍaphalah.

Hin.	- Kaith
Ben.	- Kathbel
Mah.	- Kavaṭh
Kan.	- Belada-mara
Tam.	- Viḷā-maram
Tel.	- Velaga
Mal.	- Viḷāvu
Eng.	- Wood apple tree, elephant apple tree

Botanical Name: Feronia elephantum Corr (Syn. Feronia limonia (Linn) Swingle; Crataeva vallanga Koen)

Natural Order: Rutaceae

Habitat: Indigenous in S. India. Cultivated in many parts of India.

Description: This is a medium sized, armed, deciduous glabrous tree with straight, axillary thorns. The bark is dark-grey with deep vertical cracks. The leaves are odorous, alternate, imparipinnate. Leaflets are 5-7, opposite, obovate and crenate at tip. The flowers are dull-red, in axillary cymes. The fruit is globular with a woody hard ring; the seeds are many, embedded in an edible pulp.

Parts Used: Bark, fruits, flowers, seeds, leaves, oil of seeds.

Medicinal Action:

Rasa	: Sweet, sour and astringent. Astringent and sweet (the oil)
Guṇa	: Light and dry (the unripe fruits) Heavy (the ripe fruits)
Vīrya	: Hot (the unripe fruits) Cold

The unripe fruits aggravate vāta and pitta, are constipative, appetizing, aromatic and relieve pruritus. They are harmful to the voice and engender diseases of the throat. They are useful in toxicosis.

The ripe fruits alleviate all the doshas, are constipative, aphrodisiac, difficult to digest, beneficial to the throat and voice, and alleviate tuberculosis, vomiting, fatigue, lethargy, distention of abdomen, thirst, cough, hiccough, and dyspnoea, diseases of impure blood and toxicosis.

The seeds are beneficial in angina, palpitation, headaches, herpes and toxicosis.

The oil of the seeds alleviate kapha and pitta, are constipative, and are useful in hiccough, vomiting and toxicosis.

The flowers also are used in toxicosis.

The leaves alleviate vomiting, diarrhoea and hiccough.

Therapeutic Hints:

1. The flowers are used as collyrium in cases of poisoning (SS, kalpa, 1, 69-71).
2. The juice of the fruit is used to antidote rat poison. (SS, kalpa, 7, 38) and to relieve hiccough (SS, uttara, 50, 25).
3. The stalks are used as collyrium in certain eye-diseases (SS, uttara, 17, 7).
4. An oil medicated with this drug is used as a douch in menstrual diseases (KS, dhātrī-chikitsā).

References: CS, sūtra, 25, 40; 27, 136-137; AS, sūtra, 7; uttara, 1; SS, kalpa, 7, 40).

Karamardakah

Synonyms: Vana-kshudrā, Karāmlah, Supushpah, Dṛdha-kaṇṭakah, Kshīra-phalah, Sushenah, Pāṇimardakam, Kṛshṇa-pāka-phalam, Āvighnah.

Hin.	- Karaundā
Ben.	- Karamehā
Mah.	- Karavand
Kan.	- Kavaḷi-kāyi-giḍa, Karavaḍī
Tam.	- Perukatachedi
Tel.	- Okacheṭṭu, Kalivi
Mal.	- Karaṇṭa, Kaṭāvu

Botanical Name: Carissa carandas Linn (Syn. Carissa congesta Wight)

Natural Order: Apocynaceae

Habitat: Wild throughout India.

Description: A large thorny shrub with small oval leaves and white jasmine like flowers. The fruit is dark purple when ripe.

Varieties: There is a smaller variety called Karamardikā (Carissa spinarum Linn).

Parts Used: Fruits and root

Medicinal Action:

Rasa	: Sour and bitter (the unripe fruits) Sweet (the ripe, and dried fruits)
Guṇa	: Heavy (the unripe fruit) Light (the ripe, and dried fruits)
Vīrya	: Hot (the unripe fruit) Cold (the ripe, and dried fruits)

The unripe fruits aggravate kapha and pitta, are constipative, appetizing and are used in thirst. It vitiates the blood.

The ripe fruits alleviate vāta and pitta, are appetizing and are beneficial in bleeding from internal organs.

The dried fruits have the same medicinal properties as the the ripe fruits.

The root is laxative and are useful in worms.

References: CS, sūtra, 27, 161; SS, sūtra, 46, 156; AS, sūtra, 7, 203.

Karanjah

Synonyms: Nakta-mālah, Pūtikah, Pūtipatrakah, Kaiḍaryah, Kali-mārah, Vṛttaphalah, Guccha-pushpakah.

Hin.	-	Karanj, Kiramāl
Ben.	-	Dahar karanja
Tel.	-	Kānuga-chettu
Tam.	-	Pongam maram
Kan.	-	Honġe
Mal.	-	Ponnam
Eng.	-	Indian Beech tree

Botanical Name: Pongamia glabra Vent (Syn. Dalbergia arborea Willd; Galedupa indica Lamk; Pongamia pinnata (Linn) Merr)

Natural Order: Leguminosae

Habitat: All over India on the banks of rivers and streams.

Description: A semi-evergreen, medium sized tree with a spreading shading crown and smooth grey bark. Leaves are pinnately compound, alternate, with five to seven leaflets each. Leaves have dark green colour, and are shiny when young. Flowers are pendant racemes of liliac-rose colour. Fruit is a pod, ovate and woody.

Varieties: According to one classification, there are six varieties :

1. Chirabilva

Synonyms: Nakta-mālah, Karanjakah

2. Prakīryah

Synonyms: Pūtikaranjah, Putikah, Kalikārakah

3. Shaḍ-granthah

4. Markaṭī

5. Angāra-vallarī

6. Karamardah

According to another classification, there are five varieties :

1. Mahā-karanjah

Synonyms: Mada-hastinikā

2. Ghṛta karanjah

3. Pūti-karanjah

4. Guccha-karanjah and

5. Karanjikā

Parts Used: Bark, leaves, flowers, fruits and oil.

Medicinal Action:

Rasa : Bitter, astringent and pungent
Guṇa : Light (the fruits and leaves)
Light, sharp and unctous (the oil)
Vīrya : Hot
Vipāka : Pungent

It alleviates all the three doshas, strengthens the teeth and vision, is a purgative and is beneficial in abdominal tumours, haemorrhoids, ulcers, pruritus, fever, toxicosis, menstrual disorders, eczema, worms, skin diseases, ascites, urinary disturbances and enlargement of spleen.

The fruits alleviate kapha and vāta, are useful in headaches, corneal opacity, worms, skin diseases, haemorrhoids and urinary disorders.

The leaves alleviate kapha and vāta, slightly aggravate pitta, are purgative and used in haemorrhoids, worms, ulcers and oedema.

The flowers alleviate all the doshas.

The tender sprouts alleviate kapha and vāta, are appetizing, digestive and beneficial in haemorrhoids, skin diseases, worms, oedema and toxicosis.

The oil alleviates kapha and vāta, slightly aggravates Pitta, is a laxative, analgesic, useful in worms, eye diseases, skin diseases, pruritus, ulcers, urinary disorders and headaches. They cause, when used in excess, bleeding from internal organs.

Therapeutic Hints:

1. It is useful in worms, urinary disorders (including diabetes) and bleeding from internal organs (SS, sūtra, 46, 197-198; uttara, 45, 25).
2. The bark is used in the form of decoction in washing ulcers and wounds (AHr̥, sūtra, 29, 76).
3. The roots are used as errhine (SS, sūtra, 39, 6).

References: CS, sūtra, 5, 73; 13, 10; vimāna, 7, 17; AS, sūtra, 7).

Kāravellakam

Synonyms: Kaṭhillam, Ugrakāṇḍam.

Hin.	- Karelā
Ben.	- Karalā
Mar.	- Kārale
Tam.	- Pāgal
Tel.	- Kākara cheṭṭu
Mal.	- Pāval
Kan.	- Hāgala-giḍa
Eng.	- Momordica, Bitter gourd

Botanical Name: Momordica muricata Willd (Syn. M. charantia Linn)

Natural Order: Cucurbitaceae

Habitat: Cultivated throughout India.

Description: This is a branched monoecious herb. The leaves are alternate, simple, petiolate, sub-orbicular, dentate, cordate and palmately 5-7 lobed, with obovate-oblong lobes. The flowers are yellowish in colour, in axillary racemes. The fruit is an oblong berry with compressed seeds.

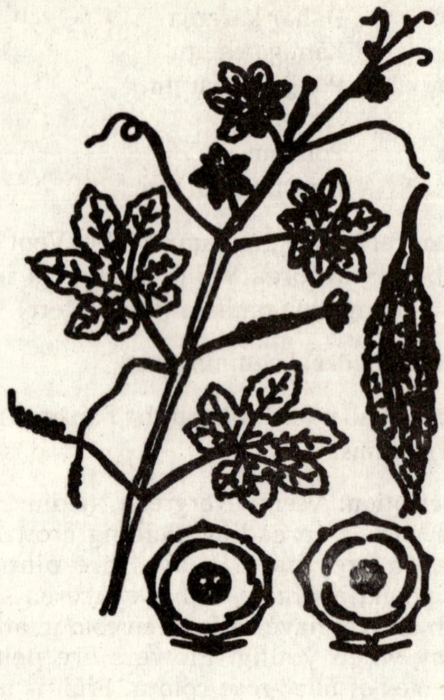

Varieties: There is a bigger variety called Kāravallī.

Synonyms: Sukāṇḍakam and Vārivallī

Parts Used: The whole plant.

Medicinal Action:

Rasa	: Bitter Bitter and pungent (Kāravallī)
Guṇa	: Light
Vīrya	: Cold
Vipāka	: Pungent

It alleviates kapha and pitta, does not aggravate vāta, purifies the blood, is laxative, appetizing, non-aphrodisiac, and is beneficial in fever, anaemia, urinary disorders, worms, anorexia, cough, ulcers, skin diseases, pruritus, jaundice, gout, dyspnoea, eruptive fevers and cholera.

The leaves aggravate pitta, are anthelminthic and are pathyā.

The flowers are useful in bleeding from internal organs.

References: AS, sūtra, 7, 122; SS, sūtra, 46, 269; 39, 5.

Karavīrah

Synonyms: Śata-kumbhah, Pratihāsah, Aśvamārakah, Divya-pushpah, Śveta-pushpah.

Hin.	-	Kaner
Ben.	-	Karabī
Mah.	-	Kanera
Kan.	-	Kanagile
Tam.	-	Karavīram
Tel.	-	Ganneru
Mal.	-	Kaṇavīram
Eng.	-	Sweet-scented Oleander
Vernacular	-	Kaṇavīr (Ḍalhaṇa)

Botanical Name: Nerium odorum Soland (Syn. N. indicum Mill; N. odoratum Lam)

Natural Order: Apocynaceae.

Habitat: Extensively cultivated throughout the greater parts of India.

Description: This is an evergreen shrub with a silvery-grey bark. The leaves are simple, entire, linear-lanceolate or oblong, rigid and leathery with a stout midrib and many parallel nerves. The flowers are red, pink or white, in terminal cymes. The fruit is cylindrical, rigid and straight with linear, ribbed seeds.

Varieties: There are four varieties based on the colour of the flowers (1) white, (2) red, (3) yellow and (4) black. The red variety has the synonyms of Chandālah, Lagudah and Bhūtadrāvī. They all have similar medicinal properties.

Medicinal Action:

Rasa	: Bitter, pungent and astringent
Guṇa	: Sharp and light
Vīrya	: Hot

It is classified as one of the Upa-Vishas (lesser poisons). It alleviates kapha and vāta, is constipative, promotes vision and is beneficial in urinary disorders, skin diseases, worms, ulcers, haemorrhoids, pruritus, blisters and boils, and fever ad toxicosis.

The red variety is also useful in headache.

Note:

1. Karavīra is to be purified by boiling it in milk by means of dolā-yantra (RJN, Vol. III, page, 338).
2. Sugar-candy given internally with buffalo's milk or curds or the bark of the arka plant antidotes the adverse effects of Karavīra (ibid, page. 355).

Karīram

Synonyms: Gūdhapatram, Śāka-pushpam, Kaṭūphalam, Grandhilam, Tīkshna-sāram, Kaṇṭtakī, Meru-bhūrakam, Mṛdu-phalam, Chakrakam.

Hin. - Karīl
Mah. - Nevatī
Kan. - Nishpatige
Tel. - Veṇturu-cheṭṭu

Botanical Name: Capparis decidua Edgew (syn. C. aphylla Roth)

Natural Order: Capparidaceae

Habitat: Cutch, Sind, Baluchisthan, W. Rajasthan, Punjab, Upper Gangetic Plain, Madhya Pradesh, Gujarat and Deccan.

Description: A densely branching shrub or a small tree, with scanty, small leaves found only on young shoots. As a young plant, it forms rounded bushes consisting of densely interlaced twigs which completely hide the stem. Leaves are small, linear-oblong, acute and pungent. Flowers are corymbs, red or scarlet in colour. Fruit is a pink berry, globose and many-seeded.

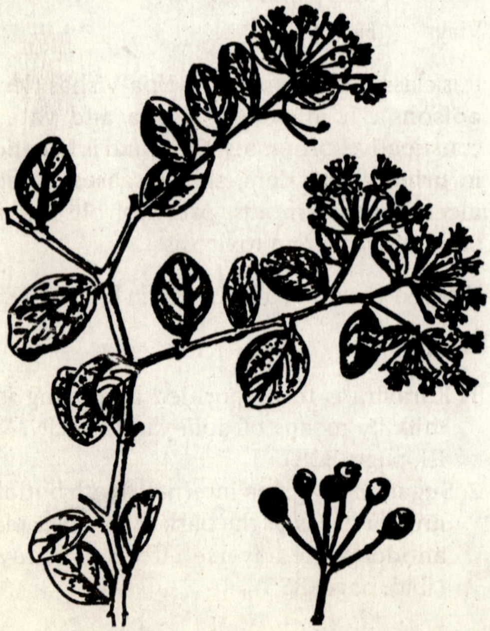

Medicinal Action:

Rasa : Bitter, pungent and astringent
Bitter, pungent, astringent and sweet (the fruits)
Astringent (the flowers)
Guṇa : Dry and vikāsī (the fruits)
Vīrya : Hot
Vipāka : Pungent

It alleviates kapha and vāta, is a laxative, diaphoretic and is beneficial in anorexia, all kinds of colic, vomiting, pruritus, ulcers, haemorrhoids, oedema, dyspnoea and toxicosis, worms. It causes distention of abdomen.

The fruits alleviate kapha, are constipative, a heart-tonic and are useful in urinary disorders and haemorrhoids. They also cleanse the mouth.

The flowers alleviate kapha and pitta, aggravate vāta, are laxative, diuretic and appetizing.

Note:

1. It is a desert plant (Chkp. on CS, chikitsā, 30, 82; sūtra, 27, 142) and is liked by camels (SS, sūtra, 46, 283).
2. The flowers are used for culinary purposes (SS, sūtra, 46, 283).
3. It is useful in menstrual disorders (CS, chikitsā, 30, 82)
4. It is a thorny desert plant with hidden leaves (NIS on uttara, 57, 9).

Karkata-śṛngikā

Synonyms: Kulingī, Kāsa-nāśinī, Mahāghoshā, Chakrāngī, Karkaṭī, Vana-mūrdhajā, Kulīśā, Navānganī, Chandrāspadā, Vishānī, Kālikā, Latāngī.

Parts Used: Horn like excrescences, caused by insects, (Galls).

Medicinal Action:

Rasa : Bitter and astringent
Guṇa : Heavy
Vīrya : Hot

It alleviates all the doshas, purifies the blood, and is useful in hiccough, cough, diarrhoea, tuberculosis, fever, vomiting, eructations, thirst, worms, diseases of traumatic origin, anorexia, vertigo, diseases of children and dyspnoea.

Karkoṭakī

Synonyms: Svāduphalā, Kumārikā, Manogynā, Devī, Visha-praśamanī, Bodhanā, Karkaśā, Pīta-pushpī.

Hin. - Kakonḍā, Kheksā
Tam. - Malepāvakkā, Egāravalli
Ben. - Kākrol, Ban-karela
Tel. - Āgākara-cheṭṭu
Mah. - Kanṭṭi, Kartoḷi
Kan. - Māḍa-hāgala, Kārchi-baḷḷi
Mal. - Vempāval

Botanical Name: Momordica diocia Roxb ex Willd

Natural Order: Cucurbitaceae

Habitat: Throughout India, ascending to 5, 000 ft. in the Himalayas.

Description: This is a perennial, dioecious climber with tuberous roots and glabrous stems. The leaves are broadly ovate, entire, deeply 3-5 lobed. The flowers are solitary and yellow. The fruits are ovoid or ellipsoidal, 2.5 - 6.3 cms. long, shortly beaked, and densely echinate with soft spines. The seeds are slightly compressed and irregularly corrugated.

Varieties: There is another variety - Vandhya-karkoṭakī.

Synonyms: Nāgārih, Sarpadamanī, Devī, Manogynā, Visha-kanṭakinī, Yogīśvari, Sarva-bhūta-pramardinī, Pathyā, Putradātrī, Sukandā, Śri-kandā, Sugandhā, Kumārī.

Parts Used: Fruits, root, leaves and tubers.

Medicinal Action:

Rasa : Pungent and bitter
Sweet (the fruits)
Guṇa : Light (the fruits)
Vīrya : Hot
Vipāka : Pungent

It alleviates all the dosha, is a laxative, appetizing, and is beneficial in skin disease, nausea, anorexia, cough, fever, leucoderma, headaches, dyspnoea and toxicosis.

The fruits alleviate all the doshas, are appetizing, and are useful in abdominal tumours, colic, skin diseases, cough, urinary disorders, fevers, leucoderma, dyspnoea, anorexia, salivation and palpitation.

The leaves alleviate all the doshas, are aphrodisiac, appetizing and are useful in worms, fever, tuberculosis, cough, dyspnoea, hiccoughs and haemorrhoids.

The tubers are used with honey in headaches.

Karma-rangah

Synonyms: Kārukah, Śuka-priyah, Bṛhaddalah, Pītaphalah, Mudgarah, Dhārāphalah, Rujākarah.

Hin. - Kamrakh
Ben. - Kāmrāngā
Tam. - Tamarattai
Mah. - Karmare
Tel. - Tamarta
Kan. - Dārehuḷi
Eng. - Carambola tree

Botanical Name: Averrhoa carambola Linn

Natural Order: Oxalidaceae

Habitat: Cultivated in gardens throughout the hotter parts of India.

Description: An ornamental tree growing to height of 20-30 ft. with beautiful evergreen foliage and clusters of pale purplish or white flowers, borne in short racemes from the bark of the old and young branches. The fruits are translucent, yellow or pale golden-brown in colour, and are elliptic in outline with three or five ribs running longitudinally.

Parts Used: Fruits

Medicinal Action:

Rasa : Sour (unripe fruits)
Sweet and sour (ripe fruits)
Vīrya : Hot
Vipāka : Pungent

The unripe fruits alleviate vāta, aggravate pitta, and are constipative.

The ripe ones are appetising, strength-giving and nutritive.

Kārpāsī

Synonyms: Tuṇḍikerī, Samudrāntā, Chavyā, Tulā, Sāriṇī, Sthūlā, Pichuh, Marudbhavā, Sūtra-pushpā, Badarī, Cchādanah.

Hin. - Kapās
Ben. - Kārpās
Mah. - Kāpaśī
Kan. - Hatti
Tam. - Parutti
Tel. - Patti-cheṭṭu
Mal. - Karuparutti
Eng. - Cotton tree

Botanical Name: Gossypium herbaceum Linn (Syn. G. indicum Lam; G. album W & A)

Natural Order: Malvaceae

Habitat: Cultivated in N. W-frontier province and Baluchisthan

Description: This is an annual herb or undershrub up to 1.5 metres high with sparsely hairy branches. The leaves are leathery and cordate, with five to seven lobes, each lobe being ovate, acute and narrowed at base. The flowers are yellow with a purple centre. The fruit is rounded and beaked, with large, greenish seeds.

Varieties: There are two other varieties :

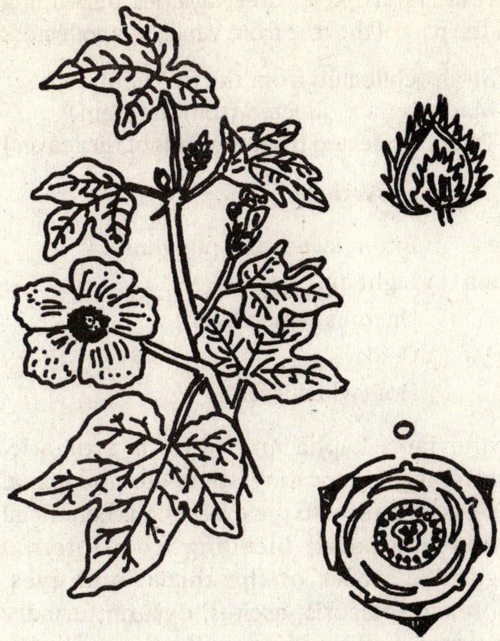

1. Vana-kārpāsī (the tree which grows in forests)

Synonyms: Tri-parṇī, Bhāradvājī, Kṛshṇānjanī, Kālī, Vana-sarojinī, Bahu-mūrtī, Vanajā, Araṇya-kārpāsī.

Hin. - Van-kapās
Kan. - Kāḍu-hatti

2. Kālānjanī

Synonyms: Kṛshṇābhā, Śilānjanī, Kṛshṇānjanī, Kālī.

Hin. - Kalī-kapās,
Kan. - Kariya-hatti

Parts Used: Root, bark, flowers, fruits, seeds and cotton.

Medicinal Action:

Rasa : Sweet and astringent (Kārpāsī)
Pungent and sour (Kālānjanī)
Guṇa : Light (Kārpāsī)
Unctous and heavy (the seeds)
Vīrya : Slightly hot (Kārpāsī)
Hot (Kālānjanī)
Cold (Vana-kārpāsī)

Kārpāsī alleviates all the doshas, is strength giving, galactagogue, and is beneficial in thirst, burning pains, vertigo, syncope, skin-diseases, diarrhoea and vomiting.

The leaves alleviate vāta, purify the blood and are diuretic. They are useful in earache, tinnitus (noises in the ear), boils in the ear, suppuration and haemorrhages.

The fruits are used in discharge from the ears. The seeds aggravate Kapha, are aphrodisiac and galactagogue.

The root is useful in leucorrhoea.

Vana-kārpāsī is nutritive, appetizing and is of use in external wounds and ulcers. The root is galactagogue and is used in glandular enlargements and alcoholism (SS, sūtra, 39, 7; 163 uttara, 47, 34).

Kālānjanī is beneficial in dyspepsia, worms and ascites.

Therapeutic Hints:

1. The root is give in certain forms of insanity (AS, uttara, 47).
2. The smoke of the burning seeds relieves cough (CS, chikitsā, 18, 75).

Karpūrah

Synonyms: Sphaṭikah, Chandrah, Sitābhrah, Hima-vālukā, Himopalah, Śita-rajah, Bhūtikah, Tushārah, Śaśīnduh, Śaśānkah.

Hin. - Kapūr
Tam. - Karpūrakam
Tel. - Karpūramu
Eng. - Camphor tree

Botanical Name: Cinnamomum camphora Nees & Eberm

Natural Order: Lauraceae

Habitat: Planted in some gardens in India up to 4,000 ft. in the N.W. Himalayas. Successfully cultivated at Dehra Dun, Saharanpur, Calcutta, Nilgiris and Karnataka.

Description: A glabrous evergreen tree with alternate long-petioled, ovate or oblong or lanceolate-oblong, three-nerved shining leaves. Both the sides of the leaves are usually uniformly coloured; rarely the lower surface is slightly paler. Flowers are small occuring in axillary panicles.

Varieties: There are two varieties -

1. Pakva - Camphor which is artificially collected
2. Apakva - Camphor which is collected when it is deposited.

Apakva karpūra is further divided into three types, based on the colour:

a) Īśāvāsah (which is Bhṛsha-śveta, pure white)
b) Hima (which is Pāṇḍura, pale-white)
c) Protāśraya (which is Śveta),

Karpūra is further of three varieties, depending on the part of the tree from which it is collected:

1. Śirah (collected from the tips of branches)
2. Madhyama (collected from the stem)
3. Talam (collected from the ends of the leaves)

Medicinal Action:

Rasa : Bitter, sweet and pungent
Guṇa : Light and soft
Unctous (when fresh)
Vīrya : Cold
Hot (when fresh)

It alleviates kapha and pitta, is aromatic, emaciating, intoxicating, stimulates the sexual urge, is beneficial to the eyes, and is beneficial in burning pains, bleeding from internal organs, diseases of the throat and eyes, anorexia, toxicosis, ascites, dysuria, urinary disorders, foul-smelling stools, thirst, obesity and external injuries.

Camphor which is fresh causes burning pains. That which is old, however, relieves burning pains and is of use in tuberculosis.

Īśāvāsa-karpurah is laxative, aphrodisiac and is useful in insanity, intoxication, fatigue, thirst, burning pains, cough, and tuberculosis. Hima-karpurah is useful in excessive sweating, burning pains, obesity and thirst. Prostāśraya-karpūrah, in addition to the usual properties, also purifies the blood.

References: SS, sūtra, 46, 483-485; 202-204; CS, sūtra, 5, 77; chikitsā, 28, 153; AS, sūtra, 12.

Kāśah

Synonyms: Sukāṇḍah, Kāsekshuh, Nādeyah, Nīrajah, Kākekshuh, Ikshu-rasah, Śirih, Darbha-patrakah, Vāyasekshah, Lekhani, Kāṇḍakāṇḍakah, Angārakhah.

Hin. - Kān
Ben. - Keśe-ghās
Mah. - Kasāyi, Kāunsu
Kan. - Kājalu, Kāsalu
Tam. - Nāṇalū
Tel. - Rellu-gaḍḍi
Mal. - Nannana
Eng. - Thatch grass

Botanical Name: Saccharum spontaneum Linn

Natural Order: Graminae

Habitat: Throughout India in the warmer parts ascending up to 6,000 ft. in the Himalayas.

Description: This is a pernnial grass with slender culms which are green, grey, ivory or white, hard and often hollow in the centre. The leaves are long, linear, narrow or very narrow or sometimes reduced to the mid-rib. The inflorescence is a panicle varying in length, and in colour from pale or greyish-white to purplish grey.

Varieties: There is another variety called Miśi.

Medicinal Action:

Rasa : Sweet and bitter
Sweet (Miśi)
Guṇa : Unctous
Vīrya : Cold
Vipāka : Sweet.

It alleviates pitta, is an aphrodisiac, strength-giving, appetizing, refreshing, laxative, purifies the blood and is beneficial in burning pains, dysuria, tuberculosis, urinary calculi, bleeding from internal organs and diseases of traumatic origin.

Therapeutic Hints:

1. It increases the milk in lactating mothers and is diuretic (CS, sūtra, 4, 12, 15).
2. It relieves urinary disorders and haemorrhages (SS, sūtra, 38, 75). and is useful in calculi of the Pitta type (ibid, chikitsā, 7, 9).

Kaserukā

Synonyms: Kaseruh, Guṇḍa-kandah, Kshudra-mustā, Sūkareshṭah, Sugandhih, Gandha-kandukah.

Hin. - Kaseru, Kesur
Ben. - Keśur
Mah. - Kacharā
Kan. - Sekina-gaḍḍe
Tel. - Guṇḍa-tungagaḍḍi, Namma-dumpa

Botanical Name: Scirpus grossus Linn (Syn. S. kysoor Roxb)

Natural Order: Cyperaceae

Habitat: More or less throughout India.

Description: This is a large, perennial, glabrous herb with stout root stocks which, in the dry season, produce dark-coloured hard, globose tubes, clothed and matted with hairs. The leaves are radical. The spikelets sub-globosely ovoid, in corymbiform decompound, terminal umbels. The nuts are obovoid, ash-grey or black in colour.

Varieties: There are two varieties, the bigger one called Rājakaserukā and the smaller one called Chinchoḍhah (which resembles Mustā in shape).

Medicinal Action:

Rasa : Astringent, slightly sweet, bitter and pungent.
Guṇa : Heavy
Vīrya : Cold

It alleviates pitta, is galactagogue, aggravates kapha and vāta, purifies the blood, is constipative, aphrodisiac, and is beneficial in burning pains and eye-diseases.

The flowers alleviate pitta and are useful in jaundice.

Kaṭabhī

Synonyms: Śouṇḍī, Pāṭalī, Kiṇihī, Madhureṇuh, Kshudra-śyāmā, Kaiḍaryah, Śyāmālā

Varieties: There is a white variety called Śveta-kaṭabhī.

Synonyms: Girikarṇikā, Śirīshpatrī, Kālindī, Śatapādā, Mahā-śvetā, Vishaghnikā, Mahā-śouṇḍī

Medicinal Action:

Rasa : Pungent
Guṇa : Dry
Vīrya : Hot

It alleviates kapha and vāta, is an aphrodisiac and is beneficial in flatulent distension of abdomen, abdominal colic and tumours, indigestion, urinary disorders, haemorrhoids, fistulous ulcers, worms, skin diseases and toxicosis.

References: SS, kalpa, 5, 17-18.

Katakam

Synonyms: Cchedanīyam, Slakshṇam, Toya-prasādanam, Chakshushyam, Śodhanātmakam, Ambu-prasādana-phalam, Tikta-phalam, Guccha-phalam.

Hin.	-	Nirmalī
Tam.	-	Tettāmaram
Tel.	-	Chilla-jinjalu, Iṇḍupa-ginjalu
Kan.	-	Chali-bīja, Chilliya-mara
Mal.	-	Teṭṭā-maram
Eng.	-	Clearing nut tree

Botanical Name: Strychnos potatorum Linn

Natural Order: Loganaceae

Habitat: Konkan, N. Kanara, Madhya Pradesh, Deccan and South India.

Description: A moderate sized glabrous tree attaining 12 m. with a black, cracked and scaly bark. Leaves are nearly sessile, ovate or elliptic, glabrous, shining and opposite. Flowers rather large, white, occuring as glabrous, nearly sessile cymes. Seeds are circular, shining, with short appressed silky hairs, and yellow colour.

Parts Used: Root, fruits and seeds.

Medicinal Action:

Rasa : Pungent, bitter, sweet and astringent
Astringent and sweet (the seeds)
Guṇa : Light, lekhana, viśada and Cchedana.
Heavy (the seeds)
Vīrya : Cold

The plant alleviates kapha and vāta, removes impurities from water, is appetizing, promotes eyesight and is beneficial in thirst, burning pains, abdominal tumours, colic, worms, urinary disorders, eye diseases and toxicosis.

The unripe fruits aggravate vāta, promotes eye-sight and are useful in bleeding from internal organs, thirst, fainting fits and toxicosis.

The ripe fruits aggravate pitta, are emetic, diaphoretic, and are beneficial in oedema, anaemia, catarrh, jaundice and toxicosis.

The seeds alleviate kapha and vāta, purify water, are beneficial to the eyes, and are used in urinary calculi, dysuria, thirst, eye-diseases, urinary diseases, headache and toxicosis.

The root is very useful in all skin diseases.

Note: The fruits are used to cleanse the water (SS, sūtra, 42, 11).

Therapeutic Hints:

1. It is an antidote to certain poisons (CS, sūtra, 4, 11).
2. The fruits are very beneficial to the eyes (KS, kalpa, 10, 31) and are useful in retention of urine (KS, khila, 144, 45).

References: SS, chikitsā, 7, 7; sūtra, 45, 17).

Kaṭphalah

Synonyms: Soma-valkah, Mahākumbhā, Bhadrā, Ugragandhah, Kaiṭaryah, Śrīparṇikā, Kumudikā, Kumbhī, Tvak-phalah.

Hin. - Kāyphal
Tam. - Marudam
Tel. - Kāya-phala, Gummaḍi-regu
Ben. - Kāyaphal
Kan. - Kiru-śivani
Vernacular - Kāyphal (NIS on SS, sūtra, 38, 14)
Eng. - Box myrtle; Bay-berry

Botanical Name: Myrica nagi Thunb (Syn. M. sapida Wall)

Natural Order: Myricaceae

Habitat: Sub-tropical Himālayas from the Ravi eastwards at 3,000-6,000 ft. Khasia Hills and Sylhet.

Description: This shrub is branching and partially evergreen and varies in height from 2 to 12 ft. The flowers appear in May, before the leaves are fully expanded. The fruits are small and globular, resembling berries, which are at first green, but become nearly white. They consist of a hard stone, enclosing a two-lobed and two-seeded kernel. On the outside of the stone are small grains and over these is a crust of dry greenish-white wax.

Medicinal Action:

Rasa : Astringent, bitter and pungent
Guṇa : Sharp
Vīrya : Hot

It alleviates kapha and vāta, is appetizing and is beneficial in fever, urinary disorders, haemorrhoids, cough, dyspnoea, diseases of the throat and mouth, anorexia, severe burning pains, abdominal tumours, dyspepsia, sprue, nausea and anaemia.

Therapeutic Hints:

1. It is used as a dusting powder over ulcers and wounds. (KS, chikitsā, 18).
2. It is useful in thirst and bleeding from internal organs (CS, chikitsā, 4, 73).

References: SS, sūtra, 38, 43.

Kattṛṇam

Synonyms: Rouhisham, Devajagdham, Sougandhikam, Bhūtikam, Śyāmakam, Dhūpagandhikam, Bhūtidam, Dhyāmakam.

Hin. - Rohish-soundhiyā, Gandhe-javās
Ben. - Rām-karpūr, Agam-ghās
Mah. - Rohish-gavat
Eng. - Roshā grass

Botanical Name: Cymbopogon schoenanthus (Linn) Spreng. (Syn. Andropogon schoenanthus Linn)

Natural Order: Graminae

Habitat: Hotter parts of India.

Varieties: There is a bigger variety.

Medicinal Action:

Rasa : Pungent, bitter and astringent

It alleviates kapha and pitta, purifies the blood, is auspicious, increases breast-milk, and is beneficial in fever, cough, dyspnoea, heart-diseases, sore-throat, visūchikā, indigestion, abdominal colic and injuries caused by sharp instruments (as in surgery).

Therapeutic Hints:

1. It increases breast-milk (CS, sūtra, 4, 12)
2. It is useful in cough (SS, uttara, 52, 14), dyspnoea and fever of the Vāta and Kapha kinds (AS, chikitsā, 1).

References: CS, sūtra, 2, 13.

Kaṭukī

Synonyms: Tiktā, Kāṇḍeruhā, Chakrāngī, Arishṭā, Śakulādanī, Tikta-rohiṇika, Kaṭu-rohiṇī, Matsya-śakalā, Kṛishṇa-bhedā, Aśoka-rohiṇī, Āmaghnī, Śata-parvā, Sādanī, Mahoushadī.

Hin. - Kuṭkī
Ben. - Katkī
Kan. - Kaṭuka-rohiṇi
Tam. - Kaḍuga-rohiṇi

Botanical Name: Picrorhiza kurroa Royle ex Benth

Natural Order: Scrophulariaceae

Habitat: Alpine Himalayas, from Kashmir to Sikkim, 9,000-15,000 ft.

Description: This is a low, more or less hairy, herb with perennial, woody, bitter rootstocks as thick as the little finger and clothed with withered leaf-bases. The leaves are serrate and rather coriaceous with a rounded tip and narrow base. The flowers are stout and longer than the leaves, white or bluish in colour. The fruit which is a capsule is ovoid, acute, 1.3 cms. long.

Parts Used: Root

Medicinal Action:

Rasa : Bitter, and slightly pungent
Guṇa : Light and dry
Vīrya : Cold
Vipāka : Pungent

It alleviates kapha and pitta, purifies the blood, is appetizing, purgative, heart tonic, and is beneficial in fevers, intermittent fevers, urinary disorders, cough, burning pains, skin diseases, worms, urticaria, anorexia, dyspepsia, tuberculosis, jaundice, heart diseases, dyspnoea and toxicosis.

Purification: It is washed in hot cow's milk and later used for medicinal purposes.

References: SS, uttara, 42, 111; AS, uttara, 42.

Kaṭu-tumbī

Synonyms: Piṇḍa-phalā, Rājaputrī, Kaṭukālābunī, Nṛpātmajā, Phalinī, Tikta-tumbī, Tikta-bījā, Ikshvākuh, Kshatriya-varā.

Hin. - Kaḍavi tombī
Ben. - Tikta Lau
Mal. - Kaḍu bhopḷā
Kan. - Kahī-sore
Tam. - Shurai
Tel. - Ānapa-kāyi, Sora-kāyi
Mal. - Kaippacharum
Eng. - Bitter Bottle Gourd

Botanical Name: Wild variety of Lagenaria vulgaris Ser

Natural Order: Cucurbitaceae

Medicinal Action:

Rasa : Pungent and bitter

Guṇa : Light and sharp
Vīrya : Cold
Vipāka : Pungent
Sweet (the leaves and fruits)

It alleviates vāta and pitta, is an emetic, heart tonic, laxative, and is beneficial in cough, dysuria, toxicosis, oedema, ulcers, abdominal colic, vomiting, fever, anaemia, worms and dyspnoea.

The leaves and fruits alleviate pitta and are diuretic.

Therapeutic Hints:

1. It relieves cough, dyspnoea, vomiting, ulcers, intermittent fever, swellings and is useful in retention of placenta (SS, śārīra, 10, 24).
2. The fresh, tender leaves are used as external application (CS, chikitsā, 14, 57).

Kemukā

Synonyms: Supatrā, Dala-malinī, Kelūṭah, Svalpa-viṭapah, Svādukandah, Polinī.

Hin.	- Kenā, Kevā
Ben.	- Kevū
Tam.	- Kuravam
Mah.	- Kobī, Pevā

Botanical Name: Costus speciosus (Koen) Sm

Natural Order: Zinziberaceae

Habitat: More or less throughout India upto an altitude of 4,000 ft. Particularly common in Bengal and Konkan.

Description: A rhizomatous-rooted plant of dwarf or semi-drawf habit with an attractive foliage and leafy stem. It grows to about 4 ft high, with oval leaves spirally arranged on the leafy stem and bearing at its apex a spike of pure white flowers, about 4 inches long.

Medicinal Action:

Rasa : Bitter, sweet and pungent
Guṇa : Light and dry
Vīrya : Cold
Vipāka : Pungent

It alleviates kapha and pitta, aggravates vāta, is appetizing, digestive, heart tonic, aphrodisiac, constipative and useful in fever, skin diseases, cough, urinary disorders, haemorrhoids, diseases of impure blood, vertigo and thirst.

Ketaki

Synonyms: Sūchikāpushpah, Jambukah, Krakachacchadah, Nṛpapriyah, Pāmśulā, Dīrghapatrā, Sthiragandhā, Kaṇṭadalā, Tīkshṇapushpā, Dhūlipushpikā, Chāmara-pushpā.

Hin.	- Kevdā
Ben.	- Keyā
Mal.	- Kaita paḷḷiyambu
Tam.	- Tāḷanchedi
Kan.	- Kedige
Tel.	- Gājangi, Mogali

Eng. Screw Pine, Caldera Bush

Botanical Name: Pandanus odoratissimus Roxb (Syn. P. tectorius Solend ex. Parkinson)

Natural Order: Pandanaceae

Habitat: Sea coast of the Indian peninsula on both sides and the Andamans.

Description: This is a large, gregarious shrub with the branched stem being supported by aerial stilt roots. The bark is pale-brown and smooth, the leaves are glaucous green, leathery, caudate-acuminate with spinous margins. The male spikes are numerous, sessile, enclosed by a long, cream-coloured fragrant spathe. The fruit is scarlet, ovoid and drooping, composed of 50-60 drupes.

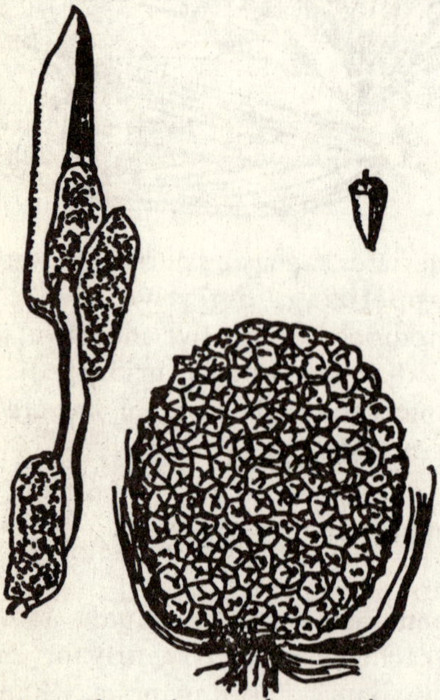

Varieties: There is another variety called Svarṇa-ketakī

Synonyms: Laghu-pushpā, Sugandhinī

Medicinal Action:

Rasa : Pungent, bitter and sweet
Sweet (the fruits)

Guṇa : Light
Vīrya : Hot
Slightly hot (the fruits)

It alleviates kapha and antidotes poison. Svarṇa-ketakī alleviates kapha, antidoes poison and is beneficial to the eyes.

The flowers of both varieties alleviate kapha and vāta, enhance the complexion, and are useful in fevers. The keśara is used in pruritus and skin diseases. The fruits alleviate kapha and vāta and are useful in urinary disorders.

Khadirah

Synonyms: Rakta-sārah, Gāyatrī, Danta-dhāvanah, Kaṇṭakī, Bālapatrah, Bahu-śalyah, Yagnikah, Tikta-sārah, Kushṭhahṛt, Khādyapatrī.

Hin. - Khair, Katthā
Ben. - Kuth
Tam. - Vodalai
Tel. - Chanḍra-cheṭṭu
Mal. - Kari-nāli
Kan. - Kaggali-mara, Kāchu
Eng. - Brown-barked Acacia

Botanical Name: Acacia catechu Willd (Syn. Mimosa catechu Roxb; Acacia wallichiana Dec

Natural Order: Leguminosae

Habitat: Punjab, N. W. Himalayas, Madhya Pradesh, Bihar, Konkan and Deccan.

Description: This is a small sized tree from fifteen to twenty feet high. The bark is thick, and branches spreading. Leaves are bi-pinnately compound, flowers are numerous, whitish or pale yellow. The fruit is a legume, two to five inches long with five to eight seeds. The tree flowers in the rainy season.

Varieties: There is a white variety called Śveta-khadirah.

Synonyms: Soma-valkalah, Kadarah

Parts Used: Bark and the extract called Khadira-sāra (the product which is got by boiling the decoction of Khadira wood and inspissating it).

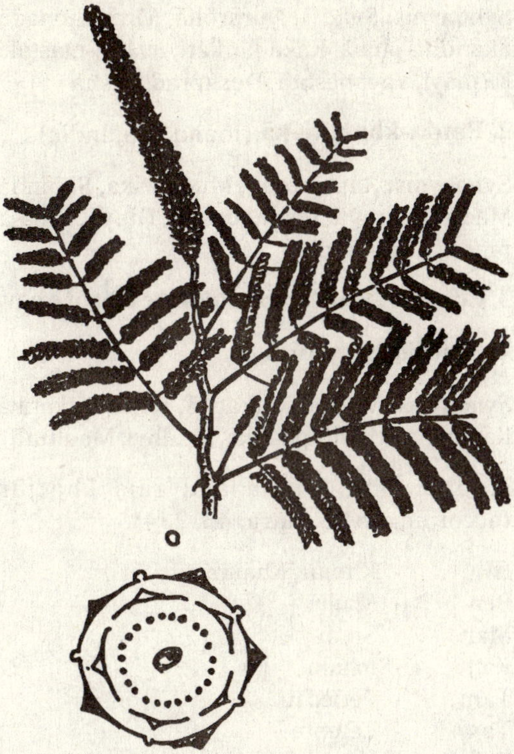

Medicinal Action:

Rasa : Astringent and bitter (Khadira)
Sweet (the gum)
Astringent, pungent and bitter (Śveta-khadira)

Guṇa : Viśada (Śveta-khadira)

Vīrya : Cold (Khadira)
Hot (Śveta-khadira)

Khadira alleviates kapha and pitta, purifies the blood, strengthens the teeth, is a digestive and is beneficial in pruritus, skin diseases, cough, anorexia, obesity, worms, urinary disorders, fever, leucoderma, oedema, dyspepsia and anaemia.

Śveta-khadira alleviates kapha and vāta, promotes healing of ulcers, and is useful in skin diseases, pruritus, worms, diseases of the mouth and toxicosis.

The extract alleviates kapha, purifies the blood, promotes healing of ulcers, and is beneficial in diseases of the mouth and throat, urinary disorders, worms, skin-diseases, obesity and haemorrhoids.

The gum is strength-giving and an aphrodisiac.

Therapeutic Hints:

1. It is useful in pruritus (CS, sūtra, 4, 17) and especially in skin diseases (ibid, 23, 40).
2. The decoction is useful in certain urinary disorders (SS, chikitsā, 11, 9).
3. Medicated ghee prepared from khadira-sāra is useful in skin diseases and bleeding (CS, chikitsā, 7, 135).
4. The decoction of Khadira is used in skin diseases, diseases of throat, urinary disorders and glandular swellings (AS, chikitsā, 21).

References: CS, kalpa, 1, 8; chikitsā, 7, 97; 18, 64; sūtra, 4, 11; 3, 3; SS, sūtra, 38, 8-9; chikitsā, 10, 13; 9, 66, AHr̥. sūtra, 2, 42; AS, sūtra, 16.

Kharbūjam

Synonyms: Daśāngulam, Madhuphalā, Shad-rekhā, Vr̥tta-karkaṭī, Tikta-phalā, Madhupākā, Shanmukhā

Hin. - Kharbūjā
Ben. - Kharmuj
Tam. - Mulampazham

Botanical Name: Cucumis melo Linn

Natural Order: Cucurbitaceae

Habitat: Extensively cultivated throughout India, particular in the hot and dry north-western area.

Description: This is an annual or creeping herb with large, soft, hairy leaves and spherical, ovoid or elliptic fruits of varying colour and size.

Parts Used: Fruits

Medicinal Action:

Rasa : Bitter, sweet and slightly sour (the unripe fruits)
Sweet (the ripe fruits)

Guṇa : Heavy and unctous

Vīrya : Cold

Vipāka : Sour (the unripe fruits)

The unripe fruits, if eaten in excess may induce bleeding from internal organs and dysuria.

The ripe fruits alleviate vāta and pitta, are a laxative, aphrodisiac, diuretic, strength-giving, refreshing, nutritive and are beneficial in ascites, burning pains, and insanity.

Kharjūrī

Kharjūrī is of four main varieties, viz.

1. Grāmya Kharjūrī

Synonyms: Svādvī, Durārohā, Mṛduchchadā, Skandha-phalā, Kāka-karkaṭi, Svādu-mastakā Kashāyī, Yavaneshṭā, Dushpradharshā

2. Piṇḍa-kharjūrikā (found in S. India)

Synonyms: Rāja-jambū, Mudgarikā, Sapiṇḍā, Madhura-sravā, Phalapushpā, Dīpyā, Sthala-piṇḍā, Rasā-bhidhā.

3. Cchohar, which resembles the teat of a cow.

4. Madhu-Kharjūrī

Synonyms: Madhu-Karkaṭikā, Koka-karkaṭikā, Kaṇṭakinī, Madhuphalikā, Mādhvī, Madhurā

Madhu, bhū, piṇḍa and rāja kharjūrī (according to SS, sūtra, 46, 334).

Hin. - Khojūr, Khajūr
Ben. - Khejūr
Mar. - Śindī
Kan. - Īchalu
Tam. - Perīcchu
Tam. - Kāṭenṭu
Tel. - Īta-chettu
Eng. - Wild Date, Date Palm

Botanical Name: Phoenix dactylifera Linn (Syn. P. farinifera Roxb; P. pusilla Gaertin; P. sylvestris Roxb).

Natural Order: Palmae

Medicinal Action:

Rasa : Sweet

Guṇa : Heavy and unctous

Vīrya : Cold

Vipāka : Sweet

The unripe fruit aggravates all the doshas. The ripe fruit alleviates all the doshas, is appetizing, heart tonic, refreshing, nutritive, aphrodisiac, strength-giving, causes flatulence and is beneficial in tuberculosis, diseases of traumatic origin, dyspnoea, bleeding from internal organs, vomiting, fever, injuries, thirst, excessive hunger, cough, intoxication, alcoholism, syncope, dyspepsia and anorexia.

Therapeutic Hints:

1. It is valuable in fatigue (CS, sūtra, 4, 16).
2. The dried fruit is useful in bleeding from internal organs (CS. chikitsā, 4, 71). and colic of the pitta type (SS, uttara, 42, 108).
3. The leaves and stems are used in tuberculosis and bleeding from internal organs (CS, sūtra, 27, 116).
4. It however increases abdominal flatulence (AS, sūtra, 7).

References: CS, 27, 127; SS, sūtra, 46, 310; AHṛ, sūtra, 10, 32.

Kodravah

Synonyms: Kora - dūshah

Hin. - Kodo, Kodra
Kan. - Haraka
Ben. - Kodoā dhān
Mah. - Harīk, Kodrū
Tam. - Varagu
Tel. - Ārikalu, Āḷḷu
Eng. - Kodo millet

Botanical Name: Paspalum scrobiculatum Linn (Syn. P. commersonii Lam)

Natural Order: Gramineae

Habitat: Throughout the hotter parts of India, wild or cultivated.

Description: This is an annual grass, with culms upto 90 cm. high, is often tufted, with a very short rhizome; leafy from the base upwards. The leaves are two-ranked, stiff and erect. The inflorescence is of two or more sessile alternate spikes.

Varieties: There are many varieties, one of them being Vana-kodravah or Uddālah.

Medicinal Action:

Rasa : Sweet, bitter and astringent
Sweet and astringent (Vana-kodravah)
Guṇa : Dry and heavy
Dry (Vana-kodravah)
Vīrya : Cold
Hot (Vana-kodravah)

It alleviates kapha and pitta, aggravates vāta, is appetizing, emaciating, constipative, delays micturition, and is beneficial as diet in ulcers. It causes fatigue and syncope, but is useful in toxicosis.

Vana-kodravā has more or less the same actions.

References: AS, sūtra, 7, 30; SS, sūtra, 20, 5; AHṛ, sūtra, 6, 11.

Kokilākshah

Synonyms: Kākekshah, Ikshurah, Kshurakah, Kāṇḍekshuh, Khaggalī, Ikshugandhā, Śṛgālaghaṇṭī, Vajrakaṇṭakah, Ikshu-vālikā, Pikekshaṇā.

Hin. - Tālmakhānā
Ben. - Kaṇṭakūlika, Kuliakhārā
Mah. - Vikharā
Kon. - Koḷavaḷike
Tel. - Nīru-gobbī, Golimiḍi-cheṭṭu

Botanical Name: Hygrophila spinosa T. Anders (Syn. Asteracantha longifolia Nees; Ruellia longifolia Roxb)

Natural Order: Acanthaceae

Habitat: Throughout India in moist places.

Description: This is a stout herb with unbranched, numerous, erect, hairy stems. The leaves are tapering at the base, sessile, appearing in whorls of six. Each of the six leaves has nearly straight, sharp, yellow spines. The flowers occur in whorls of eight, purple-blue in colour. The fruit, a capsule is about 8 mm long, linear-oblong and pointed with four-eight seeds.

Parts Used: Roots, leaves and seeds

Medicinal Action:

Rasa : Sweet, sour and bitter (roots)
Sweet and bitter (leaves)
Sweet, bitter and astringent (seeds)
Guṇa : Heavy, unctous and sticky
Vīrya : Cold

The plant alleviates pitta, is appetizing, strength-giving, aphrodisiac, refreshing, purifies the semen, and is beneficial in rheumatism, gout, diarrhoea, thirst, urinary calculi, urinary disorders, oedema, diseases of impure blood and eye-diseases.

The leaves alleviate vāta, and are useful in oedema, abdominal colic, flatulence, ascites, anaemia, toxicosis, constipation and retention of urine.

The seeds alleviate pitta, aggravate vāta and kapha, fecilitate conception, are constipative, strength-giving, are useful in burning pains and purify the blood.

Kośāmrah

Synonyms: Ghana-skandah, Vanāmrah, Jantupādapah, Kshudrāmrah, Raktāmrah, Lākshāvṛkshah, Suraktakah,

Hin. - Kośambh
Nepal - Chuchi-ām
Ben. - Keoḍā
Assam - Ban-ām
Tel. - Tummeda-māmiḍi
Vernacular - Kośambha, Kousimbha
(NIS on SS, sūtra, 45, 124)

Botanical Name: Mangifera sylvatica Roxb

Natural Order: Anacardiaceae

Habitat: Common in Nepal, Sikkim, Eastern Himālayas at 300-1,300 m, Assam, Khasi hills and Andaman Islands.

Description: This is a tall, evergreen tree, upto 45 m. high, with a straight bole, 15 m. long and 3 m. in girth. The fruits are ovate, elliptic, variable / in size, 8-10 cm. long; the flesh is thin, slimy and fibreless. The stone is less furrowed than that of an ordinary mango.

Parts Used: Root, fruits, fruit-pulp and oil.

Medicinal Action:

Rasa : Sour (unripe fruits)
Sweet (ripe fruits)
Bitter, sour and
sweet (the oil)
Guṇa : Heavy (unripe fruits)
Light (ripe fruits)

Unctous (the fruit-pulp)
Vīrya : Hot (the fruits)
Vipāka : Sweet (the fruit pulp)

The root alleviates kapha and is beneficial in skin diseases, oedema, bleeding from internal organs and ulcers.

The unripe fruits alleviate vāta, aggravate kapha and Pitta, are constipative and cause oedema.

The ripe fruits alleviate kapha and vāta and are appetizing,

The fruit-pulp alleviates vāta and pitta, is appetizing and strength-giving.

The oil is appetizing, digestive, laxative, strength-giving and is useful in worms, skin diseases and ulcers (SS, chikitsā, 31, 5).

References: SS, sūtra, 45, 124; 46, 207.

Kośātakī

Synonyms: Svāduphalā, Supushpā, Karkoṭakī, Pīta-pushpā, Dhārāphalā, Dīrghaphalā, Sukośā, Dhāmārghavah.

Hin. - Karwi tarui
Ben. - Goshālatā, Jhinga
Mah. - Śirāḷī
Kan. - Hīre-kāyi
Tam. - Pistankai
Tel. - Bīra-kāyi
Mal. - Puichenggah
Eng. - Ridged or Ribbed Gourd

Vernacular Ghusuṇḍī, Torayi (NIS on SS, sūtra, 37, 17; 46, 262)

Botanical Name: Luffa acutangula (Linn) Roxb

Natural Order: Cucurbitaceae

Habitat: Throughout India.

Description: This is a large monoecious climber with palmately 5-7 angled or lobed leaves. The male flowers have 3 stamens in 10 to 20 flowered racemes; the female flowers are solitary, in same axils as males. The fruits are 15-30 cm long, cylindrical or club-shaped, with 10 prominent almost wing like, longitudinal ribs or ridges.

Varieties:

I. There are four varieties according to Ḍalhaṇa (SS, sūtra, 11, 11).
II. There are two other varieties :

1. Mahā-kośātakī

Synonyms: Hastighoshā, Mahāphalā, Dhāmārgovah, Hastiparṇah.

Hin. - Ghia-korui

2. Tikta-kośātaki

Synonyms: Kṛatacchidrā, Jālinī, Kṛtavedhanā, Kshveḍā, Sutiktā, Ghaṇṭalī, Mṛdangaphalikā

Hin. - Kadvi-korui
Ben. - Jhingā
Mah. - Kaḍū-doḍakī
Kan. - Kāḍu-hīre
Tel. - Aḍavi-bīra
Eng. - Bitter Luffa

Botanical Name: Luffa acutangula (Linn)Roxb. var amara (Roxb) C.B.C. clarke

Medicinal Action:

Rasa : Sweet (Kośātakī and Mahā-kośātakī)
Bitter, astringent and slightly pungent(tikta-kośātakī)
Pungent and bitter (the fruits of Tikta-kośātakī)
Guṇa : Unctous (Kośātakī and Mahā-kośātakī)
Dry and light (Tikta kośātakī)

Vīrya : Cold
Vipāka : Pungent (Tikta kośātaki)

Kośātakī alleviates kapha and pitta, slightly aggravates vāta, is a laxative, appetizing, an aphrodisiac, strength-giving and useful in fever, cough, worms and dyspnoea.

Mahā-kośātakī alleviates vāta and pitta, is a laxative, an aphrodisiac, promotes healing of wounds, purifies the blood and produces intestinal worms.

Tikta-kośātakī alleviates all three doshas, is an emetic, a laxative, and is beneficial in anaemia, skin diseases, diseases of the liver, haemorrhoids, swellings, cough, ascites, jaundice, abdominal tumours and toxicosis.

The fruit of Tikta-kośātakī also alleviates all three doshas, is purgative, heart-tonic, appetizing, and useful in cough, anorexia, urinary disorders, fever, skin diseases and dyspnoea. The seeds are used as errhine in headaches.

References: SS, sūtra, 11, 11; 37, 17-19, 5; 46, 262-263; AC, sūtra, 14, 5.

Krishṇabījam

Synonyms: Śyāma-bījam

Hin. - Kālādāna
Ben. - Nīl-kamalī

Botanical Name: Ipomoea hederacea (Linn) Jacq.

Natural Order: Convolvulaceae

Habitat: Throughout India, upto 6,000 ft. in the Himalayas.

Medicinal Action:

Guṇa : Unctous

It alleviates kapha, is a laxative and is useful in fever, swellings, ascītes, constipation, diseases of the head and flatulence.

Kuberākshah

Synonyms: Latākaranjah, Krakachikā, Tinagacchikā, Vāriṇī, Tīriṇī, Vallī, Kanṭakinī, Vajrabījakah, Dusparśah.

Hin. - Kaṭ-karaunj
Ben. - Nāṭā
Mah. - Sāgar-goṭā
Kan. - Gajjega-baḷḷi
Tam. - Kaḷarkodi
Tel. - Gacchha
Mal. - Kaḷanchi
Eng. - Bonduc seed, Fever-nut, Boduc nut

Botanical Name: Caesalpinia bonducella Fleming (Syn. C. crista Linn)

Natural Order: Leguminosae

Habitat: Throughout the hotter parts of India upto 2,500 ft. in the hills, common in Bengal and S. India.

Description: This is a prickly shrub with a light brown bark. The leaves are paripinnate with six to ten leaflets, stipulate. The rachis and branches are armed with recurved prickles. The leaflets are opposite, oblong or elliptic and membranous. The flowers occur as racemes, yellow in colour. The fruit is a heavy, dehiscent, prickly pod with shining, lead coloured seeds.

Medicinal Action:

Rasa : Astringent, pungent and bitter
Pungent (the leaves)
Bitter (the flowers)

Vīrya : Hot (all parts)

It alleviates vāta, antidotes metallic poisons, is constipative and is beneficial in urinary disorders, convulsions, skin diseases, haemorrhoids, ulcers and worms.

The leaves and flowers alleviate kapha and vāta.

The seeds are appetizing and are useful in abdominal colic and abdominal tumours.

Kubjakah (See also Śatapatrī)

Synonyms: Bhadra-taruṇī, Vṛtta-pushpāh, Ati-kesarah, Kharvah, Mahāsahah, Kaṇṭakāḍhyah, Bṛhat-pushpah, Vāri-kaṇṭakah, Alikulasankulah.

Hin.	- Kujai
Ben.	- Kūjā, Golāp
Mah.	- Kaṇṭe-śevantī
Eng	- Himalayan Musk Rose

Botanical Name: Rosa brunonii Lindl (Syn. R. moschata Hook. f.)

Natural Order: Rosaceae

Habitat: Temperate and Western Himalayas, from Murree to Nepal, 2,000-11,000 ft.

Description: A large climbing shrub with stout, scattered prickles. The leaves are pinnate, the leaflets 5-9, and serrate. The inflorescence pubescent, the flowers very numerous, white, fragrant with musky odour. The fruits are globose or ovoid, and orange-red or dark-brown.

Varieties: There is a red variety, Rakta-kubjakah, besides the white one.

Medicinal Action:

Rasa	: Sweet
Anurasa	: Astringent
Vīrya	: Cold

It alleviates all the three doshas, particularly pitta, is aromatic, a laxative, aphrodisiac, purifies the blood and is of use in bleeding from internal organs.

The flowers alleviate vāta and pitta, enhance the complexion and relieve burning pains.

Rakta-kubjaka alleviates all the doshas, purifies the blood and is of use in scorpion bite.

Therapeutic Hints: The flowers are used as collyrium in eye-diseases (SS, uttara, 17, 8).

Kukuradruh

Synonyms: Kukundarah, Tāmra-chūḍah, Sūkshmapatrah, Mṛduchchadah.

Hin.	- Kukuroudā
Ben.	- Kukursunga, Bhang-rūd
Tam.	- Narakarandai
Mah.	- Kukurbandā

Botanical Name: Blumea lacera DC (Syn. Conyza lacera Burm)

Natural Order: Compositae

Description: This is an annual herb with a strong odour of turpentine. The stem is erect, 1-3 ft. high, ash-coloured, usually densely glandular-pubescent. The lower leaves are petioled, often incised or lyrate, the upper ones are sub-sessile, elliptic-oblong or obovate, finely silky, pubescent on both sides and serrate. The flowers are yellow, in short axillary cymes and terminal panicles.

Medicinal Action:

Rasa : Pungent and bitter
Vīrya : Hot

It alleviates kapha, purifies the blood and relieves burning pains and thirst.

The fresh root if kept in the mouth is useful in ulcers, toothache, bleeding from the gums and all other diseases of the mouth.

Kulanjanah

Synonyms: Gandhamālah, Tīkshṇa-mūlah, Mahābharī-vachā.

Hin.	-	Kulinjan
Ben.	-	Mahābari-vach
Kan.	-	Rāsmī, Dumparāsme
Guj.	-	Kalinjan
Tel.	-	Dumparāshṭrakamu
Tam.	-	Ārdukam, Perarattai
Mal.	-	Aratta
Eng.	-	Greater Galangal

Botanical Name: Alpinia galanga Willd (Syn. Galanga major Rumph; Maranta galanga Linn)

Natural Order: Zinziberaceae

Habitat: Mainly in the E. Himalayas and S.E. India.

Description: A herb, 1.8 to 2.4 metres in height with tuberous aromatic root-stock. The leaves are oblong-lanceolate, acute, glabrous 30-60 cm long. The flowers are greenish white, streaked with red, in dense-flowered panicles, about 30 cms long. The capsules are orange or red and globose.

Medicinal Action:

Rasa : Pungent and bitter
Vīrya : Hot

It alleviates kapha and vāta, is appetizing, a heart tonic, soothing to the throat, the voice and is beneficial in diseases of the mouth, diseases of the throat and cough.

Kulatthah

Synonyms: Tāmrabījah, Śveta-bījah, Siletarah, Kālavṛntah.

Hin.	-	Kulthi
Kan.	-	Huruḷi-giḍa

Mah. - Kulīth, Hulagā
Mal. - Koliu
Tam. - Koḷḷu
Tel. - Ulavalu
Eng. - Horse gram

Botanical Name: Dolichos biflorus Linn (Syn. D. uniflorus Lamk)

Natural Order: Leguminosae

Habitat: Himalayas to Ceylon, ascending to 3,000 ft. in Sikkim, sometimes cultivated.

Description: This is an annual, twining, downy plant with trifoliate, stipulate leaves. The leaflets are lanceolate or oblong, entire and downy. Flowers are yellow coloured; the fruit is a large compressed, heavy pod with greyish seeds.

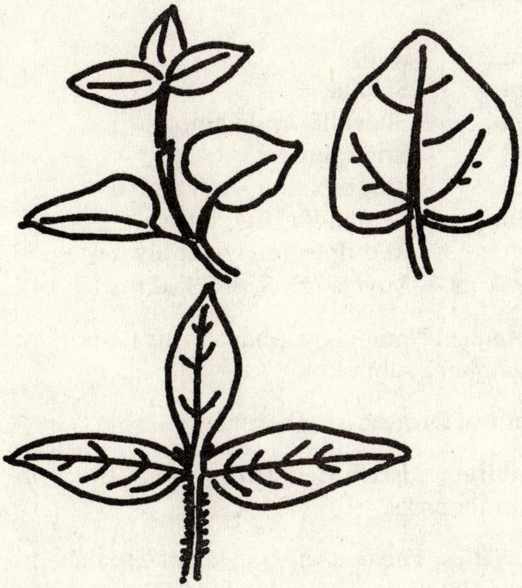

Medicinal Action:

Rasa : Astringent and pungent
Guṇa : Dry, light and vidāhi.
Vīrya : Hot

It alleviates kapha and vāta, aggravates pitta, is constipative, nutritive, lessens perspiration, and is beneficial in abdominal tumours, calculi, diseases of Medas, cough, urinary disorders, hiccough, catarrh, flatulence, excessive sweating, fever, worms, headache, renal colic, chest pain, retention of urine, eye-diseases, haemorrhoids, skin diseases, oedema, enlargement of liver, dyspnoea and toxicosis.

Therapeutic Hints:

1. It aggravates pyrosis and acidity (CS, sūtra, 25, 40).
2. The soup of Kulatthah, given with dāḍima, rock-salt and black-pepper relieves colic of the vāta type (SS, uttara, 42, 93; sūtra, 46, 372).

Kumārī

Synonyms: Dīrghapatrikā, Ghṛta-kumārī, Aphalā, Surasā, Kanyā, Suvahā, Bahupatrī, Sthūleruhā, Amarā, Ajarā, Kaṇṭakaprāvṛtā, Vipulasravā, Gṛha-kanyā, Atipichchilā, Adalā, Sukaṇṭaka, Kapilā, Bhṛngeshṭā,.

Hin. - Ghīkumār
Ben. - Ghrita kumāri
Kan. - Loḷi-sara
Tam. - Chiru-kattāḻai
Tel. - Musāmbram
Mal. - Kattavāḻa
Eng. - Small Aloes; Indian Aloes

Botanical Name: Aloe vera Tourn ex. Linn (Syn. Aloe barbadensis Mill; A. indica Royle)

Natural Order: Liliaceae

Habitat: Most parts of India.

Description: This is a dwarf plant with dense, aggregated, sword-shaped leaves with horny prickles on margins. The flowers are reddish-yellow or green, borne in scape. The fruit is a capsule.

Medicinal Action:

Rasa : Bitter and sweet
Guṇa : Unctous
Heavy (the flowers)
Vīrya : Cold

It alleviates all the three doshas, is a purgative, strength giving, nutritive, aphrodisiac, promotes vision, bestows longevity, and is beneficial in abdominal tumours, enlargements of spleen and liver, vomiting, fever, knotty tumours, burns and scalds, weals, bleeding from internal organs, eye-diseases, cough, dyspnoea and toxicosis.

The pulp from the central part of the stem, in addition, especially alleviates pitta and is anthelmintic.

The flowers alleviate vāta and pitta and are anthelmintic.

Kumbhikā

Synonyms: Vāriparṇī, Vārimūlī, Khamūlikā, Ākāśamūlī, Kutṛṇam, Kumullā, Jalavalkalam, Śvetaparṇī, Aśukumbhī, Pānīyapṛshṭhaja, Khalī.

Medicinal Action:

Rasa : Bitter, sweet and pungent
Guṇa : Light and dry
Vīrya : Cold

It alleviates all the doshas, purifies the blood, and is a laxative. It is contraindicated in fever and tuberculosis.

Kumudam

Synonyms: Kairavam, Chandrakāntam, Gardabham, Sougandhikam, Gandhasomam, Sitotpalam, Dhavalotpalam, Śītalakam, Kuvalayam.

Hin. - Koi
Ben. - Sāluka
Tam. - Shevalli, Arakkāmbal
Tel. - Errakaluva
Mal. - Kaktotpalam, Arākambal
Kan. - Kennaidile, Kendāvare
Eng. - Red-flowered water lily
Vernacular - Kuyiyā (Ni S on SS, sūtra 13, 14)

Botanical Name: Nymphaea lotus Linn (Syn. Nymphaea rubra Roxb)

Natural Order: Nymphaceae

Habitat: Distributed throughout India in warmer parts.

Varieties: The texts also speak of Utpalakam, Rakta-kumudam (also called Hallakam and Somākhyam) and Utpalinī (also called Nīlotpalinī, Kumudvatī and Indīvariṇī).

Medicinal Action:

Rasa : Sweet and bitter
Guṇa : Unctous and slimy
Dry and heavy (the seeds)

Vīrya : Cold
Vipāka : Sweet

Kumudam alleviates pitta and kapha, purifies the blood and is beneficial in debility and burning sensation.

Utpalakam is beneficial in debility, burning sensation, vomiting, vertigo, worms and fever.

Utpalinī is useful in fever, cough, thirst, debility and vomiting.

Therapeutic Hints:

1. It is useful in high-coloured urine (CS, sūtra, 4, 15).
2. The white flowered variety is useful in haemorrhages (SS, uttara, 40, 121).

References: SS, sūtra, 13, 14; 38, 52; 46, 285; AS, sūtra, 13, 3).

Kundah

Synonyms: Aṭṭa-hāsah, Sadāpushpah, Śukla-pushpah, Muktā-pushpah, Manoharah, Makarandah, Mahāmodah, Tāra-pushpah, Damanah, Bhṛnga-bandhū.

Hin. - Kundphūl
Kan. - Kastūri-mallige, Suragi
Tel. - Molla
Mal. - Kundam, Kurakuttimulla
Mah. - Mogra, Kāgdā
Eng. - Common Jasmine, Downy Jasmine

Botanical Name: Jasminum pubescens Willd (Syn. Jasminum multiflorum Andr; Nyctanthes pubescens Retz).

Natural Order: Oleaceae

Habitat: Throughout India

Description:

1. This is a large scandent, tomentose shrub with villous branches and young parts. The leaves are opposite, simple, ovate, acuminate, and more or less pubescent beneath. The white flowers are borne in compact, short, pedunculate cymes.
2. The flowers are white in colour and devoid of any fragrance (NIS).

Medicinal Action:

Rasa : Pungent, bitter, sweet and astringent
Guṇa : Light
Vīrya : Cold

It alleviates kapha and pitta, is appetizing, digestive, laxative, heart-tonic, and is useful in headaches, swellings, dyspepia, diseases of impure blood and toxicosis.

References: SS, uttara, 51, 38.

Kunkumam

Synonyms: Kāśmīrajam, Vahlikam, Raktam, Sankocham, Kusumātmajam, Pītanam, Rakta-chandanam, Agni-śekharam, Dīpakam, Aruṇam, Piśunam, Śatam, Jāgudam.

Hin. - Jāfrān, Kesar
Mah. - Kesar
Kan. - Kunkuma-kesari
Eng. - Saffron

Botanical Name: Crocus sativa Linn (Syn. C. officinalis Pers)

Natural Order: Iridaceae

Habitat: Cultivated in Pampur at 5, 300 ft. in Kashmir.

Description: This is a perennial herb with a solid, depressed-globular corm about an inch in diameter. The leaves produced from the new buds are few, very closely placed, sessile and form an erect tuft. This is closely invested in its lower part by large, membranous, thin scales. The flowers are borne on very short peduncles. The fruit is an oblong, membranous, three-celled capsule, each cell bearing numerous, sub-globose seeds.

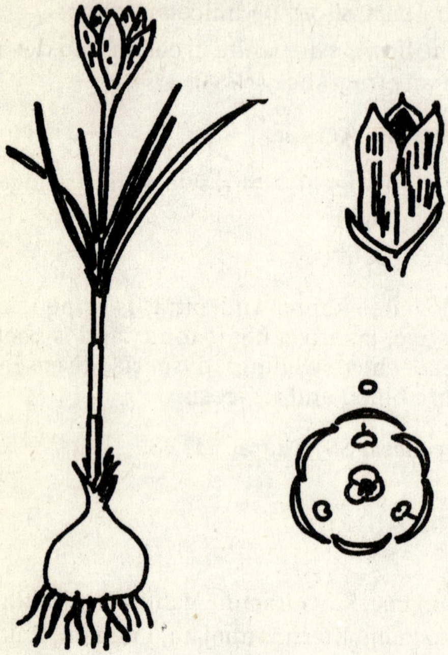

Varieties: There is another variety - Tṛṇa-kunkumam.

Synonyms: Gandhādhikam, Tṛṇa-gouram, Tṛṇāsram, Gandhi-tṛṇam, Tṛṇa-pushpam).

Parts Used: Dried stigmas and tops of the styles.

Medicinal Action:

Rasa : Bitter and pungent
Guṇa : Unctous and sharp
Vīrya : Hot

It alleviates kapha and vāta, is aromatic, a laxative, appetizing, strength-giving, enhances complexion reduces perspiration, and is beneficial in cough, sore throat, toxicosis headaches, ulcers, worms, vomiting, blemishes on the skin, pruritus, eye-diseases, the skin diseases known as Sidhma, and melancholia.

Tṛṇa-kunkumam is particularly useful in oedema, thirst, skin diseases and dyspepsia (Āma-dosha).

Test: The best variety of Kunkumam is that found in Kashmir, which has fine, delicate filaments, is reddish in colour and has the odour of the lotus flower.

The medium variety is that which has fine, delicate filaments, is yellowish-white in colour and has the odour of Ketakī.

The inferior variety is that which has coarse filaments, is whitish in colour, and has the smell of honey.

Therapeutic Hints:

1. It is useful in insect-bites and stings (SS, kalpa, 8, 49-51).
2. References : SS, sūtra, 38, 24, 25; 46, 237.

Kupīluh

Synonyms: Kāraskarah, Kimpākah, Visha-tinduh, Visha-mushṭī, Vishadrumah, Gara-drumah, Ramyaphalah, Kupākah, Kālakūṭakah, Chipiṭah.

Hin. - Kuchalā
Ben. - Kuchilā
Mah. - Kājra, Kuchalā
Tam. - Eṭṭe-koṭṭai, Visha muṭṭi, Eṭṭai-maram
Mal. - Kānniram
Tel. - Mushiṇi-cheṭṭu
Kan. - Kāsarka, Kāsarakāyi
Eng. - Vomit nut

Botanical Name: Strychnos nux-vomica Linn

Natural Order: Loganiaceae

Habitat: Forests of Gorakhpur, Orissa, Bihar, Maharastra, N. Kanara, Deccan, West Coast of Tamil Nadu, in deciduous forests and upto 4,000 ft. in Travancore.

Description: A deciduous tree sometimes reaching 30 m in height, often with short, sharp, strong, axillary spines, with thin, grey, smooth or rough bark. Leaves are opposite, acute, glabrous and shining with a rounded base. Flowers are numerous, greenish-white occur in compound cymes. Fruits are globose, orange-red when ripe with discoid seeds, concave on one side and convex on the other.

Varieties: There is another vareity called Kākapīlu or Kākatindukah.

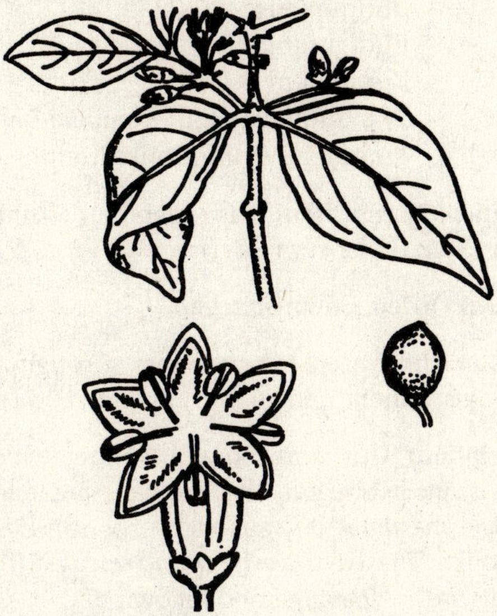

Medicinal Action:

Rasa : Excessively bitter, pungent and astringent

Guṇa : Light and dry,
Heavy and viśada (ripe fruits)

Vīrya : Hot
Cold (the unripe fruits)

Vipāka : Sweet (the ripe fruits)

It alleviates kapha and vāta, purifies the blood, is appetizing, analgesic, both constipative and laxative, and is beneficial in skin diseases, pruritus, emaciation, ulcers, jaundice, anaemia, haemorrhoids, fever and toxicosis.

The unripe fruits aggravate vāta and are constipative.

The ripe fruits alleviate all three doshas and are used in urinary disorders and diseases of impure blood.

Purification: The seeds are purified by soaking them in Kānjika for three days or by frying them with ghee (AP, 6, 112).

References: AHṛ, sūtra, 15, 30.

Kuruṇṭakah

Synonyms: Kanakah, Pīta-saireyakah, Kinkirātah, Pītapushpakah, Pītāmlānah, Sahacharah.

Hin. - Kaṭsareya, Vajradanti
Ben. - Kānṭajāti
Mah. - Koraṇṭa
Kan. - Muḷḷu-goraṇṭi, Hasiru.-goraṇṭi, Gorantige
Tel. - Muḷḷu-goraṇṭa-cheṭṭu
Tam. - Chemmuḷḷi, Mullu. - kurugam
Mal. - Chemmuḷḷi, Veṭṭilakoḍi
Vernacular. - Kaṇṭa-śeluā (NIS on SS, sūtra, 38, 6).

Botanical Name: Barleria prionitis Linn (Syn. Barleria pubiflora Benth)

Natural Order: Acanthaceae

Habitat: Throughout the hotter parts of India.

Description: An attractive, evergreen shrub, 2-4 feet in height, armed with axillary sharp spines and bearing large orange-coloured, bell shaped flowers, mostly in the rainy season.

Varieties: There are four varieties of the plant, based on the colour of the flowers :

1. Saireyakah (White)

Synonyms: Śveta-pushpah, Kaṭasārikā, Sahācharah

2. Kuruṇṭakah (Yellow)

3. Ārtagalah (Blue)

Synonyms: Dāsī, Nīla-jhintī, Nīlapushpī

4. Kurubakah (Red)

Synonyms: Raktāmlānah, Raktapushpah, Rāgaprasavakah, Subhagah, Śona-jhiṇṭikah.

Medicinal Action:

Rasa	:	Sweet, bitter and pungent (Saireyakah) Bitter and astringent (Kuruṇṭakah) Bitter and pungent (Ārtagalah and Kurubakah)
Guṇa	:	Unctous (Saireyakah)
Vīrya	:	Hot (all varieties) Cold (Kuruntakah, according to some texts).

Saireyakah alleviates kapha and vāta, strengthens the teeth, purifies the blood, antidotes poison, and is beneficial in pruritus and skin diseases. It removes wrinkles and turns grey hairs into black.

Kuruṇṭakah also alleviates kapha and vāta, is appetizing, and is useful in pruritus, oedema, discolouration of the skin and diseases of impure blood.

Ārtagalah alleviates kapha and vāta, and is beneficial in oedema, pruritus, abdominal colic, skin diseases, ulcers, discolouration of skin and diseases of the teeth.

Kurubakah alleviates all three doshas, enhances the complexion, and is useful in oedema, colic, cough, dyspnoea and toxicosis.

Therapeutic Hints: It antidotes poison, alleviates kapha, purifies ulcers and wounds and is useful in urinary disorders (including diabetes), skin diseases fever, vomiting and pruritus (SS, sūtra, 38, 6-7).

Kūshmāṇḍam

Synonyms: Pushpaphalam, Pītapushpam, Bṛhatphalam, Suphalā, Sthiraphalā, Kunjaphalā, Nāgapushpaphalā, Karkoṭakā, Grāmya-karkaṭī, Timisham.

Hin.	-	Peṭhā
Ben.	-	Kumrā
Mah.	-	Kohoḷā
Tam.	-	Kalyāṇa-pūchiṇi
Guj.	-	Bhurānkoḷān-bel
Tel.	-	Būdigummaḍi
Mal.	-	Kumbaḷam
Kan.	-	Biḷi-kumbaḷā, Būdi-kumbaḷa-baḷḷi
Eng.	-	Pumpkin, White Gourd Melon

Botanical Name: Benincasa hispida (Thunb) Cogn (Syn. B. cerifera Savi)

Natural Order: Cucurbitaceae

Habitat: Cultivated more or less throughout the plains of India, and on the hills upto 4,000 ft.

Description: This is an annual climber which spreads upto twelve feet. The leaves are simple and petiolate, the petiole being about twelve inches long and rough. The leaves are hairy and serrated. The flowers are polypetalous and yellow.

Varieties: There are two other varieties :

1. Pīta-kūshmāndam or Guḍayogaphalā and
2. Kūshmāṇḍi or Karkāru

Parts Used: Fruits, leaves and stems.

Medicinal Action:

Rasa : Sweet

Guṇa : Heavy, dry and abhishyandī
Light (mature fruits)

Vīrya : Cold

Vipāka : Sweet

Tender fruits alleviate vāta and pitta, purify the blood, are nutritive, strength giving, aphrodisiac, and are useful in urinary disorders, retention of urine, dysuria, urinary calculi, thirst, anorexia and debility of old age.

Mature fruits alleviate all the doshas, are heart tonic, appetizing, digestive and useful in insanity

The leaves and stems alleviate Kapha and Vāta, are appetizing and beneficial in urinary calculi.

References: CS, sūtra, 27, 113; AS, sūtra, 6, 109.

Kushṭham

Synonyms: Pāribhāvyam, Vyāpyam, Pākalam, Utpalam, Jaraṇam, Bhāsuram, Nīrujam, Rujā, Kimjalkam.

Hin. - Kūṭ
Ben. - Kur, Pāchak

Botanical Name: Saussurea Lappa C. B. Clarke (Syn. Aplotaxis auriculata DC)

Natural Order: Compositae

Habitat: Kashmir, 8,000-12.000 ft.

Description: This is a tall, robust, perennial herb with an erect, 1.2 to 2 metre high, simple stem. The leaves are membranous, irregularly toothed, the basal ones being very large, triangular with a long lobately winged stalk. The stem leaves are smaller with two half-stem-clasping lobes at the base. The flower-heads are dark blue-purple. The fruit is a compressed achene. The root is very light, in crooked twisted pieces with longitudinal ridges, texture very firm. Odour, somewhat aromatic; taste, bitterish at first, but soon becoming hot, pungent and biting.

Medicinal Action:

Rasa : Pungent, bitter and sweetish

Guṇa : Light

Vīrya : Hot

It alleviates kapha and vāta, enhances the complexion, bestows longevity, is aphrodisiac and is beneficial in skin diseases, herpes, scabies, pruritus, cough, dyspnoea, fever, hiccoughs, toxicosis, diseases of impure blood, vomiting and thirst. It is used externally in rheumatism. It is especially used in diseases of children.

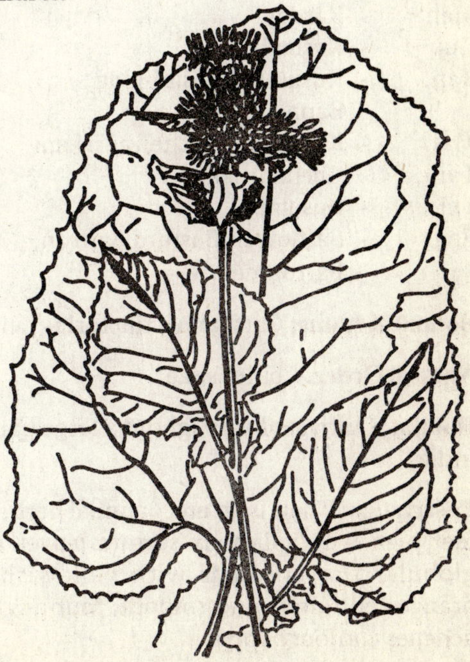

Therapeutic Hints:

1. Its external application relieves skin disease (CS, sūtra, 3, 28); it is also used as a dusting powder (ibid, 3, 10); and is useful in impotency (ibid, 4, 12), and headaches (ibid, 3, 23), and is considered to be emaciating (ibid, 4, 9).
2. When used with gold, pippali, honey, ghee and vachā, it is an excellent tonic which enhances the mental and physical development of children (SS, śārīra, 10, 68).
3. An oil medicated with this drug is used in bleeding from the navel, etc. of new born infants (AS, uttara, 1).

References: SS, sūtra, 38, 24; 14, 35; CS, sūtra, 25, 40; 4, 13.

Kusumbham

Synonyms: Pāvakam, Vahniśikham, Lohitam, Grāmyam-kunkumam, Mahārajanam.

Hin.	-	Kusum, Kardayi
Ben.	-	Kusumphūl
Mah.	-	Karḍayī
Guj.	-	Kusumbo
Kan.	-	Kusumbe, Kuśibi-giḍa, Baṇṇada-hūvu
Mal.	-	Kuyumpapū, Chendūrakam
Tam.	-	Chendurukku
Tel.	-	Kusumbā
Eng.	-	Safflower, Bastard Saffron, Parrot seed

Botanical Name: Carthamus tinctorius Linn.

Natural Order: Compositae

Habitat: Cultivated throughout a large part of India.

Description: Their is an erect annual herb, 1-3 feet high with spinosely serrate leaves and globular flower-heads with yellowish or orange-red florets and smooth, four-angled, achenes without pappus.

Medicinal Action:

Rasa	:	Pungent (the oil)
		Sweet and astringent (the seeds)
		Sweet (the flowers)
		Sweet, sour and pungent (the leaves)
Guṇa	:	Dry (the flowers)
		Dry and heavy (the leaves)
		Heavy and unctous (the seeds)
		Heavy and sharp (the oil)
Vīrya	:	Hot (all parts)
Vipāka	:	Pungent (all parts)

The leaves which are used as vegetable-food aggravate pitta, alleviate kapha, are appetizing, a laxative, diuretic and are useful in haemorrhoids and rectal fistulae.

The flowers alleviate kapha and vāta, aggravate pitta, are purgative and are useful in preventing and removing greying of hair.

The oil aggravates all the three doshas, increases bleeding from internal organ, diminishes strength and eye-sight, causes itching in the eye-lids, but is useful in worms and urinary disorders. The oil is considered to be one of the most injurious of all oils (SS).

Note: The leaves are used for culinary purposes (CS, sūtra, 27, 101).

References: CS, sūtra, 13, 10; SS, sūtra, 46, 48.

Kuṭajah

Synonyms: Mallikāpushpah, Śakrāśah, Varatiktakah, Vatsakah, Girimallikā, Pāṇḍurah, Kouṭajah, Rakta-nāśakah, Kālingah, Sangrāhī, Pāṇḍudrumah, Mahāgandhah. Indrayava (the Seeds)

Hin.	- Kurchi, Kureya
Ben.	- Kurchi
Mah.	- Kuḍā
Tam.	- Veppalai
Mal.	- Kuḍajam
Tel.	- Kodiśa-cheṭṭu
Kan.	- Korasigina-giḍa

Botanical Name: Holarrhena antidysenterica Wall (Syn. Echites antidysenterica Roxb)

Natural Order: Apocynaceae

Habitat: More or less throughout India, ascending to 4,000 ft. in the Himalayas.

Description: This is a small, deciduous tree with rough, brown bark which exfoliates in small flakes. The leaves are opposite, ovate-oblong, rounded at base, membranous, subsessile, simple and entire. The flowers are white, in terminal cymes. The fruit is a round follicle and seeds have a tuft of long, silky hairs at the apex. The stem bark is brittle, thick, often twisted or quilled, colour dirty white or snufflike. Surface rugous, soft internally; taste slightly bitter at first which soon becomes intensely increased. the root bark is reddish brown, less thick than the stem, studded with prominent small, warty growths; taste very bitter.

Varieties:

I. There are two varieties - Black and White.
II. It is also classified into two other varieties:

1. Male - which has bigger fruits, white flowers, long leaves and red and thick bark.
2. Female - which has small fruits, round greyish-red flowers and white bark.

Parts Used: Bark, flowers and seeds.

Medicinal Action:

Rasa	: Pungent, bitter and astringent
Guṇa	: Light and dry Unctous (the male variety)
Vīrya	: Cold

It alleviates kapha and pitta, purifies the blood, is appetizing and is beneficial in haemorrhoids, diarrhoea, thirst, bleeding from internal organs, menorrhagia, etc.

The flowers alleviate kapha and pitta, aggravate vāta, purify the blood and are useful in skin diseases, diarrhoea and worms.

The seeds (Indrayava) alleviate all three doshas, and are beneficial in fever, abdominal colic, bleeding from internal organs, burning, diarrhoea, vomiting, haemorrhoids, herpes, skin diseases and gout.

Therapeutic Hints:

1. It is useful in haemorrhoids and pruritus (CS, sūtra, 4, 11).
2. It is specific for (some kinds of) diarrhoea (AHṛ, uttara, 40, 49), and bleeding piles (AS, sūtra, 13, 3).
3. Its bark is used for external application in skin diseases (CS, sūtra, 3, 15).
4. A paste of the flowers given along with the juice of āmalakī and honey is useful in all kinds of urinary disorders (including diabetes) (SS, chikitsā, 11, 8).

References: CS, sūtra, 2, 7; 1, 83; 25, 40; 3, 14; kalpa, 5, 14, SS, sūtra, 6, 33; 11, 11;; 38, 6, 27.

L

Lakshmaṇā

Synonyms: Putrajananī, Nāgapatrī, Putradā, Nāginī, Asrabinducchadā.

Description: The leaves are full of small red dots (NIS).

Parts Used: Stem and tuber

Medicinal Action:

Rasa : Sweet
Vīrya : Cold

It alleviates all the three doshas, bestows longevity, facilitates conception, is an aphrodisiac and is useful in ulcers.

Substitute: If this plant is not available, Nīlīkandā is to be used in its place.

References: Ḍalhaṇa on SS, śārīra, 2, 32; Indu on AS, śārīra, 1; AS, śārīra, 1, 61; CS, sūtra, 27, 101.

Lakuchah

Synonyms: Kshudrapanasah, Likuchah, Ḍahuh, Airāvatah, Amlakah, Dṛḍha-valkalah, Kārshyah, Sthūlaskandhah, Granthimatphalah.

Hin. - Barhat, Lahu
Ben. - Mādār, Dheu, Dahu
Tam. - Irapala, Ottipilu
Mah. - Vaṭār, Wotomba
Tel. - Kamma-regu

Kan. - Vāṭehuḷi, Gaja-nimbe
Mal. - Puḷinchakkamaram, Kattupilavu
Eng. - Monkey Jack

Botanical Name: Artocarpus lakoocha Roxb

Natural Order: Moraceae

Habitat: Sub-Himalayan tract upto 4,000 ft. from Kumaon eastwards to Assam, and southwards to Burma and the Andamans, Bihar, Orissa, Madhya Pradesh, in the west-coast Konkan southwards to Malabar and Travancore.

Description: A tall deciduous tree, upto 20 m in height, with a large, spreading crown and clear straight bole. The bark is dark-brown, exfoliating in small round woody peels, reddish inside. The leaves are elliptic, oblong or ovate base broadly cuneate, pinnatifid. The inflorescence is solitary.

Parts Used: Fruit

Medicinal Action:

Rasa : Sweet and sour
Guṇa : Heavy (the unripe fruit)
Vīrya : Hot (the unripe fruit)

The unripe fruit aggravates all the three doshas, vitiates the blood, is constipative, an anaphrodisiac, harmful to the eyes and causes dyspepsia.

The ripe fruit aggravates kapha, alleviates vāta and Pitta, is appetizing, aphrodisiac and constipative.

References: SS, sūtra, 46, 155; 20, 13; AS, sūtra, 9.

Lāmajjakam

Synonyms: Sunālam, Amrṇālam, Layam, Laghu, Ishṭakāpathikam, Sevyam, Naladam, Avadātakam, Dīrghamūlam, Jalāśrayam.

Hin. - Lāmjak, Lakhvī
Ben. - Kārankus
Mah. - Lāvaj, Pivalāvāla
Tel. - Tell-vaṭṭi-vellu
Kan. - Kari-lāvancha
Eng. - White khus-khus grass

Botanical Name: Andropogon jwarancusa Jones (Syn. Cymbopogon jwarancusa Schult)

Natural Order: Gramineae

Description: This is a highly aromatic grass growing upto six feet high with densely tufted roots. The leaves are about two feet long and 0.2 inches broad.

Habitat: Himālayas, from Kashmir to Assam, ascending to 10,800 ft., and in the north-western plains, reaching down to Mumbai.

Varieties: It is a variety of Uśīra (SS, sūtra, 39, 9, Ḍalhaṇa).

Medicinal Action:

Rasa : Bitter and sweet
Guṇa : Light
Vīrya : Cold

It alleviates all the three doshas, particularly vāta and pitta, purifies the blood, is digestive, constipative, and is beneficial in skin diseases, excessive perspiration, dysuria, burning pains, bleeding from internal organs, thirst, toxicosis fatigue, syncope, fever, abdominal colic, vomiting, ulcers, and herpes.

Note: The plant which is fragrant, with a firm, thin and long root is considered superior.

References: CS, sūtra, 3, 29; 25, 40; AS, sūtra, 13, 3.

Lāngalikā

Synonyms: Kalikārī, Dīptā, Garbhaghātinī, Agnijihvā, Vahniśikhā, Vahnivakrā, Halinī, Viśalyā, Naktā, Indrapushikā, Vidyujjvālā, Vraṇahṛt, Pushpasourabhā, Svarṇapushpā, Śakrapushpā, Anantā, Garbhanut.

Hin. - Kalihāri
Ben. - Bisha lāngali
Kan. - Koḷi-kuṭuma, Śivarakti-baḷḷi, Nīru-hippali
Tel. - Potti-dumpa, Aḍavi-nābhi,
Tam. - Kāndal
Mal. - Mettonni

Botanical Name: Gloriosa superba Linn

Natural Order: Liliaceae

Habitat: Throughout tropical India, ascending upto 7,000 ft. on the hills. Common in Karnāṭaka.

Description: This is a handsome climber, climbing by leaf-tip tendrils. The stem-tubers are large and forked, resembling a country plough. The leaves are ovate-lanceolate and almost sessile with tips which are tendril like, serving as hold-fasts. The flowers are showy, bright-orange in colour. The fruit is a linear-oblong capsule. The plant flowers sometime between October and December.

Medicinal Action:

Rasa : Bitter, pungent and astringent
Guṇa : Sharp and light
Vīrya : Hot

It alleviates vāta and kapha, aggravates pitta, is a laxative, abortifacient, and is beneficial in skin diseases, ulcers, oedema, haemorrhoids, abdominal colic, worms, toxicosis, pruritus, and emaciation. It assists the expulsion of foreign matter. Its exernal application alone may also cause abortion.

Therapeutic Hints: A medicated oil prepared from Lāngalī and a few other drugs is useful in diseases of the ear lobes (SS, chikitsā, 25, 19) and is used as application in skin diseases (CS, chikitsā, 7, 109).

Note: Lāngalī is to be purified by immersing it in cow's urine for a day (AP, 6, 112).

Laśunah

Synonyms: Rasonah, Arishṭah, Mlechhakandah, Mahoushadah, Śuklakandah, Mahākandah, Vātārih, Dīrghapatrakah, Kaṭukandah, Bhutaghnah, Urgagandhah, Yavaneshṭah.

Hin. - Lasun
Ben. - Rasun
Kan. - Beḷḷuḷḷi
Tam. - Veḷḷuḷḷi
Mah. - Lasūn
Eng. - Garlic

Botanical Name: Allium sativum Linn

Natural Order: Liliaceae

Habitat: Widely cultivated in India.

Description: This is a bulbous plant with linear, lanceolate leaves and a simple stem. The spathe is long and pointed. The bulb is somewhat ovate, tapering upwards and flattened below.

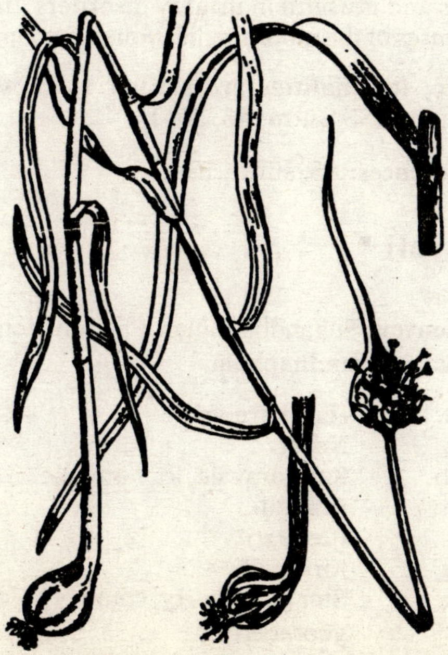

Varieties: There are two varieties, white and red.

Medicinal Action:

Rasa : Sweet, saline, bitter, pungent and astringent.
Pungent (the root)
Bitter (the leaves)
Sweet (the seeds)
Astringent (the stalk) and
Saline (the tip of the stalk)

Guṇa : Sharp, unctous, slimy and heavy

Vīrya : Hot

It alleviates kapha and vāta, is strength-giving, nutritive, an aphrodisiac, digestive, laxative, brain tonic, promotes good complexion and vision, bestows longevity and is beneficial to the throat. It aids in the healing of wounds and fractures.

It is useful in diseases of the heart and skin, continuous fever, rheumatism, constipation, abdominal tumours, anorexia, oedema, haemorrhoids, dyspepsia, worms, sprue, cough, dyspnoea, urinary disorders, menstrual disorders, cataract, night blindness, intermittent fevers, dysuria, urinary calculi, enlargement of spleen, tuberculosis and gout.

Therapeutic Hints:

1. Persons using Laśunah should avoid exertion of mind and body, sun's rays, anger, milk, jaggery and drinking much water. On the other hand, wine, meat and sour substances can be partaken of (BP).
2. It is especially useful in diseases of Vāta and abdominal tumours (AS, sūtra, 13).
3. It can be used as an article of daily diet (SS, sūtra, 46, 221).
4. It is an excellent rejuvenative if ingested during the months of Pushya and Māgha (winter and beginning of spring) (KS, kalpa, 35).
5. It should be avoided by pregnant women,

children, women in puerperium, in fever, diarrhoea, jaundice, vomiting, dyspnoea, etc. (KS, Kalpa).

6. It is useful along with goat's milk in hiccough (SS, uttara, 50, 23).
7. A soup prepared from Laśuna is valuable in diseases of Vāta (KS, khila, 4, 64).
8. Laśuna is contraindicated in diseases of kapha and pitta, in aged people, in severe hiccough and dyspnoea, and in persons who have just been administered the śodhana therapy (KS, kalpa, 5, 31-34).
9. A linctus prepared from one pala of laśuna and two palas of ghee is to be taken regularly with honey before meals. The diet is to consist of rice and milk. If this is continued for an year, it will confer a long life and good health (ibid, 89-90).

References: CS, sūtra, 27, 276; 2, 5; 3, 5; vimāna, 7, 17; KS, kalpa, 5, AHṛ, sūtra, 6, 109-111; AS, sūtra, 7, 162-165.

Latā-kastūrikā

Synonyms:

Hin. - Mushk-dāna
Kan. - Kāḍu-kastūri, Kastūri-beṇḍe
Mah. - Kasturi-bheṇḍa
Tel. - Kastūri-beṇḍa
Tam. - Vettilai-kastūri
Mal. - Kāṭṭu-kastūri
Eng. - Musk Mallow

Botanical Name: Abelmoschus moschatus Moench (Syn. Hibiscus abelmoschus Linn)

Natural Order: Malvaceae

Habitat: Cultivated in the hotter parts of India. In S. India according to Ḍalhaṇa (SS, sūtra, 46, 204).

Description: This is an erect herb, from 2 to 6 ft. high with usually palmate, five to seven lobed leaves, and large, yellow flowers with a crimson centre. The fruit is a oblong-lanceolate pod or capsule, with a large number of small seeds which are scented, greyish-brown, reniform and compressed.

Medicinal Action:

Rasa : Sweet and bitter
Guṇa : Light and sharp
Vīrya : Cold

It alleviates kapha and vāta, is aphrodisiac, chedana, diuretic, heart tonic, beneficial to the eyes and is useful in urinary disorders, thirst, diseases of the mouth, salivation and vomiting.

Note: Its qualities are similar to those of Karpūra (SS, sūtra, 46, 204).

References: AS, sūtra, 12.

Lavalī

Synonyms: Sugandha-mūlah, Pāṇḍuh, Komala-valkalā, Skandhaphalā.

Hin. - Harphāre-vaḍī
Ben. - Noyāl
Mah. - Kath-amvaḷe, Rāy-amvaḷe
Tam. - Aranelli
Tel. - Rāsusari
Kan. - Kiru-nelli
Eng. - Star gooseberry, country gooseberry

Botanical Name: Cicca acida (Linn) Merrill (Syn. Cicca disticha Linn; Phyllanthus distichus Muell)

Natural Order: Euphorbiaceae

Habitat: Frequently cultivated in homeyards and gardens in India.

Description: A deciduous tree with a grey, smooth bark. The wood is light-brown and moderately hard. The leaves are alternate; branchlets resemble pinnate leaves. The flowers are small and monoecious; the fruit is a capsule.

Medicinal Action:

Rasa : Sweet, sour, astringent and slightly bitter
Guṇa : Heavy, dry and viśada
Vīrya : Cold

It alleviates kapha and pitta. aggravates vāta, purifies the blood, is appetizing, aromatic, heart tonic and is beneficial in haemorrhoids and urinary calculi.

Note: The root is fragrant, while the bark is soft and whitish-grey in colour (Ḍalhaṇa on SS, sūtra, 46, 189).

References: Chkp. on CS. sūtra, 27, 145; AS, sūtra, 7.

Lavangam

Synonyms: Devakusumam, Śrīsamgyam, Kalikottamam, Bhṛngāram, Sushiram, Tīkshṇam, Vārijam, Śekharam, Lavam, Prasūnam, Divyam, Grahaṇīharam, Toyādhipriyam, Vāripushpam, Gīrvāṇakusumam, Chandanapushpam.

Hin. - Loung
Ben. - Langa
Kan. - Lavanga
Eng. - Cloves

Botanical Name: Caryophyllus aromaticus Linn (Syn. Syzygium aromaticum (Linn) Merr & LM; Eugenia aromatica Kuntze)

Natural Order: Myrataceae.

Habitat: A native of Moluccas. Cultivated in S. India.

Description: This is a tree with yellow-green, soft-bark, growing to about thirty feet high. The leaves are opposite, dark-green and aromatic, the flowers being fragrant, in cymes. The fruit is a fleshy berry, about an inch in length. The dried flower buds form the cloves of commerce.

Parts Used: The dried flower buds, and the oil.

Medicinal Action:

Rasa : Pungent and bitter
Guṇa : Light, sharp, unctous and viśada
Vīrya : Cold

It alleviates all the three doshas, purifies the blood, is appetizing, digestive, heart tonic, is beneficial to the eyes and is used in thirst, vomiting, distension of abdomen, abdominal colic, cough, hiccough, tuberculosis, constipation, bad breath, headache and dyspnoea.

The oil alleviates kapha and vāta, is appetizing and is useful in morning sickness and vomiting of pregnant women, bleeding from the gums and toothache.

References: CS, sūtra, 5, 77; SS, sūtra, 46, 485-486.

Lavanī

Synonyms: Rāmaphalam, Rakta-tvacham, Vāsantam, Kṛshṇa-bījam, Mṛdūphalam.

Hin. - Rāmphal, Louna
Ben. - Lona, Luvani
Kan. - Rāma-phala
Mal. - Parankichchkka

Tel. - Rāma-phalamu
Tam. - Rāma-chittā

Botanical Name: Annona reticulata Linn

Natural Order: Annonaceae

Habitat: Cultivated more or less all over India; naturalized in Bengal and S. India.

Description: This is a small deciduous or semi-deciduous tree, upto 10 metres in height. The bark is rough, chocolate-brown with longitudinal fissures. The leaves are oblong-lanceolate, with an unpleasant odour. The flowers are solitary, leaf-opposed, fleshy, greenish-white, scattered on the branches.

Medicinal Action:

Rasa : Sweet, sour and astringent

It alleviates pitta, aggravates kapha and vāta, purifies the blood and is beneficial in thirst, burning, fatigue and excessive appetite.

Limpākah

Synonyms:

Ben. - Pātinebu

Botanical Name: A variety of Citrus acida Linn

Natural Order: Rutaceae

Medicinal Action:

Rasa : Sweet and slightly sour

It alleviates kapha and vāta, does not aggravate pitta, is aromatic, a heart-tonic, appetizing, and is of use in vomiting.

Lodhrah

Synonyms: Tirīṭakah, Śābarah, Gālavah, Tilvakah, Tilakah, Mārjanah, Tindukah, Laktakarmā, Śūklah, Kāṇḍa-hīnah, Mahā-lodhrah, Balipriyah, Vānarāghātah, Bhillataru, Hemapushpakah.

Hin. - Lodh
Assam - Bhomroti
Eng. - Symplocos bark

Botancial Name: Symplocos racemosa Roxb

Natural Order: Symplocaceae

Habitat: Throughout N.E. India, up to 2,500 ft. from the Terai of Kumaon to Assam.

Description: This is a small, evergreen tree with a light-grey, thin, easily pulverizable soft smooth bark. The leaves are simple, alternate, exstipulate, ovate-lanceolate, bright-green, leathery and narrowed to base. The flowers are small, white and fragrant, in axillary spikes. The fruit is a globose, purple, glabrous, faintly-ribbed drupe. The flowering season is from December to May.

Variety: There is another variety called Kramukah.

Synonyms: Paṭṭikālodhrah, Sthūlavalkalah, Jīrṇapatrah, Akshibheshajah, Bṛhatpatrah, Lākshāpra-sādanah, Śveta-lodhrah, Bṛhaddalah.

Botanical Name: Symplocos paniculata Wall

Habitat: Himalayas upto 9,000 ft. from the Indus to Assam and Khasia Hills.

Parts Used: Bark and flowers.

Medicinal Action:

Rasa : Astringent
Astringent, bitter and sweet (the flowers)
Guṇa : Light
Vīrya : Cold
Vipāka : Pungent (the flowers)

It alleviates kapha and pitta, purifies the blood, is constipative, promotes vision and is beneficial in bleeding from internal organs, dysentery, diarrhoea, swelling, toxicosis, anorexia and uterine bleeding.

The flowers alleviate kapha and pitta and are constipative.

Therapeutic Hints:

1. It is constipative, hastens healing of fractured bones and wounds (CS, sūtra, 4, 9, 15) and stops haemorrhages (ibid, 4, 18).
2. Its paste is applied in diseases of eyelids (AS, uttara, 12), in skin diseases, excessive sweating and bad smell from the body (CS, sūtra, 3, 5, 12, 29).
3. It is used as dusting powder in skin diseases (CS, sūtra, 3, 10).

References: CS, sūtra, 5, 22; SS, sūtra, 6, 23; uttara, 45, 25; AHṛ, sūtra, 27, 48; AS, sūtra, 16.

Loṇī

Synonyms:

Hin.	-	Khursa, Khulphā
Ben.	-	Lunia, Bara-lunia
Mah.	-	Ghoḷ
Tam.	-	Pachiri, Paijiri
Kan.	-	Doddagoṇi-soppu
Tel.	-	Pāyala-kūra, Goḷi-kūra
Eng.	-	Purslane, Garden Purslane

Botanical Name: Portulaca oleracea Linn (Syn. Portulaca sativa Haw)

Natural Order: Portulacaceae

Habitat: All over India

Description: A prostate, succulent, annual herb with a short and erect stem bearing a number of lateral branches which lie prostate on the ground; they grow to a length of 4-20 inches and are green or reddish in colour. The leaves are alternate at the base, subopposite or opposite at the ends of branches and crowded round the flowers. Flowers are without stalks and are yellow in colour. The seeds are minute, blackish brown in colour and are covered with concentric lines of tubercles.

Varieties: There is a variety called Bṛhat-loṇī or Gholikā.

Medicinal Action:

Rasa	:	Pungent and sour (Loṇī) Sour (Bṛhat Loṇī)
Guṇa	:	Dry and heavy
Vīrya	:	Hot

Loṇi alleviates kapha and vāta, is appetizing, and is useful in haemorrhoids, dyspepsia and toxicosis.

Bṛhat Loṇī aggravates vāta, alleviates kapha and pitta, is a laxative, bestows longevity and is beneficial in stammering, ulcers, abdominal tumours, cough, urinary disorders, swellings, sprue, haemorrhoids, eye-diseases, skin diseases, diarrhoea and dyspnoea.

M

Māḍah

Synonyms: Māḍadrumah, Dīrghah, Dvajavṛkshah, Vitānakah, Madyadrumah, Mahakārī.

Hin.	-	Mād, Māri
Mah.	-	Berli, Surmāḍa
Kan.	-	Baini-mara
Tam.	-	Kūndarapanai, Tippili
Mal.	-	Irampana
Eng.	-	Bastard Sago, Toddy or Fish-tail palm

Botanical Name: Caryota urens Linn

Natural Order: Palmae

Habitat: Moist forest regions of the West and East coasts and in the cool and shady villages of Chota Nagpur, Orissa, Bengal and Assam upto 5,000 ft. above sea level.

Description: This is a lofty, handsome palm, with a smooth, cylindrical, annulated trunk, 40-60 ft. high and 1 1/2 ft. diameter, bearing large leaves. The leaves spring successively from the trunk for a good distance below the summit. They are bipinnate with leaflets shaped like a fish-tail. Flowers are borne on pendulous inflorescences.

Medicinal Action:

Rasa : Astringent
Vīrya : Cold

It aggravates all the three doshas, is appetizing, engender burning sensation and relieves fatigue and thirst.

Madanah

Synonyms: Cchardanah, Piṇḍīnaṭah, Piṇḍītakah, Karahāṭah, Marubaka, Śalyakah, Vishapushapakah, Pichukah, Muchukundah, Kaṇṭakī, Kaiṭaryah, Rāṭah, Granthiphalah, Ghaṇṭālah, Basti-śodhanah, Dhāraphalah.

Hin.	-	Mayin
Vernacular	-	Mayaṇaphal (NIS on SS, sūtra, 38, 6)
Kan.	-	Mangari-kāyi, Mangāre
Tel.	-	Manga-cheṭṭu
Tam.	-	Pungārai, Marakkārai
Mal.	-	Mangakāyi
Mah.	-	Geḷ
Eng.	-	Emetic Nut

Botanical Name: Randia dumetorum Lamk (Syn. Posoqueria dumetorum Roxb; Gardenia dumetorum Retz)

Natural Order: Rubiaceae

Habitat: Sub-Himalayan tract from the Rawalpindi district eastwards, ascending in Sikkim upto 4,000 ft. southwards extends into Chittagong and Penisular India.

Description: A small, deciduous shrub with long, stout, axillary spines and a grey bark. The leaves are usually opposite, obovate, obtuse or acute, narrowed into a sharp petiole, glabrous and hairy. The flowers are large and fragrant, pure white at first and later greenish or yellowish. The fruit is a globose or ovoid, yellow berry with a thick, leathery paricarp and compressed seeds. The flowers appear from April to June.

Varieties: There are two varieties, white and black.

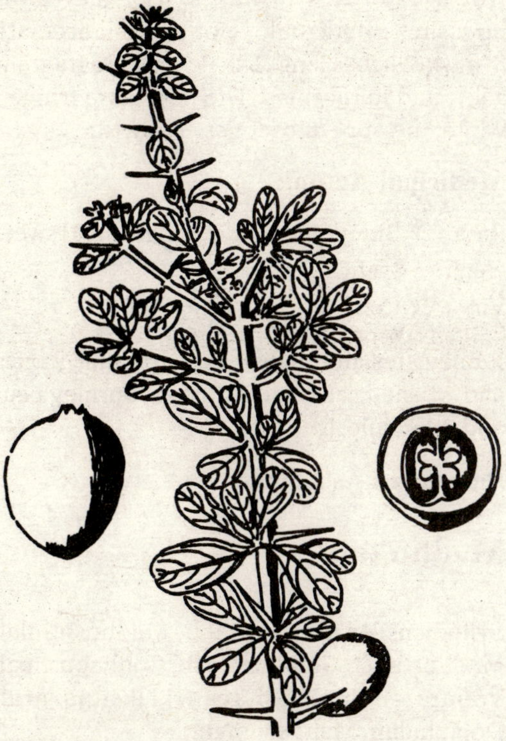

Medicinal Action:

Rasa : Sweet, bitter and pungent
Guṇa : Light, dry and lekhana
Vīrya : Hot

It alleviates kapha and vāta, is an emetic, a purgative, and is beneficial in abscesses, catarrh, ulcers, skin diseases, flatulence, swellings, abdominal tumours, fever, and haemorhoids and toxicosis.

Therapeutic Hints:

1. It is used as an emetic (CS, sūtra, 2, 7-8).
2. Its fruit is made into a paste with a little sour wine and applied in glandular swellings (SS, chikitsā, 18, 45).

Madayantikā

Synonyms: Timirah, Kokadantī, Dvivṛntā, Mendikā, Nakharanjakah, Medikā, Rāgagarbhā, Sugandhapushpā, Rāgāngī, Yavaneshṭā,

Hin. - Henā, Mehdī
Vernacular - Medī, Mehdī (Ḍalhaṇa)
Ben. - Mendi
Tam. - Marudroni, Kuravagam
Tel. - Goraṇṭa
Mal. - Mailānchi
Kan. - Goranṭṭe-giḍa
Eng. - Henna plant

Botanical Name: Lawsonia alba Lam (Syn. Lawsonia inermis Linn)

Natural Order: Lythraceae

Habitat: Cultivated all over India.

Description: This is a glabrous, deciduous shrub with tetragonous, spinescent branchlets and greyish-brown, thin bark. The leaves are opposite, simple and ovate-lanceolate. The flowers are greenish-yellow and fragrant, in large panicled cymes. The fruit is a capsule with pyramidal seeds.

It alleviates kapha, is an emetic and is useful in skin diseases and burning sensation.

The seeds are constipative, emaciating and are beneficial in fevers.

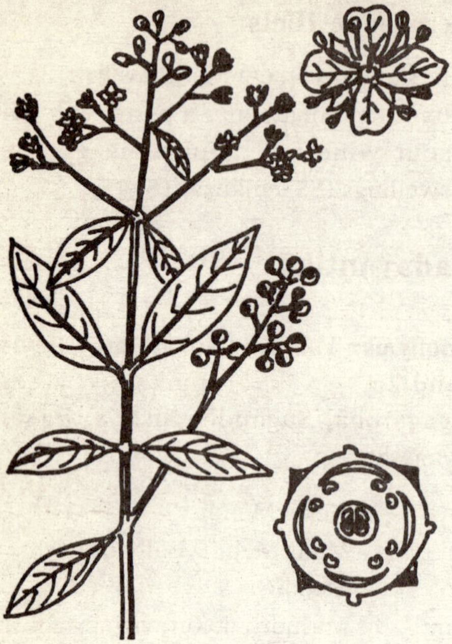

Therapeutic Hints:

1. It is useful in diarrhoea (CS, chikitsā, 8, 129).
2. The leaves are used to colour the nails (NIS on SS, chikitsā, 25, 43).
3. It is used to antidote poison (AS, sūtra, 8, 40).

Mādhavī

Synonyms: Atimuktā, Suvasantā, Parāśrayā, Kāmukah, Maṇḍapah, Bhṛamarotsavah, Sugandhā, Chandravallī, Bhadralatā, Bhūshaṇā, Puṇḍrakalatā, Tripuṭā, Śrīmatī, Nepālī, Grīshmakā, Lutā, Vanamālikā.

Hin.	-	Mādhavī-latā
Ben.	-	Mādhavī-latā, Madhu-mālti
Mah.	-	Pīta-beḷa, Kastur-mogra
Tel.	-	Mādhaya-tīga, Potu-vaḍla
Tam.	-	Aḍigam
Eng.	-	Clustered Hiptage
Kan.	-	Kāḍu-iruvantige

Botanical Name: Hiptage madablota Gaertn (Syn. H. benghalensis Kutz, Gaertnera racemosa Roxb)

Natural Order: Malphigiaceae

Habitat: Maharashtra, Western Ghats, Karnataka, Tamil Nadu, Assam, Nepal and the Andamans, in damp places.

Description: This is a large, handsome, evergreen climbing shrub with a brown bark which exfoliates in flakes. The leaves are opposite, elliptic-oblong or ovate-lanceolate, from 4-6 inches long. The flowers are fragrant, silky, and in racemes. The petals are fringed, white, the uppermost ones yellowish.

Medicinal Action:

Rasa	: Bitter, pungent, astringent and sweet.
Guṇa	: Light
Vīrya	: Cold

It alleviates all the doshas, particularly pitta, and is beneficial in cough, ulcers, burning pains and tuberculosis.

References: AHṛ, sūtra, 3, 34.

Madhūkah

Synonyms: Madhu-vṛkshah, Madhushṭhīlah, Madhusravah,Guḍapushpah, Rodhapushpah, Vānapṛsṭhah, Mādhavah, Tīkshṇasārah, Ḍolāphalah, Mahādrumah.

Hin.	-	Maua
Vernacular	-	Mahuā (Ḍalhaṇa)
Kan.	-	Ippe-mara
Tel.	-	Ippa-cheṭṭu
Tam.	-	Madhūkam
Mal.	-	Iruppa
Mah.	-	Mohācha-vṛksh
Eng.	-	The Mahwa tree, the Indian Butter tree

Botanical Name: Bassia latifolia Roxb

(Syn. Madhuca indica J. F. Gmel; M. latifolia (Roxb) Macbride)

Natural Order: Sapotaceae

Habitat: Distributed over most parts of India.

Description: A large deciduous tree with a wrinkled bark. Leaves are leathery and clustered near the end of the branches. Young leaves are coppery red. Flowers are cream-coloured with plum coloured calyces. They appear from February to April when the tree is almost leafless. The tree blooms at night and the flowers drop off at dawn. The fruit is a green juicy berry.

Varieties: There is another variety called Madhūlikā.

Synonyms: Dīrghapatrakah, Jalajah, Hrasvapushpaphalah, Svāduh and Golikā.

Medicinal Action:

Rasa : Sweet, bitter and astringent
Sweet (the flowers and fruits)
Sweet and astringent (the oil)

Guṇa : Heavy, unctous and vikāsī (the flowers)
Heavy and unctous (the fruits) Slimy (the oil)

Vīrya : Cold (all parts)

Vipāka : Sweet (the fruits)

It alleviates vāta and pitta, aggravates kapha, is nutritive, aphrodisiac and beneficial in burning pains, ulcers, fatigue and worms.

The flowers alleviate vāta and pitta, are a heart-tonic, nutritive and are cooling.

The fruits alleviate vāta and pitta, purify the blood, are an aphrodisiac, a heart tonic, nutritive, constipative, strength giving, and are useful in thirst, burning pains, dyspnoea, cough, tuberculosis and diseases of traumatic origin.

The bark is beneficial in bleeding from internal organs, and as a healing and anti-suppurating agent.

The oil alleviates kapha and pitta and is used in fever and burning pains.

The extract (Sārah) alleviates kapha and vāta and is used as errhine.

Madhūlika is strength-giving, bestows longevity and cures vomiting.

References: CS, sūtra, 3, 21; 27, 128, chikitsā, 15, 146; AS, sūtra, 6, 109-110; SS, sūtra, 38, 39-40; chikitsā, 18, 23.

Makhānnam

Synonyms: Padmabījābham, Pānīyaphalam

Hin. - Makhāna
Mah. - Makhane
Eng. - Fox nut; Gorgon fruit

Botanical Name: Euryale ferox Salisb

Natural Order: Nymphaeaceae

Habitat: Common in fresh water tanks, and jheels of north-central and western India.

Medicinal Action: Its medicinal properties are similar to those of Padmabījah (seeds of lotus)

Mālatī

Synonyms: Sumanā, Jātī, Vāsantī, Yuvatī, Mallikā, Medinī, Muktā, Madayantikā.

It alleviates kapha and pitta, purifies the blood, is emetic, beneficial to the eyes and useful in diseases of the mouth, ulcers, worms, skin diseases, discharge from the ear and ulcers in the mouth, (see Jātī).

Mallikā

Synonyms: Bhadravallī, Priyā, Soumyā, Vanachandrikā, Bhūpadī, Śīta-bhīruh, Tṛṇa-śūnyah, Gourī, Nārīshṭā, Sitā, Madayantī, Pramodinī, Damayantī, Madanīyā.

Hin.	- Bel
Ben.	- Mallikā, Bel
Kan.	- Mallige, Duṇḍu - mallige, Eḷu - Eḷusuttina-mallige
Mah.	- Mogarā
Tel.	- Malli
Tam.	- Malligai
Mal.	- Cherupichchakam, Nalamalli
Eng.	- Double Jasmine

Habitat: Bengal, Deccan and the Carnatic.

Botanical Name: Jasminum sambac Ait (Syn. Nyctanthes sambac Linn)

Natural Order: Oleaceae

Habitat: Cultivated throughout India.

Description: This is a dwarf, spreading bushy shrub, 2-4 ft. high, with attractive glabrous leaves and producing in the hot season, attractive, white, sweet scented flowers in great profusion.

Varieties: There is another variety called Vṛttamallikā.

Synonyms: Vaṭapatrā, Kumārikā, Sugandhāḍhyā, Vṛttapushpā, Muktābhā, Modinī.

Medicinal Action:

Rasa	: Bitter and pungent Bitter (the leaves)
Guṇa	: Light
Vīrya	: Hot

It alleviates vāta and pitta, is an phrodisiac, and is beneficial in diseases of the mouth and eyes, skin diseases, ulcers, anorexia, boils, pruritus and toxicosis.

The flowers alleviate vāta.

Note: The plant is used as a vegetable and alleviates pitta (SS, sūtra, 46, 286).

Māmsarohiṇī

Synonyms: Atiruhā, Vṛttā, Charmakashā, Vasā, Prahāravallī, Vikaśā, Vīravatī, Kaśāmamsī, Rasāyanī, Sulomā, Lomakaraṇī, Chandravallabhā.

Hin. - Rohan
Ben. - Rohaṇ
Tam. - Śemmaram
Kan. - Svāmimara
Eng. - Redwood tree

Botanical Name: Soymida febrifuga A. Juss (Syn. Swietenia febrifuga Roxb)

Natural Order: Meliaceae

Habitat: Dry forests of the W. Peninsula extending northwards to Merwara, the Mirjapur Hills and Chota Nagpur.

Description: A lofty deciduous tree with a straight bole and bitter, bluish-grey, dark-brown or greyish-brown bark which exfoliates in large plates. The leaves are pari-pinnate, the leaflets are 3-6 pairs, alternate and greyish-green. The flowers are bisexual and greenish-white; petals are obovate, narrowed into claw and twisted. The fruit is a five-valved, black, smooth capsule with many, flat, imbricate seeds which are winged at both ends. Flowers and young leaves appear in April-May; fruits appear in July-August.

Varieties: There is a variety called Rohinī.

Medicinal Action:

Rasa : Astringent
Vīrya : Hot

It alleviates all the three doshas, is an aphrodisiac, a laxative, appetizing, wound-healing and is beneficial in bleeding of internal organs, all varieties of sprue, worms and sore throat.

Rohiṇī particularly alleviates vāta, is appetizing and is useful in cough, worms, diseases of impure blood. and dyspnoea.

Mānakah

Synonyms: Māmakandah, Mahāpatrah, Vistīrṇaparṇah, Chchatrapatrah, Bṛhachchadah.

Hin. - Mān kand, Gorūmā
Ben. - Mān Kachu
Mah. - Ambara kand
Eng. - Giant taro

Botanical Name: Alocasia indica Schott

Natural Order: Araceae

Habitat: Cultivated in Assam and Bengal as a food crop. It is also an ornamental plant.

Description: This is a tall aroid with a succulent swollen stem from 4 to 8 inches in diameter, and an underground rhizome.

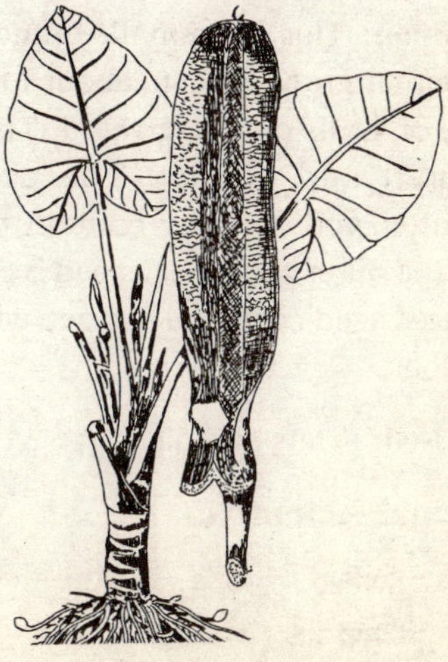

Medicinal Action:

Rasa : Pungent and sweet
Vīrya : Cold

It is beneficial in swellings and bleeding from internal organs.

References: SS, sūtra, 46, 306-307.

Maṇḍapī

Synonyms: Bhūśimbikā, Rakta-bījā, Tribījā, Sneha-bījakā, Bhūṃijā, Bhūchaṇakā

Hin. - Mūng-phalī
Ben. - Chini-badam
Mah. - Bhuyīmūng
Kan. - Nela-kaḍale
Tam. - Verkaḍalai
Mal. - Nela-kaḍalaka
Tel. - Veru-sanagalu
Eng. - Ground Nut, Peanut, Monkey Nut.

Botanical Name: Arachis hypogaea Linn

Natural Order: Leguminosae

Habitat: Widely cultivated in India, especially in Chennai, Mumbai, Madhya Pradesh, Hyderabad and Karnataka.

Description: This is a small, branched herb which either grows erect to about 1 to 2 feet in height, or trails on the ground. The flowers are small and yellow. The cylindrical reticulated pods usually contain two seeds within the outer shell. Each seed is covered by a coloured seed-coat, and has two white fleshy cotyledons.

Parts Used: Fruits and oil.

Medicinal Action:

Rasa : Sweet
Guṇa : Unctous

It aggravates vāta and kapha, and is constipative.

Manjishṭhah

Synonyms: Vikasā, Jingī, Samangā, Kālameshikā, Maṇḍūkaparṇī, Bhaṇḍīrī, Kālā, Yojanavallikā, Vastraranjinī, Raktāngī, Raktayashṭih, Yojanaparṇikā, Nāgarakumārikā, Rasāyanī, Hariṇī, Chitralatā, Jananī, Vijayā, Cchatrinī, Rāgāḍhyā, Aruṇā, Jvarahantrī, Hemapushpī.

Hin. - Manjiṭ,
Eng. - Indian Madder

Botanical Name: Rubia cordifolia Linn

Natural Order: Rubiaceae

Habitat: Throughout India in hilly districts.

Description: A perennial climber with scurfy branches. The leaves are whorled, simple, entire, cordate, petioled, rough on the upper surface and hairy below. The flowers are small, yelloyish white and hairy. The root is creeping and short with many cylindrical rootlets of the size of guills, brownish and thin.

There are three other varieties - Cholayojanī, Kounjī and Simhalī.

Medicinal Action:

Rasa : Sweet, bitter and astringent
Guṇa : Heavy
Light and unctous (the leaves and stem)
Vīrya : Hot

It alleviates kapha, purifies the blood, enhances complexion and voice, and is beneficial in swellings, toxicosis, diseases of ears and eye, diarrhoea, ulcers, skin diseases, herpes urinary diseases, fever, menstrual disorders, abdominal colic, haemorrhoids, worms and bleeding from rectum.

The leaves and stems alleviate vāta and pitta and are appetizing.

Therapeutic Hints:

1. It enhances complexion and lustre of the skin (CS, sūtra, 4, 10).
2. It alleviates Pitta (SS, sūtra, 39, 8).
3. It is an effective antidote to poisoning by rats (AS, uttara, 46; sūtra 15, 38).

Maricham

Synonyms: Palitam, Śyāmam, Veṇujam, Yavanapriyam, Vallījam, Śuddham, Kolakam, Dharmapattanam, Ūshaṇam, Vṛttaphalam, Śākāngam, Śiro-vṛttam, Sarvahitam, Kṛshṇam

Hin. - Kāli-marich
Ben. - Gol marich
Mah. - Mirre
Kan. - Meṇasu
Tel. - Miryālu
Mal. - Kuru-mulagu
Tam. - Miḷagu
Eng. - Black Pepper

Botanical Name: Piper nigrum Linn

Natural Order: Piperaceae

Habitat: Cultivated in hot and damp parts of India.

Description: This is a stout glabrous climber with stems which are much thickened at the nodes. The leaves are broadly ovate, acuminate, glabrous, petiolate with a rounded base. Flowers are in spikes of variable length. The fruit is globose, yellow first and red when fully ripe.

Varieties: There is a white variety called Sita-maricham.

Synonyms: Śītottham, Sita-vallījam, Vālukam, Bahulam, Dhavalam and Chandrakam.

Hin. - Safed marich
Ben. - Sāda marich

Medicinal Action:

Rasa : Pungent and bitter
Pungent (Sita maricham)

Guṇa	: Light, dry and sharp (dry maricham) Light (Sita-maricham) Heavy and slightly sharp (fresh maricham)
Vīrya	: Hot Slightly hot (fresh maricham and Sita maricham)
Vipāka	: Sweet (fresh maricham)

Dried marich alleviates kapha and vāta, aggravates pitta, is appetizing, Cchedi, non-aphrodisiac, and is beneficial in dyspnoea, cough, worms, abdominal colic, heart diseases, urinary disorders and haemorrhoids.

When fresh, it does not aggravate pitta, and acts as an expectorant.

Sita-maricham alleviates kapha and vāta, antidotes poison, is non-aphrodisiac, beneficial to the eyes and bestows longevity.

Therapeutic Hints: It is used as collyrium in some eye-diseases (SS, kalpa, 11, 13). Its fruit is used is an errhine (SS, sūtra, 39,).

References: CS, sūtra, 4, 9, 11, 13, 17; 27, 298; 3, 12; chikitsā, 23, 193-194; SS, sūtra, 46, 225, 224.

Mārishah

Synonyms: Mārshah, Bāshpakah.

Hin.	- Marsā, Choṭi-chaulai
Ben.	- Naṭīya sāg, Ban-note
Mah.	- Tānḍulja, Māṭh
Kan.	- Harive-soppu, chivike-soppu
Tel.	- Perugu-toṭa-kūra
Guj.	- Dambho
Tam.	- Ārumatha-thanda

Botanical Name: Amaranthus lividus Linn (Syn. A. blitum Linn, Hook. f; A. oleraceus Linn)

Natural Order: Amaranthaceae

Habitat: Cultivated as a pot-herb in India, particularly in sub-mountainous districts.

Description: An erect, ascending or prostrate annual herb. The stems are slender to stout, simple or branched, green to reddish or yellow. The leaves are mostly glabrous, long petioled, lamina ovate to rhomboid ovate. The flowers are green, in slender or stout terminal spikes and axillary cymose clusters.

The texts speak of Mārishah as having Dīrgha-nāla (long stem) and reddish, dotted leaves.

Varieties: There are two varieties - White and red. The red variety is Amaranthus gangeticus Linn.

Medicinal Action:

Rasa	: Sweet
Guṇa	: Heavy (the white variety) Slightly heavy (the red variety)
Vīrya	: Cold
Vipāka	: Pungent (the red variety)

The white variety alleviates pitta, aggravates kapha and vāta, is constipative, appetizing and is beneficial in bleeding from internal organs and dyspepsia (Vishamāgni).

The red variety aggravat kapha, is alkaline (Sakshāra) and a laxative.

References: CS, sūtra, 27, 100; AS, sūtra, 7, 139.

Mārkaṇḍikā

Synonyms: Bhūmicharī, Mṛdurechanī, Pītapushpī, Mahoushadhī, Svarṇapatrī, Kalyāṇī, Rechanī.

Hin.	- Bhui-khakkasa, Hindisana, Sunnamakki, Sanāy,
Ben.	- Kankarol bhed, Sona-pāt
Guj.	- Mathi-avalya

Kan. - Nelāvare, Nelāvarike
Mah. - Sonāmukhi
Tel. - Seema-nela-tangeḍu
Tam. - Nilāvirai
Mal. - Nilavāka
Eng. - Tinnevelly Senna

Botanical Name: Cassia angustifolia Vahl

Natural Order: Leguminosae

Habitat: South India

Description: This is a bushy herbaceous plant with paripinnate leaves. The leaflets are five to eight in number. The flowers are in racemes and the fruit is a oblong, slightly curved pod with smooth, papery valves.

Medicinal Action: It antidotes poison, is purgative, emetic and is useful in skin diseases, cough, ascites, abdominal tumours, enlargement of liver and spleen, dyspepsia, intermittent fever, jaundice and anaemia.

Marubakah

Synonyms: Maruttakah, Maruh, Phaṇī, Phaṇijjakah, Prasthapushpah, Samīranah, Kharapatrah, Gandhapatrah, Bahuvīryah, Śītalakah, Jambīrah, Kulasourabhah.

Hin. - Muruvā
Ben. - Maruyā
Kan. Maruga
Mah. - Sabjā, Marvā
Eng. - Sweet Marjoram

Botanical Name: Origanum marjorana Linn (Syn. Majorana hortensis Moench)

Natural Order: Labiatae

Habitat: Extensively cultivated In India.

Description: This is a perennial herb with a creeping elongated woody root stock, and numerous, bluntly quandrangular, pubescent, purple stems. The leaves are opposite, spreading, stalked, pubescent, and broadly ovate or rhombic-ovate and entire. The flowers are sessile or almost so, arranged in twos or threes, purplish-pink in colour. The achenes are avoid, slightly compressed and brown.

Varieties: There are two varieties - a white one (used in medicine) and a dark variety (used for pūjā purposes).

Medicinal Action:

Rasa : Pungent, and bitter
Guṇa : Light, Dry and sharp
Vīrya : Hot
Vipāka : Pungent

It alleviates kapha and vāta, aggravates pitta, is appetizing, aromatic, digestive, heart tonic, purifies the blood, antidotes the poison of spiders, etc. and is beneficial in skin diseases, fever, worms, pruritus, anorexia, dyspnoea, diseases of the heart, abdominal colic and distention of abdomen.

References: CS, kalpa, 1, 23.

Māshah

Synonyms: Kuruvindah, Dhānya-vīrah, Vṛshankurah, Māmsalah, Balāḍhyah, Pitryah, Pitṛ-bhojanah, Bījaratnah, Balī.

Hin. - Urid
Ben. - Māshkalāi
Tam. - Ulundu
Tel. - Minu-vulu
Mal. - Ulunna
Kan. - Uddu
Eng. - Black-gram

Botanical Name: Phaseolus mungo Linn

Natural Order: Leguminosae

Habitat: Extensively cultivated all over India.

Varieties: There is another variety - Rāja-māshah.

Synonyms: Mahāmāshah, Chapalah, Chavalah, Nṛpochita, Dīrghabījah, Nṛpamāshah, Nīlamāshah, Nishpāvah, Dīrghaśimbī, Kshuvah, Kshudhābhijanakah.

Hin.	-	Loliyā, Chourā
Ben.	-	Barbaṭikalāi
Mah.	-	Aḷasunde, Chavaḷyā
Kan.	-	Aḷasande-baḷḷi
Tam.	-	Karāmaṇi
Mal.	-	Koṭṭapayaru
Eng.	-	Chinese bean, Cow peas

Botanical Name: Vigna catjang Walp. (Syn. V. cylindrica skeels)

Medicinal Action:

Rasa : Sweet and astringent

Guṇa : Heavy and unctous

Heavy, dry and viśada (Rāja-māshah)

Vīrya : Hot

Māshah alleviates vāta, aggravates kapha and pitta, is galactagogue an aphrodisiac, appetizing, nutritive, strength-giving, increases the quantity of faeces, aggravates bleeding from internal organs and is beneficial in haemorrhoids, the type of colic called pariṇāma-śūla, dyspnoea, fatigue and torticollis.

It is regarded as a suitable diet for those who do manual work. It is said to cause obesity and nourish the muscles.

Rāja-māshah aggravates vāta and pitta, alleviates Kapha, is a laxative, appetizing, aphrodisiac, refreshing, strength-giving and galactagogue. It is said to be the least desirable among the pulses (Śimbhī-dhānya).

Therapeutic Hints:

1. It is considered the least beneficial among the pulses (CS, sūtra 25, 39; AHṛ, sūtra, 6, 25). However, it is aphrodisiac, hard to digest, strength-giving, alleviates Vāta, and increases the quantity of faeces (CS, sūtra, 27, 24).
2. It increases breast-milk (SS, sūtra, 46, 34).
3. A paste of the powder is used for the therapeutic procedure called Śiro-basti (AHṛ, sūtra, 22, 29).
4. Its powder is a valuable styptic (AS, sūtra, 36, 10).

References: CS, sūtra, 2, 32; 4, 13; 13, 89; chikitsā, 2(3), 14; 2(1), 49; 14, 123; AS, sūtra, 7, 33; 17, 40; AHṛ, sūtra, 6, 21-22; 7, 33; 3, 12; 22, 29.

Māshaparṇī

Synonyms: Kṛshṇavṛntā, Parṇinī, Pāṇḍulomaśā, Ṛshiproktā, Hayapuchchī, Kāmbojī, Simhapuchchikā, Mahāsahā, Ārdhramāshā, Māmsamāshā, Mangalyā, Aśvapuchchī, Kalyāṇī, Vajramūlī, Visāraṇī, Śāliparṇi, Bahuphalā, Svayambhūh, Sulabhā, Viśambhikā, Sūryaparṇī, Pāṇḍurā.

Hin.	-	Māshoṇi, Mashvan
Vernacular	-	Māshavanī (Ḍalhana)
Tam.	-	Kāṭṭualandu
Ben.	-	Māshāni
Mah.	-	Rān-uḍīd
Tel.	-	Kāru-minumulu
Kan.	-	Kāḍu-uddu

Botanical Name: Teramnus labialis Spreng (Syn. - Glycine labialis Linn)

Natural Order: Leguminosae

Habitat: Throughout India.

Description: This is a very variable, climbing or wide-spreading, hairy herb with leaves three-foliate, the leaflets membranous or sub-coriaceous, elliptic and ovate-oblong. The flowers are red, pink, purple or white in lax, axillary racemes. The pods are narrowly linear, straight or recurved with oblong, truncate or slightly rounded, smooth, dark brown seeds.

Medicinal Action:

Rasa : Bitter and sweet
Guṇa : Dry
Vīrya : Cold

It aggravates kapha, alleviates vāta and pitta, purifies the blood, is nutritive, an aphrodisiac, constipative, strength-giving, enhances the complexion, promotes growth of hair and is beneficial in swellings, fever, burning pains, bleeding from internal organs, cough, tuberculosis and diseases of traumatic origin.

Therapeutic Hints:

1. It is said to enhance the immunity of the body (CS, sūtra, 4, 9; AHṛ, sūtra, 15, 8).
2. It is also said to be aphrodisiac (CS, sūtra, 4, 12) and to increase breast-milk (SS, sūtra, 38, 35-36).

Masūrah

Synonyms: Rāgadālih, Mangalyā, Pṛthubījakah, Sūrah, Kalyāṇabījah, Gurubījah, Masūrakah, Vrīhikānchanah, Gabholikah, Tāmbūlarāgah, Hālāsakah, Pittabheshajam, Satīnāh, Chaṇakāh.

Hin.	-	Masur
Ben.	-	Masur
Tel.	-	Masara-pappu, Siri-senaga-pappu
Kan.	-	Kirugulḷi

Botanical Name: Lens esculenta Moench (Syn. L. culinaris Med; Ervum lens Linn)

Natural Order: Leguminosae

Habitat: A cold weather crop throughout India.

Description: This is an annual with a stem 6-18 inches high, erect, slender and weak, with many long branches ascending from the base. The leaves are numerous, alternate, spreading, and very shortly stalked. The leaflets are sessile, alternate or sub-opposite, entire and narrowly lanceolate-oblong. Flowers are small, pale blue and in racemose clusters of 2-4. The pod is broadly oblong or squarish, laterally compressed, about 1/2 inch long. Seeds, about 1/6 inch in diameter, lenticular with the edge sharp or blunt.

Varieties: There are two varieties : Masūra proper (which is black) and Mangalyakā (which is pale-white) (Ḍalhaṇa on SS, sūtra, 46, 30).

Medicinal Action:

Rasa : Sweet and astringent
Astringent and bitter (the leaves and stem)
Guṇa : Light, bry and viśada
Vīrya : Cold

It aggravates vāta, alleviates kapha and pitta,

enhances the complexion, is constipative, heart tonic, emaciating, appetizing, beneficial to the eyes, causes abdominal tumours, and sprue, and is useful in dysuria and bleeding from internal organs.

References: CS, sūtra, 27, 28; AHṛ, sūtra, 6, 17.

Māyāphalam

Synonyms: Mayiphalam, Chchidrāphalam, Keśaranjanam, Śiśubheshajam

Hin. - Majūphal

Botanical Name: Quercus infectoria Oliv

Natural Order: Fagaceae

Habitat: Greece, Asia Minor and Syria.

Description: This is a shrub or rarely a small tree, erect with irregular spreading branches and brownish-grey bark. The leaves are alternate, stalked, broadly oval- or obovate-oblong, rounded at both ends and rather shallowly cut into large rounded teeth or lobes.

Medicinal Action:

Rasa : Astringent
Guṇa : Dry and light
Vīrya : Cold
Vipāka : Pungent

It alleviates kapha and pitta, aggravates vāta, is appetizing, constipative, and removes debility and looseness of joints.

Mayūra-śikhā

Synonyms: Sāhasra-madhukchchada

Medicinal Action:

Rasa : Sweet, astringent and sour
Guṇa : Light
Vīrya : Cold
Vipāka : Sour

Action-Uses: It alleviates kapha and pitta, and is beneficial in dysuria, diarrhoea and diseases of children.

Methikā

Synonyms: Methinī, Dīpanī, Bahupatrikā, Vedhanī, Gandhabījā, Jyothih, Gandhaphalā, Vallarī, Chandrikā, Manthā, Miśrapushpā, Kairavī, Kunchikā, Bahuparṇī, Munīndudhā, Pītabījā.

Hin. - Methi
Kan. - Menṭe-gida, Mentya
Tam. - Vendayam
Tel. - Mentulu
Mal. - Uluva
Eng. - Fenugreek

Botanical Name: Trigonella foenum-graceum Linn

Natural Order: Leguminosae

Habitat: Punjab and Kashmir. Cultivated in many parts of India.

Description: This is an annual herb 1-2 feet high with an erect, slightly branched, cylindrical, hollow stem and tapering root. The leaves are alternate, trifoliate, entire, ciliate and longstalked, while the leaflets are shortly stalked, glabrous, oblongovate and blunt or emarginate at the apex. Flowers are sessile, solitary in the axils of the leaves and pale-yellow in colour.

Varieties: There is a wild variety dalled Vejikā.

Medicinal Action:

Rasa : Bitter and pungent
Guṇa : Dry and light
Vīrya : Hot

It alleviates vāta and kapha, is constipative, non-aphrodisiac, appetizing, a heart tonic, strength-giving, and aggravates bleeding from internal organs. It relieves fever, anorexia, vomiting, gout, cough, haemorrhoids and tuberculosis. It cures many diseases of horses.

Vejikā aggravates vāta.

Reference: Ḍalhaṇa on SS, sūtra, 46, 253.

Miśreyā

Synonyms: Madhurika, Tālaparṇī, Miśih, Śāleyah, Śītaśivah, Vanajā, Avākpushpī, Cchatrā, Samhitapushpikā, Surasā, Trishāharī, Tāpasapriyā, Ghoshavatī, Gandhādhikā, Śata-pushpā.

Hin.	- Sonf
Ben.	- Mauri
Kan.	- Sabbasige,
Mah.	- Baḍī-sonf
Tel.	- Pedda-jeelakarra,
Eng.	- Fennel seeds

Botanical Name: Foeniculum vulgare Mill

Natural Order: Umbelliferae

Habitat: Extensively cultivated in India.

Description: This plant which grows upto 1 ft. in height has pinnately compound, dark green leaves, and yellowish, small sized flowers. The fruit is small, oval-shaped, slightly compressed on either side and yellowish-brown in colour.

Medicinal Action:

Rasa	: Bitter, pungent and sweet Pungent and sweet (the distilled water)
Guṇa	: Unctous
Vīrya	: Cold
Vipāka	: Pungent

It alleviates all the three doshas, fecilitates conception, purifies the blood, increases breast-milk, is aphrodisiac, appetizing, strength-giving, laxative and is useful in fever, abdominal colic, burning pains, eye-diseases, thirst, ulcers, vomiting, diarrhoea, indigestion, enlargement of the spleen, worms, tuberculosis, and haemorrhoids and diseases of traumatic origin.

The distilled water alleviates pitta, is appetizing, digestive and relieves thirst, vomiting and burning pains.

References: SS, chikitsā, 38, 44.

Muchukundā

Synonyms: Kshatravṛkshah, Chitrakah, Prativishṇukah, Dīrgha-pushpah, Bahupatrah, Sadalah, Muṇḍīvṛkshānukārakah, Harivallabhah, Supushpah, Raktaprasavah, Arghyārh-alakshaṇah.

Hin.	- Kanak champa, Mechkand
Tam.	- Cembolavu, Senolugu
Tel.	- Lolugu-cheṭṭu
Ben.	- Muskunda

Botanical Name: Pterospermum acerifolium Willd

Natural Order: Sterculiaceae

Habitat: Most parts of India.

Description: An evergreen tree, upto 24 metres in height, with a clean bole upto 12 metres. The bark is greyish-brown. The leaves are variable in size and shape, entire or variously lobed, oblong, cordate or sometimes peltate. The flowers are large, axillary, solitary or in pairs, white and fragrant. The capsules are oblong, 5-angled, dark brown and woody; seeds winged and brown.

Medicinal Action:

Rasa	: Bitter and pungent
Vīrya	: Hot

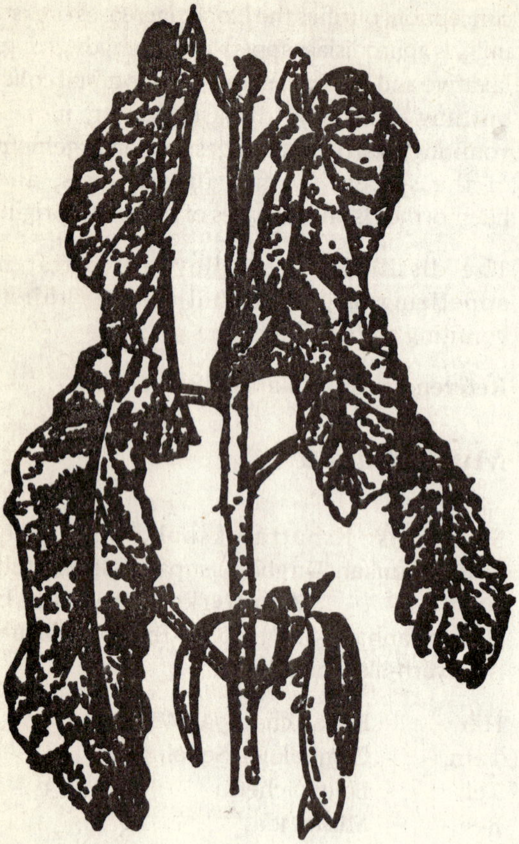

It alleviates kapha and pitta, purifies the blood, and is beneficial in cough, diseases of throat, skin diseases, oedema, ulcers, pruritus and toxicosis.

The flowers are useful in headaches.

References: SS, chikitsā, 18, 10.

Mudgah

Synonyms: Sūpaśreshṭhah, Varṇārhah, Rasottamah, Bhuktipradah, Hayānandah, Suphalah, Vājibhojanah.

Hin. - Moong
Tam. - Pachchaipayaru
Kan. - Pachche hesaru
Tel. - Pesara-cheṭṭu
Mal. - Cherupayaru
Eng. - Green gram

Botanical Name: Phaseolus radiatus Linn (Syn. P. aureus Roxb)

Natural Order: Leguminosae

Habitat: Widely cultivated all over India.

Varieties: There are many varieties based on the colour e.g. white, dark, yellow, green, black, etc. (SS, sūtra, 13, 12).

Medicinal Action:

Rasa : Sweet and astringent
Guṇa : Light and dry
Vīrya : Cold
Vipāka : Pungent

It alleviates kapha and pitta, does not excessively vitiate vāta, purifies the blood, is beneficial to the eyes and is useful in fever, ulcers, diseases of the throat and eyes, urinary disorders and indigestion.

Therapeutic Hints:

1. Mudga is regarded as the best among pulses (SS, sūtra, 25, 38).
2. It is beneficial for all living beings (SS, sūtra, 20, 5).

References: CS, sūtra, 27, 23; chikitsā, 3, 156-157; SS, sūtra, 46-29, 367, 373, 374; chikitsā, 23, 12; 17, 43; AS, sūtra, 7, 36; AHṛ, sūtra, 6, 17; 41; KS, bhojana.

Mudgaparṇī

Synonyms: Kākamudgā, Sahā, Śimbiparṇikā, Kshudrasahā, Śimbhī, Mārjāragandhikā, Hrasvā, Śūrpaparṇī, Kurangikā, Kośila, Vanodbhavā, Vanamudgā, Araṇyamudgā.

Hin. - Mugavan
Vernacular - Mugavani (Ḍalhaṇa)

Ben. - Mugani
Mah. - Sānamūng, Rānmūg
Guj. - Magavalyā
Kan. - Avare-giḍa, Kāḍu-hesaru
Tam. - Elippayaru, Nalippayar
Mal. - Cheruvidukol
Tel. - Pilli-pesolu, Pilli-pesaru

Botanical Name: Phaseolus trilobus Ait (Syn. Dolichos trilobatus Linn)

Natural Order: Leguminosae

Habitat: Throughout India.

Description: A diffuse, spreading herb with many branches prostrate on the ground and reaching a length of even 6 ft. The stem is slender, wiry, angled, sparsely pubescent and tinged with purple. The leaves are trifoliate, alternate, with large, oblong-ovate stipules. Flowers are small, yellow in few flowered cluster-like racemes on long axillary peduncles. The fruit is a cylindric pod with small, sub-cylindric and dark brown seeds.

Medicinal Action:

Rasa : Bitter and sweet
Guṇa : Light and dry
Vīrya : Cold

It alleviates all the three doshas, is an aphrodisiac, constipative, beneficial to the eyes, styptic and is useful in tuberculosis, swellings, fever, burning pains, sprue, haemorrhoids, diarrhoea, cough, gout and worms.

Therapeutic Hints: It enhances immunity (CS, sūtra, 4, 9; AS, sūtra, 15, 6; AHṛ, sūtra, 15, 8) and is an aphrodisiac (CS, sūtra, 4, 12).

References: SS, sūtra, 38, 35

Mukushṭhakah

Synonyms: Vanamudgah, Kṛmīlakah, Amṛtah, Araṇyamudgah, Vallīmudgah, Rājamudgah, Nigūḍhakah, Kulīnakah.

Hin. - Moṭh
Ben. - Vanmudga, Vanmūg
Mah. - Maṭakyā
Tel. - Aenugu-pesalu, Lankali
Eng. - Aconite-leaved Kidney Bean

Botanical Name: Phaseolus aconitifolius Jacq

Natural Order: Leguminosae

Habitat: Himalayas to Ceylon, tropical region upto 4,000 ft. in the North-West.

Description: A diffuse, trailing herb with many branches prostrate on the ground. The leaflets are usually deeply trilobed. The flowers are small and yellow in few clustered racemes on long axillary peduncles.

Medicinal Action:

Rasa : Astringent and sweet
Guṇa : Light
Vīrya : Cold

It alleviates kapha, aggravates vāta, is appetizing, constipative, and is beneficial in haemorrhoids, abdominal tumours, bleeding from internal organs, fever, burning pains, vomiting, and tuberculosis. It facilitates growth of worms, but is useful as an article of diet.

The soup alleviates kapha and pitta, purifies the blood, is aphrodisiac, nutritive, appetizing, digestive and beneficial to the eyes.

Mūlakam

Synonyms: Hariparṇam, Bhūmikshāram, Nīlakandam, Nīlakaṇṭham, Mahākandam, Ruchivyam, Hastidantakam, Rājālukam, Karukandakam, Dīrghamūlakam, Dīrghapatrakam, Mṛtkshāram, Kandamūlam, Śankhamūlam, Kshāramulam, Śimbīphalam.

Hin. - Mūli
Ben. - Mulā
Mah. - Mūḷā
Kan. - Mulangi
Tam. - Muḷḷangi
Mal. - Kanakapala
Eng. - Garden radish

Botanical Name: Raphanus sativus Linn

Natural Order: Cruciferae

Habitat: Cultivated all over India upto 16,000 ft.

Description: This is an annual or biennial bristly herb with a white or brightly coloured tuberous root stock. Stems are simple or branched and erect. The basal leaves are long and coarsely toothed, while the cauline leaves are simple and linear. The flowers are in long terminal racemes, usually white or lilac with purple veins. The fruits are inflated with a long tapering beak.

Varieties: BP classifies Mūlaka into two varieties : small and big. Other texts mention varieties such as Chāṇakyamūlakam.

Synonyms: Vāneyam, Vishṇuguptakam, Sthūlamūlam, Mahākandam, Kouṭilyam, Marusambhavam, Miśram, Gṛnjanam, Piṇḍamūlakam, etc.

Medicinal Action:

Rasa : Pungent
Guṇa : Light and sharp (the small variety and the expressed oil)
Heavy and dry (the big variety)
Vīrya : Hot
Vipāka : Pungent (the oil)

The small variety alleviates all the three doshas, is digestive, appetizing, beneficial to the voice, and is useful in fever, dyspnoea, diseases of the nose, throat and eyes, heart diseases, abdominal tumours and haemorrhoids.

The big variety aggravates all three doshas. If however, it is partaken of along with unctous substances (like ghee etc.) it alleviates all three doshas.

The dried root alleviates all three doshas, antidotes poison and relieves swellings.

The flowers alleviate kapha and pitta, while the fruits alleviate kapha and vāta.

The leaves are digestive. If tender leaves are taken with unctous substances, they alleviate all three doshas. If taken without them, they aggravate kapha and pitta.

The oil alleviates kapha and vata, is a laxative and beneficial in worms, skin diseases, urinary disorders, headaches and haemorrhoids.

A soup prepared out of Mūlaka alleviates kapha, is beneficial in salivation, stiffness of jaw and neck, urinary disorders, anorexia, catarrh and cough.

Therapeutic Hints:

1. A paste of the dried root is used as external application in certain skin-diseases (AS, chikitsā, 20).
2. It is useful in intestinal worms (CS, vimāna, 7, 17).
3. There is a poisonous variety which causes vomiting, hiccoughs, oedema, discolouration and unconsciousness (SS, kalpa, 2, 5; AS, uttara, 40).

References: CS, sūtra, 14, 31; 27, 168; chikitsā, 28, 172-SS, sūtra, 37, 9; 40, 5; 45, 115; 46, 46, 47, 240, 241, 372; KS, khila, 4, 40; AHṛ, sūtra 6, 102-105.

Muṇḍanikā

Synonyms: Śrāvaṇī, Muṇḍī, Bhūtaghnī, Palankashā, Kadambapushpā, Aruṇā, Kumbhalā, Bhikshuh, Śravaṇa-śīrshikā, Tapodhanā, Pravrajita, Parivrāji.

Hin. - Gorak-muṇḍi
Ben. - Murmuria
Mah. - Boḍtharā
Tam. - Vishṇukarandai, Koṭṭaka
Kan. - Karaṇḍe, Mūdugaṭṭina-giḍa
Tel. - Tella-boḍa-taramu
Mal. - Aṭakāmaṇiyam

Botanical Name: Sphaeranthus indicus Linn (Syn. S. hirtus Willd; S. mollis Roxb)

Natural Order: Compositae

Habitat: Throughout India, ascending the Himalayas up to 5,000 ft. from Kumaon to Sikkim.

Description: An annual, much branched aromatic herb, with a glandular hairy stem and branches cylindric with toothed wings. The leaves are simple decurrent, ovobate-oblong, rounded or sub-acute, glandular hairy, spinous serrate or dentate. The ovary is inferior, one-celled and achenes are angular and glabrous.

Varieties: There is a bigger variety - Mahā-muṇḍī (Synonyms:Mahā-śrāvaṇikā, Bhūkadambikā, Avyathā, Kroḍachūḍā, Mātā, Sthavirā, Bhūkanda, Alambushā, Cchinnagranthikā, Vṛddhā).

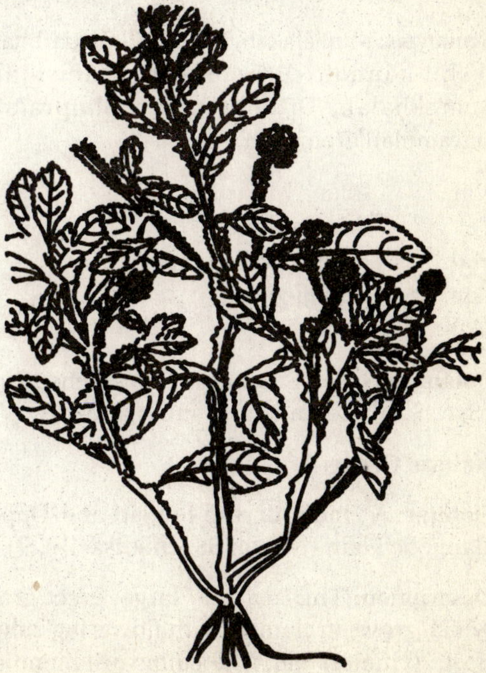

Medicinal Action:

Rasa : Bitter, sweet and astringent (Muṇanikā)
Bitter and sweet (Mahā-muṇḍi)
Guṇa : Light and sharp
Vīrya : Hot
Vipāka : Pungent

Muṇḍanikā alleviates kapha and vāta, is a purgative, brain tonic, strength-giving, bestows longevity, and is beneficial in glandular swellings, dysuria, worms, anaemia, elephantiasis, anorexia, epilepsy, enlargement of spleen, obesity, haemorrhoids, insanity, menstrual disorders, cough, skin diseases, diarrhoea, vomiting, dyspnoea and toxicosis.

Mahā-muṇḍī alleviates vāta, is appetizing, beneficial to the throat and voice and relieves urinary disorders. It has all the medicinal properties of Muṇḍanikā.

Munjah

Synonyms: Munjātakah, Bāṇah, Sthūladarbhah, Ikshu-kāṇḍah, Bṛhmaṇyah, Vānīrajah, Sumekhalah, Dṛḍhamūlah, Bahuprajah, Dūramūlah, Ranjanah.

Hin. - Mūnj
Tel. - Munja-darbha
Mal. - Munja, Mekhalapullu
Kan. - Munji-giḍa
Mah. - Moḷ

Botanical Name: Saccharum bengalense Retz (Syn. S. ciliare Anders; S. mumja Roxb).

Natural Order: Grámineae

Habitat: N. India, in the Punjab and Upper Gangetic Plain (NIS on SS, chikitsā, 39, 9).

Description: This is a very large, erect grass which grows in clumps, with flowering culms up to 6 metres tall. The culms are biennial, pale, solid, pithy, smooth with an inconspicuous growth ring and root zone. The leaves are glaucous green, rough on the margins, with dense hairs close to the ligule. The panicle is pale cream to dark reddish purple, and 30-60 cms long.

Varieties: There is another variety - Bhadra-munjah.

Synonyms: Bāṇah, Tejanah, Chakshu-veshṭanah.

Medicinal Action:

Rasa : Sweet and astringent
Vīrya : Cold

It alleviates all the three doshas, is an aphrodisiac, auspicious and is beneficial in burning pains, thirst, herpes, dyspepsia, dysuria and diseases of the eyes.

References: CS, siddhi, 2, 22, SS, sūtra, 45, 18.

Murā

Synonyms: Talaparṇī, Gandhakuṭī, Surabhī, Bhūrigandhā, Gandhinī, Gandhamādinī.

Medicinal Action:

Rasa : Bitter, sweet, astringent and pungent
Guṇa : Light
Vīrya : Cold

It alleviates vāta and pitta, purifies the blood, is auspicious, aromatic and is beneficial in fever, skin diseases, cough, dyspnoea, gout, burning, vertigo, thirst, syncope, toxicosis.

References: AS, uttara, 9.

Mūshikaparṇī (Mūshika-karṇī)

Synonyms: Ākhuparṇī, Vṛshaparṇī, Mūshakarnī, Bhūmicharā, Chitrā, Dravantī, Śambarī, Bhūdharāśrayā, Kṛśikā, Indurakarṇī, Nyagrodhī,

Vṛśchikakarṇī, Bahukarṇikā, Mātā, Chaṇḍā, Bahupādikā, Pratyakśreṇī, Vṛshā, Ādhibhū, Suvarṇī.

Hin.	-	Bhopalī, Mūshākāni
Ben.	-	Indurkāni
Mah.	-	Undīrkāni, Bhopanī
Kan.	-	Valli haruhe, Ili-kivi-giḍa

Botanical Name: Ipomea reniformis Chois (Syn. Salvinia cuscullata Roxb).

Natural Order: Convolvalaceae

Description: A creeping herb, rooting at nodes, The leaves are up to 1.9 cm long, kidney shaped or ovate-cordate, broader than long and toothed. The flowers are axillary and yellow, with hairy sepals. The plant flowers in the rainy season and cold weather.

Varieties: There are two varieties viz. small and big.

Parts Used: The whole plant.

Medicinal Action:

Rasa : Pungent, bitter and astringent

It alleviates kapha and pitta, is a digestive and is useful in flatulence, fever, abdominal colic, worms and urinary disorders.

Therapeutic Hints:

1. The tender leaves are used in medicine (AS, chikitsā, 22).
2. It is used externally in swellings (CS, chikitsā, 17, 72).
3. The leaves are given internally in worms (SS, uttara, 54, 27).

References: CS, sūtra, 4, 11.

Mushkakah

Synonyms: Mokshakah, Mushtih, Mūrkhakah, Mochakah, Kshāraśreshṭhah, Kshāravṛkshah, Ghanṭakah, Tīkshṇah, Kālasthalī, Vanavāsī, Kshudrapāṭalī, Jaṭāluh, Vishāpahah.

Hin.	-	Banpalās, Moshā,
Vernacular	-	Mokhak, Mokhaḍ (Ḍalhaṇa)
Ben.	-	Ghanṭa-pārūl,
Kan.	-	Maggārti-mara, Ganṭe
Mah.	-	Mokhāḍā, (K)
Tam.	-	Mogalinga
Tel.	-	Mokkapu-cheṭṭu, Kaṇapa-cheṭṭu

Botanical Name: Schrebera swietenioides Roxb

Natural Order: Oleaceae

Habitat: Sub-Himalaya Tract from Kumaon eastwards, Madhya Bharat, Rajasthan.

Description: A moderate-sized, deciduous tree with grey branches which are thickened at the nodes. The leaves are opposite, exstipulate, with ovate, entire leaflets which often have oblique bases. The flowers are yellowish-brown, fragrant, nocturnal, in terminal trichotomous cymes. The fruit is a loculicidal two-valved pear-shaped capsule with eight seeds ending in long wings. The tree flowers in February-May; the fruits are borne in September-November.

Varieties: There are two varieties, white and black.

Medicinal Action:

Rasa : Pungent, bitter and sour
Vīrya : Hot

It alleviates kapha and vāta, is constipative, appetizing, digestive, beneficial in enlargements of spleen, abdominal tumours, ascites, obesity, pruritus, dysuria, renal colic, worms, vomiting, earache and toxicosis.

The flowers alleviates kapha and pitta and are useful in skin diseases.

The gum alleviates vāta and pitta, is an aphrodisiac and used in tuberculosis.

The fruits are appetizing, purgative, and are beneficial in abdominal tumours, urinary disorders, haemorrhoids, anaemia, ascites and sterility (impurities of sperm).

Note: The flowers are used for culinary purposes (SS, sūtra, 46, 284) and are valuable in skin diseases (ibid).

References: Chkp. on CS, Chikitsā, 15, 189; 26, 192-193; Ḍalhaṇa on SS, sūtra, 11, 11; 38, 20; AS, uttara, 40; sūtra, 39, 10; AHṛ, sūtra, 15, 32.

Mustā

Synonyms: Ambudharah, Meghah, Ghanah, Rājakaserukah, Varāhah, Abdah, Gāngeyah, Kuruvindakah, Jīmūtah, Vṛshadhvankshī, Nādeyah, Paripelavah, Kuruvindah, Ambubhṛtah, Abhranāmakah, Vāleyah, Sugandhih, Granthilā.

Hin.	- Mothā
Ben.	- Muthā
Mah.	- Mothe
Tam.	- Korai -kilangu, Ambudam
Kan.	- Tunge-hullu, Koranāri-geḍḍe, Chekina-geḍḍe
Tel.	- Tunga-musti, Bhadra-musta
Mal.	- Karimuttana

Botanical Name: Cyperus rotundus Linn

Natural Order: Cyperaceae

Habitat: Throughout India; common in waste grounds, gardens and roadsides in open areas and up to an elevation of 6,000 ft.

Description: An erect, glabrous herb growing to a height of 3-9 inches with perennial underground stems spreading over a large area. Leaves are dark green, glabrous, rather thick linear and very acute at the tips. The tubers are roundish, nutlike, sweet-smelling round and black externally ,white internally.

Varieties: There are two other varieties :

1. Nāgaramustā

Synonyms: Nādeyī, Kacheharuhā, Chūdālā, Chakrāngī, Piṇḍamustā, Anukesarā, Uchchaṭā, Śiśirā, Kalāpinī.

Botanical Name: Cyperus scariosus R. Br

2. Bhadramustā

Synonyms: Kurubilvam, Kuṭannaṭam, Himā, Balyā, Granthimah.

Medicinal Action:

Rasa : Bitter, astringent and pungent
Astringent, bitter, pungent and sour (Bhadramustā)

Vīrya : Cold

It alleviates kapha and pitta, purifies the blood, is appetizing, digestive, constipating, brain-tonic, aromatic, enhances the complexion and is beneficial in thirst, fever, anorexia, worms, diarrhoea, ulcers, burning pains, pruritus, dyspepsia and abdominal colic.

Therapeutic Hints:

1. That variety which grows in damp and wet areas is considered superior.
2. It is emaciating, digestive, purifies breast-milk, relieves thirst and pruritus, and is constipative and appetizing (CS, sūtra, 4, 9, 11, 12, 14; 25, 40).
3. A decoction of mustā and ginger is beneficial in spring season (AS, sūtra, 4, 27).

References: SS, sūtra, 38, 54-55; KS, vishesha-kalpa; AS, sūtra, 16, 18, 40; 12, 17; AHṛ, sūtra, 15, 40.

N

Nāḍī-śākā

Synonyms: Kāla-śakā, Nāḍikā, Paṭṭa-śakah

Hin. - Pāṭ, Paṭuyā
Ben. - Pāṭ
Mah. - Moṭhe-chonche
Kan. - Chunchula-giḍa
Tel. - Periṇta-cheṭṭu
Mal. - Vakk
Eng. - Jute plant

Botanical Name: Corchorus olitorious Linn.

Natural Order: Tiliaceae

Habitat: Wild in most parts of India.

Description: This is a herbaceous annual, with straight slender stems, about 10 feet high under cultivation. It has glabrous leaves, small yellow flowers and roughly globular pods with copper-coloured seeds.

Medicinal Action:

Rasa : Bitter (one variety)
Sweet (another variety)
Guṇa : Slimy (the sweet variety)
Vīrya : Cold (the sweet variety)

The bitter variety is beneficial in skin diseases and worms. The sweet variety aggravates kapha and vāta, and is constipative.

The dried leaves, called Nalitam, alleviate kapha and pitta and relieve fever. The water in which the leaves are infused is appetizing, health-giving and alleviates pitta.

Nāgakesarah

Synonyms: Chāmpeyah, Kesarah, Mahaushadham, Rājapushpah, Nāgapushpah, Phalakah, Svaraghātanah, Suvarṇākhyah, Bhujangākhyah, Shaṭpadapriyah, Pushpa-rechanah, Kinjalkah, Pinjarah.

Hin. - Nāgkesar
Kan. - Nāgasampige-mara
Tel. - Nāgakesaramu
Mal. - Nagachampakam

Tam. - Nāgeśuram
Velutta - Champakam
Eng. - Iron wood tree

Botanical Name: Mesua ferrea Linn (Syn. M. penduculata Wight; M. speciosa Choisy).

Natural Order: Guttiferae

Habitat: Most parts of India.

Description: A medium-sized to large, handsome, evergreen tree, often buttressed at the base, with a dense crown, and grey and smooth bark. Leaves are opposite, very variable, glabrous, shining above, generally covered with a wax-like white powder underneath, and lanceolate. Flowers are solitary, fragrant, white with a central bunch of yellow stamens. Fruits are ovoid, pointed, 1-4 seeded. Seeds are upto 2.5 cm in diameter, dark brown, shining.

Medicinal Action:

Rasa : Bitter and astringent
Guṇa : Light and dry
Vīrya : Slightly hot

It alleviates kapha and pitta, purifies the blood, is a digestive and is beneficial in fever, pruritus, toxicosis, thirst, excessive perspiration, vomiting, nausea, bad odour, skin diseases, herpes, palpitation, urinary disorders, gout, diseases of the throat, headaches, haemorrhoids and vomiting.

References: SS, sūtra, 38, 24.

Nāgarangah

Synonyms: Nārangah, Tvak-sugandhah, Mukhapriyah, Airāvatikah, Vaktrādhi-vāsanah, Yogī, Gandhāḍhyah.

Hin. - Nārangī, Santarā
Ben. - Nranga - ebuka, kamalā - nebu
Mah. - Nāring, Santrā
Tel. - Nārangam, Nārinja
Mal. - Nārana
Kan. - Kittale-mara, Heraḷe-giḍa
Eng. - Sweet orange, Mandarin orange Loose-skinned orange

Botanical Name: Citrus reticulata Blanco

Natural Order: Rutaceae

Habitat: Met with throughout India.

Description: This is a bushy, evergreen, glabrous, moderate-sized tree with rather small and slender leaves; with short, almost wingless petioles. The fruit is globose or sub-globose, flattened on the top, with thin, loose rind easily separating from the segments, bright orange or scarlet orange when fully ripe. The pulp is juicy, sweet to sub-acid.

Varieties: There are two varieties according to BP.

Medicinal Action:

Rasa : Sweet and slightly sour
Guṇa : Heavy and viśada
Vīrya : Hot

It alleviates vāta, is aromatic, a laxative, strength-giving, an aphrodisiac, beneficial in fatigue, worms and abdominal colic.

Nāgārjunī

Synonyms: Yoginī, Laghu-dugdhikā,

Hin. - Dūdhī-kalav, Duddhī, Dudhiyā
Ben. - Dudūle, Dudhyā, Dudhi
Mah. - Thor-dudhī, Laghu-dudhī

Botanical Name: Euphorbia thymifolia Linn

Natural Order: Euphorbeaceae

Habitat: Throughout India in the plains and lower hills.

Description: A small, prostrate, annual herb with many, more or less hairy, often pink stems. The leaves are small, alternate, slightly crenate in upper part, with unequal halves. The nerves are obscure, often pink. The inflorescence consists of a cup-shaped, small involucre. The fruit is a hairy, three-valved capsule with rounded lobes. The plant flowers during rains and after.

Varieties: There are two other varieties :

1. Dugdhikā

Synonyms: Kshīrātmikā, Marudbhavā, Svāduparṇī, Grāhiṇī, Kachcharā, Tāmramūlī

2. Dugdhaphenī

Synonyms: Payahphenī, Payasvinī, Lūtārih, Vraṇaketuh, Gojāparṇī

Medicinal Action:

Rasa : Sweet, bitter, pungent and slightly saline.
Bitter, pungent and sweet (Dugdhikā)
Pungent and bitter (Dughdaphenī)

Guṇa : Dry
Heavy and dry (Dugdhikā)

Vīrya : Hot (Nagārjunī and Dugdhikā)
Cold (Dugdhapheni)

Nāgārjunī alleviates kapha and vāta, is a heart tonic, nutritive, an aphrodisiac, constipative, promotes conception, and is beneficial in urinary disorders, skin diseases and worms.

Dugdhikā alleviates kapha, aggravates vāta, promotes conception, is a diuretic, laxative and aphrodisiac, and is useful in skin diseases and worms.

Dugdhaphenī antidotes poison, is appetizing, and if used properly bestows longevity and good health. It assists in the healing of ulcers.

Nāgavallī

Synonyms: Tāmbūlī, Nāginī, Divābhīshṭā, Āmodajanani, Saptaśirā, Phaṇivallī, Soumyā, Bhujagalatā, Bhakshya patrā, Mukharāgakarī, Hṛdyā, Śrama-bhanjanī, Parṇagṛhāśayā, Mukhabhūshaṇā, Bahulā, Anantā, Pātālavāsinī, Yāvanīpriyā, Amṛtā, Kāmajananī.

Hin. - Pān
Tam. - Vettilai
Kan. - Vīlyada-baḷḷi
Tem. - Tamalapāku
Mah. - Nāgavel
Mal. - Vettila
Eng. - Betel leaf plant

Botanical Name: Piper betle Linn

Natural Order: Piperaceae

Habitat: Cultivated in hotter and damper parts of India.

Description: This is a shrub with semi woody stems climbing by short adventitious rootlets. The young parts are glabrous. The leaves which are bright green and thick are alternate, broadly ovate, slightly cordate, entire, and petioled. The fruits are sparingly produced and when produced, immersed in the fleshy spike.

Varieties: There are a number of varieties, e.g. Śrīvāṭī, Amlavāṭī, Śātasī, Sadāśira, Amlasarā, Paṭulikā, Hesanīya etc. They have many properties in common.

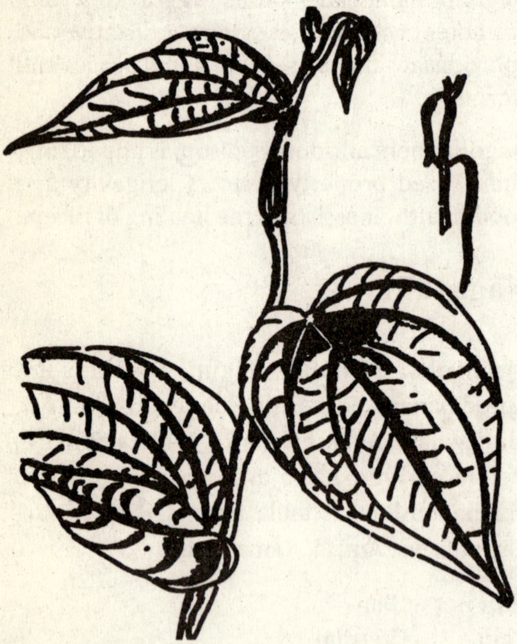

Medicinal Action:

Rasa : Pungent, bitter, sweet and astringent
Guṇa : Dry, light, sharp and viśada.
Vīrya : Hot

It alleviates kapha and vāta, is appetizing, strength giving, is cchedana, stimulates the sex urge, induces burning pains and bleeding from internal organs, and is beneficial in bad breath, fatigue, catarrh, cough and worms.

The fruits alleviate kapha and vāta are aromatic and a heart-tonic.

Therapeutic Hints:

1. It relieves excess salivation and is useful in diseases of throat (SS, chikitsā, 24, 22).
2. It is beneficial after rising from bed, after meals, after bathing and after emesis (ibid, 24, 23-24).
3. The leaves when chewed with the fruits of pūga (betel), jāti, lavanga, kaṭuka and kakkola and extract of karpūra cleanse and purify the mouth (CS, sūtra, 5, 77).

Nalah

Synonyms: Śunyamadhyah, Dhamanah, Mṛdupātrah, Vamśapatrah, Cchidrāntah, Kukshirandhrah, Kīchakah, Dīrghavamśah, Mṛthypushpah, Nartakah, Poṭagalah, Randhrī.

Description: The grass is like Dūrva in appearance, but with hollow stalks (Ḍalhaṇa).

Varieties: There is a bigger variety called Mahānalah.

Synonyms: Devanalah, Vanyah, Nalottamah, Sthūlanalah, Suranālah, Sthūladaṇḍah.

Medicinal Action:

Rasa : Sweet, astringent and bitter
Sweet and slightly astringent (Mahānalah)
Vīrya : Cold

It alleviates kapha and pitta, purifies the blood, is appetizing, strength giving, diuretic and is beneficial in dysuria, burning pains, herpes, urinary disorders, heart diseases, and menstrual disorders.

The bigger variety is considered superior.

Therapeutic Hints:

1. Its root is externally applied in haemorrhages (CS, chikitsā, 4, 102).
2. It is used both externally and internally in dog-bites (AS, uttara, 46).
3. It is useful when applied externally in swelling of Pitta type (SS, sūtra, 37, 4).

References: SS, sūtra, 38, 10-11, 75; chikitsā, 5 8; AS, sūtra, 16, 18; AHṛ. sūtra, 15, 24.

Namaskāri

Synonyms: Lajjāluh, Śamīpatrā, Samangā, Anjalikārikā, Raktapādī, Tāmra, Khadirakā, Sankochinī, Prasāriṇī, Gaṇḍamālikā, Bahoushadhi.

Hin.	-	Lajjāvati
Ben.	-	Lājak
Mah.	-	Lājāḷu, Sankoraṇī,
Tam.	-	Toṭṭalshurungi, Toṭṭāl-vāḍi
Guj.	-	Riśāmaṇī
Mal.	-	Toṭṭalvāḍi
Tel.	-	Munugudāmaramu, Nidragannikā
Kan.	-	Nāchike-giḍa, Muṭṭidare-muniva
Eng.	-	Sensitive plant

Botanical Name: Mimosa pudica Linn

Natural Order: Leguminosae

Habitat: Naturalised more or less throughout India.

Description: A diffuse undershrub, with stems and branches sparingly prickly. Leaves sensitive, bi-pinnate and petiolate. Leaflets are linear-oblong with small bristles below. Flowers occur as globose heads on penduncles which are up to 1 inch in length, and are pinkish in colour. Fruit is a pod, flat, consisting of 3-6 seeded joints.

Varieties: There is another variety - Viparīta Lajjāluh, which is smaller in size but has bigger leaves.

Parts Used: Entire plant.

Medicinal Action:

Rasa	:	Bitter, astringent and pungent
		Pungent (Viparīta-lajjāluh)
Vīrya	:	Cold
		Hot (Viparīta-lajjāluh)

It alleviates kapha and pitta, purifies the blood, and is beneficial in bleeding from internal organs, diarrhoea, menstrual disorders, oedema, burning pains, fatigue, ulcers, skin diseases and dyspnoea.

Therapeutic Hints: It is valuable in diarrhoea, in promoting healing of wounds and fractures and in ulcers (AHṛ, 15, 38; AS, sūtra, 16, 32; uttara, 49).

Nandīvṛkshah

Synonyms: Tūṇī, Tunnakah, Śrīpatih, Āpītah, Tuṇikah, Kachchakah, Nandakah, Pītakah, Kāntah, Gaṇerukah, Kanakah, Kuṭheraka

Hin.	-	Tūn
Kan.	-	Biḷi-gandhagiri, Mogemara
Tel.	-	Nandī-vṛkshamu
Mal.	-	Maḍagiri-vembu
Tam.	-	Tūn
Eng.	-	Toon tree, White Cedar

Botanical Name: Cedrela toona Roxb.

Natural Order: Meliaceae

Habitat: Most parts of India.

Description: A large, deciduous tree with a thin, rusty-brown, rough bark. The leaves are paripinnate, with 10-15 pairs of lanceolate, oblique, acuminate leaflets which are glossy above and pale beneath. The white and fragrant flowers occur in panicles. The fruit is a smooth, ovoid, brown capsule, with numerous winged seeds.

Medicinal Action:

Rasa : Bitter, sweet, astringent and pungent
Guṇa : Light
Vīrya : Cold
Vipāka : Pungent

It alleviates all the three doshas, is aromatic, nutritive, constipative, aphrodisiac, purifies the blood, and is beneficial in ulcers, skin diseases, bleeding from internal organs, burning pains, headaches, white patches on skin, pruritus and glandular swellings.

References: SS, sūtra, 38, 46-49; AS, sūtra, 15, 38; 16, 32.

Nārikelah

Synonyms: Dṛḍhaphalah, Lāngalī, Kūrchaśīrshakah, Jungah, Skandhaphalah, Tṛṇarājah, Sadāphalah, Sadāpushpah, Śirahjalah, Puṭodakah, Rasaphalah, Dṛḍhanīrah, Nīlataruh, Payodharah, Mutkaṇah, Kouśikaphalah, Jaṭāphalah, Muṇḍaphalah, Viśvāmitraphalah, Tryakshaphalah, Toyagarbhah.

Hin. - Narial
Ben. - Nārikel
Kan. - Tengu, Tengine-mara
Tel. - Tenikāyi-cheṭṭu, Kobbari-cheṭṭu
Tam. - Tennamaram
Mal. - Tena
Mah. - Nāraḷ
Eng. - Cocoanut palm

Botanical Name: Cocos nucifera Linn

Natural Order: Palmae

Habitat: Cultivated in the hot, damp regions of India, especially near the sea.

Medicinal Action:

Rasa : Sweet
Guṇa : Heavy and unctous
Vīrya : Cold
Vipāka : Sweet

The fruits alleviate vāta and pitta, aggravate kapha, purify the blood, are a heart-tonic, nutritive, strength-giving, a diuretic, an aphrodisiac, constipative, hard to digest and beneficial in emaciation, thirst, tuberculosis, diseases of traumatic origin, fatigue and bleeding from internal organs. They cause internal worms.

The tender fruits particularly alleviate pitta, purify the blood, and are useful in fever, thirst, vomiting and burning pains.

The ripe fruits aggravate pitta, are appetizing, constipative, an aphrodisiac, strength-giving, nutritive and engenders burning pains if used in excess.

The dry fruit is appetizing, constipative, strengthgiving, nutritive, hard to digest and causes burning pains.

Tender cocoanut water alleviates pitta, is appetizing, a heart tonic, diuretic, an aphrodisiac, strength-giving, and relieves thirst, vomiting and syncope.

The flowers are constipative, and are useful in bleeding from the rectum, bleeding from internal organs, urinary disorders and polyuria in women.

The oil alleviates vāta and pitta, is nutritive, a brain tonic, an aphrodisiac, and is beneficial in suppression and retention of urine, urinary disorders, dyspnoea, cough, tuberculosis and diseases of traumatic origin (SS, sūtra, 45, 120; AS, sūtra, 6, 109).

References: CS, sūtra, 27, 130; kalpa, 1, 8, SS, sūtra, 46, 180, 310, 433; 45, 43-44, 120; AS, sūtra, 7, 175; 5, 19; AHr̥, sūtra, 6 119.

Nartakah

Synonyms: Nr̥tyakuṇḍah, Bhūcharā, Malīyasah, Kaṭhinah, Rāgikā, Gucchakaṇiśaha, Lāncchanah, Bahupatrakah, Madhūlikā.

Hin. - Maduā, Nartaka
Ben. - Marua
Mah. - Nāchaṇi, Nāyalī
Kan. - Rāgi
Tam. - Rāgi, Keḷva-rāgi
Tel. - Rāgulu
Eng. - Finger Millet, Rāgi

Botanical Name: Eleusine corocana Gaertn

Natural Order: Graminae

Habitat: Cultivated in all parts of India.

Description: This is an erect annual grass, from 2 to 4 ft. high with tufted stems. The stems are somewhat laterally flattened, bearing when mature, a whorl of digitate, straight or slightly incurved spikes. The spikelets are numerous, about seventy, arranged alternately, each spikelet containing four to seven seeds. The seeds are nearly globose, or somewhat flattened, varying in colour from reddish brown to nearly white.

Medicinal Action:

Rasa : Astringent, bitter and sweet
Guṇa : Light
Vīrya : Cold

It alleviates all the doshas, particularly pitta, purifies the blood, is refreshing and strength-giving.

Nikochakam

Synonyms: Chāruphalam, Abhiśukah, Sankocham, Jala-gojakam, Pistam, Sukūlakam, Dantīphalasamākr̥tī, Kollaphalam

Hin.	- Pistā
Mah.	- Piste
Tel.	- Pista
Eng.	- Pistachio Nut

Botanical Name: Pistacia vera Linn

Natural Order: Anacardiaceae

Habitat: Found mostly in North India (Ḍalhaṇa)

Medicinal Action:

Rasa : Sweet and bitter
Guṇa : Heavy and unctous
Vīrya : Hot

It aggravates pitta, alleviates kapha and vāta, purifies the blood, is a laxative, nutritive, strength giving and is useful in abdominal colic.

References: SS, sūtra, 46, 187.

Nīlā

Synonyms: Meghavarṇā, Kutsalā, Dūlī, Klītakikā, Kālā, Nīlapushpika, Grāmīṇā, Madhuparṇikā, Ranjanī, Śrīphalā, Tutthā, Tūṇī, Droṇikā, Śyāmā, Śodhinī, Bhāravāhī, Mochā, Asitā, Rangapatrī, Gandhapushpā, Sthiraraṅgā, Vṛntikā, Chāraṭī, Anjanakeśikā.

Hin.	- Nil
Mal.	- Avari
Tel.	- Nīli-cheṭṭu
Tam.	- Nīlam
Kan.	- Oḷḷe-nīli
Eng.	- Indigo plant

Botanical Name: Indigofera tinctoria Linn

Natural Order: Leguminosae

Habitat: Widely cultivated in many parts of India.

Description: A small shrub clothed with adpressed white hairs. The leaves are imparipinnate, with 7-11 entire leaflets. The stems are slightly covered with silvery hairs. The flowers are in profuse, axillary recemes. The fruit is a linear, cylindrical and straight pod.

Varieties: There is a bigger variety called Mahānīlī (Synonyms : Amarā, Rājanīlikā, Tutthā and Keśārhā).

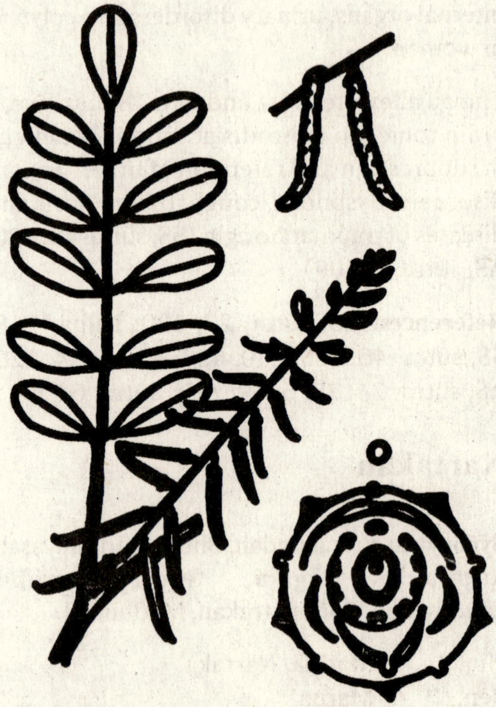

Medicinal Action:

Rasa : Bitter and pungent
Vīrya : Hot

It alleviates kapha and vāta, is a laxative, beneficial to the hair, and is useful in ascites, synocope, heart diseases, vertigo, gout, flatulence, rheumatism, moles etc. on the skin, cough, abdominal tumours, fever, skin-diseases, worms, toxicosis, enlargement of spleen, headaches and ulcer.

The bigger variety is considered superior.

Nimbah

Synonyms: Niyamanaha, Netā, Pichumandah, Satiktakah, Ariṣṭah, Sarvatobhadrah, Subhadrah, Pāribhadrakah, Śukapriyah, Śīrshaparṇah, Yavaneshṭah, Varatvachah, Cchardanah, Hinguniryāsah, Pītasārah, Ravipriyah, Arkapādapah, Kākaphalah, Viśīrṇaparṇah, Cchardignah, Kaiṭaryah.

Hin. - Nim
Mah. - Kaḍu nimb
Tel. - Vepa-cheṭṭu
Kan. - Bevu, Bevina mara
Tem. - Vembu
Mal. - Veppu
Eng. - Margosa tree

Botanical Name: Azadirachta indica A Just (Syn. Melia azadirachta (Linn)

Natural Order: Meliaceae

Habitat: Wild in the dry forests of the Deccan. Is often planted all over India.

Description: A medium-sized to large tree with a straight trunk, elegant in form and evergreen. Leaves are compound, long and pendant, crowded at the ends of branches. Young leaves are pale, tender, green and tinted with red. Flowers are small, white and sweet scented. Blossoms appear in the first week of April. Fruits are yellow berries, about 1 inch long.

Varieties: There is a bigger variety - Mahānimbah (Synonyms: Drekā, Karmukah, Vishamushṭikh, Keśamushṭih, Ramyakah, Kshīrah, Kākaṇḍah, Himadrumah, Gairikah, Giripatrah. Hin. Bakāyan). See also Kaiṭaryah.

Medicinal Action:

Rasa : Sweet and bitter (the ripe fruits)
Bitter and pungent (all other parts)
Bitter and astringent (Mahānimbah)

Guṇa : Light and unctous (the unripe fruits)
Unctous, heavy and slimy (the ripe fruits)
Light (all other parts)
Dry (Mahānimbah)

Vīrya : Cold
Hot (unripe fruits)

Vīpāka : Pungent

The tender, fresh leaves aggravate vāta, are constipative and are beneficial in bleeding from internal organs and diseases of the skin and eyes.

The leaves alleviate pitta, aggravate vāta, and are useful in anorexia, skin diseases, eye-diseases, worms and toxicosis.

The old leaves assist in the healing of ulcers.

The flowers alleviate kapha and pitta, and are anthelmintic.

The young stalks and leaves are beneficial in cough, dyspnoea, haemorrhoids, abdominal tumours, worms and urinary disorders.

The unripe fruits are purgative and are beneficial in urinary disorders, skin diseases, abdominal tumors, worms and haemorrhoids.

The ripe fruits alleviate kapha, and are used in bleeding from internal organs, eye-diseases, tuberculosis and diseases of traumatic origin. The seed-pulp and oil are used in worms and skin-diseases.

The root and bark alleviate pitta and kapha, purify the blood, are useful in diseases of children, are constipative, promote suppuration, and are used in ulcers, worms, skin diseases, oedema, vomiting, burning in the chest, fatigue, toxicosis, cough, fever, thirst and anorexia.

Mahā-nimbah alleviates kapha and pitta, antidotes poison, purifies the blood, is constipative and is useful in worms, sciatica, vomiting, nausea, skin diseases, burning pains, ulcers, intermittent fevers, palpitation, urinary disorders, cholera, abdominal tumours, urticaria, haemorrhoids and dyspnoea.

Therapeutic Hints:

1. It relieves pruritus (CS, sūtra, 4, 11).
2. The decoction of nimba is useful in certain kinds of prameha (urinary disorders, including diabetes) (SS, chikitsā, 11, 9), and to purify breast-milk (ibid, 17, 43).
3. The ghee medicated with the bark is useful in skin diseases and bleeding from external organs (CS, chikitsā, 7, 135).
4. The smoke emitted by the leaves, flowers, root bark and fruits is considered auspicious and beneficial (KS, kalpa, 1, 35).
5. The gum-resin (niryāsa) is used as collyrium in eye-disease (SS, uttara, 12, 13, 14).
6. The flowers are used for culinary purposes (SS, sūtra, 46).
7. The seeds are emetic (CS, sūtra, 2, 7-8); and are externally applied in knotty tumours of the Kapha kind (AS, uttara, 31).
8. The root is also considered to be an emetic (SS, sūtra, 39).
9. The root is valuable in sciatica. (CSS, Page 268).

References: CS, sūtra, 3, 3; SS, sūtra, 46, 197, 262-270, 370; 45, 115; 19,28; uttara, 19, 12; chikitsā, 20, 55; AS, sūtra, 12, 73; 29, 76; chikitsā, 21.

Nimbūkah

Synonyms: Amla-jambīrah, Vahnidīpyah, Amlasārah, Dantāghātah, Śodhanah, Jantumārī, Rochakah.

Hin.	-	Kāgjinembu
Ben.	-	Patinebu
Tel.	-	Nimma
Kan.	-	Nimbe haṇṇu
Tam.	-	Elumichai

Botanical Name: Citrus medica var. acida of Watt (Syn. C. aurantifolia (Christm.) Swingle)

Natural Order: Rutaceae

Description: This is a small tree, armed with strong, axillary spines. The leaves are alternate, one foliate with a winged petiole; the leaflets are elliptic or ovate-lanceolate, usually serrate, coriaceous, glabrous and gland dotted. The flowers are bisexual, white and fragrant, solitary or in axillary cymes. The fruit is an ovoid oblong or globose berry. The flowering season is in April or May.

Medicinal Action:

Rasa : Sour
Guṇa : Light and sharp
Vīrya : Hot

It alleviates all the doshas, particularly vāta, is digestive, appetizing, and is beneficial in worms, ascites, fatigue, abdominal colic, anorexia, acute fever, cholera, salivation, constipation, dyspepsia, gout, vomiting, dyspnoea, diseases of the throat, tuberculosis, rheumatism, and abdominal tumours. It is not beneficial to the eyes.

The ripe fruit is considered more useful.

Nirguṇḍī

Synonyms: Indrāṇikā, Sindhuvārakah, Śukrāṇī, Anantah.

Hin. - Sambhālu
Ben. - Nisindā
Kan. - Lakkigiḍa
Tam. - Veṇṇacchi
Tel. - Vāvila-cheṭṭu
Mal. - Indrāṇi
Eng. - Five-leaved chaste tree

Botanical Name: Vitex negundo Linn

Natural Order: Verbenaceae

Habitat: Throughout India in the warmer areas.

Description: This large shrub or sometimes small slender tree has a thin, grey bark. The branchlets are quadrangular and whitish. The leaves are apposite, and three or five foliate. The leaflets are lanceolate, acute and petioled. Almost all the leaves are glabrous above and whitish beneath. The flowers which grow in pedunculate cymes are bluish-purple in colour. The fruit which is a ovoid or globose drupe, is black when ripe.

The flowers are blue in colour (NIS on SS, sūtra, 38, 18).

Varieties: There are two varieties -

1. Blue variety viz. Nīla-nirguṇḍī

Synonyms: Bhūtakesī, Śīta-bhīruh, Kartarīpatrah, Vanajā, Marutpatrī

2. White variety viz Śveta-nirguṇḍī

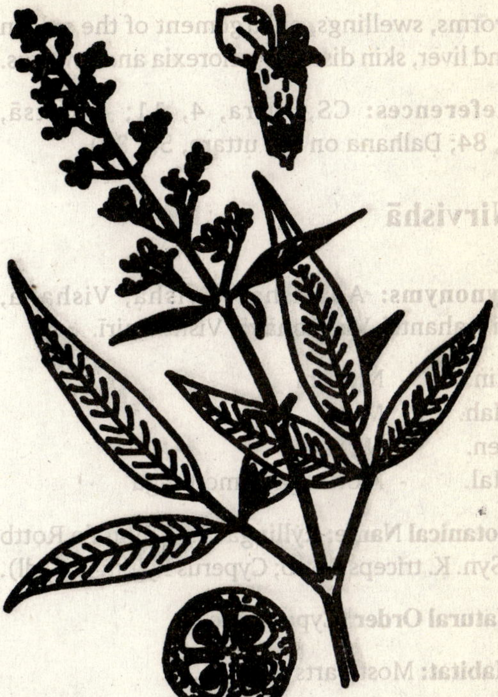

Medicinal Action:

Rasa : Bitter, astringent and pungent (white variety)
Pungent and bitter (blue variety)
Guṇa : Light and dry (both varieties)
Vīrya : Hot (both varieties)

Both varieties alleviate kapha and vāta, strengthen memory, the hairs and eyes and enhance the complextion.

The white variety is beneficial in sore throats, sciatica, fevers, catarrh, cough, dyspnoea, abdominal colic, swellings, worms, anorexia, skin diseases, vomiting and joint pains.

The blue variety is useful in menstrual disorders, cough, swellings and distension of abdomen.

The leaves alleviate kapha and vāta and are anthelmintic.

The flowers of the wild plant are useful in

worms, swellings, enlargement of the spleen and liver, skin diseases, anorexia and pruritus.

References: CS, sūtra, 4, 11; chikitsā, 8, 84; Ḍalhaṇa on SS, uttara, 52, 30).

Nirvishā

Synonyms: Apavishā, Vivishā, Vishahā, Vishahantrī, Vishābhāvā, Visha-vairī.

Hin. - Nirvishi
Mah. - Mustu
Ben. - Nirbishi
Mal. - Mottenga, Pimottenga

Botanical Name: Kyllinga monicephala Rottb (Syn. K. triceps Rottb; Cyperus kyllingia Endl).

Natural Order: Cyperaceae

Habitat: Most parts of India.

Description: This is an erect, creeping sedge, up to one foot high with well-developed rhizomes and linear leaves as long as or shorter than the stem. The inflorescence is a solitary, globose, terminal, white spike.

Medicinal Action:

Rasa : Pungent
Vīrya : Cold

It alleviates kapha and vāta, promotes healing of wounds and ulcers, purifies the blood and antiotes most poisons.

Nishpāvī

Synonyms: Grāmajā, Phalinī, Nakhapūrvikā, Maṇḍapā, Śimbī, Gucchaphalā, Chipiṭā.

Hin. - Sem
Ben. - Bārā, Makhānasim
Mah. - Ghevḍā, Pāvaṭā
Kan. - Avare, Holadavare-baḷḷi
Tel. - Anumulu
Mal. - Veḷḷavara
Tam. - Veḷḷavarai
Eng. - Cow gram, Flat bean

Botanical Name: Dolichos lablab Lin

Natural Order: Leguminosae

Habitat: Found in all parts of India.

Description: This is a perennial, twining or creeping herb with trifoliate leaves and flowers which are white, reddish or purple, borne on axillary racemes. The fruit is a flat or inflated, linear or broad pod, 1 to 5 inches long. The seeds are globose, ovate or flattened, varying in colour from white to dark black.

Medicinal Action:

Rasa : Astringent and sweet
Guṇa : Dry and heavy
Vīrya : Hot
Vipāka : Sour

It alleviates kapha and pitta, aggravates vāta, is a brain tonic, appetizing, constipative, and cleanses the throat.

The yellow variety is considered superior.

Therapeutic Hints:

1. It should not be taken along with milk (CS, sūtra, 26, 84).
2. Its decoction is used as an emetic in cases of poisoning (AS, sūtra, 8, 38).

References: CS, sūtra, 27, 33, 100.

Nīvārah

Synonyms: Tāpasah, Araṇyadhānyah, Munidhānyah, Tṛṇodbhavah, Prasāditah, Rasikah, Prasādhikah

Assam. - Phutki, Putidal
Hin. - Tīnī, Jangalī-dāl

Ben. - Uridhān
Mah. - Deva-bhat
Tam. - Vallipullu
Tel. - Nivvari-dhānyamu
Vernacular - Ulajī-dhānyam, Tulajī-dhanyam (Ḍalhaṇa)

Botanical Name: Hygroryza aristata Nees

Natural Order: Gramineae

Habitat: Common in low-lying areas and often covers paddy fields in Assam during the rains.

Description: This is a floating, perennial, glabrous grass with culms 1.0 - 1.5 ft. long and narrowly oblique grains.

This is a variety of rice having red awl (rakta-śūka) (NIS on SS, sūtra, 20, 5).

Medicinal Action:

Rasa : Sweet and astringent
Guṇa : Unctous and light
Vīrya : Cold

Action-Uses: It alleviates pitta, aggravates kapha and vāta, is constipative, auspicious, emaciating, and diminishes the quantity of urine.

Rice prepared out of nīvārah aggavates vāta, is appetizing, and is beneficial in enlargement of liver and spleen, ulcers and bleeding from internal organs.

References: SS, sūtra, 20, 5; 46, 21; CS, sūtra, 27, 17; chkp. on CS, chikitsā, 29, 50.

Nyagrodhah

Synonyms: Vaṭah, Raktaphalah, Śṛngī, Skandhajah, Dhruvah, Kshīrī, Vaiśravaṇāvāsah, Bahupādah, Vanaspatih, Vṛkshanāthah, Yamapriyah, Nandī, Bhaṇḍīrah, Jaṭālah, Viṭapī, Mahacchāyah, Yakshāvāsah, Rohiṇah, Avarohī.

Hin. - Bar
Kan. - Āladamara
Tam. - Ālamaram
Tel. - Marri-cheṭṭu
Mal. - Perāl
Eng. - Banyan tree

Botanical Name: Ficus bengalensis Linn (Syn. F. indica Roxb)

Natural Order: Moraceae

Habitat: Most parts of India.

Medicinal Action:

Rasa : Astringent
Guṇa : Dry and heavy
Vīrya : Cold

It alleviates kapha and pitta, is constipative, haemostatic, enhances the complexion and is beneficial in herpes, burning pains, ulcers, menstrual disorders, fever, thirst, syncope, swellings, vomiting, bleeding from internal organs and haemorrhages.

Therapeutic Hints:

1. The tender sprouts are used to prevent abortion (CS, śārīra, 8, 24).
2. The cold infusion of the tender leaves is used as styptic and in diarrhoea of the Pitta kind (CS, sūtra, 27, 105).
3. A medicated ghee prepared from Nyagrodha and other drugs is useful in swellings of Pitta variety (SS, chikitsā, 23, 11; AS, chikitsā, 19).
4. It is also useful in anaemia and jaundice (SS, sūtra, 37, 29; uttara, 44 27).
5. Its stem is used for brushing the head (AHṛ, sūtra, 2, 2)
6. The decoction of the bark is used externally in menstrual disorders (AS, uttara, 39).

References: CS, chikitsā, 3, 258; 4, 86-87; 21, 73; sūtra, 27, 105; SS, sūtra, 8, 38; 48-49; uttara, 40, 85; chikitsā, 11, 7; śārīra, 2, 32; AS, chikitsā, 4; uttara, 42.

P

Palāṇḍuh

Synonyms: Yavaneshṭah, Durgandhah, Mukhadūshakah, Sukhandakah, Niketanah, Nīchabhojyah, Lohitakandhah, Tīkshnakandah, Śūdrapriyah, Dīpanah, Kṛmighnah, Mukhagandhakah, Bahupatrah, Viśvagandhah, Mukundakah.

Hin. - Pyāj
Ben. - Peyāj
Kan. - Irulli
Tel. - Ullipayi
Eng. - Onion
Tam. - Uḷḷi

Botanical Name: Allium cepa Linn

Natural Order: Liliaceae

Habitat: Extensively cultivated all over India.

Description: This is a bulbous plant, with a fistulous scape which is swollen near the base. The scape appears in the second year, is about one metre high and bears greenish-white flowers. The leaves are rather cylindrical.

Varieties: There is another variety - Rāja-palāṇḍuh

Synonyms: Nṛpāhvayah, Rāja-priyah, Dīrghapatrah, Rakta-kandah.

Medicinal Action:

Rasa : Pungent and sweet
Guṇa : Heavy and unctous
Sharp (Rāja-palāṇḍu)
Vīrya : Not hot
Vipāka : Sweet

It alleviates all the doshas, is appetizing, an aphrodisiac, strength-giving, and is beneficial in vomiting, abdominal colic, abdominal tumours, fever, ascites, cough, pruritus, ear-ache, insect-bites and accumulation of phlegm in the chest.

Rāja-palāṇḍu induces drowsiness and is useful in sore-throat.

The seeds are aphrodisiac and are beneficial in dental caries and urinary disorders.

Note: It resembles Rasona as far as the medicinal properties are concerned, although it is inferior to it (AHr. sūtra, 6, 112).

References: SS, sūtra, 46, 246.

Pālankyah

Synonyms: Madhurā, Kshurapatrikā, Supatrā, Snigdhapatrā, Grāmiṇā, Grāmya-vallabhā, Vāstukākārā.

Hin. - Palanki, Chukandar
Ben. - Pālang sāk
Mah. - Pālakh
Tam. - Vasaiyilaikkirai
Tel. - Dumpā-bacchali
Eng. - Garden spinach
Vernacular - Pālank, Pālak (Ḍalhaṇa)

Botanical Name: Spinacia oleracea Linn

Natural Order: Chenopodiaceae

Habitat: Most parts of N. India.

Description: An erect, annual, smooth herb 30-60 cm.high with leaves alternate, ovate-oblong, obtuse or acute, variously lobed, smooth, soft and succulent. The flowers are unisexual, greenish, the male flowers terminate in leafless spikes; the female ones in axillary clusters. The fruits are hard, compressed utricles, enclosed in a spined, capsule-like body.

Medicinal Action:

Rasa : Slightly pungent, and sweet
Guṇa : Heavy, slimy and dry
Vīrya : Cold

It alleviates pitta, aggravates kapha and vāta, purifies the blood, is constipative, nutritive and is beneficial in dyspnoea, syncope and toxicosis.

Therapeutic Hints:

It aggravates vāta, alleviates kapha and pitta, is constipative, dry and useful in polyuria (SS, sūtra, 46, 261; AHṛ sūtra, 6, 84).

References: CS, sūtra, 27, 100; SS, sūtra, 42, 11; 46, 256.

Palāśah

Synonyms: Kimśukah, Parṇah, Brahmopanetā, Yāgninakah, Raktapushpakah, Kshāra-śreshṭhah, Brahma-vṛkshah, Samidvarah, Kāshṭhah, Vātapothah, Triparṇah, Kṛmighnah, Vakrapushpakah, Suparṇi.

Hin. - Dhāk
Ben. - Palās
Tel. - Moduga
Kan. - Muttaga
Tam. - Palāś
Mal. - Pilācham
Eng. - Bastard teak

Botanical Name: Butea frondosa Koen. ex Roxb (Syn. B. momosperma (Lam) Kuntze).

Natural Order: Leguminosae

Habitat: Common throughout the greater part of India up to 4,000 ft, except in very arid parts.

Description: A small to medium sized deciduous tree, untidy in growth and ragged in shape with a twisted and gnarled bark. Its bark is fibrous and of greyish colour. Leaves are three lobed, large, rough textured and swollen at the base. Flowers are bright, flaming scarlet-orange and borne during April-May. Pods are one seeded and pendulous.

Varieties: There are four varieties, based on the colour of the flowers -white, red, blue and yellow (RN, 10, 273-277)

Medicinal Action:

Rasa : Pungent, bitter and astringent

Guṇa : Unctous
Light and dry (the fruits)

Vīrya : Hot
Cold (the flowers)

Vipāka : Pungent
Sweet (the flowers)

It alleviates all the three doshas, is appetizing, an aphrodisiac, laxative, promotes union of fractured bones, and is beneficial in ulcers, abdominal tumours, sprue, haemorrhoids, worms, diseases of the anus, enlargement of the spleen and menstrual disorders.

The flowers aggravate vāta, alleviate kapha and pitta, purify the blood, are constipative and are useful in dysuria, thirst, burning pains, gout, skin diseases and pruritus.

The fruits alleviate kapha and vāta, are beneficial in urinary disorders, haemorrhoids, worms, skin diseases, abdominal tumours, ascites and abdominal colic.

The seed are useful in pruritus, scabies, and other skin disorders.

The seeds are useful in removing cataract, opacity of the cornea and other eye-diseases.

The stems are believed to bestow longevity.

The gum is constipative and is useful in sprue, cough, excessive perspiration and diseases of the mouth.

The oil alleviates kapha and pitta.

Therapeutic Hints:

1. A medicated ghee prepared from the leaf-juice relieves bleeding from internal organs (haemorrhages) (SS, uttara, 45, 29).
2. The extract from the fruits relieves diarrhoea of the Pitta type and dysentery (CS, chikitsā, 19, 59). The stalk is used as a styptic (ibid, 4, 89).
3. A paste of the fresh leaves relieves burning pain (SS, uttara, 39, 285).
4. A medicated ghee prepared from palāśa and certain other drugs is useful in impotence and knotty tumours (SS, śārīra, 218).
5. It is one of the plants used for preparing kshāras (SS, sūtra, 11, 11).
6. The juice extracted by burning the tree is used externally in skin diseases (CS, sūtra, 3, 15). The exact process as described by Chkp is: The tap root of the tree is cut and a vessel is kept under it. The tree is then to be set fire to. The juice which collects in the vessel is to be used.

References: SS, sūtra, 6, 26; 46, 121; uttara, 42, 20; CS, sūtra, 2, 13; chikitsā, 23, 101; AHṛ, sūtra, 15, 41.

Panasah

Synonyms: Phaṇasah, Kaṇṭaki-phalah, Atibṛhatphalah, Apushpah, Phaladah, Sthūlakaṇṭaphalah, Āśayah, Mahāsarjah, Champakālu, Mūlaphaladah.

Hin. - Kathar
Ben. - Kāṇṭāl
Tel. - Panasa
Kan. - Halasina-mara
Tam. - Palāchu
Mal. - Pilāvu, Jakka
Eng. - Indian Jack Tree
Vernacular. - Kaṭahal (Ḍalhaṇa)

Botanical Name: Artocarpus heterophyllus Lam (Syn. A. integrifolia Linn)

Natural Order: Moraceae

Habitat: Indigenous to India.

Description: This is a tree with big fruits which are prickly on the outer surface (NIS on SS, sūtra, 9, 4; 46, 199).

This is a large, evergreen tree with a dense crown and rough bark. The leaves are entire in adult and slightly three lobed in saplings, ovate-oblong, leathery, dark green and glossy above. The flowers are yellowish-green.

Medicinal Action:

Rasa : Sweet (ripe fruits and seeds)
Sweet and astringent (unripe fruits)
Bitter (the flowers)
Guṇa : Unctous and heavy (the fruits)
Heavy (the seeds and flowers)
Vīrya : Cold

The ripe fruits alleviate vāta and pitta, aggravate kapha, and are nutritive, refreshing, strength-giving, hard to digest, aphrodisiac and are beneficial in bleeding from internal organs, tuberculosis and diseases of traumatic origin.

The unripe fruits aggravate vāta and pitta, alleviate kapha, are constipative, strength-giving and are beneficial in obesity.

The seeds are aphrodisiac, constipative and diuretic. The flowers cleanse the mouth.

References: SS, sūtra, 46, 181; nidāna, 2, 12, CS, sūtra, 27, 143-144; AHr, sūtra, 6, 119.

Pārasīka-yavānī

Synonyms: Tīvrā, Turushkā, Madakāriṇī, Dīpyah, Śyāmah, Kuberah.

Hin. - Khurāsāni - jamāni
Tel. - Khurāsāni-omamu
Eng. - Henbane

Botanical Name: Hyoscamus niger Linn

Natural Order: Solanaceae

Habitat: From Kashmir to Garhwal, 5,000-11,000 ft.

Description: An erect, more or less hairy and viscid herb with a disagreeable, heavy odour. Stems are robust. Leaves are alternate, rarely entire. Radical leaves spreading, stalked and toothed. Flowers are pale yellow-green and nearly sessile. Fruit is a capsule with compressed seeds.

Medicinal Action:

Rasa : Pungent
Guṇa : Light and dry
Virya : Hot

It alleviates kapha, aggravates vāta, is appetizing, digestive, constipative, an intoxicant, an aphrodisiac and is beneficial in worms, abdominal colic and dyspepsia.

Its other properties are similar to Yavānī.

Pāribhadrah

Synonyms: Palāśī, Raktapushpah, Phalabhadrah, Prabhadrakah, Kaṇṭakī, Pārijātakah, Mandārah, Kaṇṭa- kimśukah, Kṛmighnah Rakta-keśarah, Bahupushpah, Nimbataruh, Vasavah.

Hin. - Pangrā, Pharhad
Ben. - Pālitā-mandār
Tel. - Bādida-cheṭṭu
Kan. - Hālivāṇa-mara, Hongara
Tam. - Kaliyāṇamurukku
Mal. - Muḷḷumurikā
Eng. - Indian Coral Tree

Botanical Name: Erythrina indica Lam (Syn. E. variegata Linn var orientalis (Linn) Merr).

Natural Order: Leguminosae

Habitat: Throughout India in deciduous forests in Andaman and Nicobar Islands.

Description: A small to medium sized quick growing tree. Branches are close to each other; the bark is smooth. Leaves are elegant, variegated and trifoliate. Flowers are large, scarlet coloured, occuring in racemes. The flowering period is from February to April. The fruit is a pod, curved and pointed, containing 5-10 kidney shaped seeds.

A thorny tree distributed in Eastern India, with red flowers, and leaves like those of Rohiṇī (NIS on SS, kalpa, 3, 9).

Medicinal Action:

Rasa : Pungent
Vīrya : Hot

It alleviates kapha and vāta, is appetizing, and is beneficial in worms, obesity, anorexia, oedema and urinary disorders.

The flowers alleviate pitta and are useful in diseases of the ear.

Note:

1. Ḍalhaṇa describes it as being a thorny tree with red flowers and leaves resembling rohiṇī, which grows mainly in the Eastern part of India (NIS on SS, uttara, 58, 48).
2. This tree is also made use of for preparing kshāra (AS, sūtra, 39, 10; AHṛ, sūtrā, 30, 8).
3. It is used to purify and cleanse water (SS, kalpa, 3, 9).

Pārijātah

Synonyms: Prājaktah, Hāra-śṛngara-pushpah, Sephālikā, Nala-kunkumakah, Rāga-pushpī, Khara-patrakah.

Hin.	-	Har-singār
Ben.	-	Seuli
Tel.	-	Pagaḍa-malle
Kan.	-	Pārijāta-mara
Tam.	-	Manjapu
Mal.	-	Manapu-maram
Eng.	-	Weeping nyctanthes, Night Jasmine

Botanical Name: Nyctanthes arbortristis Linn

Natural Order: Oleceae

Habitat: Himalayan ranges from the Chenab to Nepal, Assam, Bengal, Madhya Bharat southwards to the Godavari. cultivated in many parts of India.

Description: A large, deciduous tree with lenticellate, drooping, four angled branches which are rough all over with stiff white hairs. The bark is light brown and rough. The leaves are opposite, enstipulate, ovate, entire or distantly toothed with acute base. The flowers are whitish or purple, fragrant, sessile, in fascicles of short trichotomous cymes. The fruit is a orbicular compressed, two-celled capsule. The tree flowers in August-September. The flowers blossom at night and drop off in the morning; the fruits appear from November-February.

Medicinal Action:

Rasa : Pungent and bitter
Bitter (the leaves)
Guṇa : Dry
Vīrya : Hot

It alleviates vāta and is beneficial in tuberculosis, rheumatism and flatulence.

The leaves are useful in fevers of all kinds and sciatica.

The bark and leaf-stalks are useful in cough.

Therapeutic Hints:

It is useful in a particular form (udaka-meha) of urinary disorder (SS, chikitsā, 11, 9).

Pārīshah

Synonyms: Phalīśah, Kapi-chūtah, Kamaṇḍaluh, Gardabhāṇdah, Kandarālah, Kapītanah, Supārsvakah, Brahma-vṛkshah.

Hin.	-	Paper-pipal
Ben.	-	Palās-pipal
Tel.	-	Gangarāvi-cheṭṭu
Kan.	-	Kandarola, Hūvarasi
Tam.	-	Pūvaraśu
Mal.	-	Pūvarachu
Tuḷu	-	Jogi-mara
Eng.	-	Portia tree, Indian tulip tree, Umbrella Tree
Vernacular	-	Gandha-muṇḍa (according to Chkp. on CS, chikitsā, 3, 258).

Botanical Name: Thespesia populnea Soland ex. Correa (Syn. Hibiscus populneus Linn)

Natural Order: Malvaceae

Habitat: Coast forests of India, largely grown as a roadside tree in tropical regions.

Description: A quick growing, evergreen, littoral tree with a dark -brown bark, and with young parts clothed with peltate scales. The leaves are alternate, stipulate, cordate, entire, petiolate and palmately seven-nerved. The flowers are solitary, axillary, yellow fading to purplish-pink. The fruit is a loculicidal capsule which yields an yellow dye. The flowers and fruits appear all the year round; the seed seldom ripens.

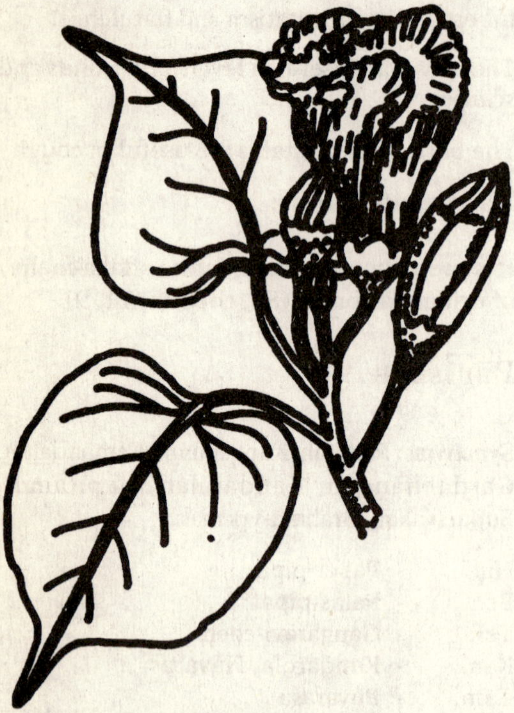

Medicinal Action:

Rasa : Sweet, sour and astringent
Astringent (the root)
Sweet (the fruit-pulp)

Guṇa : Unctous

It alleviates vāta and pitta, aggravates kapha, is an aphrodisiac, difficult to digest, causes intestinal worms and is beneficial in heart diseases, burning pains and diseases of the throat.

Parkaṭī

Synonyms: Plakshah, Jatī, Karparī, Chārudarśinī, Śṛngī, Varohaśākhī, Vaṭī, Aśvatthī, Gardabhaṇḍah, Kapītanah, Kshīrī, Supārśvah, Plavakah.

Hin.	- Pākhar
Ben.	- Pākur
Tel.	- Juvvi-cheṭṭu
Kan.	- Basari, Jubbi
Tam.	- Jovi, Icchi
Mal.	- Chelā
Mah.	- Pimparī, Pākarī, Bassarī

Botanical Name: Ficus lacor Buch-Ham (Syn. F. infectoria Roxb)

Natural Order: Moraceae

Habitat: Plains and lower hills of India.

Description: A large, evergreen tree with drooping branches and numerous aerial roots. The bark is smooth and brownish-green. The leaves are 5-10 cms long broadly ovate-elliptic, leathery, hairy, shining and bluntly acuminate. The receptacles are in axillary pairs, blood-red when ripe (They ripen from March-May).

Madicinal Action:

Rasa : Pungent and astringent
Vīrya : Cold

It alleviates kapha and pitta, purifies the blood and is beneficial in ulcers, menstrual disorders, diseases of the female generative organs, burning pains, swellings, bleeding from internal organs, syncope, vertigo and delirium.

Therapeutic Hints:

1. It reduces the frequency of micturition (CS, sūtra, 4, 15). It is also used in dhūma-pāna (ibid, 5, 22).
2. Its bark powder is used locally in menstrual disorders (AS, uttara, 39).
3. The tender leaves are used as vegetable (CS, sūtra, 27, 105.
4. It is used in the preparation of an agada (CS, kalpa, 6, 3).

References: CS, sūtra, 27, 164

Parpaṭakah

Synonyms: Varatiktah, Pāmśuh, Kavachah, Araktah, Śītah, Kalapāngah, Kṛshṇa-śākah, Raktapushpah, Kaṭupatrah, Rajah, Reṇuh, Tṛshṇārih, Kalpāngī.

Medicinal Action:

Rasa : Bitter
Guṇa : Light
Vīrya : Cold
Vipāka : Pungent

It alleviates kapha and pitta, aggravates vāta, purifies the blood, is constipative and is beneficial in vertigo, fevers, thirst, burning pains, anorexia, lethargy, vomiting and urinary disorders.

References: CS, sūtra, 4, 14; AHṛ, sūtra, 6, 76; AS, sūtra, 12, 72.

Parūshakam

Synonyms: Giripīlu, Roshaṇam, Nāgadalopa-mam, Parāvatam, Nīlacharman, Nīla-maṇḍalam, Parāparam, Alpāsthī.

Hin. - Pharsā, Dhamin
Ben. - Phalsā, Shukri
Tel. - Cchiṭṭīta
Tam. - Palisa, Tadachi
Kan. - Buttiyadippe, Taḍasale
Mah. - Parpakā
Vernacular - Phālasā (Ḍalhaṇa)

Botanical Name: Grewia subinacqualis DC

Natural Order: Tiliaceae

Habitat: Extensively cultivated throughout India.

Description: The leaves resemble those of Dhanvana. The fruit is soft and has a small stone. (NIS on SS, sūtra, 38, 43).

This is a small tree or a large straggling herb with a rough, grey bark. The leaves are variable in shape, broadly cordate to ovate with an oblique base, irregularly toothed. The flowers are yellow, in axillary clusters. the drupe is globose, of the size of a pea, red or purple in colour, indistinctly lobed.

Medicinal Action:

Rasa : Sour and pungent (unripe fruits)
Sweet (ripe fruits)
Guṇa : Light
Vīrya : Hot (unripe fruits)
Cold
Vipāka : Sweet (ripe fruits)

The unripe fruits alleviate kapha and vāta and aggravate pitta.

The ripe fruits alleviated pitta and vāta, purify the blood, are nutritive, refreshing, appetizing, constipative, heart tonic and are beneficial in swellings, thirst, burning pains, fever and tuberculosis.

The bark alleviates vāta and pitta and is useful in urinary disorders. inflammation of the genital organs and dysuria.

The leaves are used to fecilitate healing of ulcers and skin eruptions.

Therapeutic Hints:

1. It is purgative, used as a gargle and valuable in fatigue, fever, and diseases of vāta and pitta. (CS, sūtra, 4, 13, 16; 27, 128; chikitsā, 22, 62).
2. It relieves colic of the pitta kind (SS, uttara, 42, 108). Its fruit is considered to be the best among those having an astringent taste (SS, sūtra, 46, 334).

Note: Dalhana describes it as having leaves resembling those of Dhanva, and refers to two varieties, a tree and a shrub (NIS on SS, sūtra, 38, 43; 46, 172).

References: SS, sūtra, 46, 172, 390; 38, 43-44; śārīra, 2, 9; AS, sūtra, 16, 7; AHṛ, sūtra, 15, 13.

Pāshāṇa-bhedakah

Synonyms: Aśmaghnah, Śilābhedah, Upalabhedah, Nagabhit, Śailagarbhajah, Śvetā, Bhinna-yojanī.

Medicinal Action:

Rasa : Sweet, astringent and bitter
Guṇa : Heavy and unctous
Vīrya : Cold

It alleviates all the three doshas, is a diuretic, and is beneficial in urinary disorders, thirst, dysuria, urinary calculi, menstrual disorders, haemorrhoids, abdominal colic, diarrhoea, heart diseases, enlargement of spleen, abdominal tumours, ulcers, dyspnoea and convulsions.

Therapeutic Hints:

1. It is diuretic (CS, sūtra, 4, 15) and is said to relieve dysuria of the vāta type (SS, uttara, 59, 17).
2. A medicated ghee prepared from it is useful in urinary calculi of the vāta kind (SS, chikitsā, 7, 5-8).

References: AS, sūtra, 15, 35.

Pāṭalā

Synonyms: Karbūramoghā, Ambuvāsinī, Phaleruhā, Kṛshṇavṛntā, Kālavṛntā, Toyādhivāsinī, Tāmrapushpī, Kumbhīkā, Vasanta dūtī, Sthiragandhā, Kāmadūtī, Abhipriyā, Madhudūtī, Alivallabhā.

Hin. - Pār, Pāḍari
Ben. - Pārul
Guj. - Pādal, Kākach
Kan. - Pādari-mara

Tam. - Padiri-maram
Mah. - Paḍhaḷ, Pāḍali
Tel. - Kallgoṭṭu-cheṭṭu, Kāru-kolli

Botanical Name: Stereospermum suaveolens DC.

Natural Order: Bignoniaceae

Habitat: Throughout India in drier localities.

Description: This is a large, deciduous tree with the young parts hairy. The bark is grey, exfoliating in large, flat scales. The leaves are imparipinnate, with elliptic, acute or acuminate, leathery leaflets which are deeply serrate on young trees and entire on old ones. The flowers are dark purple, fragrant and downy in panicles. The fruit is a straight, dark grey capsule.

A tree with fragrant flowers (NIS on SS, uttara, 47, 51).

Varieties: There are a few other varieties such as Śveta-pāṭalā, Kāshṭhapāṭalā etc. (RN, 9, 152).

Medicinal Action:

Rasa : Bitter and pungent
Sweet and astringent (the flowers)
Bitter, sweet and astringent (the fruits)

Guṇa : Heavy (the fruits)

Vīrya : Slightly hot
Cold (the fruits)

It alleviates all the three doshas, purifies the blood, is useful in swellings, flatulence, distension of the abdomen, vomiting, dyspnoea, anorexia, thirst and vomiting.

The flowers alleviate kapha and vāta, purify the blood, are a heart-tonic and are beneficial in burning pains, and diarrhoea.

The fruits are useful in hiccoughs, bleeding from internal organs and dysuria.

Therapeutic Hints:

1. Its bark is a purgative (SS, sūtra, 39, 4).
2. It is considered valuable in swellings (CS, sūtra, 4, 16).
3. Its kshāra is said to relieve dysuria, retention of urine, etc. (SS, uttara, 58, 46).

Note:

1. Its flowers impart a fragrance to water (SS, sūtra, 45, 12; AS, sūtra, 6, 28).
2. Its bhasma is used to purify and cleanse impure water (AS, sūtra, 8, 80).

References: SS, sūtra, 46, 287; CS, sūtra, 2, 11-13; AHṛ, sūtra, 167-168.

Pātālagaruḍī

Synonyms: Cchilihiṇḍah, Mahāmūlah, Vatsādanī, Somavallī, Tiktāngā, Souparṇī, Dīrghakāṇḍā, Dṛḍhakāṇḍā, Mahābalā, Dṛḍhalatā, Vikrāntā, Vāsanī.

Hin.	-	Cchireṭa
Ben.	-	Śilindā, Huyer
Mah.	-	Bhuyapāḍ, Vasanvel

Botanical Name: Cocculus villosus DC (Syn. C. hirsutus (Linn) Diels)

Natural Order: Menispermaceae

Habitat: Tropical and subtropical India from the foot of the Himalayas to South India.

Description: A climbing shrub with the young parts densely covered with soft hairs. The leaves are ovate-oblong, mucronate, sometimes three-lobed, grey-tomentose and petiolate. The male flowers are yellow, in cymose panicles while the female ones are axillary. The fruit is a small, purplish-black drupe. The flowering period is from January to March.

Medicinal Action:

Rasa : Sweet

It alleviates all the three doshas, purifies the blood, is an aphrodisiac, appetizing, nutritive and relieves burning pains and toxicosis.

Patangam

Synonyms: Raktasāram, Surangam, Ranjanam, Paṭṭaranjakam, Pattūram, Kuchandanam, Patrāngam, Rakta-kāshṭham, Surangadam, Patrāḍhyam, Bhāryāvṛksham.

Hin.	-	Bakam
Ben.	-	Bakam
Tel.	-	Patangi-cheṭṭu
Kan.	-	Patangada-mara
Tam.	-	Partangi
Mal.	-	Chappanam
Eng.	-	Sappan Wood, Brasilitto

Botanical Name: Caesalpinia sappan Linn

Natural Order: Leguminosae

Habitat: South India and Bengal, usually cultivated as a hedge plant.

Description: This is a tree or a straggling shrub with a few small prickles. The leaves are paripinnate with twenty or thirty, oblique-oblong close leaflets. The flowers are yellow while the fruit is a pod with a hard beak. The shrub flowers in the rainy season.

Medicinal Action:

Rasa : Pungent, bitter, sour and sweet
Guṇa : Dry
Vīrya : Cold

It alleviates all the doshas, purifies the blood, promotes healing of wounds and ulcers, is aromatic, and is useful in insanity, fevers, dysuria, urinary calculi, boils and vesicles.

Pāṭhā

Synonyms: Ambashṭhā, Pāpachelī, Kuchelā, Cchinnaveśikā, Prāchīnā, Yūthikā, Sthāpanī, Śreyasi, Viddhakarṇikā, Ekāshṭhīlā, Vanatiktakā, Tiktapushpā, Śiśirā, Mālatī, Vṛttaparṇī, Triśirā, Trivṛt, Raktaghnī, Vishahantri, Aviddha-karaṇī.

Hin.	-	Pāḍh
Ben.	-	Ākanādi
Kan.	-	Pāḍavali, Agilu-śuṇṭhi, Hāḍe-baḷḷi
Mal.	-	Kaṭṭuvalli
Mah.	-	Paharvel, Pahaḍ-mūḷ
Tam.	-	Appāṭṭā, Vaṭṭa-tiruppi
Tel.	-	Visha-boddi, Pātha-cheṭṭu
Eng.	-	Velvet leaf
Vernacular	-	Pāḍh (Ḍalhaṇa)

Botanical Name: Cissampelos pareira Linn

Natural Order: Memispermaceae

Habitat: Throughout tropical and subtropical India.

Description: A tomentose sub-erect or climbing shrub with nearly circular often peltate leaves with the petiole as long as the blade. The flowers are small and greenish while the fruit is an ovoid, red drupe. The plant flowers in the rainy season.

Varieties: There is a smaller variety viz. Laghu-pāṭhā.

Medicinal Action:

Rasa : Bitter and pungent
Guṇa : Light and sharp
Vīrya : Hot

It alleviates all three doshas, purifies the blood, promotes healing of fractures and is beneficial in fever, abdominal colic, vomiting, skin diseases, diarrhoea, heart diseases, burning pains, pruritus, dyspnoea, worms, ulcers, toxicosis, ascites and abdominal tumours.

Therapeutic Hints:

1. It relieves fever and purifies breast-milk (CS, sūtra, 4, 12, 16; SS, chikitsā, 17, 44).
2. It is valuable in all forms of diarrhoea, colic of the kapha variety and in knotty growths (SS, uttara, 40, 114; 42, 111; śārīra, 2, 14).
3. It is used externally in ulcers of the kapha variety (SS, chikitsā, 1, 115). It is also used in diabetic carbuncles (ibid, 12, 9).

References: CS, sūtra, 27, 88; SS, sūtra, 14, 35; 37, 13; 38, 6-7.

Paṭolah

Synonyms: Svādupūrvā, Svādishṭhā, Janavallabhā, Rājapūrvā, Suśākā, Svādupatraphalā.

Hin. - Palwal, Parwal, Kaḍave-parwal
Ben. - Paṭol
Guj. - Kadava-paṭol
Kan. - Paḍavala-kāyi, Kahi-paḍavala
Tel. - Cheti-poṭla, Chedu-poṭla
Mal. - Paṭolam
Tam. - Kombuppudalai, Paeppuḍa

Botanical Name: Trichosanthes cucumerina Linn (Syn. T. dioica Roxb)

Natural Order: Cucurbitaceae

Habitat: Throughout India

Description: The stems of this plant are slender, extensively climbing, more or less scabrous and wooly. The leaves are 3 by 2 inches, ovate-oblong, cordate, acute, dentate, not lobed, rigid and rough on both surfaces. The flowers are dioecious. The fruit is nearly spherical or oblong, acute, smooth and orange-red when ripe with compressed, ellipsoid seeds.

Varieties: There are two other varieties :

1. Rāja-paṭolah

Synonyms: Mekī, Parvagā, Pīluparṇikā, Rājanāmā, Vṛttabījā, Parvajā.

2. Tikta-paṭolah

Synonyms: Kulakah, Kaṭuphalah, Karkaśacchadah, Rājīphalah, Pāṇḍuphalah,

Tiktottamah, Bījagarbhah, Kusṭhārī, Kāramardahah, Pancharājīphalah, Amṛtaphalah.

Botanical Name: Trichosanthus dioica Roxb.

Medicinal Action:

Rasa : Sweet
Pungent and bitter (Tiktapaṭolah)
Guṇa : Light and unctous
Vīrya : Hot (all varieties)
Vipāka : Sweet (fruits of Tikta-paṭolah)

It (the fruits) alleviates all the three doshas, purifies the blood, is an aphrodisiac, digestive, appetizing, nutritive, strength-giving, heart-tonic, and is beneficial in fevers, cough, worms and tuberculosis.

The root is purgative, the stems alleviate kapha, and the leaves, pitta.

Tikta-paṭolah alleviates all the doshas, purifies the blood, is a laxative, appetizing, digestive, and is useful in pruritus, skin diseases, fevers, burning pains, herpes, diseases of the eyes, thirst and worms.

Therapeutic Hints:

1. It is said to relieve thirst and anorexia (CS, sūtra, 4, 11, 14).
2. It is used externally to relieve pruritus (ibid, 3, 8).
3. The leaves and fruits are used for culinary purposes (SS, sūtra, 46, 268).
4. The decoction of the buds is used as an eye-wash in eye-diseases (AS, uttara, 14).
5. A medicated ghee prepared from the plant is valuable in bleeding from internal organs and skin diseases (SS, chikitsā, 7, 135).
6. A gruel prepared from Paṭola is refreshing, appetizing, alleviates pitta and kapha and is useful in fever, worms, and skin diseases (SS, sūtra, 46, 370-371).
7. The fine powder of Paṭola and certain other drugs is used in ascites (CS, chikitsā, 13, 119-123).

References: CS, sūtra, 27, 96; chikitsā, 21, 59; SS, uttara, 39, 226, 246; sūtra, 38, 33-34; AS, sūtra, 16, 9; 18, 28; AHṛ, sūtra, 15, 15.

Perukam

Synonyms: Dṛḍha-bījam, Māmsalam, Pītam, Vartulam, Madhurāmlakam.

Hin. - Lāl-sapharī, Sapharī
Mah. - Perū
Kan. - Chepe-mara
Tam. - Koyyāpaḷam
Tel. - Jāmi-cheṭṭu
Mal. - Malampera
Eng. - Guava

Botanical Name: Psidium guajava Linn

Natural Order: Myrtaceae

Habitat: Throughout India.

Description: This is a small tree, with the bark smooth, thin, greenish-grey, peeling off in thin flakes. The leaves are simple. entire, exstipulate, gland dotted, elliptic-oblong, nearly glabrous above, downy below. The flowers are white coloured and axillary. The flowers season is from August to September.

Medicinal Action:

Rasa : Astringent, sweet and sour

Vīrya : Cold

It aggravates kapha, alleviates vāta and pitta, is an aphrodisiac and is useful in insanity.

Pīluh

Synonyms: Śītasahah, Sramsī, Guḍa-phalah, Sahasrāmsī, Śākhī, Śyāmah, Karabha-vallabhah.

Hin. - Pilu
Ben. - Pilu
Mah. - Diar, Goḍ-pilu
Kan. - Goṇi-mara
Tam. - Ughāiputtai, Karkoḷ
Tel. - Varagogu
Mal. - Pīlumaram

Botanical Name: Salvadora oleoides Decne (Syn. S. persica Linn; S. indica Wight)

Natural Order: Salvadoraceae

Habitat: Arid regions of Punjab and Western India.

Description: A shrub or a small tree with a short twisted trunk and drooping branches, and a grey or whitish grey bark. The leaves are linear-lanceolate, coriaceous while the flowers are sessile, greenish-white, minute in paniculate spikes. The drupes are globose, usually yellow when ripe with greenish-yellow seeds.

Varieties: There is a bitter variety called Mahāpīluh.

Synonyms: Mahāphalah, Rāja-pīluh, Madhu-pīluh.

Parts Used: Fruits

Medicinal Action:

Rasa : Pungent, astringent, bitter, sweet and sour.
Sweet (Mahā-pīluh)

Guṇa : Unctous and sharp
Light (the oil)

Vīrya : Hot

It alleviates kapha and vāta, purifies the blood, is a laxative, appetizing, engenders burning pains, and is beneficial in haemorrhoids, abdominal tumours, gout, enlargement of the spleen, flatulence, ascites and toxicosis.

Mahā-pīluh alleviates pitta, antidotes poison, is appetizing and an aphrodisiac.

The oil alleviates kapha and vāta.

Therapeutic Hints:

1. It is useful in fevers, and leucoderma (CS,

sūtra, 4, 16; chikitsā, 9, 28).

2. A medicated ghee prepared from Pīlu and a few other drugs is very useful in tuberculosis (KS, rāja-yakshma).
3. The fruit is used as an errhine (CS, sūtra, 2, 4-5).

Note:

1. The stalk is not to be used for brushing the teeth (AS, sūtra, 3, 21).
2. The fruit is mainly found in northern parts of India (Chkp on CS, sūtra, 27, 145).
3. The fruits are much relished by camels (SS, uttara, 55, 43).

References: SS, sūtra, 46, 195; uttara, 11, 5-6.

Pippalah

Synonyms: Bodidruk, Aśvatthah, Chalapatrah, Gajāśanah, Keśavālayah, Kṛshṇāvāsah, Chaityavṛkshah, Nāgabandhuh, Devātmā, Māhādrumah, Kunjarāśanah, Pavitrakah, Yājnikah, Śrīmān, Guhyapushpah, Sevyah, Dhanuṛvrkshah, Kshiradrumah, Guhyapatrah.

Hin.	-	Pipal
Ben.	-	Aśvattha
Tel.	-	Rāvi-cheṭṭu
Kan.	-	Araḷī-mara
Tam.	-	Araśa-maram
Mal.	-	Arayāl
Mah.	-	Pimpal
Eng.	-	Sacred Peepul

Botanical Name: Ficus religiosa Linn

Natural Order: Moraceae

Habitat: Throughout India.

Medicinal Action:

Rasa : Astringent, sweet and bitter
Guṇa : Heavy and dry
Vīrya : Cold

It alleviates kapha and pitta, purifies the blood, is hard to digest, enhances complexion, diminishes the amount of urine and is beneficial in ulcers, wounds, burning pains and menstrual disorders.

The ripe fruits alleviates pitta, purifies the blood, is a heart-tonic and is beneficial in burning pains, vomiting, tuberculosis, anorexia and toxicosis.

Therapeutic Hints:

1. It reduces the frequency of urination and is used in dhūmapāna-therapy (CS, sūtra, 4, 15; 5, 22).
2. The leaves are used as vegetables (ibid, 27, 195).
3. It increases intelligence, strength and life span (AS, uttara, 1).

References: CS, sūtra, 27, 164; kalpa, 1, 8; SS, sūtra, 38, 48; AS, sūtra, 3, 21.

Pippalā

Synonyms (of the fruits): Māghadī, Kṛshṇā, Chapalā, Chanchalā, Kaṇā, Upakulyā, Kolyā,

Vaidehī, Tiktataṇḍulā, Souṇḍī, Kaṭī, Ūshaṇā, Sūkshma-taṇdulā, Kaṭubījā, Dantaphalā.

Synonyms (of the root): Pippalīmūlam, Granthikam, Chavikāśirah, Kaṭugranthim, Chaṭakā, Kolamūlam, Sarva-granthikam, Jaṭā.

Hin. - Pipal, Pipla-mūl
Ben. - Pipul
Tel. - Pippaḷḷu
Kan. - Hippali-baḷḷi
Tam. - Tippili,
Mal. - Tippali
Eng. - Long Pepper

Botanical Name: Piper longum Linn

Natural Order: Piperaceae

Habitat: Hotter Parts of India.

Description: This shrub has an erect, thick and jointed root-stock and numerous stems which are ascending or prostrate, much branched, cylindrical, stout and finely pubescent. The leaves are numerous, sub-acute, entire, glabrous, dark green and shining above and pale and dull beneath. The fruit is very small, ovoid, completely sunk in a solid, fleshy spike which is oblong, erect, blunt, blackish-green and shining.

Parts Used: Fruits and roots.

Medicinal Action:

Rasa : Pungent (dried fruits and root)
Sweet (fresh fruits)
Guṇa : Heavy and unctous (fresh fruits)
Light and unctous (dried fruits)
Light, dry and sharp (the root)
Vīrya : Slightly hot (dried fruits)
Cold (fresh fruits)
Vipāka : Sweet (fruits)

The fresh fruits aggravate kapha and alleviate pitta.

The dried fruits alleviate kapha and vāta, aggravate pitta, are laxative, appetizing, an aphrodisiac, bestow longevity and are useful in dyspnoea, cough, ascites, fevers, skin-diseases, abdominal colic, abdominal tumours, urinary disorders, haemorrhoids, enlargement of the spleen and hiccoughs.

If taken with honey, it is appetizing, an aphrodisiac, a brain tonic, and is beneficial in obesity, fevers, dyspnoea and cough. If taken with jaggery, it is useful in chronic fevers, cough, dyspepsia, anorexia, dyspnoea, anaemia and worms.

The roots alleviate kapha and vāta, aggravate pitta, are purgative, digestive, appetizing, and are used in ascites, flatulence, abdominal tumours, enlargement of spleen, worms, dyspnoea, tuberculosis, abdominal colic and cough.

Therapeutic Hints:

1. It is appetizing, and relieves cold and catarrh (CS, sūtra, 4, 9, 17).
2. It is useful in colic of the kapha variety (SS, uttara, 42, 110).
3. The fruits are used as errhine and to induce vomiting (CS, sūtra, 39, 6).
4. It has an affinity for the throat and relieves hiccough (CS, sūtra, 4, 10-14).
5. The roots are appetizing, digestive and relieve flatulence and colic (ibid, 25 ,40).
6. Pippali taken in gradually increasing doses is an excellent rejuvenative (CS, chikitsā, 1, 3, 32-35; SS, chikitsā, 5, 12; uttara, 39, 216).
7. A medicated ghee prepared from this and certain other drugs is useful in dyspnoea, cough, rheumatic pains etc. (CS, chikitsā, 18, 36).

References: SS, sūtra, 38, 22-23; 46, 433; uttara, 42, 21; CS, sūtra, 27, 287; vimāna, 1, 116; 7, 21.

Piyālakah

Synonyms: Priyālah, Kharaskandhah, Chārakah, Bahula-valkalah, Rājādānah, Tāpaseshṭah, Sannakadruh, Dhanushpaṭah, Moksha-vīryah, Hasannakah, Snehabījah, Lalanah, Sāradrumah (NIS on SS, sūtra, 38, 43-49).

Hin.	- Piyal
Ben.	- Piyāl
Kan.	- Morave-mara
Mal.	- Mūral
Tel.	- Sāra-poppu-cheṭṭu, Moraḷi-paṇḍu
Tam.	- Śārapparuppu, Kattu-ma
Mah.	- Chaura
Vernacular	- The fruit-pulp is known as Chārulī (Ḍalha)

Botanical Name: Buchanania lanzan Spreng (Syn. B. latifolia Roxb)

Natural Order: Anacardiaceae

Habitat: Throughout India in dry deciduous forests; in N. W. India from the Sutlej to Nepal ascending to 3,000 ft.

Description: A moderate-sized, almost evergreen tree with the bark 1.3 cm thick, black, tough, tersellated with prominent squares; the cracks being deep and narrow. Leaves are oblong, obtuse or emarginate, simple and entire. The flowers are bisexual, greenish-white, sessile in pubescent panicles. The fruit is a black, edible, laterally compressed, two-valved drupe. The fruits appear in April-May.

Medicinal Action:

Rasa	: Sweet and sour Sweet (the fruit-pulp and oil) Astringent (the root)
Guṇa	: Heavy and unctous
Vīrya	: Cold Slightly hot (the oil)

It alleviates vāta and pitta, aggravates kapha, purifies the blood, is hard to digest, strength-giving, a laxative, nutritive and is beneficial in fever, burning pains, thirst, diseases of traumatic origin and tuberculosis.

The fruit-pulp alleviates pitta,while the oil alleviates vāta and pitta and aggravates kapha.

The root alleviates kapha and pitta and purifies the blood.

References: AS, sūtra, 6, 7; SS, sūtra, 46, 205.

Potakī

Synonyms: Upodakī, Kalambī, Picchila, Mohinī, Mada-śākah, Viśālā, Valipodakī, Vṛshchikapriyā.

Hin. - Poi
Ben. - Puiśāk
Tel. - Bacchali
Kan. - Basale
Tam. - Basalakkirai
Mah. - Māyāḷ
Eng. - Indian Spinach

Botanical Name: Basella rubra Linn

Natural Order: Basellaceae

Habitat: Throughout India, wild or cultivated.

Description: This is a perennial twining herb, with leaves up to 5 inches by 3 inches, which are broadly ovate, and pointed at the apex. The young stems and leaves are markedly fleshy.

Medicinal Action:

Rasa : Astringent, pungent, and sweet
Guṇa : Unctous and slimy
Vipāka : Sweet

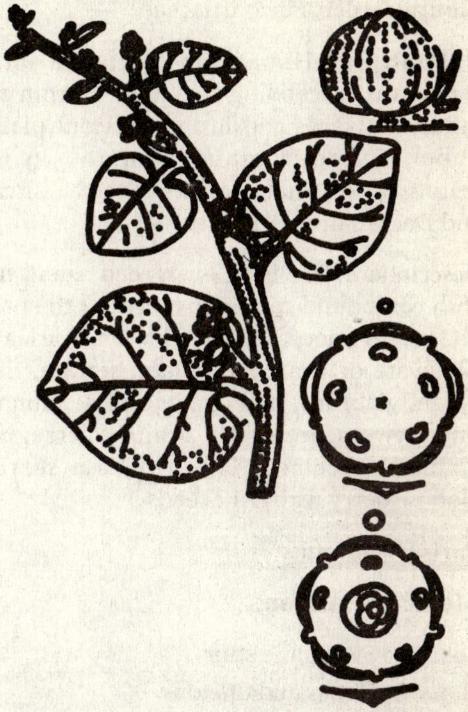

It aggravates kapha, alleviates vāta and pitta, is strength giving, appetizing, nutritive, causes drowsiness and lethargy and relieves bleeding from internal organs. It is harmful to the throat.

Therapeutic Hint: If taken with til, it causes diarrhoea (CS, sūtra, 26, 89; SS, sūtra, 20, 14).

References: CS, sūtra, 27, 94; 2, 33.

Prāchināmalakam

Synonyms: Pānīyāmalakam, Raktakam, Prāchīnārangam.

Hin. - Pāniāmlak
Ben. - Paniālā
Kan. - Chanchali-mara, Ara - nelli
Tel. - Neru-nelli
Eng. - Puneala Plum

Botanical Name: Flacourtia cataphracts Roxb (Syn. F. jangomas (Lour.) Raeu)

Natural Order: Flacourtiaceae

Habitat: Sub-Himalayan tract and outer Himalayas, ascending to 4,000 ft from the Indus eastwards and in the adjacent plains, upper Gangetic plain, common in the Peninsula, W. Ghats, forests of the N. Circars and Deccan upto 3, 000 ft.

Description: This is an evergreen, small tree with compound spines or thorns at the base. The bark is smooth and dark brown. The leaves are ovate or ovate-lanceolate, serrate, thin, tough, glabrous, pale-green and acuminate. The flowers are small, white in irregular glabrous racemes. The fruit is a scarlet, globose berry with 8-12 seeds.

Parts Used: Fruits

Medicinal Action:

Rasa : Sweet and sour

Guṇa : Heavy and unctous

Vīrya : Hot

It alleviates all the three doshas, is constipative, appetizing, and is useful in fevers, thirst and toxicosis.

When ripe, it aggravates kapha and pitta and alleviates vāta.

Note:

1. It is useful in antidoting gara-visha (CS, sūtra, 27, 146; SS, sūtra, 46, 158).
2. It is found in Eastern India (NIS).

References: Chkp on CS, sūtra, 27, 146 and NIS on SS, sūtra, 46, 158.

Prasāraṇī

Synonyms: Rājabalā, Gandālī, Kaṭambharā, Gandhādhyā, Pratānikā, Gandhabhadrā, Saraṇī, Śaranā, Bhadraparṇī, Suprasarā, Chandraparṇī, Chāruparṇī, Balyā.

Hin. - Khip, Gandhāli
Ben. - Gandhahāduliā
Kan. - Kaḷḷana-chouri, Sāraṇe-giḍa
Tel. - Gontima-goru-cheṭṭu, Gontima-gomaru
Mah. - Hiranvel, Chāndabel
Tam - Mudiyāra-kundil

Botanical Name: Paederia foetida Linn

Natural Order: Rubiaceae

Habitat: Central and E. Himalayas, up to 5,000 ft. extending to Calcutta and Malay Peninsula.

Description: This is a slender, twining shrub, foetid when bruised. The leaves are petiolate, opposite, ovate or lanceolate, usually ovate, with a broad or narrowed base. The stipules are ovate lanceolate and bipid. The flowers are violet, shortly pedicelled, in cymes. The fruit is orbicular.

Medicinal Action:

Rasa : Bitter and pungent

Guṇa : Heavy

Vīrya : Hot

It alleviates all the three doshas, is a laxative, strengthgiving, an aphrodisiac, nutritive, beneficial to the eyes and voice, promotes healing of wounds and fractures and is beneficial in gout, haemorrhoids, swellings, and fevers.

References: CS, chikitsā, 28, 166; SS, chikitsā, 15, 44-45.

Priyanguh (see also Kanguh)

Synonyms: Gandhaphalā, Govandanī, Vishvaksenā, Kṛshṇapushphī, Kāntā, Kṛśāngī, Mahilāhvā, Gundrā, Kārambhā, Govarṇā, Bhedinī, Mangalyā, Phalapriyā, Vṛttā, Subhagā, Pītā, Anganāpriyā, Śubhā, Śyāmā, Phalinī (Ḍalhaṇa).

Varieties: There is another variety called Gandha-priyanguh.

Medicinal Action:

Rasa : Bitter and astringent
Sweet and astringent (fruits and seeds)
Guṇa : Heavy and dry (fruits and seeds)
Vīrya : Cold

It alleviates vāta and pitta, purifies the blood, and is useful in diarrhoea, maelena, foul odour, excessive perspiration, burning pains, fever, abdominal tumours, thirst, toxicosis, vomiting and vertigo.

The fruits alleviate kapha and pitta, are constipative, strength-giving, and cause flatulence and distension of the abdomen.

The seeds alleviate kapha and pitta, are constipative and strength-giving.

Gandha-priyanguh alleviates vāta and pitta, purifies the blood, is an aphrodisiac, is beneficial to the hair, and scalp and is useful in vomiting, vertigo, burning pains, fever, insanity, perspiration, skin diseases, thirst, abdominal tumours, alcoholism, bleeding from internal organs and toxicosis.

Note: The flowers are used as collyrium (SS, sūtra, 17, 8-10).

References: CS, sūtra, 3, 26; 4, 9, 15, 18, 20; 27, 17; SS, sūtra, 14, 36; 6, 22-23; 38, 45, 46, 21; AHṛ, sūtra, 6, 12 15, 37-39.

Pṛkkā

Synonyms: Spṛkkā, Latā, Koṭivarshā, Marunmālā, Lankārikā, Samudrāntā, Samudrakāntā, Kuṭilā, Devaputrikā, Brāḥmaṇī, Panchaguptirasā, Sukumārā, Chaṇḍah, Asak, Gagounā, Sugandhā, Piśunā.

Medicinal Action:

Rasa : Sweet, bitter, pungent and astringent
Vīrya : Cold
Vipāka : Sweet

It alleviates all the three doshas, purifies the blood, is a heart-tonic and an aphrodisiac, and is beneficial in skin diseases, pruritus, excessive perspiration, burning pains, fevers, cough, syncope, urinary calculi, dysuria and toxicosis.

Note: According to Dalhana, it is an aromatic plant with curved flowers, found in North India (NIS on SS, sūtra, 38, 24).

References: CS, chikitsā, 23, 77; SS, sūtra, 38, 24-25; AHṛ, sūtra, 15, 43.

Pṛśniparṇī

Synonyms: Pṛthakparṇī, Pṛshṭiparṇī, Tanvī, Kroshṭuka-pucchikā, Triparṇī, Pūrṇaparṇī, Kalaśī, Simha-lāngalī, Chitraparṇī, Anghrivallikā, Dhāvanī, Guhā, Dīrghapatrā, Mekhalā, Brahmaparṇī, Vishṇuparṇī, Śvapucchā.

Hin. - Piṭhvan, Dabra
Ben. - Chākulia, Śankarjata
Tel. - Kolapanna-cheṭṭu
Kan. - Ondele-honne
Tam. - Sittirappaladai, Kottunkaḍambai, Śittamalli
Mah. - Pīṭhvan
Guj. - Pṛshṭiparṇī
Vernacular - Pīṭhavanī (NIS on SS, sūtra, 38, 4)

Botanical Name: Uraria picta Desv

Natural Order: Leguminosae

Habitat: Tropical zone, Nepal, Chota Nagpur and Bengal.

Description: This is an erect, sparsely branched perennial herb, about 90 to 180 cm high. The leaves are very variable, 1-3 foliate, and blotched white. The leaflets are usually 4-6, linear-oblong or lanceolate, obtuse and mucronate. The flowers are purple, in dense cylindrical racemes. The fruit is a 3-6 jointed, polished, glabrous, usually white coloured pod.

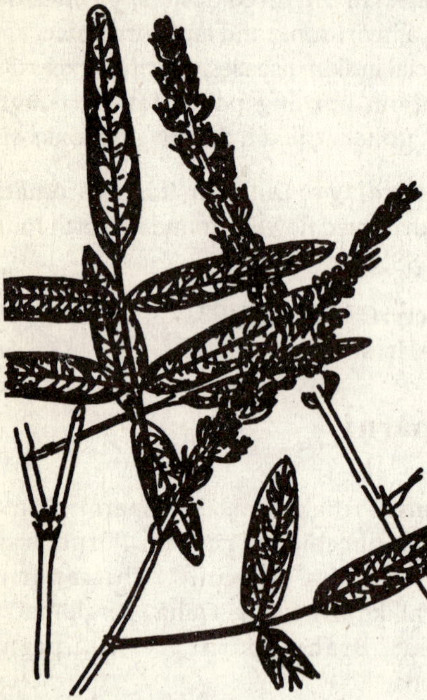

Medicinal Action:

Rasa : Sweet, bitter and pungent
Guṇa : Light
Vīrya : Hot

It alleviates all the three doshas, purifies the blood, is a laxative, an aphrodisiac and is beneficial in burning pains, fever, dyspnoea, diarrhoea, thirst, worms, cough, gout, insanity and ulcers

References: CS, sūtra, 2, 11, 20; 4, 16; 5, 65; 25, 40.

Pudinah

Synonyms: Vyanjanah, Vāntihārī, Ruchīshyah Śokaśobhanah, Sugandhipatrah, Ajīrṇaharah, Pūtihā.

Hin. - Pudīna
Punj. - Pudnahasna
Kan. - Pudīna
Eng. - Spearmint, Garden mint

Botanical Name: Mentha spicata Linn (Syn. M. spicata var viridis Linn)

Natural Order: Labiatae

Habitat: Western Himalayas, Kashmir, 5,000-10,000 ft., Punjab, Kumaon and Garhwal.

Description: A glabrous perennial with robust or slender, tomentose stems. The leaves are sessile, ovate-lanceolate, acute, coarsely dentate, smooth above, glandular below. The flowers are lilac coloured, in loose, cylindrical, slender, interrupted spikes.

Medicinal Action:

Rasa : Sweet
Guṇa : Heavy

It is appetizing, a heart-tonic, constipative, decreases the amount of urine, and is beneficial in cough, alcoholism, dyspepsia, cholera, diarrhoea, sprue, worms and chronic fevers.

Pūgah

Synonyms: Guvākah, Khapurah, Pūgī, Kramukah, Ghoṇṭā, Kapītanah, Dīrghapādapah, Dṛḍhavalkalah, Kalkataruh, Chikkaṇah, Tantusārah, Suranjanah, Gurvākah.

Hin. - Supāri
Ben. - Gua
Tel. - Poka-cheṭṭu
Kan. - Aḍike-mara
Tam. - Kamuku
Mal. - Kamuku
Kon. - Phopaḷa
Eng. - Betel nut palm, Areca palm

Botanical Name: Areca catechu Linn

Natural Order: Palmae

Habitat: Cultivated in the coastal regions of southern Mumbai, Chennai and Mysore, Bengal and Assam.

Description: This is a tall, erect tree with a slender stem and smooth, greenish grey bark. The leaves are alternate, while leaflets are numerous, crowded, glabrous and linear or linear-lanceolate. The flowers are monoecious, and greenish-yellow in colour. The fruit is ovoid, orange, fleshy and fibrous.

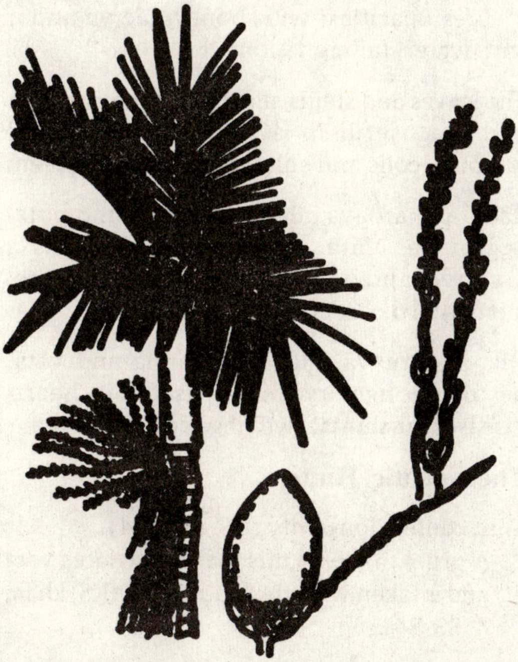

Parts Used: Nuts and Gum

Medicinal Action:

Rasa	: Astringent, sweet and slightly pungent
Guṇa	: Heavy and dry
	Heavy and abhishyandī (when unripe)
Vīrya	: Cold

It alleviates kapha and pitta, is appetizing, a laxative and is used in worms, bad breath and anorexia.

When unripe, it is abhishyandi, hard to digest and harmful to the eyes.

The nuts, after they are boiled alleviate all the doshas.

The ripe nuts aggravate vāta, alleviate kapha and are a laxative. The dried nuts are appetizing and digestive.

The gum aggravates pitta, alleviates vāta and is an intoxicant.

Note: The nuts, if used without the betel leaves causes swellings and anaemia.

References: CS, sūtra, 5, 77; SS, sūtra, 46, 201; chikitsā, 24, 29.

Punarnavā

Synonyms: Viśākhah, Kaṭhillah, Śothaghnī, Śaśivāṭikā, Vṛschīrah, Dīrghapatrah, Varshābhūh.

Hin.	-	Sānṭ
Vernacular	-	Sāṭaḍī (Ḍalhaṇa)
Ben.	-	Punarnaba
Tam.	-	Mūkkirattai
Tel.	-	Aṭika-māmiḍi, Galjeru
Kan.	-	Komme-beru, Sanāḍikā, Gaṇajali
Mah.	-	Ghetuli
Eng.	-	Spreading Hog-weed

Botanical Name: Boerhaavia diffusa Linn (Syn. B. repens Linn)

Natural Order: Nyctaginaceae

Habitat: A weed throughout India.

Description: The plant is a very diffusely branching perennial with the branches ascending or prostrate. The stem is slender and swollen at the nodes. Leaves are opposite, shortly petioled and 1/2 - 1 inch long. The upper surface is green and the lower white. Flowers are very small and red. Fruit is small and easily gets separated from the plant. The root is tough, white and starchy when cut.

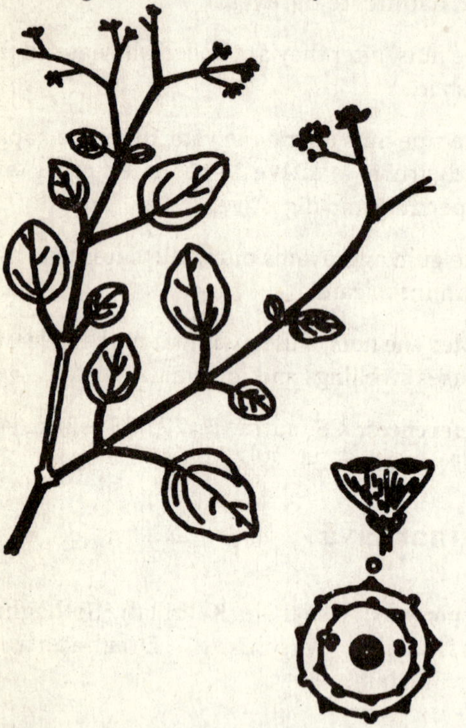

Varieties: There are three varieties of Punarnavā :

1. White variety (Śveta-punarnavā)

2. Red variety (Rakta-punarnavā)

Synonyms: Krūrah, Rakta-patrikā, Rakta-kāṇḍā, Prāvṛshāyaṇī, Maṇḍalapatrikā, Śilāṭikā, Vaiśākhī, Śoṇapatrakah, Rakta-pushpikā.

3. Blue variety (Nīla-punarnavā)

Synonyms: Śyāmā, Kṛshṇākhyā.

Medicinal Action:

Rasa : Sweet, bitter, astringent and pungent (Śveta-punarnava)
Bitter (Rakta-punarnavā)
Bitter and pungent (Nīla-punarnavā)

Guṇa : Dry and light (all varieties)

Vīrya : Hot (Śveta and Nīla-punarnavā)
Cold (Rakta-punarnavā)

Vipāka : Pungent (Rakta-punarnavā)

Śveta-punarnavā alleviates kapha and vāta, purifies the blood, is appetizing, a laxative, bestows longevity and is beneficial in cough, dyspnoea, heart diseases, abdominal colic, anaemia, swellings, hernia, ulcers, ascites, haemorrhoids, anorexia, trauma and toxicosis.

It cures many eye diseases when applied as anjanā (collyrium). When applied with ghee, it cures opacities; with honey, lacrymation; with water, failing vision; etc.

The leaves and stems alleviate kapha and vāta and are useful in dyspepsia, abdominal tumours, colic and enlargement of the spleen.

Rakta-punarnavā alleviates kapha and pitta, aggravates Vāta, purifies the blood, is a laxative and is beneficial in swellings, menstrual disorders, and anaemia.

Nīla-punarnavā alleviates kapha and vāta, bestows longevity and is useful in heart-diseases, anaemia, swellings and dyspnoea.

Therapeutic Hints:

1. It confers longevity (CS, sūtra, 4).
2. A gruel made of this plant alleviates vāta and is taken with curds and ghee (KS, khila, 4, 53-54).

References: CS, sūtra, 4, 13-18; 2, 12-13; 27, 94; SS, sūtra, 38, 4-5; 46, 254-255.

Punnāgah

Synonyms: Purushākhyah, Rakta-vṛkshah, Deva-vallabhah, Nāgapushpah, Kumbhīkah, Tungah, Rakta-keśarah, Pāṇḍu-nāgah, Pāṭalādrumah.

Hin.	-	Punnāg, Pulāk
Ben.	-	Punnāg
Tel.	-	Ponna cheṭṭu, Sura-ponna
Kan.	-	Sura-honne
Tam.	-	Punnai, Nameru-maram
Mah.	-	Uḍkaṇi
Mal.	-	Cherupunna
Eng.	-	Alexandrean Laurel, Pinnay oil tree, Dilo oil
Vernacular	-	Rāja-champakah, Surapatī (Ḍalhaṇa)

Botanical Name: Calophyllum inophyllum Linn

Natural Order: Guttiferae

Habitat: Coastal region of S. India, Andaman Islands and grown throughout India as an ornamental tree.

Description: It is a moderate sized, very ornamental, evergreen tree. The bark is smooth and dark-brown. Leaves are dark green and shining, with wavy margins and an acute base. Petioles are long and stout. Flowers are fragrant, pure white, occurring as racemes, 10-15 cms long. Fruit is globose, smooth and yellowish with scanty pulp.

Medicinal Action:

Rasa : Sweet and astringent
Vīrya : Cold

It alleviates kapha and pitta, purifies the blood, is aromatic and is beneficial in bleeding from internal organs.

The flowers alleviate vāta and kapha, are an aphrodisiac and relieve abdominal colic.

References: SS, sūtra, 38, 24-25.

Pushkaramūlam

Synonyms: Padma-varṇakam, Poushkaram, Kāśmīram, Śvāsārih, Vīram, Śūlaghnam, Brahmatīrtham, Mūlam.

Hin.	-	Pośakar mūl
Kash.	-	Poshkar

Botanical Name: Inula racemosa Hook

Natural Order: Compositae

Habitat: Temperate and alpine W. Himalayas, 5,000-14,000 ft and Kashmir 5,000-7,000 ft.

Description: This is a stout herb, up to 5 ft. high with leathery leaves which are rough above and densely hairy beneath. The radical leaves are long-stalked and elliptic-lanceolate. The flower-heads are yellow, numerous, 1.5-2 inches in diameter, in racemes. The fruit is a long-slender achene with a reddish pappus.

Parts Used: Root

Medicinal Action:

Rasa : Bitter and pungent
Vīrya : Hot

It alleviates kapha and vāta and is beneficial in dyspnoea, hiccoughs, cough, rheumatism, fevers, anorexia, anaemia, swellings and distension of abdomen.

References: CS, sūtra, 25, 40; SS, uttara, 42, 120

Putranjīvah

Synonyms: Putrajīvah, Pavitrah, Garbhadah, Suta-jīvakah, Apatyajīvah, Siddhidah, Ślīpadāpah, Yashṭīpushpah.

Hin. - Jiaputā, Panijiyā
Ben. - Jiaputa
Tam. - Karupilai
Tel. - Putrajīvi, Kuduru-jīvī
Kan. - Putrajīva

Botanical Name: Putranjiva roxburghii Wall

Natural Order: Euphorbiaceae

Habitat: Throughout tropical India, wild and cultivated.

Description: This is an evergreen tree with pendant branches, nearly glabrous except for the young shoots, with corky, pale bark. The leaves are dark green, shining, elliptic-oblong, acute and alternate. Flowers are dioecious. The fruit is a drupe 1.3 - 2 mm long, ellipsoid, rounded or pointed at the apex, narrowed at the base and very hard.

A tree with leaves like those of Jambīra and fruits which are rounded at the middle with narrowed apex (NIS on SS, uttara, 31, 8).

Medicinal Action:

Rasa : Sweet and pungent
Guṇa : Heavy and dry
Vīrya : Cold

It aggravates kapha, alleviates pitta, is a laxative, a diuretic, an aphrodisiac, is beneficial to vision, fecilitates conception and is useful in thirst and burning pains.

Therapeutic Hints: It is considered to be useful in elephantiasis (SS, chikitsā, 19, 61).

R

Rājādanī

Synonyms: Kshīrī, Kshīra-śuklakah, Nṛpah, Dṛḍhaskandhah, Kapīshṭah, Priya-darśanah, Rāja-phalah, Kshīra-vṛkshah, Nimba-bījah, Madhuphalah, Guccha-phalah, Śrīphalah.

Hin. - Kshīri, Khirani
Ben. - Khīrkhejur
Guj. - Khiraṇi
Kan. - Khiraṇī-mara
Tam. - Palla
Mah. - Rāyṇī, Khiraṇī

Botanical Name: Mimusops hexandra Roxb

Natural Order: Sapotaceae

Habitat: Upper Gangetic plain, Central and S. India, Gujarat, Deccan and Śrīharikoṭa.

Description: A small tree. The bark is blackish-grey and smooth, when young it is studded with branchlets and leaf clusters which degenerate into conical protuberances. The leaves are alternate, exstipulate, simple, entire, coriaceous, elliptic-obovate, emarginate and glabrous. The flowers are pale-yellow. The fruit is an ellipsoid, reddish-brown berry. The flowers appear from November-February; fruits from April-July.

Medicinal Action:

Rasa : Sweet and astringent
Guṇa : Heavy and unctous
Vīrya : Cold
Vipāka : Sour

Action-Uses: It alleviates vāta and pitta, is refreshing, an appetizing, aphrodisiac, a heart-tonic, nutritive and relieves urinary disorders.

References: CS, sūtra, 27, 243; SS, sūtra, 42, 11; 46, 166.

Rāsnā

Synonyms: Rāshnā, Rasanā, Surasā, Sarpagandhā, Nākulī, Palankashā, Suvahā, Śreyasī, Sugandhamūlā, Rasāḍhyā, Elāparṇī, Yuktarasā, Droṇa-gandhikā, Bhujangākshī.

Varieties: There are three varieties i.e. (1) Mūla-rāsnā, (2) Patra-rāsnā (both of which are considered superior) and (3) Tṛṇa-rāsnā.

Medicinal Action:

Rasa : Bitter
Guṇa : Heavy
Vīrya : Hot

It alleviates vāta and kapha, purifies the blood, is a digestive and is beneficial in swellings, dyspnoea, abdominal colic, ascities, cough, fevers, gout, intermittent fevers, hiccough, rheumatism, tremors and toxicosis.

Therapeutic Hints:

1. It relieves pain in the sides (CS, sūtra, 3, 25).

2. When applied externally, it is very useful in relieving coldness (CS, sūtra, 25, 40).
3. A gruel prepared from rāsnā is valuable in Vāta diseases (KS, khila, 4, 53-54).

References: CS, sūtra, 4, 13.

Reṇukā

Synonyms: Kapilā, Kountī, Hareṇuh, Bhasmagandhikā, Kṛtāntā, Rājapatrī, Nandinī, Khara-nādinī, Dvijā, Varamukhī, Mahilā, Saparṇikā, Pāṇḍupatnī, Śiśirā, Śāntā, Vṛttā, Dharmiṇī, Haimavatī.

Medicinal Action:

Rasa : Bitter and pungent
Guṇa : Light
Vīrya : Cold
Vipāka : Pungent

It alleviates kapha and vāta, aggravates pitta, is appetizing, a digestive, abortifacient, brain-tonic, and is useful in pruritus, skin diseases with itching, thirst, burning pains, bad breath and toxicosis.

References: AS, uttara, 2.

Revaṭ-chīnī

Synonyms: Pītā, Gandhinī, Pītamūlikā, Amla-parṇī.

Hin. - Revaṭchīnī
Ben. - Rauchīnī
Tam. - Nāṭṭi-revalchīnī
Eng. - Indian Rhubarb

Botanical Name: Rheum emodi Wall

Natural Order: Polygonaceae

Habitat: Sub-alpine and alpine Himalayas, 11,000-12,000 ft.

Description: It is a stout herb with woody large roots and has a leafy, broad stem streaked green and brown. The leaves are large, long, petioled, usually alternate, broadly ovate, obtuse with a cordate base. The flowers are clustered in panicled racemes, dark purple in colour. The fruit is ovoid-oblong, 13 mm. long, purple, with cordate base, and notched apex.

Medicinal Action:

Rasa : Bitter and pungent

It is strength-giving, a laxative, beneficial to the gums and teeth and is used in dyspepsia, diarrhoea, anorexia, constipation, urticaria and ulcers which are slow in healing.

Rohitakah

Synonyms: Kuśālmalī, Dāḍimapushpakah, Sadāprasūnah, Kūṭa-śālmalī, Virechanah, Raktapushpah, Sadāpushpah, Plīha-nāśanah, Rakta-prasādanah, Māmsadalanah, Yakṛtvairī.

Varieties: There is a white variety called Śveta-rohitakah

Synonyms: Sitapushpah, Lakshmīvān, Jana-vallabhah.

Medicinal Action:

Rasa : Pungent, bitter and astringent
Guna : Unctous
Vīrya : Cold

It alleviates kapha and vāta, purifies the blood, is a laxative and is beneficial in enlargement of the liver and spleen abdominal tumours, abdominal colic, ascites, worms, ulcers, eye-diseases, ear-diseases, constipation and flatulence.

Therpeutic Hints:

1. It is useful in jaundice, enlargement of the spleen, worms and abdominal tumours (CS, chikitsā, 13, 81).

2. A medicated ghee prepared from rohitaka and pancha-kola is useful in disorders of spleen (AS, chikitsā, 17).

Note: The flowers are similar to those of Dāḍima (Pomegranate) (NIS on SS, uttara, 17, 41).

Rudantī

Synonyms: Sanjīvanī, Amṛtasravā, Romānchikā, Mahāmāmsī, Chaṇapatrī, Madhusravā, Sravattoyā.

Hin. - Rudravantī
Ben. - Rudravantī
Kan. - Aluguṇi

Botanical Name: Cressa cretica Linn

Natural Order: Convolvulaceae

Habitat: Throughout India.

Description: An annual, short, slender plant not more than a foot high, with a stiff, grey, hairy stem. The leaves are ovate, lanceolate and hairy. The flowers are white or pinkish, usually in small clusters in the axils of upper leaves. The fruit is a capsule, small and when fully ripe with a solitary seed.

Medicinal Action:

Rasa : Bitter and pungent
Sour (the leaves)
Vīrya : Hot
Cold (the leaves)

It alleviates kapha and pitta, is an aphrodisiac, appetizing, bestows longevity and is beneficial in tuberculosis, worms, bleeding from internal organs, dyspnoea and urinary disorders.

Rudrāksham

Synonyms: Śivāksham, Śarvāksham, Bhūtanāśanam, Pāvanam, Tṛṇameruh, Pushpa-chāmaram.

Hin. - Rudrākh

Botanical Name: Elaeocarpus ganitrus Roxb. (Syn. E. sphaericus K. Schum)

Natural Order: Elaeocarpaceae

Habitat: Bihar, Bengal, Assam, Madhya Bharat, Bombay and Nepal, and occasionally cultivated as an ornamental tree.

Description: An ornamental tree, about 30 feet high, producing compact drooping racemes of white flowers from the axils of fallen leaves. The flowering period is March-April.

Medicinal Action:

Rasa : Sour
Vīrya : Hot

It alleviates kapha and vāta, is appetizing, auspicious, and is beneficial in headaches.

S

Śaivālam

Synonyms: Kaivarti-mustam, Jala-nīlī, Jalajam, Ambu-chāmaram, Haṭhaparṇī, Jalaśūkam, Paripelavam, Jalamustam.

Hin. - Sivāl
Ben. - Seyāla

Botanical Name: Vallisneria spiralis Linn.

Natural Order: Hydrocharitaceae

Habitat: Throughout India.

Description: A submerged, leafy, grasslike herb growing in tufts at the bottom of tanks. The leaves are long and narrow. The flowers are unisexual and dioecious. The narrow, elongate fruits ripen under water.

Medicinal Action:

Rasa : Bitter, sweet and pungent
Guṇa : Light and unctous
Vīrya : Cold

It alleviates. all the three doshas, purifies the blood, is a laxative and is useful in fevers, ulcers, skin diseases, herpes, pruritus, heat and toxicosis.

Note:

1. It is cooling when applied externally (CS, sūtra, 3, 26).
2. The root is used to purify and cleanse water (SS, sūtra, 45, 17).

Sājakah

Synonyms: Varjarī, Nālikā, Agradhānyam, Nīlakaṇā.

Hin. - Bājrā, Lahra
Mah. - Bājrī
Kan. - Sajje
Tam. - Kambu
Eng. - Spiked Millet, Pearl Millet

Botanical Name: Pennisetum typhoides (Burm. f. Stapf & Hubbard) (Syn. P. typhoideum Rich)

Natural Order: Gramineae

Habitat: Cultivated in most parts of India.

Description: This is a tall erect annual, about one to three meters high, with slender or stout culms. The leaves are lanceolate, while the inflorescence is a false spike, compact, cylindrical and greenish-yellow or pinkish.

Medicinal Action:

Guṇa : Dry and heavy
Vīrya : Hot

It alleviates kapha, aggravates vāta and pitta, is a heart-tonic, appetizing and an aphrodisiac.

Śākah

Synonyms: Krakachapatrah, Kharapatrah, Atipatrakah, Mahīruhah, Śreshṭhakāshṭhah, Sthira-sārah, Gṛhadrumah, Śarapatrah, Dīrghacchadah, Halīmakah.

Hin.	- Segun
Ben.	- Segun
Tel.	- Ṭeku
Kon.	- Sāgavāni-rūku
Tam.	- Tekku-maram
Kan.	- Tegu, Tegina-mara
Eng.	- Teak wood
Vernacular	- Sāgavān, Śrīparṇa (Ḍalhaṇa)

Botanical Name: Tectona grandis Linn. f.

Natural Order: Verbenaceae

Habitat: Most parts of India.

Description: A big tree with big leaves which are smooth on one surface and rough on the other (Ḍalhaṇa).

A large, deciduous tree, fluted near the base. Young leaves give a deep red stain when crushed. The branchlets are quadrangular, deeply channelled. The leaves are simple, ovate, elliptic or obovate entire and thickly coriaceous. The flowers are regular, sweet-scented and white. The fruit is a globose drupe covered with dense felt of branched hairs. Flowers appear from June-August and fruits from November-January.

Medicinal Action:

Rasa	: Sweet and astringent (the bark)
	Astringent and bitter (the flowers)
Guṇa	: Dry (the bark)
	Dry, light and viśada (the flowers)
Vīrya	: Cold

The bark alleviates kapha and pitta, is a laxative, and is beneficial in repeated abortions, burnings, fatigue, bleeding from internal organs, haemorrhoids and skin diseases.

The flowers aggravate vāta, alleviate kapha and pitta and are useful in urinary disorders.

References: SS, sūtra, 38, 14; chikitsā, 15, 22; kalpa, 6, 3.

Śālah

Synonyms: Sālah, Bastakarṇah, Sarjakāryah, Kārśyah, Aśvakarṇikā, Kālah, Dīrgha-śākah, Vallī- vṛkshah, Chīraparṇah, Kālakūṭah, Ajakarṇakah, Gandha-vṛkshakah, Jaraṇa-drumah, Divya-sārah, Rajodbhavah.

Hin.	- Sāl, Sākhu
Ben.	- Sāl
Kan.	- Āsina-mana, Rāḷada mara
Tel.	- Sālamu, Aepi-cheṭṭu

Mal. - Sāla-vṛksham
Eng. - Sal Tree

Botanical Name: Shorea robusta Gaertn. f.

Natural Order: Dipterocarpaceae

Habitat: Most parts of India.

Description: This is a tall, evergreen tree; the bark is rough, dark-brown, with deep vertical furrows. The leaves are alternate, simple, entire, with 10-12 pairs of secondary nerves; the stipules are large, leathery and persistent. The flowers are in unilateral racemes or panicles, with the petals grey-tomentose outside and orange inside. The flowering season is in March.

Medicinal Action:

Rasa : Pungent, bitter and astringent (the gum)
Sweet and astringent (the fruits)
Guṇa : Unctous (the gum)
Heavy and dry (the fruits)
Vīrya : Hot (the gum)
Cold (the fruits)

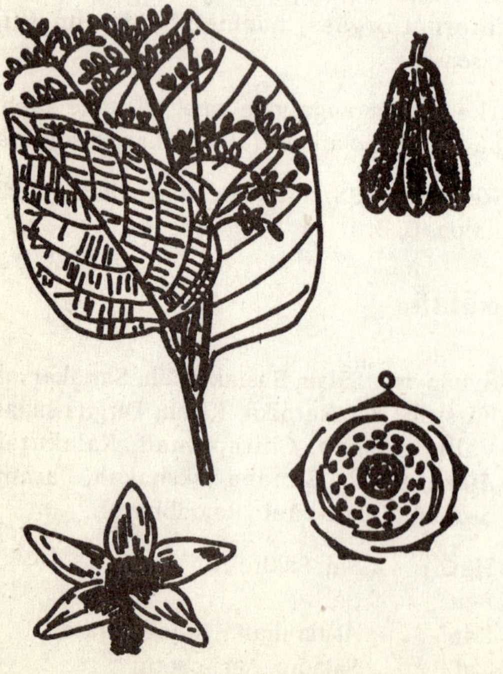

The gum alleviates kapha, purifies the blood, and is beneficial in perspiration, worms, ulcers, hernia, abscesses, deafness, diseases of the ear, menstrual disorders, bleeding from internal organs, boils, pruritus, headaches, toxicosis, anaemia, skin diseases and urinary disorders.

The fruits aggravate vāta, alleviate pitta, are constipative, emaciating, purify the blood and are useful in thirst, burning and diseases of traumatic origin. It causes flatulence and colic.

Therapeutic Hints:

1. It relieves pruritus (CS, sūtra, 4, 17).
2. The bark-powder is used to facilitate healing of wounds (SS, sūtra, 37, 27). It is used externally in Upadamśa (chancre) (SS, uttara, 31, 5).
3. Its flowers are used as an antidote to poison (SS, kalpa, 6, 22).

References: CS, kalpa, 1, 8; SS, sūtra, 38, 8-9; 46, 144; NIS on SS, chikitsā, 19, 33-34; SS, kalpa, 6, 22; AS, sūtra, 7, 181-184; uttara, 46).

Śāliparṇī

Synonyms: Sthirā, Ṣoumyā, Triparṇī, Pīvarī, Guhā, Vidārigandhā, Dīrghapatrā, Amśumatī, Vātaghnī, Tanvī, Sarvānukāriṇī, Dīrghamūlā, Śophaghnī, Kīṭavināśinī, Surūpā, Sumūlā, Suparṇikā.

Hin. - Sarivan
Ben. - Sālpāni
Tel. - Muyyāku-ponna
Kan. - Mūrele-honne
Tam. - Mel-malli, Nela-kaḍambai
Mah. - Sālavaṇ

Botanical Name: Hedysarum gangeticum Linn (Syn. Desmodium gangeticum DC)

Natural Order: Leguminosae

Habitat: Outer Himālayas, up to 5,000 ft and throughout India.

Description: This is an erect undershrub, with leaves pinnately one-foliate. The leaflet is variable is width, ovate-oblong, acute, petiolate and stipulate, with a rounded base. The flowers are white or lilac-tinged, in racemes. The fruit is a sickle-shaped, 6-8 jointed pod. The plant flowers from June to August.

Medicinal Action:

Rasa : Bitter and sweet

Guṇa : Heavy

Vīrya : Hot

It alleviates all the three doshas, is nutritive, an aphrodisiac, bestows longevity and is beneficial in fever, dyspnoea, diarrhoea, tuberculosis, traumatic diseases, cough, worms, intermittent fever, urinary diseases, haemorrhoids, toxicosis, swellings and vomiting.

Therapeutic Hints: It is useful in swellings (CS, sūtra, 4, 16).

References: CS, sūtra, 2, 20; SS, chikitsā, 11, 10.

Śallakī

Synonyms: Gajabhakshī, Hlādinī, Mahāruhā, Vasā, Mochā, Surabhī, Suvahā, Maheruṇā, Aśvamūtrī, Asruphala, Gandhavīrā, Vanakarṇikā, Suśrīkā, Gandhamūlā.

Hin. - Sālai
Ben. - Sālai
Tel. - Anduka-cheṭṭu
Tam. - Kundurukam
Vernacular - Sāla (Ḍalhaṇa)
Eng. - Indian olibanum tree

Botanical Name: Boswellia serrata Roxb

Natural Order: Burseraceae

Habitat: Most parts of India except Assam.

Description: A gregarious, deciduous tree with yellow or ash-coloured bark; the sap wood is white-brown. The leaves are imparipinnate, crowded at the tips of branches, and the leaflets are deeply toothed. The flowers are small and white, in axillary racemes. The fruit is a three-valved capsule. The tree flowers during April-May, and is leafless from March to June.

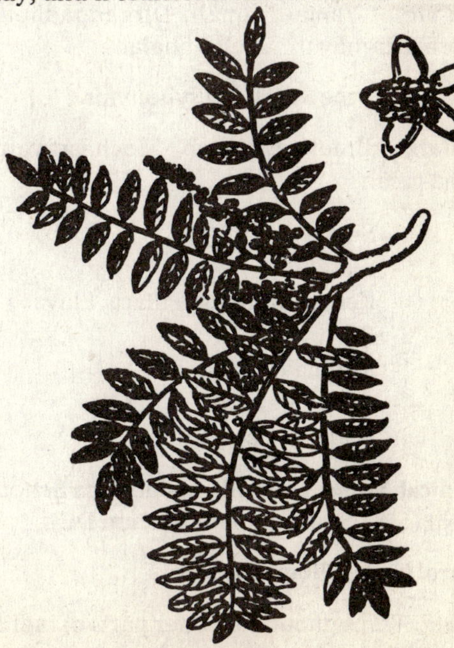

Medicinal Action:

Rasa : Astringent, bitter and sweet

It alleviates kapha and pitta, is constipative, nutritive, and is useful in diarrhoea, bleeding from internal organs, ulcers, haemorrhoids and skin diseases.

The flowers and fruits alleviate kapha and vāta, and are of value in haemorrhoids, skin diseases, and anorexia.

Note: The gum-resin of Śallakī is termed Kunduru.

Hin. - Sālai-gūgul,
Eng. - Indian olibanum or Frankincense

References: CS, kalpa, 1, 8; SS, sūtra, 38, 14-15.

Śālmalī

Synonyms: Pichhilā, Pūraṇī, Sthirāyuh, Tūliphalā, Durārohā, Rakta pushpā, Nirgandha-pushpī, Tulinī, Kukkuṭī, Kaṇṭakārī, Bahu-vīryā, Yama-drumah, Dīrghapādapā, Nissārā, Dīrghāyuh, Sthūla-phalah.

The gum has the following synonyms :

Pichhah, Śālmelīveshṭakah, Mochasrāvah, Mocha-rasah.

Hin. - Semal
Ben. - Simul
Kan. - Kempu-būrugada mara, Elava
Tel. - Būruga
Mal. - Muḷḷilavu, Pūḷa
Tam. - Ilavu, Śānmali
Eng. - Red Silk Cotton tree

Botanical Name: Salmalia malabarica Schott & Endl (Syn. Bombax malabaricum DC)

Natural Order: Bombacaceae

Habitat: Throughout the hotter parts of India.

Description: This is a very large, often buttressed, deciduous tree. The branches are whorled, spreading nearly horizontally with sharp conical prickles. The bark is grey while the leaves are palmate, and leaflets lanceolate and short petioled. The flowers are large and solitary, appearing before the leaves. The pedicels are short and thick. The fruit is a capsule, and is green, cylindrical, smooth and tapering at both ends. The tree flowers in December-January.

Varieties: There is another variely called Kūṭa-śālmalī.

Medicinal Action:

Rasa : Sweet and astringent (flowers, fruits, root and gum.
Sweet (stems)

Guṇa : Unctous, simy and dry (root)
Heavy and dry (flowers and fruits)
Heavy and unctous (gum)

Vīrya : Cold (Parts)
Vipāka : Sweet (root)

The root aggravates kapha, alleviates pitta, purifies the blood, bestows longevity, is nutritive, an aphrodisiac, strength-giving and relieves bleeding from internal organs.

The flowers and fruits alleviate kapha and pitta, aggravate vāta, purify the blood, and are constipative.

The stems alleviate pitta, are constipative and are used in swellings, burnings and heat.

The flowers and stems, if taken with ghee and rock-salt are beneficial in severe menorrhagia and metrorrhagia. They also alleviate kapha and pitta, aggravate vāta and are constipative.

The gum alleviates vāta and pitta, aggravates kapha, purifies the blood, gives protection against abortion, is strength-giving, nutritive, a brain-tonic, constipative, an aphrodisiac, bestows longevity, enhances the complexion and is useful in diarrhoea, dysentery, burning pains and bleeding from rectum.

When taken with curds, it relieves diarrhoea with colic and tenesmus. It is also used as picchābasti (SS, sūtra, 40, 113; AS, sūtra, 15, 32).

References: SS, chikitsā, 15, 9; uttara, 40, 69, 113; 45, 34; CS, chikitsā, 30, 91.

Śamī

Synonyms: Śaktuphalī, Śāntā, Keśahantrī, Śivāphalā, Mangalyā, Śubhadā, Lakshmī, Pavitrā, Pāpa-nāśinī, Kānanārih, Tungā, Keśamathanī, Samudra, Vahnigarbhā, Medhyā, Duritadamanī, Śankarī, Surabhī, Śankhuphalā.

Hin. - Chhikura
Ben. - Sain
Tel. - Jammi-cheṭṭu
Kan. - Banni-mara
Mal. - Parampu

Botanical Name: Prosopis spicigera Linn

Natural Order: Leguminosae

Habitat: Punjab, Rajasthan, Gujarat, Sind and Baluchisthan.

Description: This is a moderate-sized, nearly evergreen, thorny tree, with the branches and branchlets having conical broad-based prickles. The leaves are bipinnate, with two pairs of opposite pinnae. There are 7-10 pairs of opposite, linear-oblong leaflets. The flowers are in axillary spikes or panicles. The fruit is a slender, torulose pod, 10-26 cms. long, with 10-15 seeds in a dry, sweetish pulp. Flowers appear from March to May.

Medicinal Action:

Rasa : Astringent, bitter and pungent.
Sweet (fruits)
Guṇa : Dry and light
Heavy, dry and sharp (fruits)
Vīrya : Cold
Hot (fruits)

It alleviates kapha, is appetizing, and is beneficial in bleeding from internal organs, diarrhoea, dyspnoea, cough, vertigo, skin diseases, heamorrhoids, worms, tremors and fatigue.

The fruits aggravate pitta, are a brain tonic and are used to remove unwanted hair.

References: CS, sūtra, 27, 160; kalpa, 1, 8; SS, sūtra, 46, 193.

Śaṇah

Synonyms: Mālyapushpah, Vamanah, Kaṭutiktakah, Niśāvanah, Dīrghaśākhah, Tvaksārah, Dīrghapallavah.

Hin. - San, Saḍam
Ben. - San
Kan. - Saṇabu-giḍa

Mah. - Tāg, Ambāḍī
Tel. - Janapa-cheṭṭu
Tam. - Chaṇal, Kuttiram, Śaṇam
Mal. - Chaṇaka, Kāṭu-tendalkoḍi
Eng. - Sunn Hemp

Botanical Name: Crotalaria juncea Linn

Natural Order: Leguminosae

Habitat: Cultivated throughout India.

Description: This is a tall shrub, reaching to 244 cms in height with prominently grooved and striated stems. The leaves are simple, linear or oblong, and shiny with short, thin silky hairs. The flowers are bright-yellow in racemes. The fruit is a pod, covered over with silky hairs.

Medicinal Action:

Rasa : Sour and astringent
Guṇa : Heavy (the seeds)
Vīrya : Hot
Cold (the seeds)

It alleviates kapha and vāta, is emetic, purgative, abortifacient, induces bleeding and relieves body-ache and pain.

The fruits purify the blood and are useful in menorrhagia and metrorrhagia.

The seeds purify the blood and are constipative.

References: SS, sūtra, 37, 9; AS, sūtra, 3, 21.

Śaṇa-pushpī

Synonyms: Bṛhat-pushpī, Śana-ghaṇṭikā, Mālyapushpī, Vamanī, Lomaśā, Kaṭutiktakā, Pītapushpī, Sthūlaphalā.

Hin - Ban-shaṇa
Jhun-jhunia, Saṇhuly
Ben. - Jhanjhana, Ban-sanui
Mah. - Tirat, Tāgī
Kan. - Gijigiji
Tel. - Veḷḷaikilukiluppai
Mal. - Petandalakoṭe
Vernacular - Saṇahulī (Ḍalhaṇa)

Botanical Name: Crotalaria verrucosa Linn

Natural Order: Leguminosae

Habitat: In the tropical region of India from Himalayas to Srilanka.

Description: The plant is a diffusely much branched herb, 2-3 ft. high, with a four-angled stem. The leaves are simple, alternate, somewhat oblong and round with a wavy margin. Stipules are large, leaf-like and persistent. Flowers are rather large, 10-20, in terminal racemes, 4-8 inches long. The fruit is an oblong, cylindrical, turgid pod, with 12-15, kidney shaped seeds.

Varieties: There are two other varieties:

1. A smaller variety called Kshudraśanah

Synonyms: Sūkshmapushpah, Vishṭikā, Sūkshmaparṇī).

2. **A white flowered variety called Śvetapushpā**

Synonyms: Vṛtta-parṇī, Mahāsitā.

Medicinal Action:

Rasa : Pungent, bitter and astringent
Bitter (Kshudra-śaṇah)
Astringent (Śvetapushpā)
Vīrya : Hot (Śvetapushpā)

It alleviates all the three doshas, purifies the blood, is an emetic and is useful in dyspepsia, fever and diseases of the mouth, throat and heart.

Kshudra-śanah is an emetic, while Śvetapushpā is constipative and a narcotic.

References: CS, sūtra, 4, 23; SS, sūtra, 39, 3).

Śankhapushpi

Synonyms: Medhyā, Chaṇḍā, Supushpī, Kumbu-mālinī, Mala-vināśinī, Kīrīṭī, Śankha-gālinī, Raktapushpī, Nīla-pushpī, Vishṇu krāntā, Śukshmapatra, Vanamālinī, Vana-vilāsinī, Tilaki, Sitapushpī, Chiriṇṭi, Bhūlagnā.

Medicinal Action:

Rasa : Bitter, pungent and astringent
Guṇa : Sharp
Vīrya : Slightly hot

It alleviates kapha and pitta, bestows longevity, purifies the blood, is a laxative, appetizing, strength giving, a brain-tonic and is beneficial in worms, insanity, epilepsy, salivation, nausea, cough, skin diseases and toxicosis.

Reference: CS, chikitsā, 1, 3, 30, 31; 10, 62; SS, uttara, 52, 4.

Saptacchadah

Synonyms: Saptaparṇah, Viśāla-tvak, Śāradah, Vishama-cchadah, Vinyākah, Deva-vṛkshah, Graha-nāśah, Sūtipatrah, Guccha pushpah, Suparṇakah, Ayugma-cchadah, Bahuparṇah, Śālmalīpatrakah, Madagandhah, Gandhiparṇah, Śaradipushpah, Śuktiparṇah.

Hin. - Cchātiān
Ben. - Chhātin
Tel. - Aeḍākula-ponna cheṭṭu
Kan. - Hāle, Konḍāle-mar
Tam. - Eḷilaippālai
Mal. - Erilampāla
Kon. - Sāntnirūku
Mah. - Sātvina
Eng. - Dita bark
Vernacular - Sātavan (Ḍalhaṇa)

Botanical Name: Alstonia scholaris R. Br

Natural Order: Apocynaceae

Habitat: Throughout the moist regions of India, especially in the coast forests.

Description: This is a large, evergreen, often buttressed tree with bitter, milky juice, whorled branches and greyish-brown, bitter bark. The leaves are in whorls of five or ten, obovate, elliptic oblong or lanceolate, bright-green above and pale beneath. The flowers are greenish-white and sessile with an unpleasant smell.

A big tree which flowers in the autumn (śarad-rutu), has flowers which exude an odour like that of an elephant in rut and leaves like those of Śālmalī (NIS on SS, sūtra, 38, 6).

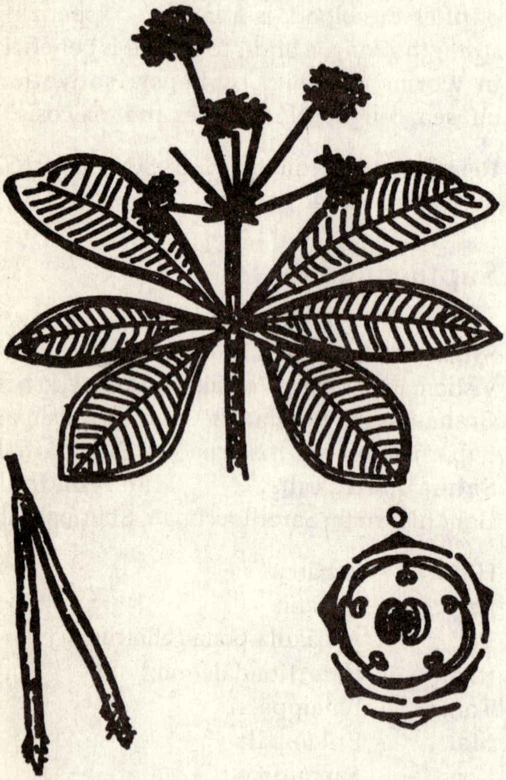

Medicinal Action:

Rasa : Astringent and bitter
Guṇa : Unctous
Vīrya : Hot

It alleviates kapha and vāta, purifies the blood, is a heart-tonic, a laxative, appetizing and is beneficial in dyspnoea, ulcers, skin diseases, worms, abdominal tumours and abdominal colic.

Therapeutic Hints:

1. It is useful in skin diseases and pruritus (CS, sūtra, 4, 11, 17).
2. Its bark is externally applied in ulcers and wounds (AS, sūtra, 38, 54).
3. Its root is used as an emetic (ibid, 14, 3), while the milky exudation is purgative (ibid, 14, 4).
4. It is one of the plants used for preparing kshāras (SS, sūtra, 11,11) It is useful in antidoting poisons and in fever and urinary disorders (ibid, 38, 6-7).

Saralah

Synonyms: Pūtikāshṭhah, Manojnah, Dhūpavṛkshah, Pītadruh, Marichapatrakah, Surabhidāruh, Chiḍā, Dīpa-vṛkshah, Tumbī, Utthitopataruh, Snigdha-dāruh.

Hin. - Chir, Saral
Mah. - Surūche-jhāḍ
Tel. - Saraḷa-devadāri-cheṭṭu
Eng. - Long leaved Pine

Botanical Name: Pinus longifolia Roxb (Syn. P. roxburghii Sargent)

Natural Order: Pinaceae

Habitat: Outer Himalayan Ranges from the Indus to Bhutan, 1,500 to 7,500 ft.

Description: A large, more or less deciduous tree with a clear, straight bole and rough branches. The bark is reddish-brown, corky outside, brick-red internally, vertically and spirally furrowed. The leaves are in bundles of three needles, nearly three cornered. The cones are on short stalks.

Parts Used: Heart wood, gum-resin.

Medicinal Action:

Rasa : Sweet, bitter and pungent
Guṇa : Light and unctous
Vīrya : Hot
Vipāka : Pungent.

It alleviates kapha and vāta, is auspicious and is useful in diseases of the ears, throat, eyes and skin, excessive perspiration, salivation, cough, syncope, ulcers, swellings and pruritus.

Reference: CS, kalpa, 1, 23; SS, sūtra, 45, 123; chikitsā, 38, 25; AHṛ, sūtra, 15, 26; AS, sūtra, 6, 306.

Śarapunkhā

Synonyms: Kālaśākah, Plīhārih, Kālikā, Nīlavṛkshākṛtih, Kāṇḍapunkhā, Bāṇapunkhā

Hin. - Sarphonkā
Tam. - Kāḷākorinil
Mal. - Korinil
Mah. - Unhāḷi
Tel. - Vempali-cheṭṭu
Kan. - Phankī, Vajrada-nīlī giḍe

Botanical Name: Tephrosia purpurea (Linn) Pers (Syn. Galega purpurea Linn)

Natural Order: Leguminoseae

Habitat: All over India and ascending the Himalayas upto 6,000 ft.

Description: A freely branching perennial under-shrub, 1/2 - 1 ft. high. The stem is woody at the base. The leaves are compound, odd-pinnate and alternate. The upper surface of the leaflet is glabrous, while the lower one is hairy. The margin is entire. Flowers are purple and arranged in a raceme. Fruit is a flat pod which breaks open longitudinally into two parts. Each leaf when torn asunder leaves a gap in the form of the letter v.

Varieties: There are two other varieties:

1. A white variety : Śveta-śarapunkha

2. A spiny variety Kaṇṭapunkhā.

The white variety is considered superior.

Medicinal Action:

Rasa : Bitter, pungent and astringent
Guṇa : Light
Vīrya : Hot

It alleviates kapha and vāta, purifies the blood, is beneficial in dyspnoea, fevers, enlargement of liver and spleen, abdominal tumours, ulcers, worms, cough, haemorrhoids, heart diseases, ascites, skin diseases, discolouration of the skin and toxicosis.

The spiny variety is said to be of use in worms and abdominal colic.

Note: Its seeds are useful in antidoting the poison generated by rat-bites (AS, uttara, 46).

Sārivā

Synonyms: Anantā, Gopī, Bhadravallī, Utpala-sārivā, Nāga-jihvā, Karālā, Sugandhā, Śyāmā, Gopi-kanyā, Āspoṭā, Kṛśodarī, Pratānikā, Kāshṭha-sārivā.

Hin.	-	Gorīsar, Ananta-mūl
Ben.	-	Syāmlatā
Kan.	-	Sogade-beru, Nāmada-beru, Kari-banṭa
Mah.	-	Upaḷasarī
Tam.	-	Nannari
Tel.	-	Pāla-sugandhī, Gede-sugandhī
Mal.	-	Nannāri, Pāravalli
Eng.	-	Indian Sarsaparilla

Botanical Name: Hemidesmus indicus R. Br

Natural Order: Asclepiadaceae

Habitat: Upper Gangetic plain, east-wards to Bengal and the Sundarbans and from Madhya-Pradesh to S. India.

Description: A perennial prostrate or twining herb with numerous, slender, glabrous stems. Leaves are very variable, glabrous, dark green, often variegated with white above, pale and sometimes silvery white below. Flowers are greenish purple with a short stalk. Seeds are long, flattened and blank.

The roots are aromatic (NIS on SS, uttara, 39, 218).

Varieties: There are two varieties - the white (sārivā) and the black (Kṛshṇa-sārivā). Kṛshṇa-sārivā has the synonyms: of Palindī, Subhadrā, Dīrgha-mūlā, Masūra-vidalā, Chandana-sārivā, Kala-ghanṭhika.

Medicinal Action:

Rasa	: Sweet and bitter
Guṇa	: Heavy and unctous
Vīrya	: Cold

It alleviates all the three doshas, purifies the blood, is an aphrodisiac, aromatic, constipative and is beneficial in skin diseases, pruritus, fever, indigestion, toxicosis, dyspnoea, cough, anorexia, diarrhoea, burning pains, menstrual disorders, thirst and bleeding from internal organs.

Kṛshna-sārivā has similar properties.

Therapeutic Hints: It enhances complexion, purifies breast-milk, and relieves fever and burning pains (CS, sūtra, 4, 10, 12, 16, 17).

References: SS, sūtra, 38, 39-40.

Sarshapah

Synonyms: Siddhārthah, Kaṭu-snehah, Rājikā-phalah, Kaṇḍūghnah, Gurughnah, Siddha-prayojanah, Tīkshṇakah, Durāgharshah, Kushṭha-nāśanah, Śveta-sarshapah.

Hin.	-	Sarson
Ben.	-	Sarisā

Tel. - Āvālu
Kan. - Sāsive-giḍa
Tam. - Kaḍugu
Kon. - Sāsama
Mah. - Śiras,
Eng. - Indian Mustard

Botanical Name: Brassica compestris Linn. var sarson Prain

Natural Order: Cruciferae

Description: This is a sparsely branched herb with generally hairy lower leaves and lower parts of the stem. The petals are narrow and do not overlap. The pods are plumpy with a slightly flattened beak, often containing one or two seeds. Seeds are light yellow or brown with a smooth seed coat and non-mucilaginous epidermis.

Varieties: There are two varieties - the white one called Sarshapah or Siddharthak and the black one called Rājakshavakah (Synonyms : Rājikā, Kṛshṇa-sarshapā, Kshudhābhijanakā, Āsurī, Jvalantī, Madhurikā. The white variety is considered superior.

Botanical Name: Brassica nigra (Linn.) Koch;

Hin. - Rāi
Mah. - Rāyi

Medicinal Action:

Rasa : Pungent and bitter (both varieties)
Pungent (the oil)

Guṇa : Sharp and slightly dry (both varieties)
Sharp (the oil)

Vīrya : Hot (both varieties and oil)

Vipāka : Pungent (both varieties and oil)

The white variety aggravates pitta, alleviates kapha and vāta, is auspicious, appetizing, a heart-tonic, and is useful in pruritus, skin diseases, abscesses, worms, abdominal colic, ulcers, swellings, haemorrhoids, toxicosis and diseases of the ears and head. It aggravates gout and bleeding from internal organs.

The leaves and stems aggravate pitta and are not conducive to health. They are constipative and lessen the quantity of urine.

The oil aggravates pitta, alleviates vāta and kapha, is useful in enlargement of the spleen, pruritus, abscesses and worms. It is an aphrodisiac, harmful to the eyes and aggravates bleeding from internal organs.

The black variety is particularly useful in abdominal tumours and enlargement of the spleen. It is similar in all other respects to the white-variety.

Therapeutic Hints:

1. The oil from the seeds is externally used in skin diseases, (CS, sūtra, 3, 6). The seeds are used as errhine (ibid, 2, 3).
2. It promotes suppuration of abscesses (SS, sūtra, 37, 9).

3. The oil from the seeds is used for cooking vegetables, etc., in urinary disorders (including diabetes) (SS, chikitaā, 11, 6). It is used as an errhine in mental illness (SS, uttara, 62, 16).

Note: The plant is harmful if used for culinary purposes (CS, sūtra, 25, 39).

References: CS, sūtra, 13, 10; 14, 31; SS, sūtra, 19, 28; chikitsā, 5, 37.

Sātalā

Synonyms: Saptala, Sārā, Vimalā, Vidulā, Nigaditā, Bhūriphenā, Charma-kashā, Dīptā, Vishāṇikā, Svarṇa-pushpī, Putravanā, Marālikā.

Medicinal Action:

Rasa : Bitter and astringent
Guṇa : Light and sharp
Vīrya : Cold
Vipāka : Pungent

It aggravates vāta, alleviates kapha and pitta, purifies the blood, is a laxative, a heart tonic and is beneficial in swellings, distension of abdomen, skin diseases, boils, ulcers, fevers, worms, abdominal tumours, ulcers in the mouth, toxicosis, and haemorrhoids.

References: Chkp on CS, kalpa, 7, 57; NIS on SS, sūtra, 38, 29; 39, 4.

Śatamūlī

Synonyms: Śatāvarī, Śatapadī, Pīvarī, Indīvarī, Ṛshyaproktā, Dvīpikā, Urdhvakaṇṭakā, Amarakaṇṭikā, Sūkshmapatrā, Supatrā, Nārāyaṇī, Svādurasā, Laghu-parṇikā, Ātma-śalyā, Jaṭamūlā, Śatavīryā, Mahoudanī, Keśikā, Viśvākhyā, Vaishṇavī, Durmarā, Varīyasī.

Hin. - Satāvar
Ben. - Śātābari
Tel. - Pilli-pīchare
Kan. - Āshāḍi, Halavu-makkalatāyi
Tam. - Paṇiyanāku
Mah. - Śātāvari

Botanical Name: Asparagus racemosus Willd

Natural Order: Liliaceae

Habitat: Throughout tropical and sub-tropical India, up to 4,000 ft. in the Himalayas, from Kashmir eastwards.

Description: This is a tall, rambling, spinous undershrub or climber with many tuberous roots. The leaves are alternate, scaly, minute, bearing tufts of cladodes in axils. The flowers are white and fragrant, occuring in racemes. The fruit is a berry, 0.64 cms in diameter. The plant flowers in the rainy season. The root is brownish-white in colour, in length from 6 to 8 inches.

Varieties: There is another variety, viz. Mahā-śatāvarī.

Medicinal Action:

Rasa : Sweet and bitter
Guṇa : Heavy and unctous
Light (the sprouts)
Vīrya : Cold

The root alleviates vāta and pitta, purifies the blood, is appetizing, a brain tonic, strength-giving, an aphrodisiac, nutritive, galactagogue, improves vision, bestows longevity and is beneficial in swellings, diarrhoea, abdominal tumours and tuberculosis.

The fresh sprouts alleviate all three doshas, are a heart tonic and are useful in gout, haemorrhoids, tuberculosis and sprue.

Mahā-śatāvari is used with benefit in haemorrhoids, sprue and eye diseases.

Therapeutic Hints:

1. It enhances intelligence, strength and memory (KS, śatāvarī K.).
2. The fresh sprouts are an aphrodisiac and alleviate all the doshas (AS, sūtra, 7, 127).
3. A medicated ghee prepared from this plant is used as an aphrodisiac (CS, chikitsā, 2, 3, 18) and relieves menstrual disorders (ibid, 8, 105) and dysentery (ibid, 19, 98).
4. A pāyasa (milk-dish) prepared from the roots is useful in cataract (SS, uttara, 17, 49).

References: CS, sūtra, 5, 65; SS, sūtra, 39, 7-8; 46, 301-302; AHṛ, sūtra, 15, 21).

Śatapushpā

Synonyms: Śatākshī, Kāravī, Tālaparṇī, Mādhavī, Misih, Sanghātapatrikā, Avākpushpī, Vajrapushpī, Śataprasūnā, Sāleyah, Aticchatra, Śiphā, Sugandhā.

Hin. - Sowā
Ben. - Sulphā
Kan. - Sabbasige
Mal. - Chatukuppa
Tel. - Pinna-sadāpa
Tam. - Śadakuppi
Eng. - Dill seeds

Botanical Name: Peucedanum graveolens Linn (Syn. Anethum sowa Kurz)

Natural Order: Umbelliferae

Habitat: Throughout India, often cultivated.

Description: The leaves are fine and delicate, the flowers are yellow.

An annual or biennial herb with a stem 1-3 ft high, erect, slightly branched, cylindrical, finely straited, smooth and pale green. Leaves are alternate, stalked, petiolate, bright-green, smooth narrowly oval-triangular in outline and usually tri-pinnate. Flowers are small, numerous, yellow, pedicelled, in umbels. The fruit is about 1/5 inch long, broadly oval in outline, smooth and rounded at both ends.

Medicinal Action:

Rasa : Pungent and bitter
Guṇa : Light and sharp
Vīrya : Hot

It alleviates kapha and vāta, alleviates pitta, is appetizing, a brain tonic and is beneficial in dysmenorrhea, fevers, ulcers, abdominal colic, and distension of abdomen.

Therapeutic Hints:

1. It is one of the drugs used in upanāha sveda (CS, sūtra, 14, 36).
2. It is an aphrodisiac and is useful in amenorrhoea, sterility and impotence (KS, kalpa).

References: CS, sūtra, 4, 13.

Śaṭhī

Synonyms: Karchūrah, Vedhyah, Mukhyah,

Drāviḍah, Kalpakah, Gandhamūlakah, Gandha-sārah, Kārśyah, Durlabhah

Hin. - Karchur
Ben. - Saṭi
Mah. - Kachorā
Kan. - Kāḍarasina, Kastūri-arishina-giḍa
Tel. - Kachoramu
Mal. - Kāṭṭu-mannal
Tam. - Kastūri-manjal
Kon. - Āmbahalaḍi
Eng. - Zedoary

Botanical Name: Curcuma zedoaria Rose

Natural Order: Zinziberaceae

Habitat: Said to be wild in the eastern Himalayas and in the moist deciduous forests of the coastal regions of Kanara.

Description: A large perennial herb with a large tuberous root stock with many palmately attached tubers. Leaves are lanceolate, smooth, tapering at the base and purplish at the centre. The inflorescence arises from the rhizome. The flowering period is usually from March to May.

Medicinal Action:

Rasa : Pungent and bitter
Guṇa : Light and sharp
Vīrya : Hot
Vipāka : Pungent

It alleviates kapha and vāta, is aromatic, appetizing, cleanses the mouth, and is beneficial in skin diseases, haemorrhoids, ulcers, worms, cough, dyspnoea, abdominal tumours, fever, enlargement of the spleen, glandular swellings, dyspepsia and epilepsy. It aggravates bleeding from internal organs.

References: AHṛ, sūtra, 6, 72.

Satīlā (Satīnā)

Synonyms: Kalāyah, Muṇḍa-chaṇakah, Hareṇuh, Reṇukah, Tripuṭah, Kaṇṭī, Ativartulah, Vartula-kalāyah.

Hin. - Maṭar
Ben. - Maṭar
Tel. - Batānīlu
Kan. - Baṭāṇi
Tam. - Paṭāṇi
Guj. - Mah.-Wāṭāṇi
Mal. - Paṭṭāṇi payaru
Kon. - Baṭṭaṇe
Eng. - Garden Pea

Botanical Name: Pisum sativum Linn

Natural Order: Leguminosae

Habitat: Cultivated generally.

Description: This is an annual herb with hollow stems ending in one or more tendrils. The leaves are pinnately compound, with auricled stipules. The flowers are white, bluish or purple coloured. The pods are straight or curved, 8-10 cms long with 6-9, green, yellow-green, blue-green, white-grey, brown or mottled, smooth and rounded or flattened seeds.

Medicinal Action :

Rasa : Astringent and sweet
Guṇa : Dry
Vīrya : Cold
Vipāka : Sweet

It aggravates vāta, alleviates kapha and pitta, purifies the blood, is appetizing, nutritive, strength-giving and relieves burning pains. It causes indigestion if eaten in excess.

Therapeutic Hints:

1. It is generally beneficial to all living beings (SS, sūtra, 20, 5). It is useful in syncope (SS, uttara, 46, 16).
2. The leaves and stalks alleviate all the doshas, are light, slightly bitter, constipative and useful in skin diseases (SS, sūtra, 46, 266; AHṛ, sūtra, 6, 72).
3. The gruel prepared from this is used in certain cases of bleeding from internal organs (SS, uttara, 45, 16).

References: CS, siddhi, 3, 8; SS, sūtra, 46, 33.

Sevam

Synonyms: Mushṭi-pramāṇam, Badaram, Sinchitikā-phalam.

Hin. - Sev
Ben. - Seb
Kan. - Sebu
Eng. - The Apple tree

Botanical Name: Pyrus malus Linn (Syn. Malus sylvestris Mill)

Natural Order: Rosaceae

Habitat: Cultivated in the Himalayas, the Punjab, Sind, N.W. Frontier Province, M. P. and the Deccan. Wild in the N. W. Himalayas, ascending to 9,000 ft.

Parts Used: The ripe fruits.

Medicinal Action:

Rasa : Sweet
Guṇa : Heavy
Vīrya : Cold
Vipāka : Sweet

It alleviates vāta and pitta, aggravates kapha, is appetizing, nutritive and aphrodisiac.

Śigruh

Synonyms: Śobhānjanah, Harita-śākah, Laghupatrakah, Tīkshṇagandhah, Śākapatrah, Upadamśakshmah, Komalapatrakah, Bahumūlah, Damśa-mūlah, Kāminīśah, Vidradhi-nāśanah, Akshīvah, Vana-pallavah, Śveta-marichah, Kaṭu-gandhah, Mechakah, Strī-chitra-hārī, Kṛshṇa-gandhah, Mūlaka-parṇī.

Hin. - Sahinjan, Sajinā
Ben. - Sajinā
Tel. - Munaga
Kan. - Nugge-mara
Tam. - Murungai
Mah. - Śevaga
Mal. - Murina
Eng. - Drumstick tree or Horse-radish tree

Botanical Name: Moringa oleifera Lam (Syn. M. pterygosperma Gaertn)

Natural Order: Moringaceae

Habitat: Most parts of India.

Description: A medium sized elegant deciduous tree with rough and corky bark. Leaves are fern-like, divided and sub-divided. The tree is leafless for a short period before it flowers from February to April. Flowers are creamy-white and honey-scented; and appear as clusters along with the leaves. The fruit is pod-like, triangular and pendulous containing many winged seeds.

Varieties: There are two varieties:

1. A white-variety called Śveta-śigruh

Synonym: Mukha-bhangah

2. A red variety called Madhu-śigruh

Synonym: Surangī

Medicinal Action:

Rasa : Pungent, sweet and bitter
Sweet and bitter (Madhu-śigruh)
Sweet (the stems)
Pungent (the flowers and the oil)
Sweet and astringent (the fruits)

Guṇa : Light, dry, sharp and slimy
Sharp (the seeds and flowers)
Unctous (the stems)
Light and sharp (the oil)

Vīrya : Hot (all other parts)
Cold (the stems)

Vipāka : Pungent

It alleviates kapha and vāta, aggravates pitta, vitiates the blood, is a heart-tonic, appetizing, constipative, an aphrodisiac, beneficial to the eyes and is used in abscesses, swellings, worms, obesity, glandular swellings, toxicosis, enlargement of the spleen, abdominal tumours, ulcers and abdominal colic.

The seeds alleviate vāta and kapha, antidote poison, are an aphrodisiac, beneficial to the eyes, and if used as an errhine relieve headaches.

The stems alleviate vāta and pitta, are appetizing, nutritive, analgesic, beneficial to the eyes and are useful in worms and alcoholism.

The flowers alleviate kapha and vāta, and are useful in abscesses, enlargements of the spleen, abdominal tumours, sprains and swellings.

The fruits alleviate kapha and pitta, are appetizing, are beneficial in colic, skin diseases, dyspnoea, abdominal tumours and tuberculosis.

The oil alleviates kapha and vāta, is a laxative, and is useful in worms, skin diseases, urinary disorders and headaches.

Therapeutic Hints:

1. It is refreshing, a heart-tonic and slightly aggravates pitta (CS, sūtra, 27, 170).
2. It is one of the drugs used for administering nāḍī-sveda (a kind of fomentation) (ibid, 14, 31).
3. The seeds are used as errhine (ibid, 2, 3-5).
4. The fruits are to be administered with tepid water in anaemia (SS, uttara, 44, 26).

References: SS, uttara, 39, 272; 42, 94; CS, sūtra, 13, 10.

Śimbikā

Synonyms: Asi-śimbī, Khanga-śimbī, Sthūla-śimbī.

Hin. - Sem, Suarā-sem
Ben. - Śem-gācch
Mah. - Khad-sāmbal
Kan. - Śambe
Tam. - Koḷiya-varai
Guj. - Eraboliya
Eng. - Sword-bean

Botanical Name: Canavalia ensiformis (Linn.) DC, (Syn. C. virosa (Roxb.) W & A)

Natural Order: Leguminosae

Habitat: Most parts of India.

Description: A woody perennial climbing bean, bearing pods, 6-12 inches long and 1-1/2 inches broad.

Medicinal Action:

Rasa : Sweet and astringent
Guṇa : Heavy
Vīrya : Cold
Vipāka : Sweet

It alleviates vāta and pitta, is strength-giving and is useful in burning pains and ulcers.

Śimśipā

Synonyms: Mahā-śyāmā, Kṛshṇa-sārā, Dhūmrikā, Tīkshṇa-sārā, Dhīrā, Yugapatrikā, Pichhilā, Kālānusāryah.

Hin. - Śīsu, Śīsav
Ben. - Śiśu
Mah. - Śisavā
Kan. - Śishmabāge, Ibaḍi-mara
Tel. - Iruguḍu-cheṭṭu
Mal. - Iruviḷ
Eng. - Sissoo wood

Botanical Name: Dalbergia latifolia Roxb.

Natural Order: Leguminosae

Habitat: Most parts of India.

Description: A fairly large tree with a full, rounded crown and a grey, thick, somewhat longitudinally furrowed, exfoliating bark. The young parts are grey and downy. The leaves are alternate, imparipinnate, with three to five leaflets, which are alternate, broad ovate, tough and acuminate. The flowers are pale white, the racemes in short axillary panicles. The fruit is a linear-lanceolate, pale-brown pod with light brown seeds.

Varieties: There are two other varieties

1. Śveta-śimśipā (a white variety)

2. Kapilā (an yellow variety)

Medicinal Action:

Rasa : Pungent, bitter and astringent
Guṇa : Bitter (Śveta-śimśipā and Kapilā)
Vīrya : Hot
Cold (Śveta-śimśipā and Kapilā)

It alleviates kapha and vāta, purifies the blood, is an abortifacient, appetizing, strength-giving, enhances the complexion, and is beneficial in tuberculosis, obesity, skin diseases, leucoderma, vomiting, worms, diseases of the bladder, ulcers, burning pains, swellings, urticaria, chronic fevers, diarrhoea and herpes.

Śveta-śimśipā alleviates pitta and relieves burning pains.

Kapilā alleviates vāta and pitta, and is useful in fever, fatigue, vomiting and hiccoughs.

Therapeutic Hints: The oil is bitter, pungent, astringent, alleviates vāta and kapha, cleanses septic ulcers and wounds and is useful in worms and skin diseases (SS, sūtra, 45, 123).

References: CS, śārīra, 8, 38; kalpa, 1, 8; AS, sūtra, 6, 106; 16, 14; AHṛ, sūtra, 15, 32.

Sindūrapushpī

Synonyms: Tṛṇapushpī, Sindūrī, Sukomalā.

Hin.	-	Sindūriyā, Jāphar, Latkan
Mah.	-	Śendrī
Ben.	-	Latkan
Kan.	-	Rangmāle
Eng.	-	Arnatto

Botanical Name: Bixa orellano Linn

Natural Order: Bixaceae

Habitat: Cultivated to a small extent in Karnataka, is grown in gardens on a hedge plant. Occurs as an escape in Travancore, Coromandel and Malabar coasts and in some districts of Mumbai, Bengal and Assam.

Description: A small evergreen tree up to 5 m in height, generally with long branches from near the ground. Leaves are simple, alternate, glabrous and emit a foetid smell when crushed. Flowers are white, pinkish or purplish, and the fruit is a reddish-brown capsule.

Medicinal Action:

Rasa : Bitter, pungent and astringent

Guṇa : Light

Vīrya : Cold

It alleviates kapha and vāta, purifies the blood, is auspicious and is beneficial in bleeding from internal organs, vomiting, headache, gout and toxicosis.

Śirīshah

Synonyms: Mṛdupushpah, Bhaṇḍikah, Śankhinīphalah, Kapītanah, Śukataruh, Śyāmavarṇah, Śītapushpah, Barhipushpah, Vishahantā, Uddānakah, Lomaśa-pushpakah, Karṇa-pūrah, Mūrdhapushpah, Svarṇapushpah, Vṛtta-pushpah, Madhupushpah.

Hin.	-	Siris
Ben.	-	Siris
Tel.	-	Dirasana-cheṭṭu
Kan.	-	Bāge-mara
Tam.	-	Vāgai-maram
Mal.	-	Nenneni

Mah. - Śirasī
Eng. - Sirissa tree

Botanical Name: Albizzia lebbeck Benth

Natural Order: Leguminosae

Habitat: Throughout India.

Description: This large, deciduous tree with a spreading crown, has a brownish-grey, rough bark and bipinnate leaves with five to nine leaflets which are obliquely oblong. The flowers are scented, and the fruit is a pod with six to twelve seeds.

Medicinal Action:

Rasa : Pungent, bitter, astringent and sweet
Guṇa : Light
Vīrya : Cold

It alleviates vāta, purifies the blood, antidotes all poisons, is an analgesic and is beneficial in scabies, skin diseases, pruritus, haemorrhoids, sweating, swellings, herpes, cough and ulcers.

Therapeutic Hints:

1. The flowers are most useful in antidoting poisons (CS, sūtra, 25, 40; SS, kalpa, 5, 17-18).
2. The fruits are useful when used as errhine (SS, sūtra, 39, 6).
3. The panchāngās (the five parts of the plant) are all useful in antidoting poison (AHṛ, sūtra, 10, 31; AS, uttara, 40).
4. The oil is used as uttara-basti in menstrual disorders (AS, uttara, 39).

References: CS, sūtra, 2, 5.

Śiva-mallikā

Synonyms: Linginī, Bahupatrā, Īśvarī, Svayambhū, Linga-sambhūtā, Chitraphalā, Chaṇḍā, Devī, Āpastambhinī.

Hin. - Śiva-lingī
Ben. - Śiva-lingini
Tel. - Linga-doṇḍa
Kan. - Linga-toṇḍe-baḷḷi
Mal. - Naiyunni

Botanical Name: Bryonopsis lanciniosa (Linn) Naud (Syn. Bryonia laciniosa Linn)

Natural Order: Cucurbitaceae

Habitat: Throughout India.

Medicinal Action:

Rasa : Pungent and bitter
Vīrya : Hot

It alleviates vāta, has a disagreeable smell, bestows longevity, is auspicious, appetizing and is beneficial in skin diseases, dyspepsia and abdominal tumours.

Śleshmātakah

Synonyms: Karbudārah, Pichchilah, Lekhasāṭakah, Śeluh, Bahuvārah, Śāpitah, Dvija-kutsitah, Gandha-pushpah.

Hin. - Nisoḍā, Labherā, Barālsoḍā
Vennacular - Lisodā (Ḍalhaṇa)
Mah. - Bhonkar
Ben. - Bahuyār, Boharī, Chālta
Kon. - Śarpaḷe
Tel. - Pedda-nakkera, Banke-nakkera
Mal. - Naruvari, Vidi-maram,
Kan. - Maṇṇaḍike, Challe-mara, Soḷḷe-mara, Chaḷḷe.
Eng. - Sepistan plum, Narrow-leaved Sepistan

Botanical Name: Cordia wallichii G. Don (Syn. C. oblique Willd var. Wallichil)

Natural Order: Boraginaceae

Habitat: Most parts of India.

Description: A middle-sized, deciduous tree with a grey or brown bark. The leaves are variable, usually broadly ovate, entire, with a cordate, three-nerved base. The flowers are small, white and fragrant, in lax cymes. The fruit is a yellow or pink, ovoid drupe with a mucilaginous, edible pulp. The tree flowers in March-April.

Varieties: There is another variety - Bhūkar-budārah (Synonyms : Laghu-Śleshmātakah).

Botanical Name: Cordia angustifolia Roxb; C. dichotama Forst. f.

Medicinal Action:

Rasa : Pungent and astringent
Sweet, astringent and bitter (unripe fruits)
Sweet (ripe-fruits)

Guṇa : Slimy and unctous
Light (unripe fruits)
Dry, heavy and unctous (ripe fruits)
Heavy (the oil)

Vīrya : Cold
Slightly cold (Bhū-karbudārah)

Vipāka : Sweet

It alleviates pitta, aggravates kapha, purifies the blood, and is useful in worms, abdominal colic, ulcers, wounds, boils, herpes and toxicosis.

The fruits are externally applied as a paste on the breasts to purify breast-milk. The unripe fruits aggravate vāta, alleviate pitta and kapha, purify the blood and are constipative. The ripe fruits alleviate vāta and pitta, purify the blood, are constipative and nutritive.

The bark is used externally in scorpion bites, insect bites, etc.

The oil aggravates kapha, alleviates pitta and vāta and is beneficial to the hair.

1. The paste of the fruits is applied over the breasts in order to purify breast-milk (CS, chikitsā, 30, 275; SS, chikitsā, 5, 10).
2. The bark is used both internally and externally in poisoning by spiders (lūta) (SS, kalpa, 8, 120).

References: CS, sūtra, 4, 11; 27, 159; SS, sūtra, 46, 193; chikitsā, 5, 10; 39, 5, kalpa, 5, 75-76; uttara, 47, 32; AS, sūtra, 6.

Snuhi

Synonyms: Snuk, Mahāvṛkshah, Guḍā, Nistrimśa-patrakah, Samanta-dugdhā, Gaṇḍīrah, Sehuṇḍah, Vajra-kaṇṭakah, Sudhā, Śākhākaṇṭah, Bahuśākhah, Vātarih, Kshīrakāṇḍakah, Bhadrah, Vyāghra-nakhah, Netrārih, Daṇḍa-vṛkshah, Śītahuṇḍah, Kuliśa-drumah, Kāṇḍa-rohakah.

Hin. - Thohar, Sehund
Ben. - Mansā sij
Tel. - Jemuḍu, Āku-chemuḍu

Tam. - Kaḷḷi, Hi-kaḷḷi
Mah. - Kate-nivadung
Mal. - Tirukaḷḷi
Kan. - Muṇḍu-gaḷḷi, Kaḷḷi-giḍa, Mūreṇina-kaḷḷi
Eng. - Milk Hedge, Indian Tree Spurge

Botanical Name: Euphorbia neriifolia Linn

Natural Order: Euphorbiaceae

Habitat: Orissa and Deccan. Cultivated elsewhere in India.

Description: This is a tree, up to 9 metres high. The leaves are alternate, simple, obovate, fleshy, green and deciduous. The stipules are modified into spines. The inflorescence of crowded csymes is seen at the end of the branches. The fruit is a glabrous capsule with globose, smooth, dorsally lined, black seeds.

Varieties: There is another variety with three ridges (Tridhārā) (Also see SS, chikitsā, 4, 31).

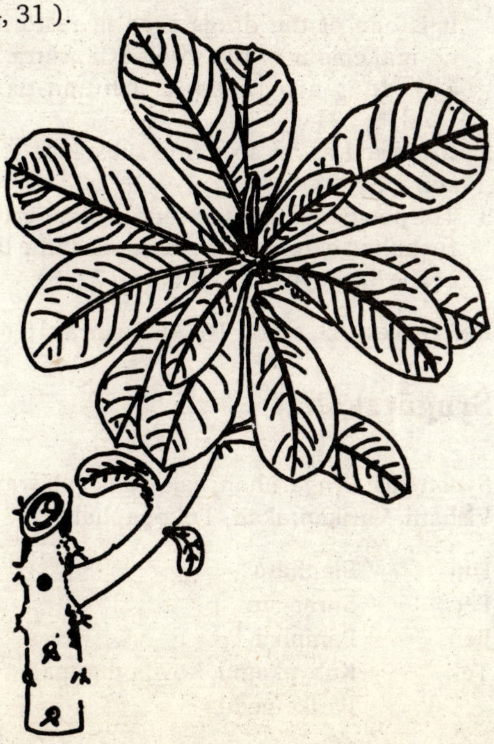

Medicinal Action:

Rasa : Pungent and bitter
Pungent (the milky juice)
Guṇa : Heavy and sharp
Light and unctous (the milky juice)
Sharp (the leaves)
Vīrya : Hot (all parts)

It alleviates vāta, antidotes poison, is appetizing, a purgative and is useful in enlargement of the spleen, urinary disorders, burning pains, skin diseases, abdominal colic, distension of abdomen, Ashṭhīla, insanity, abdominal tumours, ascites, syncope, haemorrhoids, swellings, calculi, anaemia, boils and fever.

The milky juice also alleviates vāta, is a purgative, and is beneficial in distension of the abdomen, abdominal tumours, ascites, skin diseases and toxicosis.

The leaves are appetizing, and are used in flatulence, distension of abdomen, Ashṭhila, abdominal tumours, colic, swellings and ascites.

Note:

1. Purification of the milk of Snuhī : One tola of the leaf juice of amlikā, after being filtered through a cloth is mixed with two palas of the milky juice of snuhī. The liquid is then dried in the heat of the sun. Thus dried, the milk of snuhī becomes purified and can be used when necessary (RJN, Vol.III, page 332).
2. The adverse effects can be remedied by taking internally amlikā leaves made into a paste with water (ibid, page 356).
3. Its milky exudation is a strong purgative (CS, sūtra, 25, 40). It is useful in purifying and cleansing wounds (SS, sūtra, 37, 16-17).

Somalatā

Synonyms: Soma-vallī, Yajna-netrī, Somakshīrī, Dvija-priyā, Yajna-śreshṭhā, Dhanurlatā, Gulmavallī, Indulekhā.

Hin. - Somlatā
Tam. - Koḍikaḷḷi
Kan. - Soma baḷḷi
Ben. - Somlatā
Eng. - Moon plant

Botanical Name: Sarcostemma acidum (Roxb) Voigt (Syn. S. Brevistigma W & A)

Natural Order: Asclepiadaceae

Habitat: Arid rocks in Konkan, Deccan, N. Circars, Carnatic and Bengal.

Description: A trailing, leafless shrub with jointed, green, glabrous stems. The leaves are opposite, exstipulate, simple and entire. The flowers are small, sessile, regular, bisexual, white, in terminal umbels. There are two follicles, tapering at both ends. The plant flowers from July-December.

Medicinal Action:

Rasa : Pungent, bitter and sweet
Vīrya : Cold

It alleviates all three doshas, is auspicious and is useful in burning pains, thirst and tuberculosis.

Śrīvāsah (See. Saralah)

Synonyms: Saralasrāvah, Śrīveshṭah, Vṛkshadhūpakah, Rasāveshṭah, Padmadarśanah, Pāyasah, Kshīrāhvayah, Yāsah, Rakta-Śīrshakah, Yavāsah, Sudhūpakah, Tilaparṇah.

Hin. - Gandhabirojā
Ben - Gandhabiroja
Mah. - Dhūp, Rāḷ
Tam. - Pinai-mārū
Eng. - Long-leaved Pine

Botanical Name: Resin of Pinus longifolia Roxb

Natural Order: Pinaceae

Medicinal Action:

Rasa : Sweet, bitter and astringent
Guṇa : Light and unctous
Vīrya : Hot

It alleviates vāta and kapha, aggravates pitta, is auspicious, aromatic, a laxative, an aphrodisiac and is useful in diseases of the head, eyes and larynx, perspiration, pruritus, ulcers, menstrual disorders, dyspepsia, flatulent distension, fever, skin diseases and burning pains.

The extract (sārah) alleviates kapha, is an analgesic, a diuretic, is beneficial in swellings, fever and worms.

Theraputic Hints:

1. It is one of the drugs used in restoring normal colour of the stools (CS, sūtra, 4, 15). It is also used as Dhūma-pāna (ibid, 5, 23).
2. It is used as an aromatic substance (SS, sūtra, 37, 21).
3. The powder of this and certain other drugs is applied externally in diseases of the lips of the Vāta type (SS, chikitsā, 22, 5).

References: AS, sūtra, 16; AHṛ, sūtra, 15,43.

Śṛṇgāṭakah

Synonyms: Śṛngaruhah, Jala-vallī, Jalāśrayā, Vishāṇī, Vārikaṇṭakah, Trikoṇaphalah.

Hin. - Singhāra
Pers. - Surangān
Ben. - Pāniphal
Tel. - Kubyakamu, Kovila-dumpa, Parike-geḍḍa

Mah. - Singhāḍe
Tam. - Śingāra-koṭṭāi
Mal - Karimpoḷam
Vernacular - Singhāḍā (Ḍalhaṇa)
Eng. - Singhara Nut, Water Caltrops, Water Chestnut

Botanical Name: Trapa natans Linn. var bispinosa (Roxb.) Makino (Syn. T. bispinosa Roxb; T. quadrispinosa Wall)

Natural Order: Trapaceae

Habitat: Throughout India.

Description: This is a very variable, handsome, rooted, aquatic herb. The stems are long, flexuose, ascending in the water, the submerged portions possess pairs of green spreading organs (or leaves). The leaves are floating, crowded at the upper part of stems, appearing as rosettes, rhomboidal, the lower surface reddish-purple to green, the upper green . The flowers are white, opening above the surface of water in the afternoon. The fruits are bony and turbinate.

Varieties: There are two varieties, big and small (Daḷhaṇa).

Medicinal Action:

Rasa : Astringent and sweet
Guṇa : Light
Vīrya : Cold

It alleviates pitta, aggravates kapha and vāta, purifies the blood, is a laxative, an aphrodisiac, appetizing, refreshing and is beneficial in fatigue, fevers, swellings, burning pains and vertigo.

Note: Ḍalhaṇa describes the plant as having fruits with three ridges and growing in damp regions (NIS on SS, chikitsā, 3, 61).

Therapetic Hints:

1. It is useful in urinary disorders (including diabetes) and is used for external application with ghee in visarpa of the pitta type (SS, chikitsā, 11, 10; 17, 6).
2. It is useful in bleeding from internal organs, in preventing abortion, as an aphrodisiac and preparing alcoholic drinks (āsava) (CS, sūtra, 25, 49; śārīra, 8, 24; chikitsā, 4, 71; 2, 22).

References: CS, sūtra, 27, 117; SS, sūtra, 46, 304.

Śṛngaveram

Synonyms: Ārdrakam, Kaṭubhadram, Kaṭutkaṭam, Gulmamūlam.

Fresh: Ārdraśākam, Apakrshṇakam.

Dry: Śuṇṭhī, Mahoushadhī, Viśvā, Viśvabheshajam, Kaphārī, Nāgaram, Kaṭu-granthim, Śoshaṇam.

Hin. - Ādrak, Souṇṭh
Ben - Ādā
Tel. - Śuṇṭhi
Kan. - Śuṇṭhi

Tam. - Inji, Śukku
Kon. - Ālle
Mal. - Inchi
Eng. - Common Ginger

Botanical Name: Zinziber officinale Rosc

Natural Order: Zinziberaceae

Habitat: Widely cultivated in India.

Description: This is a perennial herb with large, solid, tough, horizontal rhizome, consisting of a series of many roundish joints, pale yellow within and covered with pale silvery-brown skin. The leaves are alternate, distichous, smooth, with long, lax sheaths. The flowering stems are shorter than the leafy ones, are erect and slender with few, sessile, orange-yellow flowers.

Medicinal Action:

Rasa : Pungent and sweet (fresh)
Pungent (dry)

Guṇa : Heavy, dry and sharp (fresh)
Light and unctous (dry)

Vīrya : Hot (both)

Vipāka : Sweet (both)

Fresh ginger alleviates kapha and vāta, is a purgative, appetizing, a digestive, an aphrodisiac, beneficial to the throat and is useful in indigestion, swellings, anorexia, cough, dyspnoea, sore-throat, flatulent distension of abdomen, vomiting, constipation and abdominal colic.

Fresh ginger taken with rock salt before meals is said to be universally beneficial. It alleviates kapha and vāta, is a laxative, appetizing and relieves swellings.

Fresh ginger taken with juice of Jambīrah cleanses the mouth, and is useful in dysuria, anaemia, bleeding from internal organs, ulcers, calculi, fever, burning pains and in summer heat.

Fresh ginger is however contraindicated, if taken alone, in anaemia, skin diseases, dysuria, bleeding from internal organs, ulcers, fever, burning pains and in summer and Śarad ṛtu (autumn).

Dry ginger alleviates kapha and vāta, is constipative, appetizing, a digestive, an aphrodisiac and is beneficial in constipation, rheumatism, vomiting, dyspnoea, cough, abdominal colic, heart disease, elephantiasis,haemorrhoids and flatulent distension of abdomen.

Therapuitic Hints:

1. Dry ginger alleviates thirst, haemorrhoids, indigestion, and is useful as an errhine (CS, sūtra, 4, 11-14; 2, 5).
2. It is useful in a kind of indigestion called rasa-śeshājīrṇa, in jaundice and hiccough (SS, sūtra, 46, 511; uttara, 44, 30; 50, 22).

Reference: CS, sūtra, 4, 9; 25, 38; chikitsā, 12, 44; 13, 153; SS, sūtra, 20, 14; chikitsā, 14, 10; AHṛ, sūtra, 3, 23.

Sthalapadmiṇī

Synonyms: Padma-chāriṇī, Avyathā, Śāradā, Supushkarā, Ramyā, Sugandhamūlā, Amburuhā, Pushkariṇī, Chāraṭī.

Medicinal Action:

Rasa : Astringent, pungent and bitter
Guṇa : Light
Vīrya : Cold

It alleviates kapha and pitta, purifies the blood, strengthens the breasts, is auspicious and is useful in urinary calculi, dysuria, abdominal colic, diarrhoea, vomiting, burning pains, syncope, urinary disorders, dypnoea, epilepsy, toxicosis, cough and bleeding from internal organs.

Sudarśanā

Synonyms: Somavallī, Chakrāngī, Madhuparṇikā, Vṛshakarṇī,

Medicinal Action:

Rasa : Sweet
Vīrya : Hot

It alleviates kapha and vāta, purifies the blood and relieves swellings.

Sunishaṇṇakah

Synonyms: Sitavārah, Svastikah, Śrīvārakah, Sūchipatrah, Parṇakah, Śikhī, Vitunnah, Medhākṛt, Kuranṭah, Kukkuṭah, Chatush-parṇī.

Hin. - Chaupatte
Ben. - Sunsuniā, Susnishak
Tel. - Chenchali-kūra
Kan. - Chiṭigina-soppu
Tam. - Arai-keecrai
Mah. - Kuraḍu
Vernacular - Siribālikā (Ḍalhaṇa)

Botanical Name: Marsilea minuta Linn

Natural Order: Marsileaceae

Habitat: Throughout India in damp areas.

Description: This is a herb with a creeping rhizome, quadrifoliate leaves and bean-shaped sporocarps.

An aquatic pot-herb with leaves resembling those of chāngerī but four in number (NIS on SS, sūtra, 46, 262).

Medicinal Action:

Rasa : Astringent and sweet
Guṇa : Dry and light
Vīrya : Cold

It alleviates all three doshas, is constipative, an aphrodisiac, appetizing, a brain-tonic, bestows longevity and beneficial in fever, dyspnoea, urinary disorders, skin diseases, vertigo and burning pains.

The seeds relieve dysuria.

Therapeutic Hints: A medicated ghee prepared from this and chāngerī is useful in haemorrhoids (CS, chikitsā, 14, 234).

References: NIS on SS, uttara, 45, 16; 14, 50; AS, chikitsā 4; AHṛ, sūtra, 6, 72; 8, 42.

Sūraṇah

Synonyms: Arśoghnah, Kandah, Kandavardhanah, Suvṛttih, Vātārih, Kaṇḍūlah, Tīvrakandah, Kaṭukandah, Ollah, Ruchyakandah.

Hin. - Ol, Zamin-kand
Ben. - Ol, Jimikand
Tel. - Kanda
Kan. - Gaṇḍīra, Suvarṇa-gaḍḍe
Tam. - Karaṇaippala
Mal. - Chīnapāvu

Botanical Name: Amorphophallus campanulatus (Roxb.) Bl

Natural Order: Araseae

Habitant: Cultivated largely throughout the plains of India.

Description: This is a stout herbaceous plant which bears a large solitary mottled leaf on a long petiole, and has an underground corn which is dull-brown, hemispherical and depressed.

Varieties: There is a wild variety called Śveta-sūraṇah.

Medicinal Action:

Rasa : Astringent, pungent

Guṇa : Dry, light and viśada.

It alleviates kapha and vāta, is constipative, appetizing, digestive, causes itching and is useful in haemorrhoids, abdominal tumours, enlargement of spleen, worms, dyspnoea, cough, vomiting and abdominal colic, It is considered as the best among tubers.

It is contraindicated in certain skin diseases, bleeding from internal organs and Dadru (a kind of skin disease).

References: SS, sūtra, 46, 306-307.

Svarṇakshīrī

Synonyms: Hema-śikhā, Paṭuparnī (Katuparnī), Haimavatī, Pītapushpā, Tikta-dugdhā, Rukmiṇī, Kānchanī.

Medicinal Action:

Rasa : Bitter and pungent

Vīrya : Cold

It alleviates kapha and pitta, purifies the blood, is a laxative, and is beneficial in worms, pruritus, flatulence, skin diseases, fever, dysuria, urinary calculi, burning pains and toxicosis.

The milky juice is mixed with ghee and a few drops are put into the eyes in corneal opacity, fleshy growths and cataract.

References: CS, sūtra, 4, 9; chikitsā, 27, 36; NIS on SS, sūtra, 38, 29; 39, 4.

Śyāmākah

Synonyms: Tri-bījah, Avi-priyah, Sukumārah, Rāja-dhānyam, Tṛṇabījottamah, Muni-bhakshyah.

Hin. - Sāva

Ben. - Sāvā, Śāmulā, Śyāmā-dhām

Mah. - Sāve, Jangli-sāmā

Guj. - Sāmo

Tel. - Oddalu

Eng. - Japanese Barnyard Millet

Botanical Name: Echinochloa frumentacea Link (Syn. Panicum frumentaceum Roxb)

Natural Order: Gramineae

Habitat: Cultivated over the greater part of India, and on the Himalayas up to 6,500 ft.

Varieties: There are three varieties:

1. **Toya-śyāmākah**
2. **Ushṭra-śyāmākah (the big variety)**
3. **Ħasti-śyāmākah (NIS on SS, sūtra, 46, 21).**

Medicinal Action:

Rasa : Sweet and astringent
Guṇa : Dry and light
Vīrya : Cold

It aggravates vāta, alleviates kapha and pitta, antidotes poison, is constipative and drying.

Note: It is generally beneficial to all living beings (CS, sūtra, 2, 26; SS, sūtra, 20, 5).

Śyonākah

Synonyms: Śukanāsah, Kaṭvangah, Kaṭambharah, Aralukah, Mayūra-janghah, Priya-jīvah, Patrorṇah, Kuṭannaṭah, Pṛthaśimbhah, Tiṇṭukah, Dīrgha-vṛntakah, Bhallakah, Śillakah, Bhūtasārah, Pītavṛkshah, Phalgu-vṛntākah, Pūtipatrah, Maṇḍūkaparṇah, Jambūkah, Bhramareshṭah, Bahirjanghah, Svarṇa-valkalah.

Hin. - Arlu, Sonā-pāthā
Ben. - Sona-gācch
Guj. - Maṭamaṭṭya, Araḍūśo
Mah. - Ṭeṇṭu, Choṭā-ṭeṭu
Tam. - Pampenācheṭṭu, Vākay
Tel. - Dundilapu-cheṭṭu
Kan. - Bāgi-mara, Āne-mungu-mara, Hemmaravu
Mal. - Palakapaiyāna, Aralu,
Kon. - Chāmmuyi

Botanical Name: Oroxylum indicum Vent

Natural Order: Bignoniaceae

Habitat: Throughout India, except in the Western drier areas.

Description: A small tree, 7.5 to 12 metres high, branched at the top with a light brown, soft-bark. Leaves are opposite, very large and pinnately compound. Leaflets are glabrous and acuminate. Flowers are numerous, fetid, in large, erect racemes, lurid-purple in colour. Fruit is a capsule with very numerous seeds.

Medicinal Action:

Rasa : Pungent, bitter and astringent
Astringent, pungent and sweet (the tender fruits)
Guṇa : Dry
Light (the tender fruits)
Heavy (the unripe fruits)
Vīrya : Cold
Hot (the tender fruits)

It alleviates all the three doshas, is constipative, appetizing, strength-giving, aphrodisiac, and is useful in fevers, anorexia, rheumatism, vomiting, worms, cough, dyspnoea, diarrhoea, thirst, skin diseases, swellings and diseases of the bladder.

The tender fruits alleviate kapha and vāta, are heart-tonic, digestive, appetizing, beneficial to the throat and are used in abdominal tumours, anorexia and worms.

The unripe fruits aggravate vāta.

Note:

1. The oil can be used in the same way as balā taila (KS, Dhātrī-chikitsā).
2. It is one of the daśa-mūla (ten roots) (SS, sūtra, 38, 68-69).

References: CS, chikitsā, 23, 70; SS, chikitsā, 31, 5.

T

Tagaram

Synonyms: Kālānusāryam, Kuṭilam, Laghusham, Naṭam, Dīpanam, Vinamram, Vakram, Dadruhastam.

Hin. - Chāndni, Sugandha vālā, Muśk-vālā
Ben. - Tagar-pādukā, Asārūn
Eng. - Indian Valerian rhizome

Botanical Name: Valeriana wallichii DC

Natural Order: Valerianaceae

Habitat: Temperature Himalayas from Kashmir to Bhutan, 10,000 ft. and Khasia Hills, 4,000-6,000 ft.

Description: This is a slightly hairy, perennial herb with a thick, horizontal rootstock, and tufted stem. The basal leaves are usually 2.5 to 7.5 cms. in diameter, wing-stalked, deeply cordate-ovate, usually toothed and sharp pointed. The stem leaves are few, much smaller and entire. The flowers are white or tinged with pink, in a terminal corymb.

Varieties: There is another variety called Piṇḍa-tagaram.

Medicinal Action:

Rasa : Sweet, bitter, pungent and astringent
Guṇa : Light and unctous
Vīrya : Hot

It alleviates all the three doshas, purifies the blood, is auspicious, and is beneficial in epilepsy, diseases of the eyes, headache, insanity and skin diseases.

Therapeutic Hints: It is one of the drugs useful in colds and catarrh (CS, sūtra, 4, 17).

Tālah

Synonyms: Lekhyapatrah, Tṛṇarājah, Mahonnatah, Dīrghaskandhah, Dhvaja-drumah, Madhurasah, Chirāyuh, Dīrghapatrah, Guchchapatrah, Āsavadruh, Karapatravān, Tantu-niryāsah, Śataparvā, Tāḍī (NIS on SS, sūtra, 46, 177).

Hin. - Tār
Ben. - Tāl
Kan. - Tāḷi-mara
Tel. - Tāṭi
Kon. - Talṭamāḍḍo
Tulu. - Tāri
Tam. - Panaimaram
Mal. - Tālam
Mah. - Tāḍ
Eng. - Palmyra Palm

Botanical Name: Borassus flabellifer Linn (Syn. B. flabelliformis Roxb)

Natural Order: Palmae

Habitat: Most parts of India.

Description: A tall, deciduous palm with a black, cylindrical stem. The leaves are fan shaped, shining, folded along mid-rib, linear-lanceolate and petioled. Flowers are in spikes. The fruit is a smooth, sub-globose, dark-brown drupe. The tree flowers in March or April.

Varieties: There are two other varieties:

1. Śrītālah

Synonyms: Madhutālah, Lakshmītālah, Mṛduchhadah.

2. Hintālah

Synonyms: Sthūla-tālah, Valkapatrah, Bṛhaddalah.

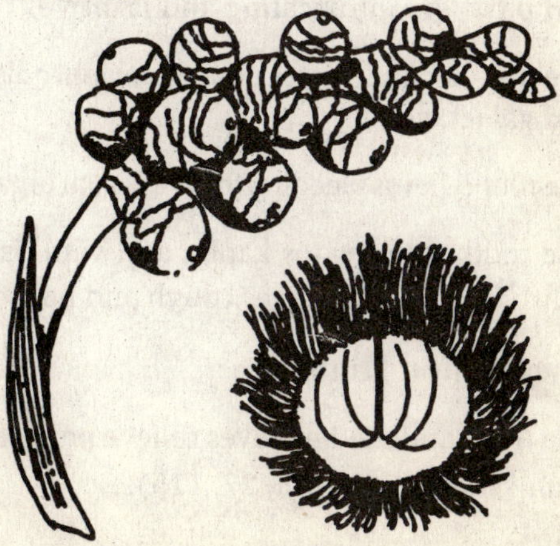

Medicinal Action:

Rasa : Sweet (all parts)
Guṇa : Heavy
Heavy and unctous (the tender fruit)
Light and unctous (the fruit pulp)
Heavy (the juice of the fruit)
Vīrya : Cold (all parts)
Vipāka : Sweet (all parts)

It aggravates kapha, alleviates vāta and pitta, purifies the blood, engenders obesity, is a laxative, strength-giving, intoxicating, nutritive, an aphrodisiac, and is useful in burning pains, tuberculosis, fatigue, worms, skin diseases and toxicosis.

The tender fruits aggravate kapha, alleviate vāta and pitta, purify the blood, are nutritive, constipative, strength-giving, an aphrodisiac, promote growth of flesh and are useful in dyspnoea, bleeding from internal organs, ulcers, burnings, diseases of traumatic origin and tuberculosis.

The ripe fruits aggravate pitta and kapha, vitiate the blood, are difficult to digest, are diuretic, an aphrodisiac and cause lethargy.

The fresh seeds aggravate kapha, alleviate vāta and pitta, and are diuretic.

The fruit-pulp aggravates kapha, alleviates vāta and pitta, are intoxicating and laxative.

The fruit-juice alleviates pitta, is an aphrodisiac and galactagogue.

The root relieves bleeding from internal organs.

The toddy aggravates kapha and vāta, is an aphrodisiac, and relieves cough and nausea.

Therapeutic Hints:

The fresh and tender leaves relieve pain and urah-kshata (CS, sūtra, 27, 115).

References: CS, sūtra, 27, 116, 130; chikitsā, 18, 154; Chkp on CS, siddhi, 11, 24; SS, sūtra, 46, 310; uttara, 51, 39; AS, chikitsā, 5.

Tāla-mūlī

Synonyms: Musalī, Khalanī, Arśoghnī, Godhāpadī, Hemapushpī, Dīrgha-kandikā, Mahā-vṛshyā, Kharjūrī, Suvahā.

Hin. - Mushali
Ben. - Tāl-muli, Tallūra
Tel. - Nelatāḍi-cheṭṭu
Kan. - Nelatāḷe
Tam. - Nilappanai
Tulu. - Nelamuṇḍa
Mal. - Nilappana
Kon. - Bhunyimāḍḍi

Botanical Name: Curculigo orchioides Gaertn

Natural Order: Amaryllidaceae

Habitat: Sub-tropical Himalayas from Kumaon eastwards and in the western Ghats from Konkan southwards.

Description: This is an erect herb with a tuberous root stock, up to 8 cms high. The leaves are crowded at base, almost spreading on the ground, linear-lanceolate, and hirsute with a white leaf sheath. The flowers are yellow, The inflorescence is an axillary scape. The fruit is a capsule with oblong, grooved, beaked seeds. The dried root is translucent, cylindrical, dark brownish in colour, in pieces about 1/2 to 1 inch in length.

The root is shaped like the tail of a rat (NIS).

Medicinal Action:

Rasa : Sweet and bitter
Guṇa : Heavy and slimy
Vīrya : Cold
Vipāka : Sweet

It alleviates vāta and pitta, aggravates kapha, bestows longevity, purifies the blood, is nutritive, an aphrodisiac, appetizing, softens the body and relieves burning pains, fatigue and haemorrhoids.

References: NIS on SS, chikitsā, 7, 18; 17, 25.

Tālīśapatram

Synonyms: Tālisam, Patrāḍhyam, Śukodaram, Mukharogaharam, Hṛdyam, Granthikāpatram, Dhātripatram, Arkavedham, Karipatram.

Hin. - Talīspatra
Ben. - Tālispatra
Nep. - Gobra salla
Eng. - Himalayan Silver Fir

Botanical Name: Pinus webbiana, Wall.

Synonyms: Abies webbiana Lindl; A. spectabilis (D. Don) Spach.

Natural Order: Pinaceae

Habitat: Sikkim and Bhutan at 9,000-13,000 ft.

Description: The tree, which is evergreen, grows to about 100 ft. high. The young shoots are covered with short brown hairs. The leaves are flattened, linear, 1.3 to 2.5 cms long. The fruit is oval shaped and bluish in colour.

Medicinal Action:

Rasa : Sweet and bitter
Guṇa : Light and sharp
Vīrya : Hot

It alleviates kapha and vāta, purifies the blood, is appetizing, a heart-tonic, beneficial to the voice and is useful in dyspnoea, cough, anorexia, abdominal tumours, dyspepsia, tuberculosis, hiccough and vomiting.

References: SS, sūtra, 39, 6; uttara,17, 25.

Tamākhuh

Synonyms: Kshārapatrā, Kṛmighnī, Dhūmrapatrikā.

Hin. - Tāmbāku
Ben. - Tāmāk
Tel. - Pogāku
Kan. - Hoge-soppu
Tam. - Pugaiyilai
Mal. - Pukayila
Kon. - Dhurāpāna
Eng. - Tobacco plant

Botanical Name: Nicotiana tabacum Linn

Natural Order: Solanaceae

Habitat: Cultivated throughout India.

Description: This is an erect, glandular-pubescent herb. Leaves are entire, oblong-lanceolate, acuminate and sessile. Flowers are rosy or reddish in colour and occur in panicled racemes. Fruit is a capsule with numerous, small, scarcely compressed seeds.

Medicinal Action:

Rasa : Bitter and pungent
Guṇa : Sharp
Vīrya : Hot

It alleviates kapha and vāta, aggravates pitta, is intoxicating, a laxative, diuretic, appetizing, emetic, causes vertigo, is harmful to the eyes and is useful in cough, dyspnoea, worms, flatulence, swellings, toothache, and lice infestation.

Tamālah

Synonyms: Kāla-skandhah, Mitadrumah, Loka-skandhah, Nīla-dhvajah, Mahābalah, Tāpichhah

Hin. - Tamāl
Ben. - Tamāl
Mah. - Jhārambī
Tam. - Chitakāmārāku
Vernacular - Patraka (Ḍalhaṇa)

Botanical Name: Cinnamomum tamala Nees & Eberm

Natural Order: Lauraceae

Habitat: Tropical and sub-tropical Himalayas, 3,000-7,800 ft., Sylhet and Khasia Hills, 3,000-4,000 ft.

Description: A small evergreen tree up to 1.4 metres in girth with dark brown or blackish, slightly rough bark. Leaves are opposite, sub-opposite or alternate, acuminate, glabrous and petioled. Flowers are about 7.5 mm long, pale-yellow in colour, appearing as pendulous panicles. Fruit is a drupe which is long, ovoid, fleshy and black.

Medicinal Action:

Rasa : Astringent and sweet
Guṇa : Heavy
Vīrya : Cold

It alleviates kapha and pitta, is nutritive, an aphrodisiac, strength giving and is useful in swellings, burning pains, boils and fatigue.

References: SS, sūtra, 39, 6; uttara, 47, 61.

Taṇḍulīyah

Synonyms: Bhaṇḍīrah, Meghanādah, Ghanasvanah, Granthilah, Bahuvīryah, Suśākah, Pathya-śākah, Sphūrjathuh, Vishaghnah.

Hin. - Cholai, Katailichaulai
Ben. - Chāmpa-natiā, Kāṇṭā-natiā
Mah. - Tānduḷajā
Tam. - Śirukirai
Tel. - Muḷḷa-toṭa-kūra
Kan. - Kirukasāle
Mal. - Cheruchira

Botanical Name: Amaranthus spinosus Linn

Natural Order: Amaranthaceae

Habitat: Throughout India.

Description: An annual, erect, glabrous herb. The stem is 1-2 ft high, hard, polished, cylindrical and much branched. The leaves are ovate-lanceolate, obtuse, sessile and pale-green.

Medicinal Action:

Rasa : Sweet
Guṇa : Light and dry
Vīrya : Cold (stems and leaves)
Hot (roots)
Vipāka : Sweet (stems and leaves)

The stems and leaves alleviate kapha and pitta, purify the blood, are appetizing, diuretic and are beneficial in vertigo, burning pains, thirst, anorexia, bleeding from internal organs, cough, haemorrhoids, tuberculosis and toxicosis.

The roots alleviate kapha and are useful in bleeding from internal organs and menorrhagia.

Therapeutic Hints:

A medicated ghee prepared from the root is used internally in cases of poisoning by rats (AS, uttara, 46).

References: CS, sūtra, 27, 95; SS, sūtra, 46, 253-259.

Tankārī

Synonyms:

Hin. - Tipāri, Tulasīpati
Ben. - Tepuria, Tekāri, Van-tepāri
Mah. - Thānmoḍi
Kan. - Boṇḍula, Buḍḍe-haṇṇu-giḍa
Mal. - Niṭṭaniduna, Mottāmpuḷī
Eng. - Cape Gooseberry, Winter Cherry

Botanical Name: Physalis peruviana Linn (Syn. P. minima Linn)

Natural Order: Solanaceae

Habitat: More or less throughout India, ascending up to 7,000 ft in the Himalayas.

Medicinal Action:

Rasa : Bitter
Guṇa : Light

It alleviates kapha and vāta, is appetizing and relieves ascites and swellings.

Tarambujam

Synonyms: Kālingam, Kṛshṇabījam, Suvartulam, Māmsaphalam, Chitraphalam, Madhura-phalam, Ghṛṇāphalam, Alpa-pramāṇakam, Śīrṇavṛntam.

Hin. - Tarbuz
Ben. - Tarmuj
Tam. - Kommāṭṭi
Mah. - Kalingad
Tel. - Pucchakāyā
Eng. - Water Melon

Botanical Name: Citrullus vulgaris Schrad (Syn. Colocynthis citrullus (Linn.) Kuntze)

Natural Order: Cucurbitaceae

Habitat: Largely cultivated throughout India.

Description: This is a trailing or climbing hispid annual with deeply or moderately divided leaves and large ovoid fruits, dark green or mottled green in colour. The fruits vary in size. The flesh is soft, spongy, and reddish or pink or yellowish-white in colour. The seeds are numerous, small, compressed and black, brownish or white in colour.

Medicinal Action:

Rasa : Sweet (the fruits)
Bitter (the leaves)
Guṇa : Heavy
Vīrya : Cold (tender fruits)

The tender fruits alleviate pitta, are constipative, nutritive, strength-giving, an aphrodisiac, refreshing and are useful in fatigue, burning pains and conjunctivitis.

The ripe fruits alleviate kapha and vāta, and aggravate pitta.

The leaves increase the quantity of blood.

Tarkārī

Synonyms:

Mal. - Tirutāli
Tel. - Tekkali, Takkīḍu
Kan. - Taggi giḍa
Tam. - Taludālai, Chiru-munnai

Botanical Name: Clerodendron phlomides Linn. (Syn. Volkameria multiflora Burm)

Natural Order: Verbenaceae

Habitat: Throughout India in the drier parts, and Baluchisthan.

Description: A shrub sometimes attaining a large size, with white stems and ovate toothed, rather brittle leaves which have a characteristic, disagreeable odour about them. Flowers are tubular, white or pink, axillary, and either solitary or in racemes.

Both Agnimanthā and Tarkārī are said to have the same properties.

Parts Used: Root-bark.

Medicinal Action:

Rasa : Bitter, pungent, astringent and sweet
Guṇa : Light and dry.
Vīrya : Hot
Vipāka : Pungent

It alleviates kapha and vāta, increases the digestive fire, and is useful in oedema, anaemia, constipation, toxicosis, chiḷḷ, haemorrhoids, flatulence and diseases of meda.

Preparations: Daśamūlārishṭa.

Therapeutic Hints:

1. The entire plant (of agnimanthā) is used internally in constipation, haemorrhoids, urinary disorders, etc. (CS, sūtra, 2, 11).
2. The fresh plant-juice is useful in obesity (AHṛ, sūtra, 14, 23)
3. The decoction relieves the pain in haemorrhoids.
4. The root powdered and given with ghee relieves urticaria.

References: SS, sūtra, 38, 10, NIS on sūtra, 38, 12; 39, 7.

Tava-kshiram

Synonyms: Yavajam, Gavayodbhavam, Palāśa-gandhā, Payah-kshīram.

Varieties: There are many varieties, whose starch is used as a substitute for arrow-root : (1) Godhūmajam, (2) Pishṭikā-taṇḍulajam and (3) Tāla-kshīram

Medicinal Action:

Rasa : Sweet
Guna : Light and dry
Vīrya : Cold

It alleviates pitta, purifies the blood, is aromatic, strength-giving, nutritive, an aphrodisiac, and is beneficial in burning pains, tuberculosis, cough, dyspnoea, anorexia, fever, thirst, jaundice, anaemia, skin-diseases, urinary calculi, dysuria, ulcers, and urinary disorders.

The starch is used as a substitute for the true arrow-root powder from Maranta arundinacea Linn.

References: AS, sūtra, 12, 29.

Tejovati

Synonyms: Tejasvinī, Tejanī, Aśvaghnī, Valkalā, Pārijātā, Śītā, Mahoujasī, Bahurasā, Kanaka-prabhā, Suvarna-nākulī, Agnidīptā, Suralatā, Agni-garbhā, Kanguṇī, Suvegā, Pārāvatapadī, Brāhmī, Vāyasī, Śailasutā, Sutailā.

Hin. - Tejabal
Ben. - Tejabal
Mah. - Tirpāni
Eng. - Toothache tree

Botanical Name: Zanthoxylum alatum Roxb

Natural Order: Rutaceae

Habitat: Hot valleys of the sub-tropical Himalayas, Punjab along the foot of the Himalayas from the Indus eastwards up th 5,000 ft., Kumaon, 5,000-7,000 ft., eastwards to Bhutan and Khasia Hills, 2,000-3,000 ft.

Medicinal Action:

Rasa : Bitter and pungent
Vīrya : Hot

It alleviates kapha and vāta, is appetizing, digestive and is beneficial in heart-diseases, diseases of the teeth and mouth, hiccoughs, indigestion, dyspnoea, haemorrhoids, toxicosis, diseases of the throat, cough, abdominal colic and rheumatism.

Tilah

Synonyms: Hema-dhānyam, Pavitrah, Pāpaghnah, Pūtadhānyah, Pitṛtarpaṇah, Jaṭilah, Snehaphalah, Pūraphalah.

Hin.	- Til
Ben.	- Til
Tel.	- Nuvvulu
Kan.	- Ūru-eḷḷu-giḍa
Tam.	- Eḷḷu, Nāvu
Mal.	- Kāreḷḷu
Eng.	- Gingelly oil plant

Botanical Name: Sesamum indicum Linn (Syn. Sesamum orientale Linn)

Natural Order: Pedaliaceae

Habitat: Cultivated all over India and Baluchisthan.

Description: This is an erect, more or less fetid and glandular, usually pubescent herb. The leaves are simple, alternate and lanceolate above, and opposite, usually ovate and toothed below. The flowers are purple or whitish with purple or yellow marks. The fruit is a capsule, oblong, erect and dehiscent from above downwards. Three varieties of seeds are black, white and red.

Varieties: There many varieties like black, white, etc. The black variety is considered superior (NIS on SS, sūtra, 46, 39).

Medicinal Action:

Rasa	: Pungent, bitter, sweet and slightly astringent.
Guṇa	: Heavy and unctous
Vīrya	: Hot
Vipāka	: Sweet

It alleviates vāta, aggravates kapha and pitta, is strength giving, constipative, a brain tonic, diminishes the amount of urine, is beneficial to skin, hair and teeth, promotes lactation, and is useful in ulcers and wounds.

Therapeutic Hints:

1. The kaṇas restore normal colour to the stools (CS, sūtra, 4, 15).
2. The paste of the seeds hastens the healing of wounds (SS, chikitsā, 1, 67; sūtra, 11, 22), and purifies ulcers (SS, chikitsā, 1, 67).
3. The kshāra is used in ascites (CS, chikitsā, 13, 170) and externally in skin diseases (CS, sūtra, 3, 14).

4. The ash (mashi) is used externally in the diseases Arūmkshi (AS, uttara, 28).
5. A paste of fried seeds of tila, sarshapa and juice of mātulunga is useful in relieving pain in eye diseases (SS, uttara, 17, 88-89).
6. A paste of tila and other drugs acts as an antidote to dog-bites (AS, uttara, 46).

References: CS, sutra 13, 12, 24, 85; 25, 27; 27, 30, 39, 109; SS, sūtra, 11, 11; 45, 112; 46, 39, 381; chikitsā, 1, 65; 32, 12; AS, sūtra, 39, 10.

Tindukah

Synonyms: Nīlasārah, Kālaskandhah, Atimuktakah, Sphūrjakah, Syandanah, Rāmaṇah, Ravah, Kṛshṇatvak, Susārah, Śiti-sārakah, Kāla-sārah.

Hin.	-	Gāb
Ben.	-	Gāb
Tel.	-	Tumiki-cheṭṭu, Tummi-cheṭṭu
Kan.	-	Bandada-mara, Bantha
Mah.	-	Tembhurṇī
Tam.	-	Tumbi
Mal.	-	Panichhi-maram
Kon.	-	Bandārūku
Eng.	-	Gaub tree

Botanical Name: Diospyros peregrina Gurke (Syn. D. embryopteris Pers; D. malabarica Desr)

Natural Order: Ebenaceae

Habitat: Throughout India.

Description: This is a medium sized, much branched, evergreen tree with the bark being almost black with a greenish tinge. The leaves are large, 13 to 20 cms long, oblong, tapering to base, glabrous, bright green when young, dark green and hairy when mature, with a thick petiole. The flowers are fragrant, pale-yellow, white or cream coloured. The fruit is sub-globose, yellowish-red when ripe supported by enlarged calyx.

Varieties: There is another variety - Kāka - tindukah.

Medicinal Action:

Rasa	: Bitter and astringent
	Astringent (unripe fruits)
	Sweet (ripe fruits)
Guṇa	: Unctous and heavy (ripe fruits)
	Unctous and light (unripe fruits)
Vīrya	: Hot
	Cold (unripe fruits)
Vipāka	: Sweet (ripe fruits)

The unripe fruits aggravate vāta, are emaciating, constipative and produce flatulence.

The ripe fruits alleviate pitta and vāta, aggravate Kapha, purify the blood and are useful in urinary disorders and urinary calculi.

The extract of the wood alleviates pitta.

References: CS, śārīra, 8, 47; SS, sūtra, 46, 168; chikitsā, 21, 10.

Tiniśah

Synonyms: Syandanah, Nemī, Sarvasārah, Bhasmagarbhah, Meshī, Jaladharah, Śakaṭah, Atimuktakah, Chitrakarmā.

Hin.	-	Sandan
Ben.	-	Tinis
Mah.	-	Tivas
Kan.	-	Nehi, Beṭṭa-honne-mara
Tel.	-	Nemmi-cheṭṭu
Mal.	-	Kāṭṭu punna
Vernacular	-	Sādaṇa (Ḍalhaṇa)

Botanical Name: Dalbergia ougeinensis Roxb (Syn. Ougeinia oojeinensis (Roxb) Hochr; Ougeinia dalbergioides Benth)

Natural Order: Leguminosae

Habitat: Sub-Himālayan tract and outer Himalayan valleys and slopes up to 5, 000 ft. from the Punjab to Bhutan, Oudh, Orissa, Bundelkhand, M. P., Mumbai and Rajasthan.

Medicinal Action:

Rasa : Astringent

Vīrya : Hot

It alleviates all the three doshas, purifies the blood, is constipative and is used in urinary disorders, skin diseases, burning pains, leucoderma, ulcers, anaemia, worms, bleeding from rectum and diseases of Medas.

References: NIS on SS, sūtra, 38, 8; kalpa, 6, 3; SS, chikitsā, 16, 43.

Trapusham

Synonyms: Vipāṇḍuh, Hastiparṇinī, Dīrghaparṇī, Mūtraphalā, Latā, Karkaṭikā, Pītapushpī, Kaṇṭāluh, Bahuphalā, Kośaphalā, Tundilaphalā, Sudhāvāsam.

Hin. - Kherā
Ben. - Śaśa
Tel. - Dosakāya
Kan. - Muḷḷu-soute-baḷḷi
Tam. - Muḷḷu-veḷḷari
Mah. - Tavase, Tauśī-kākḍī
Mal. - Muḷḷan-veḷḷari
Eng. - Common Cucumber

Botanical Name: Cucumis sativus Linn,

Natural Order: Cucurbitaceae

Habitat: Cultivated in all parts of India.

Description: This is a prostate, much-branched, hirsute monoecious herb with alternate, hispid, broadly cordate-ovate leaves. The flowers are unisexual and yellow, in axillary racemes. The fruit is oblong, cylindrical, greenish or yellow, glabrous and tubercled with whitish, obovate-oblong, entire seeds.

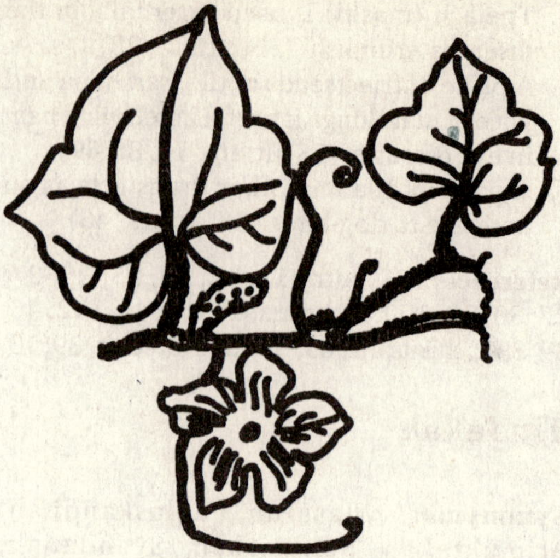

Medicinal Action:

Rasa : Sweet (tender fruits)
Sour (ripe fruits)
Guṇa : Light (tender fruits)
Heavy (ripe fruits)
Dry (the seeds)
Vīrya : Cold (tender fruits and the seeds)
Hot (ripe fruits)

The tender fruits alleviate pitta, are diuretic, and beneficial in thirst, fatigue, burning pains, bleeding from internal organs, vertigo and vomiting.

The ripe fruits alleviate kapha and vāta, and aggravate pitta.

The seeds alleviate pitta, are diuretic and are useful in dysuria and bleeding from internal organs.

References: CS, sūtra, 27, 110; 1, 81-84; SS, sūtra, 45, 120; 46, 216.

Trāyamāṇā

Synonyms: Kṛtatrāṇā, Trāyantī, Baladevā, Balabhadrā, Vārshikam, Girijā, Sukāmā,

Devabalā, Pālinī, Bhaya-nāśinī, Avanī, Anujā.

Medicinal Action:

Rasa : Astringent, bitter, sweet and pungent
Vīrya : Cold

It alleviates all the three doshas, purifies the blood, is a laxative and is useful in vomiting, fever, abdominal tumours and colic, vertigo, tuberculosis, fatigue, thirst, heart diseases, bleeding from internal organs, lethargy, haemorrhoids, afterpains and toxicosis.

References: CS, chikitsā, 12, 53; 13, 70; kalpa, 7, 59; AS, chikitsā, 1, 62-64.

Tripuṭā

Synonyms: Karaṭah, Karālāh, Rūkshaṇātmakāh, Kāṇḍikā, Lankā, Saṇḍikah.

Hin. - Khesari, Latri
Ben. - Khesāri
Mah. - Lāng, Lākh
Eng. - Chickling Vetch, Grass Pea

Botanical Name: Lathyrus sativus Linn

Natural Order: Leguminosae

Habitat: Cultivated in many parts of India up to 4,000 ft. in the Himalayas.

Description: A much-branched, sub-erect annual with stem up to 1.2 meters high. The leaves are pinnately compound; the leaflets usually two, linear-lanceolate, the upper ones modified into tendrils. The flowers are solitary, axillary, reddish-purple, blue or white. The pods are oblong, flat, slightly curved and dorsally two-winged. The seeds are 4-5 in a pod, greyish-brown or yellowish, usually spotted.

Medicinal Action:

Rasa : Sweet, bitter and astringent
Guṇa : Heavy and excessively dry
Vīrya : Cold

It alleviates kapha and pitta, excessively aggravates vāta, is appetizing, constipative, and causes lameness, paralysis of single parts, vertigo, abdominal colic, swellings, burning pains, heart-diseases and haemorrhoids.

The leaves and stem are considered beneficial to bulls.

Trivṛt

Synonyms: Mālavikā, Śyāmā, Masūrā, Kālā, Ardhachandrā, Kālindī, Susheṇī, Vidalā, Trivelā, Suvahā, Tripuṭā, Tribhaṇḍī, Rechanī, Saraṇā, Surasā, Sārā

Hin - Nisoth, Turbud
Ben. - Teori
Tel. - Tegaḍa, Tella-tegaḍa
Kan. - Tigaḍe-baḷḷi, Biḷi-nāgadanti

Tam. - Chivadai
Mah. - Niśottara
Mal. - Tigaḍe, Niśottara
Eng. - Indian Jalap

Botanical Name: Ipomoea turpethum R. Br. (Syn. Operculina turpethum (Linn) S. M.)

Natural Order: Convolvulaceae

Habitat: Throughout India up to 3,000 ft.

Description: A large climbing perennial herb, with milky juice and long, slender, fleshy root. Stems are very long, twining and much twisted together, tough and brown when old. Leaves are ovate or oblong, more or less pubescent on both sides especially when young.

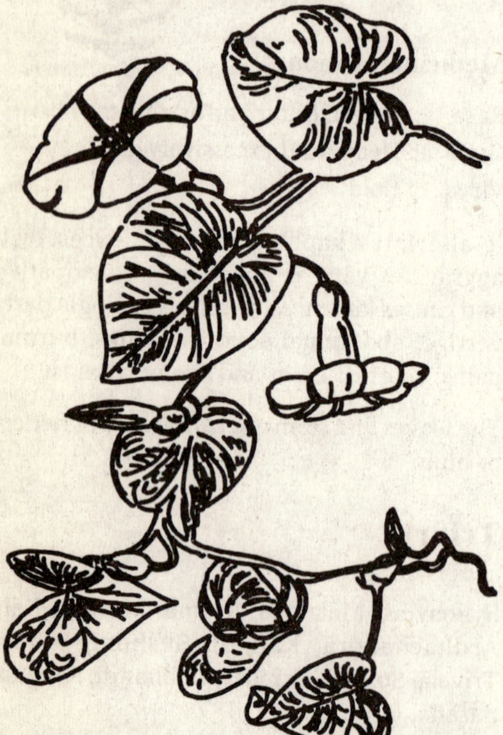

Flowers are large, occuring in cymes, whitish in colour. Fruit is a capsule which is globose.

The roots are red in colour (NIS on SS, sūtra, 39, 4).

Varieties: There are three varieties - White, black and red. The black variety is of inferior quality and should not be employed medicinally.

Medicinal Action:

Rasa : Sweet, bitter and astringent
Guṇa : Sharp and dry
Vīrya : Hot
Vipāka : Pungent

It alleviates kapha and pitta, aggravates vāta, is ideal as a purgative, and is useful in worms, ascites, skin diseases, pruritus, ulcers, sprue, swellings, anaemia, enlargement of the spleen, fever, heart diseases and gout.

The black variety is a drastic purgative and causes vertigo, syncope, burning pains etc. when used.

Therapeutic Hints:

1. The root is recommended as a purgative (CS, sūtra, 25, 400; kalpa, 7, 3).
2. When used as a vegetable in diet, it relieves colic (SS, uttara, 42, 90).

References: CS, sūtra, 4, 13; 25, 40; kalpa, 3,3-9, 71; SS, sūtra, 38, 29; 39, 4; 44, 3; uttara, 17, 30.

Tūlam

Synonyms: Tūdam, Yūpam, Kramukam, Brahmakāshṭham, Brahma-dāru, Supushpam, Surūpam, Nīlavṛntakam, Mṛdu-sāram, Dvibhūmitam.

Hin. - Tūt, Sahatūt
Ben. - Tut, Tutri
Tel. - Tūtikā, Reśme-cheṭṭu
Kan. - Kambaḷi-giḍa, Hip-nerḷe
Tam. - Musukette
Mah. - Tūte
Eng. - Silkworm Mulberry, White Mulberry

Botanical Name: Morus alba Linn (Syn. M. acedosa Griff; M. indica Linn)

Natural Order: Moraceae

Habitat: Commonly cultivated in Baluchisthan and the northern part of the Trans-Indus territory, also in the Punjab, Kashmir and the N.W. Himalayas, Karnataka.

Description: This is a shrub or moderately-sized tree with a fairly cylindrical straight bole, up to 3 metres high. The bark is dark greyish-brown and rough, with vertical fissures. The leaves are very variable, ovate, serrate or crenate-serrate, often deeply lobed. The flowers are inconspicuous and greenish.

Parts Used: Fruits.

Medicinal Actions:

Rasa : Sweet and astringent (ripe fruits)
Sour (unripe fruits)
Guṇa : Heavy
Vīrya : Cold (ripe fruits)
Hot (unripe fruits)

The ripe fruits alleviate vāta and pitta, purify the blood, are constipative, an aphrodiasiac, strength-giving, enhance the complexion and relieve burning pains.

The unripe fruits aggravate pitta and bleeding from internal organs, and are a laxative.

Tulasī

Synonyms: Surasā, Grāmyā, Surabhī, Bahu-manjarī, Apeta-rākshasī, Gourī, Bhūtaghni, Deva-dundubhih, Tīvrā, Subhagā, Vishṇu-vallabhā, Surejyā, Puṇyā, Kāyasthā, Bahu-patrī, Tridaśa-manjarī, Vaishṇavī.

Hin. - Tulsi
Ben. - Tulsi
Tel. - Tulasi
Kan. - Kari-tuḷasi-giḍa
Tam. - Tuḷasi
Mal. - Kṛshna-tuḷasi
Kon. - Kāḷi tuḷasi
Eng. - Holy Basil

Botanical Name: Ocimum sanctum Linn

Natural Order: Labiatae

Habitat: Throughout India.

Description: An annual herb with a somewhat purplish stem and a sometimes woody lower part. The leaves are elliptic-oblong, entire or serrate and softly hairy. The flowers are purplish, in racemes.

Varieties: There are two varieties - black and white, both of which have similar properties.

Medicinal Action:

Rasa : Pungent, bitter and astringent

Guṇa : Light and dry
Vīrya : Hot

It alleviates kapha and vāta, aggravates pitta, purifies the blood, antidotes all poisons, purifies ulcers and wounds, is appetizing, a heart-tonic, auspicious, causes burning sensation, and is beneficial in dysuria, skin-diseases, rheumatic pains, dyspnoea, cough, hiccough, worms, vomiting, fever, abdominal colic, catarrh and foul odour of the body.

Note:

1. The kshāra of the leaves is useful in cough (CS, chikitsā, 18, 171).
2. The leaf-juce is useful in eye-diseases (AS, uttara, 20).

References: CS. sūtra, 27, 169; vimāna, 7, 17; Chkp. on chikitsā, 23, 101; SS,sūtra, 38, 18-19; 46, 233; chikitsā, 11, 7; uttara, 62, 30; kalpa, 8, 68; AS, uttara, 42, 44.

Tumburu-phalah (the fruit of tejovati)

Synonyms: Sourabhah, Vanajah, Sanujah, Dvijah, Tīkshṇa-valkah, Tīkshṇa-phalah, Tīkshṇa-patrah, Mahāmunih, Sphuṭaphalah, Sugandhih.

Hin. - Tumru
Ben. - Nepāli-dhaniā
Mah. - Chiraphal
Tel. - Tumburulu

Botanical Name: Zanthoxylum alatum Roxb

Natural Order: Rutaceae

Habitat: Hot valleys of the subtropical Himalayas, Trans-Indus, Punjab along the foot of the Himalayas from the Indus eastwards up to 5,000 ft., Kumaon, 5,000 to 7,000 ft., eastwards to Bhutan and Khasia Hills, 2,000 to 3,000 ft.

Medicinal Action:

Rasa : Bitter, pungent and sweet.
Guṇa : Dry, light and sharp
Vīrya : Hot
Vipāka : Pungent

It alleviates kapha and vāta, is appetizing, causes burning pains and is beneficial in abdominal colic and tumours, ascites, flatulent distension of the abdomen, worms, lethargy, diseases of the eyes, ears and head, skin-diseases, heaviness of the body, dyspnoea, anorexia, dysuria and enlargement of the spleen.

Tuvarakah

Synonyms: Kaṭu-kapitthah, Kushṭha-vairī

Description: This tree which is distributed along the coastal regions of the Arabian sea resembles a Palāśa tree, while the leaves are like those of Nāga-keśara and the fruits like those of Kapittha (NIS on SS, sūtra, 45; 122; chikitsā, 31, 5).

Medicinal Action: It is useful in skin diseases and urinary diseases.

References: SS, sūtra, 45, 122; chikitsā, 13, 20-35; 31, 5; AS, chikitsā, 21; uttara, 49.

U

Udumbarah

Synonyms: Kshīra-vṛkshah, Hema-dugdhah, Sadā-phalah, Apushpa-phala-sambandhah, Yajnāngah, Śīta-valkalah, Kāla-skandhah, Jantu-phalah, Pushpa-śūṇyah, Pavitrakah, Soumyah, Krimi-kaṇṭakah, Śveta-valkalah.

Hin.	-	Gular
Ben.	-	Jagna dumar
Mah.	-	Umbar
Kan.	-	Atti-mara
Tam.	-	Atti-maram
Tel.	-	Meḍi-cheṭṭu, Atti-cheṭu
Mal.	-	Atti,
Kon.	-	Rumdi-ruku
Eng.	-	Country Fig Tree

Botanical Name: Ficus glomerata Roxb (syn. F. racemosa Linn)

Natural Order: Moraceae

Habitat: Throughout India.

Description: This is a large, deciduous tree with a few short aerial roots. The bark is grey or reddish- brown and smooth. The leaves are alternate, elliptic-lanceolate or ovate, glabrous, three-ribbed with a narrow apex. The flowers are small, found on the inner surface of fleshy hollow receptacles which can be seen in large clusters on leafless branches.

Varieties: There are two other varieties

1. Nadyudumbarah

2. Kākodumbarah.

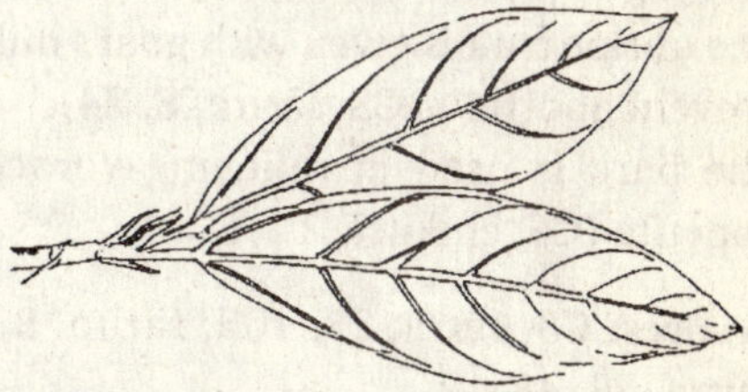

Medicinal Action:

Rasa	:	Sweet and astringent
		Astringent (the bark and unripe fruits)
Guṇa	:	Heavy and dry
Vīrya	:	Cold

It alleviates kapha and pitta, promotes healing of wounds and fractures, facilitates conception and enhances the complexion.

The bark is also a galactagogue.

The unripe fruits alleviate pitta and kapha, purify the blood, are constipative and relieve thirst. The slightly ripe fruits aggravate pitta, cause thirst and syncope, and are useful in bleeding, vomiting and menorrhagia.

The ripe fruits aggravate kapha, alleviate pitta,

purify the blood, increase the tendency to worms, are appetizing, and are beneficial in burning, thirst, excessive hunger, fatigue, swellings and syncope.

Theraputic Hints:

1. It is used in dhūmapāna and is one of the drugs which diminish the quantity of urine (CS, sūtra, 4, 15; 5, 22).
2. It is excellent for external application (AS, sūtra, 13).
3. The til oil which is extracted after bhāvanā with the milky exudation is used for medicating a tampon applied in menstrual disorders (CS, chikitsā, 30, 77-78).
4. The ripe fruits are useful in bleeding and haemorrhages (SS, uttara, 45, 23). The juice of the ripe fruits is excellent for relieving thirst (ibid, 48, 22-23).
5. The kshāra is given with honey and ghee in hiccoughs (SS uttara, 50, 20).
6. The unripe fruit is given with goat's milk to prevent abortion (CS, śārīra, 8, 24).
7. The bark is used in relieving voracious appetite (CS, chikitsā, 15, 230).

References: CS, sūtra, 27, 105; śārīra, 8, 10; SS, sūtra, 38, 48-49.

Uśīram

Synonyms: Mṛṇālam, Abhayam, Samagandhikam, Vīra-taram, Bālakam, Amṛṇālam, Jala-vāram, Haripriyam, Raṇa-priyam, Jalāmodam, Sugandhi-mūlakam, Śubhram, Lāmajjakam.

Hin. - Khus-khus
Ben. - Benāmul
Kan. - Lāvancha, Bāḷada-hullu
Tel. - Vaṭṭi-veḷḷu
Tam. - Veṭṭivār
Kon. - Bhāṇāvaḷo
Mal. - Rāmachham
Eng. - Cuscus Grass

Botanical Name: Vetiveria zizanioides (Linn) Nush (Syn. Andropogon muricatus Retz)

Natural Order: Graminae

Habitat: Practically all over India.

Description: This is a coarse perennial grass, 91 to 122 cms high with stout rhizomes.

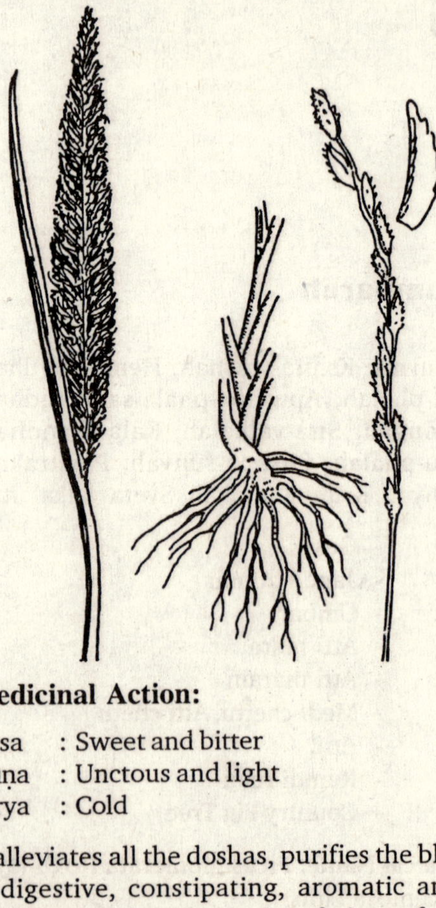

Medicinal Action:

Rasa : Sweet and bitter
Guṇa : Unctous and light
Vīrya : Cold

It alleviates all the doshas, purifies the blood, is digestive, constipating, aromatic and is beneficial in burning pains, fatigue, fevers, bleeding from internal organs, sweating, thirst, vomiting, herpes, ulcers, dysuria, and toxicosis.

Therapeutic Hints:

1. It is used in dhūmapāna (CS, sūtra, 5, 21), relieves vomiting, body pain, burning

sensation, impotence, enhances complexion (ibid, 4, 10, 12, 14, 17).

2. It is excellent for external application and in relieving sweating, skin diseases and burning pains (CS, sūtra, 25, 40).
3. It alleviates pitta (SS, sūtra, 39, 8).
4. An oil prepared from this drug and a few others is used as nasal drops in timira (cataract) of the kapha type (SS, uttara, 17, 41).

References: AS, sūtra, 12, 78-79; 13, 6; 16;, 3; AHṛ, sūtra, 10, 28.

V

Vachā

Synonyms: Ugra-gandhā, Shaḍ-granthā, Golomī, Śata-parvikā, Mangalyā, Jaṭilā, Tikshṇā, Lomaśā, Vijayā, Rakshoghnī, Kshudra-patrī, Bodhanīyā, Bhūta-nāśinī, Tīkshṇa-patrā, Śleshmaghnī.

Hin. - Vach
Ben. - Bach
Tel. - Vasa
Kan. - Baje-giḍa
Tam. - Vaśambu
Mal. - Vayampu
Kon. - Ekhaṇḍa,
Mah. - Vekhaṇḍa,
Eng. - Sweet Flag

Botanical Name: Acorus calamus Linn

Natural Order: Araceae

Habitat: Throughout India and Śri Lanka.

Description: An evergreen, aromatic shrub, from 3 to 5 ft. in height. The leaves are erect, 3-6 inches long and 1-1 1/2 inches broad. The fragrant rhizome is about 1/2 inch in breadth with many nodes.

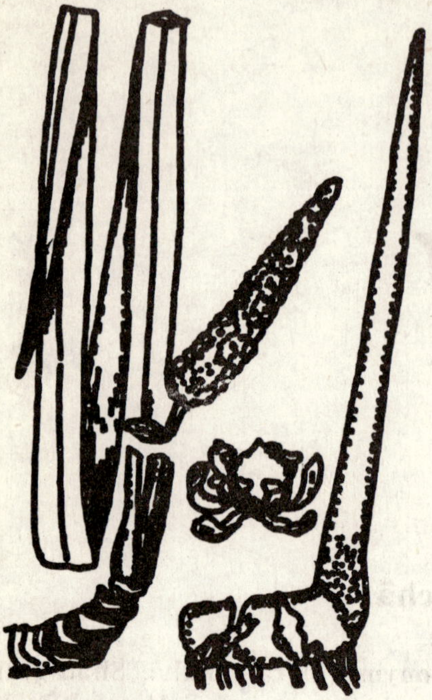

Medicinal Action:

Rasa : Pungent and bitter

Guṇa : Sharp

Vīrya : Hot

It alleviates kapha and vāta, is appetizing, a laxative, diuretic, emetic (in large quantities), brain tonic, beneficial to the throat, promotes the development of speech, bestows longevity and is useful in abdominal colic, flatulent distension, constipation, fever, swellings, insanity, epilepsy, worms, knotty growths, diarrhoea and thirst. Vachā taken daily with water or milk for a month is said to increase lustre.

Therapeutic Hints:

1. It is one of the drugs used in administering enema (CS, siddhi, 3, 14).
2. It is also used as purgative (CS, sūtra, 2, 9) and to purify breast-milk (SS, chikitsā, 17, 44).
3. It is useful in purifying ulcers and wounds (SS, sūtra, 37, 19).
4. It alleviates colic of the Kapha variety (SS, uttara, 42, 111).
5. It is one of the drugs used in fumigation (SS, sūtra, 5, 18).
6. Its decoction is used as emetic in anorexia of the Vāta type (SS, uttara, 57, 6).
7. A paste of this drug is given to infants along with gold, kushṭha and ghee as a tonic (SS, śārīra, 10, 74).

References: CS, sūtra, 3, 5; SS, sūtra, 38, 26-28.

Vamśah

Synonyms: Veṇuh, Yavaphalah, Kārmukah, Tṛṇa-ketukah, Tvak-sārah, Śataparvā, Maskarah, Kīchakah, Kaṇṭāluh, Kaṇṭakī, Mahābalah, Dṛḍhagranthih, Dṛḍhapatrah, Dhanur-drumah, Dhanushyah, Dṛḍhakāṇḍah.

Hin. - Bans
Ben. - Bans
Tel. - Veduru
Kan - Biduru
Tam. - Mūngil
Mal. - Mūngil
Kon. - Vāro
Mah. - Beṭu.
Eng. - Common Prickly Bamboo

Botanical Name: Bambusa bambos Druce (Syn. B. arundinacea Willd)

Natural Order: Graminae

Habitat: Most parts of India.

Varities: There is another vareity called Randhra-vamśah (AS, sūtra, 26, 6; AHṛ, sūtra, 17, 8).

Medicinal Action:

Rasa : Sour, astringent, bitter and sweet
Sweet, astringent and pungent (fresh sprouts)
Astringent and sweet (the grains)
Guṇa : Heavy and dry (fresh sprouts)
Dry (the grains)
Vīrya : Cold
Hot (the grains)
Vipāka : Pungent (the fresh sprouts and grains)

It alleviates kapha and pitta, purifies the blood, is diuretic, a laxative, cchedana, and is useful in skin diseases, swellings, ulcers, dysuria, urinary disorders, burning and haemorrhoids.

The young sprouts (called Karīrah) aggravate kapha, are a laxative, and relieve dysuria.

The grains (vamśa-yavah) alleviate kapha and pitta, antidote poison, are strength-giving, an aphrodisiac, a laxative, produce skin diseases and relieve urinary diseases. They diminish the amount of urine.

Randhra-vamśah is a heart-tonic, is appetizing, digestive, and is beneficial in abdominal tumours and colic and indigestion.

References: CS, sūtra, 14, 31; SS, sūtra, 46, 290; chikitsā, 18, 20; NIS on uttara, 21, 15; AS, sūtra, 26, 10; AHṛ, sūtra, 6, 99.

Vamśa-rochanā

Synonyms: Vamśī, Tunga-kshīrī, Tugā, Śubhā, Vamśa-kshīrī, Yavajā.

Hin. - Banqsolochas, Tabashir
Eng. - Bamboo manna

Medicinal Action:

Rasa : Astringent, bitter and sweet
Guṇa : Dry
Vīrya : Cold

It alleviates pitta and vāta, purifies the blood, is constipative, strength giving, nutritive, enhances the complexion and is useful in thirst, cough, dyspnoea, fever, tuberculosis, jaundice, anaemia, bleeding from internal organs, skin diseases, ulcers, dysuria, vertigo, anorexia and burning.

References: AS, sūtra, 12, 29.

Vandā

Synonyms: Vṛkshādanī, Sevyā, Kāmarūpakā, Taru-ruhā, Padma-rūpiṇī, Śikharī, Keśarūpā, Gandha-mohinī, Drupadī.

Hin. - Vandā, Bandāl
Ben. - Vāndu, Māndaḍā
Tel. - Badanike
Kan. - Kāsarahina, Bandanige
Tam. - Ucchichedi, Pulluruvi

Mah.	-	Vāndguḷ, Kām-rukh
Mal.	-	Kānirottin nel pulluṇṇi, Ittukanni
Eng.	-	Indian Mistletoe

Botanical Name: Loranthus longiflorus Der (Syn. Dendrophthoe falcata Linn. f.)

Natural Order: Loranthaceae

Habitat: More or less throughout India.

Description: A rather shrubby plant with big, thick, opposite sessile leaves, parasitic on mango and other trees. The flowers are orange or pink, long, tubular and in racemes. Berries are elongate and pink in colour. The seeds are covered with sticky pulp.

Medicinal Action:

Rasa : Astringent, sweet and bitter
Vīrya : Cold

It alleviates kapha and vāta, antidotes poison, purifies the blood, bestows longevity, is auspicious, an aphrodisiac, diuretic and is beneficial in ulcers, wounds, fatigue, hiccough and diseases of ligaments.

Vārāhīkandah

Synonyms: Gṛshṭikākandah, Mādhavī, Soukari, Kāntih, Vana-mālinī, Vishvaksenakāntā.

Medicinal Action:

Rasa : Pungent and bitter
Vīrya : Cold

It alleviates kapha and pitta, is nutritive, strength-giving, an aphrodisiac, digestive, bestows longevity, strengthens the voice, enhances the complexion and is beneficial in dysuria, urinary disorders, worms, haemorrhoids, abdominal tumours and toxicosis.

References: SS, chikitsā, 27, 10; also NIS on ibid

Vārtākī

Synonyms: Vṛntākī, Kaṇṭa-vṛntākī, Kaṇṭāluh, Kaṇṭa-patrikā, Nidrāluh, Māmsa-phalā, Mahoṭikā, Chitra-phalā, Mahatī, Kaṭphalā, Miśra-varṇa-phalā, Nīla-phala, Rakta-phalā, Śāka-śreshṭhā, Vṛtta-phalā, Nṛpa-priya-phalah.

Hin.	-	Bhaṇṭā, Baingan
Ben.	-	Begun
Tel.	-	Vankāyi
Kan.	-	Badane-giḍa
Tam.	-	Kattari-kai
Kon.	-	Vāyingaṇa
Mah.	-	Vānge, Vāyinga
Vernacular	-	Bayigaṇa (Ḍalhaṇa)
Eng.	-	Brinjal, Egg-plant, Aubergine

Botanical Name: Solanum melongena Linn

Natural Order: Solanaceae

Habitat: Widely cultivated in India.

Description: A herbaceous, prickly or sometimes unarmed perennial with ovate, sinuate or lobed leaves. The flowers are blue, in small clusters of 2-5. The berries are large, ellipsoid or elongate, in various shades of white, yellow or dark-purple, and glabrous with thick calyx. The seeds are discoid and numerous.

Medicinal Action:

Rasa : Sweet, bitter and pungent
Guṇa : Light and sharp (the tender fruits)
Heavy (ripe fruits)
Heavy and unripe (the fruit roasted in fire, when taken with oil and salt)
Vīrya : Hot
Vipāka : Pungent

According to some authorities, it alleviates pitta, aggravates kapha, is strength-giving, nutritive, heart-tonic, appetizing, and is contra-indicated in cough, dyspnoea, fever, lethargy and diseases of vāta.

According to other authorities, the tender fruits alleviate kapha and pitta, while the ripe fruits aggravate pitta. The fruits which are roasted on coal slightly aggravate pitta and alleviate kapha and vāta.

The white variety is beneficial in haemorrhoids. Its properties are said to be similar to those of eggs.

References: CS, sūtra, 27, 97, 162; SS,sūtra, 46, 269; AS, sūtra, 7, 1; uttara, 43, AHṛ, sūtra, 6, 77.

Varuṇah

Synonyms: Śveta-pushpah, Tikta-śākah, Kumārakah, Gandha-vṛkshah, Tamālah, Mārutāpahah, Sādhu-vṛkshah, Śvetadruh.

Hin.	-	Barnā
Ben.	-	Barun
Mah.	-	Vāy-varaṇā
Kan.	-	Nārumbeḷe-mara, Nīrvāla-mara
Tam.	-	Māvilingu, Ādichāraṇam
Vernacular	-	Varuṇa (NIS)
Mal.	-	Nīrvāl
Tel.	-	Urumiḍi, Uḍumudi-cheṭṭu, Ulimiḍi-cheṭṭu

Botanical Name: Crataeva religiosa Hook. f. (Syn. C. nurvala Buch-Ham)

Natural Order: Capparidaceae

Habitat: Almost all over India, wild or cultivated.

Description: It is a small to medium-sized deciduous tree, reaching up to 15 metres in height with a much-branched head of glossy foliage.

The tree is leafless in the cold seasons. Leaves are compound, with three leaflets on a common stalk. Flowers are white or yellow. Fruit is a berry, globose with dark brown, irregularly circular seeds.

Medicinal Action:

Rasa	: Sweet, bitter, pungent and astringent Sweet (fruits)
Guṇa	: Light and dry Heavy and unctous (fruits)
Vīrya	: Hot
Vipāka	: Sweet (fruits)

It alleviates kapha and vāta, aggravates pitta, purifies the blood, is a purgative, appetizing, and is useful in dysuria, urinary calculi, abdominal colic and tumours, gout, worms, abscesses, suppression of urine and heart-diseases.

The flowers alleviate vāta and pitta, purify the blood, and are constipative.

The fruits alleviate all the doshas and are laxative.

Note: The leaves are used in culinary preparations (SS, sūtra, 46, 271).

References: SS, sūtra, 38, 10-11.

Vāsakah

Synonyms: Simhaparṇī, Vṛshah, Vāsā, Āṭarūshah, Simha-mukhī, Bhishag-mātā, Vasādanī, Kaṇṭhīravī, Vājidantā, Nāsā, Pancha-mukhī, Kasanotpāṭanah.

Hin. - Arushā
Ben. - Bākas
Tel. - Aḍḍasaramu
Kan. - Āḍusoge
Tam. - Āḍatoḍai
Mal. - Āṭaloṭakam
Mah. - Aḍūḷasā
Eng. - Malabar Nut

Botanical Name: Adhatoda vasica Nees

Natural Order: Acanthaceae

Habitat: Most parts of India.

Description: This is a dense shrub with many long, opposite, ascending branches and a glabrous stem. Leaves are opposite, elliptic-lanceolate, acuminate, entire, dark-green above and paler beneath. Flowers occur as pedunculate spikes, white in colour. Fruit is a capsule containing glabrous seeds.

Part Used: Leaves, flowers and root.

Medicinal Action:

Rasa : Bitter, pungent and astringent
Guṇa : Light
Vīrya : Cold

It alleviates kapha and pitta, aggravates vāta, purifies the blood, is a heart tonic, and is beneficial in thirst, dyspnoea, cough, fever, hoarseness, vomiting, syncope, skin diseases, tuberculosis, bleeding from internal organs and jaundice.

The leaves are used in culinary preparations.

References: CS, sūtra, 3, 3; 14, 31; SS, sūtra, 46, 262-270; uttara, 45, 33; AS, sūtra, 26; AHṛ, sūtra, 6, 77.

Vāstukam

Synonyms: Hilamochikā, Śākarājah, Chakravartī, Kshāra-patrah, Bṛhat-patram.

Hin. - Bethuā-śāk, Chillī-śāk
Mah. - Chākavat
Tam. - Paruppu
Ben. - Bethua sak
Tel. - Chakravartapu-kūra
Eng. - Goose foot, Lambs quarters
Vernacular - Ṭank-chucchū (Ḍalhaṇa)

Botanical Name: Chenopodium album Linn

Natural Order: Chenopodiaceae

Habitat: Cultivated as a pot-herb.

Description: This is a herb reaching to about three metres high, erect or ascending, green or reddish in colour and inodorous. The stems are often striped. The leaves are alternate, entire, oblong, toothed, petioled and slender. Flowers are borne in clusters forming spikes. The fruit is membranous, while the seeds are compressed, smooth, shining with an acute margin.

Varieties: There is also a red variety.

Medicinal Action:

Rasa : Sweet
Guṇa : Unctous and light
Vīrya : Cold
Vipāka : Pungent

It alleviates all the three doshas, particularly kapha, purifies the blood, is a brain-tonic, appetizing, a diuretic, a laxative, digestive, strength-giving, aphrodisiac, beneficial to the eyes and voice and is useful in fever, worms, constipation, abdominal colic, haemorrhoids, anorexia, and enlargement of the spleen.

It is considered as one of the best among leafy vegetables.

Note: This is considered the best of vegetables (SS, sūtra, 46, 335).

References: SS, sūtra, 20, 5; 46, 260; NIS on chikitsā, 6, 8; CS, chikitsā, 19, 31; AS, sūtra, 7.

Vatsanābhah

Synonyms: Amṛtah, Kshvedah, Garalah, Vishah, Mahoushadhah.

Hin. - Bacchnāg, Miṭhā-bish
Ben. - Kāṭaṭh-bish
Eng. - Monk's Hood

Botanical Name: Aconitum ferox Wall

Natural Order: Ranunculaceae

Habitat: Alpine Himalayas of Nepal.

Description: The leaves are similar to those of Sindhuvārah (Vitex negundo Linn), and the shape is like that of the navel of a calf. The root is pale-white in colour, like the teat of a cow in shape, and is not longer than five angulas. No other plant is said to grow near Vatsanābhah.

This is a large shrub, three to six feet in height. The leaves are about four inches long, and highly serrated. The flowers are blue and the seeds are blackish in colour.

Medicinal Action:

Rasa : Sweet

Guṇa : Vyavāyi and unctous

Vīrya : Hot

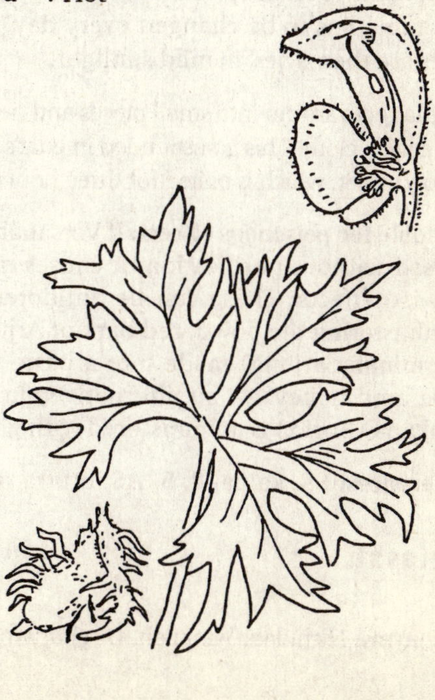

It alleviates kapha and vāta, is strength-giving, bestows longevity and is beneficial in fever, catarrh, swellings, dyspepsia, dyspnoea, cough, enlargement of spleen, ascites, sore throat, ear-ache and urinary disorders. It is externally used in swellings, glandular swellings and rheumatic pains. It is,however, to be used only after purification.

If taken daily by a person who also regularly partakes of ghee, it confers longevity. If taken for three months, it cures all skin diseases; for six months, increases sexual vigour; and for a year, cures all diseases.

It should not be used during the summer and rainy seasons, by a diseased person, by a person who is afficted by anger, pitta, hunger, thirst, vertigo and fatigue, by impotent persons, by pregnant women, children, old and aged people. While taking Vatsanābhah, pungent, sour, salty and oily food substances, sleep during day-time, and exposure to winds and sunshine should be avoided.

Purification: Vatsanābhah is purified by soaking the roots in cow's urine for three days. The urine has to be changed every day. The roots are then dried in mild sunlight.

Or, the roots are cut into small pieces and tied up in a cotton cloth. This is suspended in goat's milk or cow's milk, which is boiled for three hours.

Antidote for poisonous effects: If Vatsanābhah is used without purification, it causes many adverse effects. These can be antidoted by administering the powdered bark of Arjunah (Terminalia arjuna) made into a paste with ghee amd honey. As an alternative,purified Ṭankana (Borax) is administered with ghee.

References: SS, kalpa, 2, 5, AS, uttara, 48.

Vetasah

Synonyms: Nichulah, Vanjulah, Dīrghapatrakah, Kalanah, Manjarīnamnah, Vetrah, Vanīrah, Vidulah, Gandha-pushpakah, Sushenah.

Varieties: There is another variety, viz., Jala-vetasah (Synonyms : Nikunchakah, Nādeyah)

Medicinal Action:

Rasa : Pungent, bitter, astringent and sweet
Pungent (the sprouts)
Astringent, bitter and pungent (the leaves)
Astringent, sweet and sour (the seeds)
Bitter and astringent (Jala-Vetasah)

Guṇa : Light (the sprouts and leaves)
Dry (the seeds and Jala-vetasah)

Vīrya : Cold (all parts and Jala-vetasah)
Hot (the sprouts)

It alleviates kapha and vāta, purifies the blood, is auspicious, appetizing, a laxative, purifies wounds and ulcers and is beneficial in burning pains, swellings, haemorrhoids, menstrual disorders, ulcers, herpes, dysuria, bleeding from internal organs, urinary calculi, skin-diseases, urinary disorders and toxicosis.

The sprouts alleviate kapha and vāta.

The leaves aggravate vāta, alleviate kapha and pitta, purify the blood and are a purgative.

The seeds aggravate pitta, purify the blood and alleviate kapha.

Jala-vetasah aggravates vāta, alleviates kapha and pitta, purifes the blood, cleanses wounds and ulcers and is constipative.

Vibhītakah

Synonyms: Karsha-phalah, Vāsantah, Kalidrumah, Samvartakah, Bhūta-vāsah, Bahedakah, Kalpa-vṛkshah, Hāryah, Kāsaghnah.

Hin. - Bahera
Ben. - Bahera
Tel. - Tāḍi-kāya
Kan. - Tāre-kāyi-mara
Tam. - Akkandam
Mal. - Tānni
Kon. - Goṭinga
Mah. - Behaḍā
Eng. - Beleric Myrobalans

Botanical Name: Terminalia belerica Roxb

Natural Order: Combretaceae

Habitat: Throughout the forests of India, below elevations of about 3,000 ft, except in the dry and arid regions of Sind and Rajputana.

Description: This is a large, deciduous tree with a tall, straight, bole, growing to a height of 24-30 meters, easily recognisable by its characteristic bark and broad massive crown. The bark is bluish or ashy gray, covered with fine, numerous, longitudinal cracks. The leaves are alternate, crowded towards tips of the branches. leathery, ovate, elliptic, greyish-green, pale beneath. The flowers are pale-white or greenish-yellow with an offensive odour.

Medicinal Action:

Rasa : Pungent, bitter and astringent
Guṇa : Light and dry
Vīrya : Hot
Vipāka : Sweet

It alleviats kapha and pitta, purifies the blood, is beneficial to the hair and eyesight, is a purgative and is useful in cough, worms, heart-diseases, hoarseness, greying of hair, diseases of the nose and throat, and skin-diseases.

The fruit-pulp alleviates kapha and vāta and is beneficial in thirst and vomiting.

References: CS, sūtra, 13, 10; SS, sūtra, 38, 54; 45, 120, 179, 188, 183; 46, 200.

Viḍangām

Synonyms: Jantuhantrī, Kṛmighnī, Chitra-taṇḍulā, Amoghā, Kairalā, Vātārih, Mṛga-gāminī, Kapālī, Suchitra-bījā.

Hin. - Bāberang, Vāy-viḍang
Ben. - Biranga
Tel. - Vāyu-viḍangamu
Kan. - Vayu-viḍanga

Botanical Name: Embelia ribes Burn

Natural Order: Myrsinaceae

Habitat: Throughout India, up to 5,000 ft.

Description: A large climbing shrub having rough stems with conical, hard protruberances. The branches are stout, with a brown coloured, horizontally cracked bark. The leaves are memberanous, alternate, elliptic, gland dotted. The flowers are greenish yellow, small, in panicles. The fruit is globose, small and black when ripe.

Medicinal Action:

Rasa : Pungent and slightly bitter
Guṇa : Dry and light
Vīrya : Hot
Vipāka : Pungent

It alleviates kapha and vāta, is appetizing and is beneficial in abdominal colic and tumours, flatulent distension of the abdomen, constipation, worms, dyspepsia, vertigo, toxicosis, enlargement of the spleen, dyspnoea, cough, heart-diseases, urinary disorders and diseases of Medas.

The medicinal properties of the fruits are said to increase with the passage of time.

1. It is purgative, and is used as an errhine (CS, sūtra, 4, 11, 81).
2. It is used as an emetic (SS, sūtra, 39, 3)
3. SS has described its use as a rejuvenative (SS, chikitsā, 29, 8).

References: CS, sūtra, 4, 11; siddhi, 4, 18-24; SS, sūtra, 44, 9; 45, 115).

Vidārī

Synonyms: Vṛshya-kandā, Kshīra-śuklā, Sitā, Ikshu-gandhā,, Triparṇī, Gaja-vāji-priyā, Śṛgālikā, Viḍālikā, Bhū-kūshmāṇḍī, Svādulatā, Kanda-phalā.

Hin. - Bilai-kand
Ben. - Bhūmi-kumra, Śīmiyā
Tel. - Nela-gummaḍi, Darī-gummaḍi
Kan. - Nela-kumbala, Guḍḍa-geṇasu
Mah. - Bhui-kohaḷā, Bendariya, Ghorbel
Tam. - Phalmo-dika
Mal - Motaṭkaṇta, Gumaḍigiḍā
Kon. - Bhuynkuvāḷe
Eng. - Indian Kudzu

Botanical Name: Pueraria tuberosa DC

Natural Order: Leguminosae

Habitat: Throughout tropical India in moist regions.

A large perennial climber with very large tuberous roots. Stems are woody, up to 12 cms. in diameter. The leaves are trifoliate, while the flowers are blue or purplish-blue, in racemes, 15-30 cms. long. The pods are flat, 5-7 cms. long, densely clothed with long, silky, bristly-brown hairs.

Varieties: There is another variety called Kshīra-vidārī, (Synonyms : Payasvinī) which is Ipomoea digitata, Linn of Convolvulaceae.

Description: A perennial herb with long, ovoid or elongated tuberous roots and long, thick, twining, tough, glabrous stems. Leaves are alternate, often broader than long, deeply palmately divided. Flowers occur in paniculate cymes, and are purplish in colour. Fruit is a capsule, ovoid and four-valved. Seeds are clothed with brownish, cottony, easily detachable hairs.

Medicinal Action:

Rasa : Sweet
Guṇa : Heavy and unctous
Vīrya : Cold
Vipāka : Sweet

It alleviates vāta and pitta, aggravates kapha, purifies the blood, facilitates conception, increases breast milk, is nutritive, strength-giving, an aphrodisiac, diuretic, bestows longevity, enhances complexion and voice, and is useful in bleeding from internal organs, vomiting and burning pains and epilepsy.

Therapeutic Hints:

An oil prepared with vidārī and other drugs is used externally in spider bites (SS, kalpa, 8, 70).

References: CS, sūtra, 27, 121; chikitsā, 1, 42; SS, sūtra, 38, 4-5; 46, 300; kalpa, 8, 70; AS, sūtra, 16, 3; AHṛ, sūtra, 15, 9-10.

Vikankatah

Synonyms: Sruvāvṛkshah, Granthilah, Svādu-kaṇṭakah, Yajna-vṛkshah, Kaṇṭakī, Vyāghra-pādapī, Mṛdu-phalah, Kāka-pādah, Bahu-phalah, Danta-kāshṭhah, Pūtah, Gopa-ghoṭa.

Hin. - Kanṭāi, Bilāngra
Ben. - Bainch
Mah. - Bhekaḷ, Vehaḷi
Tam. - Kaṭukal
Tel. - Kāṇḍregu-cheḍḍu
Eng. - Governor's Plum

Botanical Name: Flacourtia indica Merr (Syn. F. ramontchi L'Herit)

Natural Order: Flacourtiaceae

Habitat: Most parts of India.

Description: A rigid, thorny bush, often bearing leaves and flowers on thorns. The bark is yellowish-red and thin. The leaves are obovate or oblong or round, and serrate. The flowers are small, dioecious, solitary or few in imperfect glabrous racemes. The fruit is a five-seeded drupe, about the size of a pea. The plant flowers in the cold season.

Medicinal Action:

Rasa : Sweet, sour, bitter and astringent
Guṇa : Light
Vīrya : Cold
Vipāka : Sweet

It alleviates kapha and pitta, purifies the blood, is appetizing, digestive, and is beneficial in jaundice, swellings, opacities of cornea, ulcers, haemorrhoids, tuberculosis, burning pains, haemorrhoids, and bleeding from internal organs.

The ripe fruits alleviate all the doshas.

Vṛddha-dārukah

Synonyms: Āvegī, Jantukah, Dīrgha-vallarī,

Koṭarapushpī, Cchagalāntrikā, Dīrgha-vālukā, Jungakah.

Hin. - Vidhārā
Ben. - Bijtarkā
Tam. - Peymuchaṭṭai
Tel. - Samudrapaṇḍu
Mah. - Vardhārā
Mal. - Samudrajogam
Eng. - Elephant Creeper

Botanical Name: Argyreia speciosa Sweet (Lettsomia nervosa Roeb)

Natural Order: Convolvulaceae

Habitat: Throughout India (except in dry western regions) up to an elevation 1,000 ft.

Description: A very large climber with stout white-tomentose stems. The leaves are ovate, acute, glabrous above and persistently white-tomentose beneath, with a cordate base. The petioles are 2-6 inches long, white-tomentose. The flowers are in sub-capitate cymes.

Varieties: There is another variety - Jīrṇa-dārukah (Synonyms : Phanjī, Supushpikā, Sūkshmapatrā, Ajarā,).

Medicinal Action:

Rasa : Pungent, bitter, astringent and sweet
Guṇa : Light and slimy
Vīrya : Hot

It alleviates kapha and vāta, is nutritive, appetizing, a brain tonic, a laxative, bestows longevity, is beneficial to the voice and is used in cough, indigestion, Upadamśa, anaemia, tuberculosis, urinary disorders, gout, worms, rheumatism and swellings.

Vṛkshāmlam

Synonyms: Tittiḍīkam, Śākāmlam, Raktapūrakam, Chukrāmlam.

Hin. - Vishāmbil, Tattaḍīk, Kokam
Ben. - Mahāda, Tentul
Kan. - Muruginahuḷi-mara, Āmasolu, Huḷisoppu
Mah. - Amsūl, Kokambasol
Tam. - Murgāl-maram
Mal. - Punampuli
Kon. - Bīruṇḍa
Eng. - Kokam butter tree

Botanical Name: Garcinia indica Chois (G. purpurea Roxb)

Natural Order: Guttiferae

Habitat: Konkan, N. Kanara, W. Ghats, S. Kanara, Coorg.

Description: A tree of moderate height with spreading or drooping branches and dark brown, smooth bark. The young twigs are cylindrical, glabrous, with four elevated lines. The leaves are petiolate, oblong-lanceolate or oblong-oval, obtuse or acute at the apex, entire, thin, glabrous bright-green and reddish when young. The flowers are small and uni-sexual. Fruit is as large as a small orange, spherical, smooth, fleshy, indehiscent and dull-red or purplish.

Medicinal Action:

Rasa : Sour, pungent and astringent
Sour (unripe fruits)
Pungent and astringent (ripe fruits)
Guṇa : Light and dry
Vīrya : Hot

It alleviates kapha, is appetizing and constipative. The unripe fruits alleviate vāta and aggravate kapha and pitta.

The ripe fruits aggravate kapha and vāta, are a heart-tonic, constipative, appetizing, and are useful in thirst, haemorrhoids, diarrhoea, ulcers and wounds, sprue, abdominal colic and tumours, heart-diseases and worms.

Therapeutic Hints: It is used as a heart-tonic (CS, sūtra, 4, 10).

References: CS, sūtra, 27, 151.

Vṛschikāli

Synonyms: Vishāṇī, Vishaghnī, Netrarogahā, Ushṭrikā, Aliparṇī, Kalikā, Āgamāvartā, Devalāngulikā, Karabhā, Bhūridugdhā, Karkaśā, Chāmarā, Svaṛnapushpā, Yugma-phalā, Bhāsurapushpa.

Hin. - Barhanta, Vichavāghās
Ben. - Bichaṭi
Mah. - Vichavā, Khāj-kolati
Tam. - Kāyanchori, Śendoṭṭi
Mal. - Koṭattūva
Kon. - Khājrakuḷli
Eng. - Nettle

Botanical Name: Tragia involucrata Linn

Natural Order: Euphorbiaceae

Habitat: Throughout India from the Punjab and outer Himalaya ranges eastwards to Assam and southwards to Travancore.

Description: This is a climber with rough, stinging hairs. The leaves are three lobed, and serrate. The fruit is a three-lobed, hairy capsule. The flowers appear from September to February.

Medicinal Action:

Rasa : Pungent and bitter
Guṇa : Slimy
Vīrya : Hot

It is a diuretic, a heart tonic, strength-giving, cleanses the mouth and is benefical in bleeding from internal organs, constipation, anorexia and hernia.

Y

Yamānī

Synonyms: Dīpyakah, Yavānikā, Ugragandhā, Bhūtikah, Bhūkadambakah, Vātārih, Śūlahantrī, Tīvragandhā, Hṛdyā, Agnivardhanī.

Hin.	- Ajwān
Ben.	- Joan
Tel.	- Omamu
Kan.	- Voma
Tam.	- Omam
Mal.	- Omam
Eng.	- Bishop's Weed

Botanical Name: Ptychotis ajowan DC (Syn. Trachyspermum ammi (Linn.) Spraque; Carum copticum Benth & Hook. f.)

Natural Order: Umbelliferae

Habitat: Cultivated extensively in Indian gardens.

Description: This is an annual herb, 1-3 ft. high with an erect, cylindrical, slender, smooth, striate and hollow stem with many branches. The leaves are few, distant and alternate, the lower ones on long stalks, and the upper on shorter ones. Flowers are very small, crowded, unisexual, borne on small umbels. The fruit is very small, ovate, rounded and brownish gray in colour.

Medicinal Action:

Rasa	: Bitter and pungent
Guṇa	: Light and sharp
Vīrya	: Hot

It alleviates kapha and vāta, aggravates pitta, is digestive, appetizing, a laxative and is beneficial in abdominal colic and tumours, ascites, flatulent distension of abdomen, enlargement of spleen, worms, haemorrhoids, vomiting, skin diseases and rheumatism.

References: CS, chikitsā, 8, 141-144; Kalpa, 12, 24.

Yāsah

Synonyms: Yavāsakah, Anantā, Bālapatrah, Adhi-kaṇṭakah, Dūramūlah, Samudrāntah, Dīrgha-mūlah, Marudbhavah, Rodanika, Triparṇikā, Gāndhārī.

Hin.	- Yavāsā, Dulāh
Ben.	- Yavāsā
Mah.	- Tambḍā-dhamāsā

Botanical Name: Alhagi maurorum Baker (Syn. A pseudalhagi (Dieb.) Desv).

Natural Order: Leguminosae

Habitat: Maharashtra, Gujarat, Sind, Punjab, Baluchisthan, Uttar Pradesh and Rajasthan.

Medicinal Action:

Rasa	: Sweet, bitter and astringent
Guṇa	: Light
Vīrya	: Cold

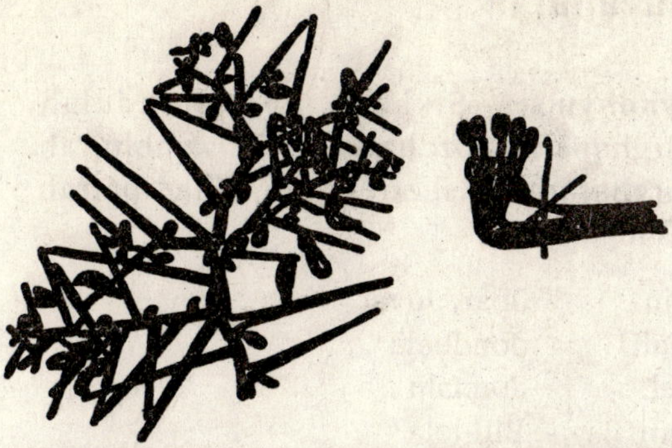

It alleviates kapha and pitta, purifies the blood, is appetizing, a laxative, strength-giving, and is beneficial in obesity, vertigo, bleeding from internal organs, skin-diseases, cough, thirst, herpes, gout, fever, vomiting and toxicosis.

References: CS, sūtra, 27, 241.

Yashṭi-madhukam

Synonyms: Klītakā, Madhu-yashṭī, Yashṭikā, Madhu-sravā, Madhukam, Vasusammitam.

Hin.	-	Mulhaṭṭi, Jeṭhi-madhu
Ben.	-	Jashṭi madhu
Kan.	-	Atimadhura
Tel.	-	Yashṭi-madhukamu, Atimadhura
Eng.	-	Liquorice root

Botanical Name: Glycyrrhiza glabra Linn

Natural Order: Leguminosae

Habitat: Baluchisthan and Sub-Himalayan tracts.

Description: This is a small shrub growing from two to four feet in height. The leaves are compound, each with four to seven pairs of leaflets which are lanceolate. The flowers are blue or violet, in loose racemes. The fruit, a legume, is about an inch long, compressed and glandular, with four to five seeds. The plant flowers in spring.

Varieties: There are two varieties - (1) Jalaja (those which grow in marshy places) and (2) Sthalaja (those which are found in dry regions).

Medicinal Action:

Rasa	: Sweet and slightly bitter
Guṇa	: Heavy and unctous
Vīrya	: Cold

It alleviates vāta and pitta, antidotes poison, purifies the blood, strengthens eyesight, improves the voice, enhances the complexion, is an aphrodisiac, strength-giving, appetizing, and is useful in tuberculosis, thirst, ulcers, swellings, vomiting, bleeding from internal organs, gout and glāni.

Therapeutic Hints:

1. Its powder is given with milk as a brain-tonic (CS, chikitsā, 1, 3, 34).
2. A pāyasa (dish made of milk) is useful in hoarseness of pitta type (SS, uttara, 53, 13).

References: SS, uttara, 45, 24.

Yavah

Synonyms: Medhyah, Sitaśūkah, Divyah, Akshatāh, Dhānyarājah, Tīkshṇaśūkah, Turaga-priyah, Śaktuh, Hayeshṭah, Pavitradhānyam, Kanchukih.

Hin.	-	Jav. Jau
Ben.	-	Jab, Jau
Kan.	-	Yava, Jave-godhi
Kon.	-	Bājri
Tel.	-	Yavalu, Bārli-bīyam
Eng.	-	Barley

Botanical Name: Hordeum vulgare Linn (Syn. H. sativum Pers)

Natural Order: Gramineae

Habitat: Cultivated chiefly in N. India and up to 13,000 ft. in the Himalayas.

Description: This is an annual, erect, stout, tufted herb, from two to four ft. in height, with few leaves which are linear-lanceolate, the upper ones close to the spike. The spikes are terminal, linear-oblong, compressed and densely flowered. It resembles wheat in habit.

Varieties: There are three varieties :

1. **Saśūka (those having bristles)** - these are superior.
2. **Niśśūka (those without bristles)** - these are also called Atiyavāh. These are considered inferior in quality.
3. **Harit (the green variety)** - these are called Stokyam. They are the most inferior of the three varieties.

Medicinal Action:

Rasa : Astringent, sweet and bitter

Guṇa : Heavy, and dry (slimy according to some texts)

Vīrya : Cold

Vipāka : Pungent

It alleviates all the three doshas (aggravates vāta according to DN, but alleviates vāta according to SS), purifies the blood, is constipative, an aphrodisiac, a brain tonic, appetizing, emaciating, strength-giving, enhances the complexion and voice, and is beneficial in cough, dyspnoea, urinary disorders, vomiting, diseases of throat and Medas, ulcers, catarrh, skin diseases, fatigue and Uru-stambhah. It is considered to be Pathya in ulcers.

Therapeutic Hints:

1. A paste of Yava is beneficial when applied over ulcers or wounds (SS, chikitsā, 1, 69).
2. It is beneficial to the throat and alleviates vāta (SS, sūtra, 46, 375).

References: CS, sūtra, 4, 13, 14, 16; SS, sūtra, 46, 41-42; 39, 7; AS, sūtra, 13, 3.

Yavanālah

Synonyms: Śikharī, Vṛttataṇḍulah, Dīrghanālah, Dṛḍhatvak, Vārisambhavah, Dīrghaśarah, Kshetrekshuh, Kharapatrah, Ikshupatrakah.

Hin. - Joār, Juvār
Mah. - Jondhaḷā
Tel. - Jonnalu
Kan. - Biḷi-joḷa
Tal. - Choḷam
Kon. - Joḷu
Eng. - Great Millet

Botanical Name: Sorghum vulgare (Linn.) Pers

Natural Order: Gramineae

Habitat: Widely cultivated in India.

Varieties: There are two varieties:

1. Dhavala-yavanālah

Synonyms: Pāṇḍurah, Tara-taṇḍulah, Nakshatrākṛtivistārah, Mouktika-taṇḍulah.

2. Tuvara-yavanālāh

Synonyms: Rakta-yavanālah.

Medicinal Action:

Rasa : Sweet

Guṇa : Dry and heavy

Vīrya : Cold

It alleviates kapha and pitta, purifies the blood, is appetizing, constipative and an aphrodisiac. It is considered to be deleterious to animals.

Dhavala-yavanālah alleviates all the doshas, is strength giving, an aphrodisiac and is useful in ulcers, abdominal tumours and anorexia.

Appendix - I & II

APPENDIX - I

Pratinidhi Dravyas (Substitute Drugs)

As the indicated drug may not be available in all seasons, and at all places, or even if available may not be suitable to a particular patient, the medical texts give a list of substitute drugs. These drugs have properties and range of action similar to that of the original ones. One of the earliest texts to mention the substitute drugs is the CSS of Vangasena, compiled in the 12th century A.D.

I. Substitute Drugs according to CSS

1.	Ahimsra	Māna-kandā
2.	Amla-vetra	Ripe Chukra
3.	Arka-parṇī, latex of	The leaf-juice of the same
4.	Bandhūka	Flowers of Punnāga
5.	Bhallātaka	Rakta-chandana
6.	Chitraka	The Kshara of Dantī, or of Apāmārga
7.	Dāḍima	Vṛkśāmla
8.	Dāru-haridrā	Haridrā
9.	Drākshā	Fruits of Kāśmarī or flowers of Madhūka
10.	Hingu-patra	Hingu
11.	Karpūra	Granthi-parṇī
12.	Lakshmaṇā	Nīla-kanda-śikhā (Mayūra-śikhā)
13.	Lāngalī	Vahni-patrī
14.	Madhu	Jīrṇa-guḍa (old jaggery)
15.	Mayūra	Cchāśā, Hamsa or Ākhu
16.	Milk	The juice of Muḍga or Masūra
17.	Mūla (root)	Tvak (bark)
18.	Nāga-pushpa	Padma-keśara
19.	Nīlotpala	Kumudā
20.	Pippalī-mūla	Chavikā, Gaja-pippalī
21.	Pṛsni-parṇī	Simha-pucchī
22.	Pushkara-mūla	Kushṭha
23.	Rakta-chandana	Fresh Uśīra
24.	Rasānjana	Dāru-haridrā
25.	Ruchaka	Viḍa-lavaṇa
26.	Rūpya	(Kānta) Loha
27.	Śāli	Shashṭika-śālī
28.	Śallakī	Śikha-piccha
29.	Sita (sugar)	Khaṇḍa (sugar-candy)
30.	Somarājī (bākuchi)	Kaṭhinī
31.	Sourāshṭra	Fruit of Prapunnāṭa (Chakra-marda)
32.	Srī-khaṇḍa	Karpūra chandana
33.	Suvarṇa	(Kānta) Loha
34.	Suvarṇa ksīrī	Kankushṭha
35.	Svarṇa-mākshika	Svarṇa-gairika
36.	Tagara-pādi	Kushṭha
37.	Tālīśa-parṇi	Svarṇa-tālī
38.	Tumburu-taila	Ārushkara
39.	Yūthikā	Jātī

II. Substitute Drugs Mentioned in BP (pūrva, 6, 1, 138-168)

1.	Ativishā	Mustā
2.	Bhārngī	Tālīśa or root of Kaṇṭakārī
3.	Dhanvayāsa	Durālabhā
4.	Jāti-pushpa	Lavanga
5.	Jīvaka	Vidārī
6.	Kākoli	Aśvagandhā
7.	Kankola	Jātī-pushpa
8.	Kānta-Loha	Tīkshṇa-loha
9.	Karpūra	Sugandhi-mustā
10.	Kastūrī	Kankola
11.	Kunkuma	Fresh flowers of Kusumbha
12.	Madhu-yashṭī	Dhātakī
13.	Medā	Śatāvarī
14.	Mouktikā	Muktā-Śuktī
15.	Mūrva	Bark of Jinginī
16.	Roupya	Roupya-makshika
17.	Ṛrddhi	Vārāhī
18.	Ruchaka	Pāmśu-lavaṇa
19.	Sourīshṭraja	Sphaṭika
20.	Suvarṇa	Suvarṇa-mākshika
21.	Tagara	Kushṭha

III. Substitute Drugs mentioned in Ayurveda Soukhyam of Toḍarānanda

1. Abhraka-sattva — Kānta-loha
2. Harītakī — Āmalakī
3. Honey — Water mixed with Khaṇḍa
4. Karikaṇā — Kukkuṭa-mastaka
5. Meda — Yashṭī
6. Naṭa — Veṇu
7. Sarshapa — Siddhārta
8. Sourāshṭrī — Kaṭibhī
9. Tagara-pādī — Veṇu
10. Vajra — Vaikrānta
11. Vetasāmla — Chaṇakāmla or Hemantāmla

IV. Substitute Drugs enumerated in Svayam-Vaidya by Tiruka (Sri Raghavendra Swamiji of Mallaḍihaḷḷi) in Kannada, 1978.

1. Amla-vetasa — Chāngerī
2. Bhallātaka — Chitraka
3. Bhārngī — Tālīsa-patra
4. Bilva — Kapittha
5. Chāngeri — Lemon-juice
6. Chitraka — Kshara of Apāmārga
7. Dantī — Chitraka
8. Drāksha — Kharjūra or Yashṭī-madhu
9. Elā — Tālīsa-patra
10. Go-ghṛta — Aja-ghṛta
11. Go-kshīra — Aja-kshīra
12. Harītakī — Vibhītakī
13. Jātī-patra — Lavanga or Jātī-phala
14. Jīraka — Kṛshṇa-jīraka
15. Kākoli — Sārivā
16. Kaṇṭakāri — Bṛhati
17. Kunkuma — Padma-kesara
18. Lavanga — Flowers of Dhātakī
19. Mahā-vṛddhī — Gokshūra
20. Mahā-vrddhī — Musalī
21. Mustā — Harītakī
22. Pippalī — Maricha
23. Pippalī-mūla — Maricha
24. Pushkara-mūla — Chandana
25. Rakta-chandana — Uśīra
26. Rāsnā — Śuṇṭhi or Pāṭhā
27. Sita and Madhu — Guḍa
28. Śuṇṭhī — Ārdraka
29. Uśīra — Chandana
30. Yashṭī — Jaṭā-māmsī

APPENDIX - II

Drug-groups

Drugs which have similar properties such as rasa, guṇa, vīrya and vipāka and similar action are classified into various groups :

A. Groups of three drugs (which are usually in equal quantities)

1. Tri-dīpya - yamānī, khoramānī and ajamoda (Vaidyaka-nighaṇṭu)
2. Tri-gandha - a. patra (tamāla-patra) tvak (dālchinī), elā (CS, chikitsā, 16, 89).
   - b. haritāla, manahśilā and gandhaka (RRS, 21, 29-30).
3. Tri-jāta - tvak, ela and patra.
4. Tri-kaṇṭaka (the three thorny plants) - kaṇṭakārī, durālabhā and gokshūra (siddhayoga)
5. Tri-karshaka - nāgara, ativishā and mustā (RN, 22).
6. Tri-kaṭu (the three pungents) - pippalī, maricha and śuṇṭhī
7. Tri-kshāra - yava-kshāra, sarji-kshāra and ṭankaṇa (RRS, 5).
8. Tri-lavana (the three salts) - saindhava, souvarchala and viḍa (SS, uttara, 42, 69). (See Tri-paṭu)
9. Tri-loha (the three metals) - suvarṇa, roupya and tāmra (RRS, 23).
10. Tri-mada - viḍanga, mustā and chitraka
11. Tri-madhura (the three sweets) - śarkara, madhu and ghṛta (RRS, 30).
12. Tri-paṭu - viḍa, saindhava and kācha (Vaidyaka nighaṇṭu)
13. Tri-phala (the three fruits)
    a) Main Triphala - harītakī, vibhītakī and amalaki (CS, sūtra, 2, 9; SS, sūtra, 38, 55).
    b) Lesser Triphala - kāśmarī, mṛdvīka and parūshaka
    c) Aromatic Triphala - jātīphala, lavanga and pūga (elā according to DN)
    d) Sweet Triphala - drākshā, dāḍima and kharjūra
14. Tri-sama - harītakī, śuṇṭhī and guḍūchi (KS, khila, 17, 32).
15. Tri-trika - triphala, trikaṭu and trijāta.
16. Tri-varṇaka - Tri-jāta (SS, sūtra, 44, 7).

B. Groups of four drugs

1. Chaturamla (the four sour drugs) - vṛkshāmla, amla-vetasa, dāḍima and badara (CS, chikitsā, 15, 111)
2. Chaturbhadraka
   a) śuṇṭhī, ativishā, mustā and guḍūchi (DN, 7).
   b) elā, tvak, tamāla-patra and maricha (ibid)
3. Chatur-bīja (the four seeds) - methikā, chandra-śūra, kṛshṇa-jīraka and yavanikā (ajamoda).
4. Chatur-jāta - tvak, elā, patra and nāga-kesara (SS, śārīra, 10, 22).
5. Chatur-sama - harītakī, lavanga, saindhava and ajamoda.
6. Chatur-sneha - ghṛta, taila, vasā and majja (SS, sūtra, 44, 47-49).
7. Chaturūshaṇa - sūṇṭhī, maricha, pippalī and pippalī-mūla.

C. Groups of five drugs

1. Panchāmlaka
   a) Kola, chakrika, mātulunga, amla-vetasa and dāḍima (CS, chikitsā, 22, 35).
   b) Kola, dāḍima, chinchā, chullikā and chakrā (RRS, 10).
   c) jambīra, nāranga, amla-vetasa, bīja-pūra and tintiḍīka (RN)
2. Panchāmṛta
   a) guḍūchī, gokshūra, mushalī, śatāvarī and muṇḍikā (RN, 22).
   b) gavya-ghṛta, dadhī, dugdha, madhu and śarkarā (DN, 7).
3. Pancha-bhadra - guḍūchī, parpaṭa, mustā, śuṇṭhī and kirāta-tikta (chakra-datta).
4. Pancha-bīja
   a) karkaṭī, trapushā, dāḍima, padma and kapikacchū
   b) rājikā, ajamoda, jīraka, tila and khasa-khasa

5. Pancha-bhṛnga - devadālī, śamī, bhṛngā, sanakā and nirguṇḍī (DN, 7, 17).
6. Pancha-gavya - gomutra, gomaya, kshīra, dadhi and sarpi (DN, 7).
7. Pancha-kashāya - vachā, vāsā, paṭola, priyangu and nimba (BP).
8. Pancha-kola - śuṇṭhi, pippalī, pippalī-mūla, chavya and chitraka (AHṛ, sūtra, 6, 166).
9. Pancha-lavaṇa - saindhava, souvarchala, biḍa, sāmudra and udbhida (RRS, 12).
10. Pancha-mūla
   a) Greater pancha-mūla - bilva, agnimantha, śyonāka, kāśmarī and pāṭalā (SS, sūtra, 38, 67).
   b) Lesser pancha-mūla - śālaparṇī, pṛśniparṇī, bṛhatī, gokshūra and kaṇṭakārī (ibid, 66)
   c) Madhyama pancha-mūla - balā, punarnavā, eraṇḍa, mudgaparṇī and māshaparṇī (DN, 7).
   d) Gokshūrādi pancha-mūla - gokshūra, badarī, indra-vāruṇī, kāsa-marda and sarshapa.
   e) Jīvaka pancha-mūla - jīvaka, ṛshabhaka, medā, mahāmedā and jīvantī
   f) Kaṇṭaka pancha-mūla - gokshūra, śatāvarī, saireyaka, himsrā and karamarda (AS, sūtra, 12, 62)
   g) Śatāvaryādi pancha-mūla - śaṭāvarī, vidārī, jīvantī, jīvaka and vishāṇī.
   h) Tṛṇa pancha-mūla - kuśa, kāsā, śara, darba and ikshu-mūla (SS, sūtra, 39, 8).
   i) Vallī pancha-mūla - guḍūchī, mesha-śṛngī, sārivā, vidārī and haridrā.
11. Pancha-pallava - āmra, jambu, kapittha, bilva and bīja-pūra.
12. Pancha-sugandhi (the five aromatics) - karpūra, kankola, lavanga, pūga and jātīphala (RN, 22).
13. Pancha-tikta (the five bitters)
   a) Paṭola, nimba, bhūnimba, rāsnā and sapta-parṇa (CS, siddhi, 8, 9).
   b) kaṇṭakārī, guḍūchi, śuṇṭhī, kushṭha and kirāta-tikta
   c) nimba (root-bark), paṭola (leaves), vāsā (bark), guḍūchi and kaṇṭakārī (BP)
14. Pancha-valkala (the five barks) - vaṭa, udumbara, aśvattha, pārīsha and plaksha (CS, chikitsā, 14, 214).

D. Group of six drugs

1. Shaḍūshana - pancha-kola and maricha (Chakra-datta)

E. Group of eight drugs

1. Ashṭa-varga - medā, mahāmedā, kākolī, kshīra-kākolī, ṛddhī, vṛddhī, jīvaka and ṛshabaka (SaS, madhyama, 19)

F. Group of ten drugs

1. Daśamūla - Greater and lesser pancha-mūlas.

Glossary of Botanical Terms

Achene	A small, hard, dry, indehicent, one-seeded fruit.
Acuminate	Tapering towards the apex and drawn to a point.
Acute	Tapering to an angle.
Adnate	Attached by the whole length.
Adventitious	Arising irregularly and not in the normal order.
Aggregate Fruit	One formed by the coherence of pistils that were distinct in flower.
Alternate	Rising singly at each node.
Amplexicaul	Stem-clasping, as the bases of some leaves or petioles.
Androecium	The entire male parts of a flower.
Annular	In the form of ring.
Anther	Part of the stamen which contains the pollen.
Apetalous	Without petals; petals missing.
Apex	The tip or distal end.
Aphyllous	Leafless.
Apiculate	Terminated by an apicula, a short, sharp, flexible point.
Apocarpus	When the carpels are free and seperate.
Appendage	An attached subsidiary or secondary part, as a projecting part or a hanging part or supplement.
Appressed	Closely and flatly pressed against; adpressed.
Arcuate	Curved or bowed.
Aril	An appendage arising from the hilum and more or less enveloping the seed, as mace of the nutmeg.
Arista	A bristle-like appendage, common in grasses.
Armed	Provided with spines or thorns.
Articulate	Jointed; provided with nodes or joints, or places where seperation may naturally take place.
Ascending	Rising up; produced somewhat obliquelY or indirectly upward; rising obliquely and then becoming erect.

Attenuate	Narrowed, tapered.
Attenuate	Showing a long gradual taper, applied to bases or apices of parts.
Auricle	An ear-shaped part or appendage, as the projections at the bases of some leaves and petals.
Awn	A bristle-like append age longer than an arista.
Axil	The upper angle formed between the axis and any organ arising from it, as that between a stem and a leaf on it.
Axile	Belonging to the axis.
Axillary	Situated in an axil.
Axis	An imaginary line around which organs are developed; any member which bears lateral subsidiary members; the stem.
Beak	A narrowed, usually solid prolonged tip; not used for leaves.
Beard	A long awn or bristle-like hair, as in some grasses; a tuft, line, or zone of pubescence, as in some corollas.
Berry	A pulpy fruit with immersed seeds; A fruit in which seeds are distributed in mesocarp and enclosed by an epicarp.
Biennial	Of two seasons duration from seed to maturity and death.
Bifid	Two-cleft, as apices of some petals or leaves.
Bisexual	Having both sexes present and functional in one flower.
Blade	The expanded part of a leaf or petal.
Bract	A modified, reduced leaf, usually on an infloresence, often bearing a flower in its axil.
Bracteole	A small bract, often on the petiole or immediately below or on the calyx.
Bristly	Bearing stiff strong hairs or bristles.
Bulb	A modified bud, usually underground and with fleshy scales or coats.
Bulbil	A small, usually axillary bulb.
Caducous	Falling off early.
Calycine	Herbaceous; resembling a calyx in texture.
Calyx	The outermost series of the parts of a flower; also the enveloping parts of a flower with only one perianth-series.
Campanulate	Bell-shaped.
Capitate	Headed; in heads; formed like a head; aggregated into a very dense or compact cluster.

Capitulum	A dense inflorescence comprised of an aggregation of usually sessile flowers;
Capsule	A dry dehiscent fruit, formed of a compound ovary; opening by one or more lines of dehiscence; A dry fruit of more than one carped breaking open to tiberate seeds.
Carpel	A single modified leaf forming on ovary or part of it and bearing the ovules.
Carpophore	The axis of an ovary from which the ripe carpels eventually separate.
Caruncle	Protuberance or peculiar growth near the attachment of a seed.
Caryopsis	An achene; some times restricted to the fruit of grasses and distinguished from the achene of Asteraceae Compositae by it origin from a superior ovary.
Catkin	A spike consisting usually of unisexual flowers without petals, solitary or twin in the axis of bracts.
Caudate	Bearing a tail-like tip.
Caulescent	Having an obvious, though not large stem.
Cauline	Belonging to or arising from the stem.
Centrifugal	Developing from the center outwards.
Centripetal	Developing from the outside towards the center.
Chaff	A small, thin, dry and membranous scale or bract.
Chartaceous	Papery.
Ciliate	Fringed with hairs; bearing hairs on the margin.
Cladod	A branch or single intenode simulating a leaf.
Clavate	Club- shaped.
Claw	The narrowed base of an organ, especially of a petal.
Cleft	Divided to or about the middle into divisions.
Coccus	A berry; in particular, one of the parts of a lobed, sometimes leathery or dry fruit with 1-seeded cells pl. Cocci.
Coma	The tuft of hairs at the end of seeds; the tuft of empty bracts at the summit of some inflo-rescences.
Compound	Formed of similar parts grouped in a whole; of leaves when composed of more than one separate leaflet.
Connate	United to one another.

Connective	The portion of a stamen distinct from the filament which connects the lobes or cells of an another.
Connivent	In contact or weakly cohering.
Convolute	Rolled up from one or both margins.
Cordate	Heart-shaped, ie more or less deeply notched at the base and in form like a conventional heart.
Coriaceous	Leathery.
Corm	A bulb-like fleshy stem or base of stem.
Corolla	The interior series of the perianth; or second whorl of floral envelops.
Corona	An inner appendage to the corolla shaped like a coronet, or a more or less interrupted outer appendage to the stamens.
Corymb	A form of centripetal inflorescence where the branches or pedicels arise at different levels but attain to nearly the same height to form a flat-topped or slightly domed cluster.
Costate	Ribbed.
Cotyledon	Seed leaf; the primary leaf whose petiole continues through the blade as a distinct midrib.
Creeper	A trailing shoot that takes root mostly throughout its length; sometimes applied to a tight-clinging vine.
Cremocarp	A dry, dehiscent, 2-seeded fruit of the Apiaceae Umbelliferae family, each half a mericarp borne on a hairlike carpophore; a schizocarp.
Crenate	Scalloped or troothed with rounded teeth.
Cristate	Crested.
Culm	The stem, usually hollow, of grases and bamboos.
Cuneate	Wedge-shaped.
Cyathium	A type of inflorescence charesteristic of genus Euphorbia; the unisexual flowers condensed and congested within a bacteate envelop from which they emerge at anthesis.
Cyclic	Worled, the opposite of spiraled.
Cyme	A centrifugal inflorescene in which the secondary or lateral branches continue to grow and may extend beyond the main axis. A flower structure in which the axes of growing parts end in flowers.
Cystolyth	A mineral concretion

	in a cell, usually of calcium carbonate.
Deciduous	Falling off, not persistent.
Decompound	Repeatedly divided or branched or compound.
Decumbent	Reclining or lying on the ground, but with the end ascending.
Decurrent	Extending down and adnate to the stem.
Dehiscence	The method or process of opening of a seed pod or another.
Deltoid	Shaped like an equilateral triangle.
Dentate	Sharply toothed, especially with teeth not pointing forward.
Dichotomous	Forked.
Diclinous	Unisexual, the stamens and pistil in separate flowers.
Digitate	Spreading like the fingers of a hand; in a compound leaf, when the leaflets are all borne at the apex of the petiole.
Dioecious	The two sexes segregated on different plants.
Disc	A development of the fleshy or elevated structure on the receptacle outside the pistil.
Distichous	Arranged in two vertical rows.
Downy	Covered with very short and weak soft hairs.
Drupe	A fruit with more or less succulent flesh enclosing a single, 1-many celled stone.
Echinate	With stout, bluntish prickles.
Elliptic	Oval in outline, being narrowed to rounded ends and windest at or about the middle.
Elongate	lengthened; stretched out.
Emarginate	with a shallow notch at the apex.
Ensiform	Sword-shaped.
Entire	With a continuous margin; not in any way indented; whole.
Epicalyx	A whorl of bracts on or just below the calyx and more or less resembling it.
Epigynous	Borne on the ovary or aparently so.
Epipetalous	bore on or arising from the petals or corolla.
Epiphyte	A plant growing on another.
Exogenous	Arising from the superficial tissues.
Fascicle	A close cluster or bundle.
Filiform	Thread-shaped.
Fimbriate	Fringed.
Fistular	Hollow throughout the length.
Foliaceous	Leaflike; said particularly of sepals and calyx lobes and of bracts that in texture, size or color look like

	mall or large leaves.
Follicle	A fruit of one carpel opening by a ventral suture to which the seeds are attached.
Frond	Leaf of fern.
Fusiform	Spindle-shaped.
Glabrous	Without any kind of hairs.
Glabrescent	With deciduous hairs and becoming glabrous.
Glacous	Sea- green of blue green.
Glochidiate	Bearing barbed bristles.
Gynophore	Stipe of an ovary prolonged within the perianth.
Haustoria	The absorbing organs of parsitic plants.
Helicoid Cyme	A sympodial determinate inflorescence, coiled like a snake-shell; with all the flowers on one side.
Herb	A plant without woody shoot system.
Hermaphrodite	With flowers bisexual.
Hirsute	Bearing long tolerably distinct hairs.
Hispid	With rough or bristly hairs.
Hypanthium	The cup like receptacle derived usually from the fusion of floral envelops and androecium, and on which are seemingly borne calyx, corolla, and stamens.
Imparipinnate	Pinnate with an odd terminal member.
Indehiscent	Not regularly opening as a seed pod or anther.
Inflorescence	A cluster of flowers on an axis.
Interpetiolar	Between two opposite petioles.
Laciniate	Irregularly cut into narrow lobes.
Lamina	The blade of a leaf.
Lanceolate	Lance shaped; much longer than broad; widening above the base and tapering to the apex.
Latex	Milky sap.
Lax	Loose, the oopsite of congested.
Leaflet	One part of a compound leaf; secondary leaf.
Legume	Simple fruit dehiscing on both sutures, and product of a simple unicarpellate ovary.
Lianous	Vinelike.
Ligulate	Strap-shaped, as a leaf, petal, or corolla.
Limb	The expanded flat part of an organ.
Linear	Several times longer than wide.
Lobe	A rounded part of a structure.
Locule	A cell or a compartment of an ovary.
Membranous	Thin and somewhat translucent.
Mericarp	A portion of a fruit

which splits away and simulates a perfect fruit.

Moniliform Resembling a string of beads.

Monoecios With the male and female parts in different flowers but on the same individual plant.

Mucronate Terminated abruptly by a distinct and obvious mucro.

Multiple Fruit One formed from several flowers into a single structure having a common axis.

Muricate Rough, due to presence of many minute spiculate excrescences on the epidermis.

Nut A hard, dry, indehiscent 1-seeded fruit; on often also applied to similar single part of a severalcelled fruit.

Ob A latin prefix, usually signifying inversion.

Obovate inverted ovate

Obovoid Shaped like an inverted egg.

Operculum A lip or cover which separates by traverse dehiscence.

Opposite Said of leaves when there are two at the some node,.

Ovoid Applied to a small body like an egg.

Orbicular Circular in outline.

Ovary That part o f the pistil which contains the ovules.

Ovate Egg-shaped.

Ovule The incipient and before fertilization.

Panicle An indeterminate branching raceme; an inflorescence in which the branches of the primary axis are racemose and the flowers pedicellate.

Pappus Tufts of hairs on some achenes or fruits, specially the scaly, bristly, hairiy or feathery modified calyx in the Asteraceae (Compositae).

Paripinnate Pinnate with an equal number of members on each side of the axis and no od terminal lone.

Pedicel The stalk of a single flower.

Peduncle The common stalk of 2- many flowers or of a complete inflorescence.

Peltate Shield-shaped; said of leaves of which the petiole is attached to the lower surface of the blade and not at the margin.

Perianth The flower envelops of 1 or 2 series, i.e. calys and corolla; more.commonly used when the two series are not differentiated or when ony one of them is present.

Pericarp	Fruit coat.
Petal	A single member of the corolla.
Petiole	The stalk of a leaf.
Phyllode	A petiole assuming the form and function of a leaf.
Pilose	Hairy with rather long, soft, distinct hairs.
Pinnate	Compound leaf when leaflets are arranged in two opposite rows on the same stach.
Pistil	The complete female part of a flower.
Plumose	Feathery or feathered.
Pod	A dehiscent dry fruit.
Procumbent	Trailing or lying flat, but not rooting.
Prostrate	Hying flot and close to the ground.
Puberlous	Slightly hairy with very short hairs.
Pubescent	Clothed with soft, rather short hairs or down.
Pulvinous	An enlargement close to the insertion of a leaf or the swollen base of the petiole.
Raceme	A centripetal inflores cence with lengthened axis and equally pedicellate flowers.
Raceptacle	That part of the axis that bears one or more organs of flowers.
Reniform	Kidney-shaped.
Rhizome	An underground stem, usually horizontal and elongated.
Rootstock	Subterranean stem; rhizome.
Rotate	Wheel-shaped; said of a gamopetalous corolla with a short tube and spreading limb.
Rugose	Thrown into wrinkles.
Runner	A slender trailing shoot taking root at the nodes.
Sagittate	like an arrowhead in form; triangular, with the basal lobes pointing downward or concavely toward the stalk.
Samara	An indehiscent winged fruit, or winged parts of a dehiscing fruit.
Saprophyte	A plant living on dead organic matter.
Scabrid	Covered with small hard hairs or points and feeling rough.
Scandent	Climbing.
Schizocarp	A dry dehiscent fruit that splits into 2 halves, each half a mericarp.
Sepal	A single member of the calyx.
Serrate	Margin when saw-toothed with the pointing forward.
Serrulate	Minutely serrate.
Sessile	Without stalk.
Sinuate	With a deeply wavy margin.

Spike	An inflorescence with sessile flowers on a usually elongate axis.
Spikelet	A cluster of 1 or more flowers each in the axil of one or a pair of bracts and subtended by 2, rarely 1 empty bracts.
Sporangium	A spore case, a sac or body bearing spores.
Stamen	The floral organ bearing anther and pollen.
Stipule	One of a pair of appendages borne on each side of the base of the leaves or petioles of many plants.
Stolon	A sucker; any basal branch that is disposed to from roots.
Succulent	Soft and juicy.
Tendril	A rotating or twisting thread like process or extension by which a plant grasps an object and clings to it for support; morphologically it may be stem or leaf.
Tepal	A segment of a perianth, usually employed when there is no distinction between the 2 series.
Terete	Cylindrical and circular in cross-section.
Tomentose	With tomentum; densly wooly or pubescent; with matted soft wool-like hairiness.
Trifoliate	With three leaves.
Tuber	A short, thickened subterranean branch beset with buds; the swollen end of a root attached to the upper end of rootstock.
Umbel	An inflorescence in which a cluster of pedicels springs from the same point.
Utricle	A membranous sac, or a bladder-like appendage.
Verrucose	Warty.
Verticillate	Arranged in a ring around the axis.
Villose	Shaggy with long, weak hairs.
Viscid	Sticky or clammy owing to an exudation.
Whorl	Applied to leaves when they are arranged in a circle around the stem.

Bibliography

Anon. - The Ayuvedic Formulary of India, Part I, 1978.

Anon. - The Wealth of India (Raw Materials), C.S.I.R., 11 Vols, 1948.

Anon. - Five Hundred Indian Plants, The Kanerese Mission Press and Book Depot, Mangalore, 1922 (Kannaḍa).

Āpte, M.V., Van-śrī-sṛshṭī, Maharāshṭra Rājya Sāhitya āṇi Samskṛtī Maṇḍal, 2 Vols, 1982 (Marāṭhī).

Bentley, Robert and Trimen, Henry. ; Medicinal Plants; International Book Distributors and Periodical Expert Book Agency, 4 Vols, First Indian Reprint, 1983.

Chopra, R.N., Nayar, S.L. and Chopra, I.C.; Glossary of Indian Medicinal Plants, C.S.I.R., 1956.

Chunekar, K.C. ; Commentary on Bhāva-prakāśā Nighaṇṭu, C, 1986 (Hindī).

Dastur, J.F.; Medicinal Plants of India and Pakisthan; D.B. Taraporewala Sons & Co. Ltd., Bombay, 1951.

Dutt, U.C. ; The Materia Medica of the Hindus, C, 1980.

Gopālaswāmiengār, K.S. ; Complete Gardening of India; The Hosali Press, Bangalore, 1935.

Gupta, Umeśa-chandra. ; Vaidyaka Śabda Sindhu, Calcutta, 1894 (Sanskrit).

Jaḍe, Śrīpāda Śāstrī. ; Sarva Vaidya Ratna, Hubli, 1963 (Kannaḍa).

Jośī, Veṇi-mādhav-śāstrī and Jośī, Nārāyaṇ Hari.; Āyurvedīya Mahā Kośa arthāt Āyurvedīya Śabda Kośa; Maharāshṭra Rājya Sāhitya āṇi Samskṛtī Maṇḍal, Bombay, 1968 (Sanskrit)

Khory, Rustomjee Naserwanjee and Katrak, Nanabhai Navrosji; Materia Materia of India and their therapeutics : Neeraj Publishing House, Delhi, First Reprint - 1981.

Kirtikar, K.R. and Basu, B.D. ; Indian Medicinal Plants; Bishen Singh Mahendra Pal Singh, in 4 vols. with 4 vols of illustrations, 1980.

Randhawa, M.S. ; Flowering Trees in India, I.C.A.R., 1957.

Sen Gupta, Vinod Lal; Āyurveda Vijnānam, Calcutta, 2 Vols. (Sanskrit).

Sharma, P.V. ; Ḍalhaṇa and his Comments on Drugs; Munshiram Manoharlal Publishers Pvt. Ltd., 1982.

Sharma, P.V. ; Dravya-guṇa Vijnāna, C, 4 Vols. 1978 (Hindi).

Tadulingam, C. and Narayana, G.V. ; A Handbook of some South Indian Weeds, Government Press, Madras, 1955.

Trikumji, Āchārya Yādavji; Dravya-guṇa Vijnānam; Śrī Śarmā Āyurveda Mandir, 2 Vols, 1978 (Sanskrit-Hindi).

Troup; The Silviculture of Indian Trees; Revised and Enlarged by the Editorial Board, Forest Research Institute and Colleges, Dehra Dun, The Controller of Publications, Delhi, 1975.

Vāsudeva Śāstrī, Viṭūri.; Vastu-guṇa Prakāśika, Saraswati Power Press, Rājahmundry, 1938 (Telugu).

Venkaṭa-kṛshṇayya, R.S.; Sachitra-mūlikā Vaidya-prakāśika, Kalānidhi Press, Bangalore, 1926 (Kannaḍa).

Venkaṭaswāmy gāru, Erra.; Vastu-guṇa-dīpikā or Dictionary of Drugs, Medicinal Plants, Eatables, etc., Guardian Press, Madras, 1919 (Telugu).

Index

A

B

C

D

M

N

O

P

Q

R

S

T

U

V

W

Z